Cheapskate's Guide to Bargain Computing

■Bill Camarda■

To join a Prentice Hall PTR Internet mailing list, point to
http://www.prenhall.com/mail_lists/

Prentice Hall PTR, Upper Saddle River, NJ 07458

Library of Congress Cataloging-in-Publication Data
Camarda, Bill
   Cheapskate's guide to bargain computing / by Bill Camarda.
     p.   cm.
   Includes index.
   ISBN 0-13-756404-X
   1. Microcomputers--Purchasing.   I. Title.
QA76.5.C346 1998
004.16'029'7--dc21   97-26393
                                     CIP

Editorial/Production Supervision: *Eileen Clark*
Acquisitions Editor: *Mark L. Taub*
Editorial Assistant: *Tara Ruggiero*
Marketing Manager: *Dan Rush*
Buyer: *Alexis R. Heydt*
Cover Design: *Scott Weiss*
Cover Design Direction: *Jerry Votta*
Interior Design: *Gail Cocker-Bogusz*
CD Web Page Design: *Cynthia L. Mason*

© 1998 Prentice Hall PTR
Prentice-Hall, Inc.
A Simon & Schuster Company
Upper Saddle River, NJ 07458

Prentice Hall books are widely used by corporations and government agencies for training, marketing, and resale. The publisher offers discounts on this book when ordered in bulk quantities.
For more information, contact

        Corporate Sales Department,
        Phone: 800-382-3419; FAX: 201-236-7141
        E-mail (Internet): corpsales@prenhall.com
Or write: Prentice Hall PTR
        Corp. Sales Department
        One Lake Street
        Upper Saddle River, NJ 07458

Printed in the United States of America

10 9 8 7 6 5 4 3 2

ISBN 0-13-756404-X

Prentice-Hall International (UK) Limited, *London*
Prentice-Hall of Australia Pty. Limited, *Sydney*
Prentice-Hall Canada Inc., *Toronto*
Prentice-Hall Hispanoamericana, S.A., *Mexico*
Prentice-Hall of India Private Limited, *New Delhi*
Prentice-Hall of Japan, Inc., *Tokyo*
Simon & Schuster Asia Pte. Ltd., *Singapore*
Editora Prentice-Hall do Brasil, Ltda., *Rio de Janeiro*

Contents

Acknowledgments

Every time I sign on to write a book, my wife Barbara takes a deep breath, because she knows what she'll be in for: long evenings taking care of our three-year-old Matthew by herself, long weekends figuring out new ways to distract him—and a husband who's grouchy, stressed, and constantly behind schedule.

Then she proceeds to cope with grace and humor, occasionally even finding time for herself. It seems as if every book I read these days is dedicated to a spouse. Boy, is that ever appropriate.

So, first and foremost, to Barbara—and to Matthew, too, my breathtaking little boy.

I also want to thank my friends who helped with specific ideas and suggestions for "cheaping out"—in particular, Dave Razler, who sent memos and e-mails that dramatically improved several chapters in this book. Dave also helped me troubleshoot and fix my own dead computer while I was meeting the deadline for this project. A talented writer, smart computer person, and all-around good guy.

Thanks to my editorial, marketing, production, and public relations team at Prentice Hall PTR—especially Mark Taub, Eileen Clark, Martha Williams, and Cynthia Mason. I've known these hard-working, talented people for a long time before having the privilege of writing this book with them. That's why I *wanted* to write a book with them. And they've been even better than I imagined.

Thanks to Jim Aspinwall, co-author of *Troubleshooting Your PC*[1] and author of the best-seller *IRQ, DMA and I/O*,[2] for his review of my manuscript—and for the important improvements he made, especially in hardware coverage. If you're in the Silicon Valley area and you're in need of PC, ISDN, or networking support services, you'll do well to contact Jim at **wb9gvf@raisin.com**.

(Of course any remaining errors are all mine.)

Finally, a tip of the hat to Amy Dacyczyn, author of *The Tightwad Gazette*.[3] She's more of a cheapskate than I'll ever be, but she has the right idea when it comes to ferreting out hype and waste unmercifully—and having fun while you're at it.

—*Bill Camarda*
July, 1997

▲ ▲ ▲ ▲ ▲ ▲ ▲ ▲ ▲ ▲ ▲ ▲ ▲ ▲ ▲ ▲ ▲ ▲ ▲ ▲

1. *Troubleshooting Your PC*, Jim Aspinwall and Mike Todd, MIS Press, November 1996, ISBN: 1558284931, $34.95.

2. *IRQ, DMA & I/O: Resolving and Preventing PC System Conflicts*, MIS Press, October 1995, ISBN: 1558284567, $24.95.

3. *The Tightwad Gazette: Promoting Thrift as a Viable Alternative Lifestyle*, Amy Dacyczyn, January 1993, ISBN: 067974388X, $12.99 (and two followup books with even more tips).

About the Author

Bill Camarda has been writing about computers and the computer industry for well over a decade. His recent books include *The Windows Sources Word 97 for Windows SuperGuide* (ZD Press), *Inside Word for Windows 95* (New Riders Publishing); *Inside 1-2-3 Release 5* (New Riders Publishing); and *OS/2 in the Fast Lane* (New Riders Publishing). He was formerly an editor at *Family Computing* magazine, one of the first magazines to specialize in helping home users make the most out of personal computer technology. A specialist in computing, networking and technology marketing, he can be reached at **bcamarda@nisnet**.

Introduction

This book is for you, if

- ✍ *You want, need, or already have a computer.*
- ✍ *You believe in the value of a dollar—and you think it is vaguely (or explicitly!) immoral to waste money.*

Computers are extraordinary tools, and for some of us, they are awesome fun, too. It really doesn't matter whether you're simply trying to get the job done, or you actually *like* noodling around with computers: There's still no excuse to waste one hard-earned dime.

The fact is, nowadays you can find awesome technology dirt-cheap. And there's some technology that isn't worth buying at any price, no matter how slick the advertising is.

That's what this book is about: Helping you figure out what you *really* need and then showing you how to get it at the lowest possible cost.

How This *Cheapskate's* Guide Will Save You Money

In this book, I'll show you exactly how (and where) to shop for the best deals in

▲ Computers

▲ Software

▲ Peripherals

▲ Internet and other on-line services

▲ Accessories and consumables

I'll also show you what to watch out for—and what new technologies aren't all they're cracked up to be.

Then I'll show you how to make the most of what you may already have. It's amazing how many people buy expensive software when their computers came with software that will do the job they need, at no additional cost.

And on the accompanying Cheapskate's CD-ROM, you'll find a comprehensive library of Windows, Macintosh, and DOS shareware and freeware. When you don't have the right software, look here first, before you visit your local computer store. This disk *could* contain practically all the software you'll ever need.

You'll also find a Web page you can use with your Internet connection and Web browser to link to some of the world's best sources of inexpensive (or free) computer stuff. It will also link to our own Cheapskate's Web site—with up-to-date information on the world's best computer bargains.

Speaking of the Internet, you'll find a lot more Internet resources in this book than I ever expected when I started writing. It turns out that, for the Cheapskates among us, the Internet is heaven on earth. I often wonder how long it can last—getting all that stuff for free on-line. Free software. Free information. You name it: While it's there, I say grab it.

Things change fast in this business. I've tried my best to focus on sound buying principles and avoid using examples that will be out of date by the time you read the book, but inevitably some of the specific deals and prices I'll mention may change. We'll try to keep you updated as best we can on our Web site, **nis.net/~bcamarda/cheapskt.htm.**

Whether you're a novice or an old hand, a PC user or a Mac aficionado, this book is designed to help you get more for your computing money. I hope you'll let me know how well I've succeeded. If you have good sources I haven't mentioned, tell me about them. I'd also like to hear about your experiences with the companies and buying techniques discussed in this book. Just e-mail me at **bcamarda@nisnet**.

Thanks for investing your hard-earned dime in *Cheapskate's Guide to Bargain Computing*. I sincerely hope you'll come to depend on this book as your ongoing resource for getting the best value in *everything* computer related.

CHAPTER 1

Buying a Computer—
The Cheapskate's Way

- First Computer versus Second Computer
- Unlimited Possibility = Unlimited Expense
- Generations: How Much Computer is Enough for You?
- What Are You Trying to Accomplish?
- Do You Need Windows 95 (or Windows 98)?
- Windows or Mac?
- Buy Now, or Wait?
- The Network Computer: For Individuals, a Pig in a Poke?
- New, Refurbed, or Used?
- Summary

This is America, where we've always believed in buying the fastest, newest, shiniest, slickest equipment possible—and we've always admired those folks who could soup up their off-the-shelf stuff even further.

Once, not so long ago, the purest manifestation of this was the automobile. Today, it's the computer. The guy at the party bragging about his new Pentium Pro multiprocessor and speedy Web connection is no different than yesterday's street racer, or from the male ostrich showing off his plumage to establish his rank.

And no wonder. It's a cliché in the computer industry that if cars had improved as fast as computers, a Rolls Royce would run a million miles an hour and get a million miles to the gallon. Then, there's the added attraction of raw, vicarious greed. In the 1990s, unfathomable amounts of money have found their way to such worthies as Bill Gates, the era's singular cultural icon.

But enough sociology. I propose that you buy computer stuff with your *brain* working on all cylinders, not your hormones. I want you to focus on buying only what you need and getting the best deals possible. I'm not saying don't buy: I love computer stuff as much as anyone. I am saying, buy smart.

▲ Understand what you want to achieve—before you start shopping.
▲ Do careful research.
▲ Be clear about your options.
▲ Don't buy on impulse.

A computer system is the third most expensive possession many people will ever buy, after a home and a car. And once you *have* a computer, there's a world of add-on software and equipment to be sorely tempted by—with more temptations arriving every week. Trust me, I know.

But next time you're getting ready to pay full price in a computer store for something that just might not be worth it, think for an instant about the future of the Social Security system. Then decide who needs the money more. The store? Or you?

The argument *for* buying a new computer every couple of years is that it'll only cost you several dollars a day, and it'll make you a whole lot more competitive. Maybe that makes sense for people who habitually *do* squeeze every ounce of performance out of their PCs, *do* have valuable old computers to sell, and *do* have $3,000 or so to shell out for new equipment every two years. (Even those folks can use the information in this book to buy smarter and save at least *some* of that money.)

But there are millions of people who simply do not have the time, energy, inclination, or money to stay on the "bleeding edge" indefinitely. They need ways to take advantage of the computer revolution, too. And they can do it for $1 a day, or much less—*not* $4 a day. This book will show how.

In this chapter, we'll scope out the computer marketplace—new, refurbished, old, and prehistoric—and I'll offer some guidelines to help you decide what you really need. In Chapter 2, I'll cover everything Cheapskates need to know to buy a new computer. Then, in Chapter 3, I'll take a close look at the refurbished and used computer marketplaces—both private and commercial sellers—and show you how to take a good hard look at a used computer.

First Computer versus Second Computer

Industry surveys show that 65 percent of the people buying a computer already own a computer. At the same time, 60 percent of American households *don't* own a computer. Arguably, the computer industry has been doing something seriously wrong to miss all those people.

For the moment, it's enough to point out that first-time and second-time computer buyers often have very different concerns. Many first-time buyers are concerned with cost, ease of use, and fundamental questions of computer literacy. Second-time buyers generally have a pretty good idea of what computers can do for them, and they may be more concerned with performance, reliability and value. Having been around the block a few times, they're more sophisticated about the marketplace, and a little less afraid to get their hands dirty. Often, they're purchasing an additional system for another member of the family, or purchasing a new system and handing down the older one.

I'll try to be respectful of these varying concerns throughout the book, but if you've gotten this far, I feel safe in making *one* assumption: You are definitely a Cheapskate.

Unlimited Possibility = Unlimited Expense

When it comes to buying computers, there's a philosophical issue lurking just under the surface that's rarely discussed. Let's talk about it.

If you're completely open to the possibility that you'll do just *anything* with your PC, it logically follows that you want the world's most powerful computer—just in case it turns out that only the most powerful computer will do what you want. That has been a reasonable argument for a very long time: People have continued to invent cool new things for personal computers to do for nearly 20 years now. And it's what has made personal computing so exciting for the millions of people who care about it most: *the idea of unlimited possibility.* (With the American frontier long closed, outer space pretty well off the table, a long-term budget deficit, and so on, society's a little short on "unlimited possibilities" nowadays.)

On the other hand, many people have a pretty good idea of what they'll be doing with their computer. Word processing. Spreadsheets. The company finances. Homework. Surfing the Web. Printing out birthday cards on an inkjet printer. Most of these applications are relatively mature by now. Microsoft Word or WordPerfect will do everything a writer can imagine, and then some. It's getting more and more difficult for software publishers to imagine compelling new features that will sell upgrades.

Moreover, with the exception of 3D games and professional design, nearly all the types of software you're likely to need will run pretty well with hardware that's nowhere near state of the art.

OK, how about the *next* generation of applications—the ones that will use high-quality full-motion video, practical and reliable speech recognition, stuff like that? Those are still largely beyond the reach of today's systems no matter *what* you buy.[1] And as far as user interfaces go, it appears you'll still be using a mouse to point and click on menus and windows for awhile yet. Direct mind-to-PC interfaces look as if they'll be in the labs for quite a while.

For the last several years, much of the new power being delivered by the latest hardware has been gobbled up by newer operating system software and newer applications. The saying in the industry is what Andy Grove (from Intel) gives us in terms of faster processors, Microsoft's Bill Gates takes away in terms of bulkier, more complex applications and operating systems. For many users, the benefits of a faster computer can therefore appear subtle indeed.

Your challenge is to determine whether newer equipment and software really meet *your* needs so much better that they're worth the stiff premium they command. The industry doesn't help much. I will.

Here's a "for instance," courtesy of Michael Slater,[2] the industry's leading microprocessor analyst. A few years ago, word processing software developers would never have considered "on-the-fly spell-checking." It would simply slow down users' computers too much. Now, with faster

▲ ▲ ▲ ▲ ▲ ▲ ▲ ▲ ▲ ▲ ▲ ▲ ▲ ▲ ▲ ▲ ▲ ▲ ▲ ▲

1.   In making these predictions, I'm painfully aware that the world is full of surprise. At the turn of the century, Lord Kelvin, the leading physicist of his day, warned students not to go into physics: All the tough problems had already been solved, he told them. A few years later, along came Einstein, Bohr, quantum mechanics . . . and physics suddenly became more exciting than ever before. That could happen to PCs—but if so, it'll almost certainly involve hardware you can't buy now, no matter how much you spend.

2.   *PC World Online* interview, February 9, 1997, © PC World Communications. All rights reserved.

processors, the slowdown doesn't matter as much, so developers add the feature. It's a cool, incremental improvement, nice to have. Is it essential to you—*enough* to be worth, say, $1,000 in incremental hardware costs? That's a different question.

If you're determined to stay on the leading edge *all* the time—if you want to be the first person on your block with Windows 98, Windows 2001, and new applications to go with them—you'll need leading-edge hardware. And you really *will* need to replace it every couple of years.

On the other hand, if you find software you really like, stick with it, get to know its nooks and crannies, keep learning all the nifty things it can already do, stay fairly cautious about software upgrades, and maintain your system properly, your next computer could last you a *very* long time.

Generations: How Much Computer Is Enough for You?

If you're buying your first computer, the next couple of pages are intended to help you get oriented. If you're an experienced user, you'll probably know some of this, but you'll still find the tables valuable in purchasing, identifying, or selling older systems.

Computers, like people, come in generations. Understanding those generations is the quickest way of focusing on what you need and want. The easiest way to identify a computer's generation—and its approximate age and performance level—is by the microprocessor it uses. This isn't foolproof; computer performance is determined by many factors. But 95 percent of the time, it's the best place to start.

> **tip** For precise details on when every microprocessor in the known universe was first introduced, see Aad Offerman's Chiplist: *http://einstein.et.tudeflt.nl/ ~offerman/chiplist.html#*. Of course it takes a while after a chip is formally introduced for it to start showing up in products.

Table 1-1 gives you a quick guide for PC compatibles; Table 1-2 offers comparable information for Macintosh computers, which use Motorola microprocessors instead of Intel-style chips. I'll tiptoe into the ongoing Windows versus Mac war a little later in this chapter and cover Mac buying in detail in Chapter 9.

Table 1–1 Generations of PC Compatibles

Generation	Speed	Dates (Approx.)	Prices (Used/Refurb)[a]	Operating System
8088/8086	4.77–10 MHz	1982–1986	$100 or less	DOS only
80286	6–20 MHz	1984–1988	$150 or less	DOS only[b]
80386	16–40 MHz	1985–1991	$100–$250	DOS and/or Windows 3.1. Faster 80386s will run Windows 3.1 comfortably.
80486	20–120 MHz	1989–1994	$250 (486SX/20, 486SX/25) $500 (486/66, 486DX4/100)	Dos and/or Windows 3.1. Later 486s will comfortably run Windows 95. Majority of machines had Windows 3.1 preloaded.
Pentium and compatibles	60–200+ MHz	1994–1998	$550–$650 (Pentium 60, 66, 75); $600–$800 (Pentium 90, 100, 120); $800 and up (Pentium 133 through 200 and beyond)	Windows 95, Windows 3.1, DOS (Windows 95 or occasionally Windows NT usually preloaded)
Pentium Pro	150–300+ MHz	1996–?	$2,000 and up (new)	Windows NT, Windows 95
Pentium II	233+ MHz	1997–?	$2,000 and up (new)	Windows NT, Windows 95

[a] For typical system with keyboard, but excluding monitor and mouse. May or may not include software. Prices as of spring 1997.

[b] Masochists will point out that Windows 3.0 can be made to run on a 286—very, very slowly.

7

In Table 1-1, I've made a point of distinguishing between DOS-only and Windows PCs. That's because this distinction generally corresponds to a division between an older, text-oriented style of computing, and a newer, graphics-oriented style. There's no such distinction on the Mac side: A Mac has always been graphical, and the unmistakable personality of a Mac hasn't changed much over the years—though big-time changes are now on the way.

Millions of people are doing useful work on DOS-only machines, using programs like WordPerfect 5.1 for word processing, Lotus 1-2-3 for spreadsheet calculations, and either a flat-file database or the extremely arcane dBASE II for database projects. Those aren't the programs I'd pick to start with today, but you *can* be productive with them. And with a going price of less than $100 for a complete used DOS system, they really are the right choice for *some* people.

Table 1–2 Generations of Macintosh Compatibles

Generation	Speed	Dates	Prices (Used/Refurb.)
68000	8 MHz	1984–1990	$100–$200
68020	16 MHz	1987–1990	$100–$200
68030	16 MHz–40 MHz	1989–1993	$200–$500
68040	20 MHz–40 MHz	1993–1996	$400–$800
PowerPC 601/601e	60 MHz–120 MHz	1994–1996	$500–$1,000
PowerPC 603/603e	75–200 MHz	1995–	$1,000–$2,000+
PowerPC604/604e	120–233+ MHz	1996–	$1,000–$2,000+

Warning! One strategy I don't recommend: Buying a pre-Windows PC with the idea of upgrading it to Windows. It will cost you much less to start with a low-end, used Windows system.

What Are You Trying to Accomplish?

People give many reasons for buying a computer: "I don't want my children to fall behind in school." "I want to play games." "I might open a business someday." Walk into a computer store, or read a computer magazine, and you're likely to get the same advice: *Buy the most powerful system you possibly can, so it will last longer.* And before you know it, you're shelling out around $2,500—or even more.

But let's step back for a moment to look at some of the most common scenarios for purchasing a computer and see if we can't do a little better than that. These scenarios will help you begin figuring out how much computer you really *need*. You may ultimately decide to buy a more powerful system, but at least you'll have made the choice yourself based on the facts, not simply fear of obsolescence.

Buying a Computer for Your Small Business

Let's say you own a small business, or you run a business out of your home.

What is it that you expect to *do* with your computer? Run the books, do invoicing? Write proposals and correspondence? Make budget projections? Send e-mail and occasionally do research on the World Wide Web? If so, is that all you *ever* expect to do with the system? For many businesses, even after they consider the matter carefully, that *is* all they'll do with the computer they're planning to purchase. (For example, many businesses set aside one computer for sophisticated managerial or creative applications but use the rest for specific tasks such as correspondence or database entry.)

OK, given those parameters, how much computer do you need? You don't want to purchase a system that's *too* ancient, simply because your business depends on the computer working reliably. On the other hand, you certainly don't need the state of the art.

You might start your shopping at the level of a fast 486 (say, a 486/66 or 486 DX/4 100) with at least 8 megabytes of RAM, running Windows 3.1. Most computer aficionados will call a system like that obsolete, and most computer stores will find them too unprofitable to sell, but they could well be all you need.

ONSALE, the leading on-line Web auction, just auctioned off a system just like that—a Dell 486 2/66 system with 8 Mb RAM, 200 Mb Hard Disk and even a 4X CD-ROM—for just $279 plus shipping. Add $200–$250 for a monitor, and you're in business. (Well, OK, you're *already* in business, but the business you're already in will have a very good computer.)

The newest version of QuickBooks and QuickBooks Pro, the leading PC accounting systems, will run on the computers we've described, though they'll run faster with 16 Mb instead of 8 Mb. (That's currently a $40–$50 upgrade.) Older versions[3] won't even need the extra memory.

Let's refine our horsepower estimate a bit. How much of your time do you expect to spend on the computer? An hour a day? Two hours? Eight? Are you a fast typist? Are you especially impatient? If so, let's bump up your hardware requirements somewhat, just to be on the safe side.

I'll get you a refurbished COMPAQ DeskPro XL 5100 Model 535 w/Pentium 100 system—that's a pretty quick computer, and it comes with DOS, Windows 3.1, 16 Mb and a 720 Mb hard drive—for $525 plus shipping from Image Microsystems (**www.imagemicro.com**). I'll add another 16 Mb, 33.6-Kbps modem, and a monitor, and I'll have a very speedy system that can run the latest software, surf the Web, you name it—all for well under $900.

OK, what *haven't* we bought?

You're not playing games, so you don't need a top-of-the-line wavetable sound card, or anything 3D. You don't need a high-speed CD-ROM, unless you're planning to spend a lot of time accessing CD-ROM databases, or unless you plan to install an extraordinary number of CD-ROM based programs. You don't need a monitor larger than 14" or 15". And you certainly don't need a top-of-the-line processor. A Pentium 90 or 100 is more than enough, and you could easily get away with much less power than that.

▲ ▲ ▲ ▲ ▲ ▲ ▲ ▲ ▲ ▲ ▲ ▲ ▲ ▲ ▲ ▲ ▲

3.   We'll discuss purchasing older versions of software in Chapter 4. One current source for older versions of QuickBooks is Software Clearance Outlet, 1-800-230-SOFT.

(Why does this matter to you? Let's say you clear 10 percent profit on your sales. If you can spend $1,000 less on a computer without sacrificing productivity, that's *$10,000* less sales you need to make. I've been around enough small businesses to know how important that can be!)

Buying a Computer for Your Family

You can spend as little or as much as you want to purchase a computer for your family.

Let's say your primary concern is to make sure your child has a computer to do homework assignments, perhaps to write reports and run some basic educational software. If that's all you need, you could get away with something like IBM PS/2 Model 56s—relatively slow 386 systems with 12-Mb RAM, 160-Mb hard drive, and a low-end monitor—all auctioned recently by ONSALE for well under $200, plus $37.95 shipping.

So your child is a really quick typist? OK, how about a refurbished Compaq 486 DX2-66 All-in-One Prolinea system with 8-Mb RAM, a 270-Mb hard drive, and a .28-dot-pitch color monitor, all for $399 plus shipping? Add DOS and Windows 3.1 for around another $75 and you have a very respectable student system.

Still not enough? A 1994-vintage Pentium P75 upgraded to 24 Mb and Windows 95 would place you *squarely* in the lap of luxury—still for well under $800 complete. Beyond this, and all you're doing is keeping up with the Joneses.

Again, the specifics are likely to change by the time you read this, and you may decide you want features that aren't in these systems. But the point is, no matter what anyone tells you, *you don't have to spend $2,000!*

• *What about Games?*

Games may be your biggest obstacle in buying a cost-effective computer for your family. Serious gamers want every ounce of power they can afford—and a few tons of power they can't afford, for good measure. There's no such thing as a powerful enough computer for people who are desperately into Quake.

As the Cheapskate in your family, are you considering a $2,500 computer system instead of a $1,000 system purely because someone in your household wants the best possible gaming experience?

If so, you have options. One is to say no.

If that's not heresy enough, try this: Buy the computer as if you never plan to let a game anywhere near it. Then, with a quarter of the money you save, spend $150–$200 on a separate game system that hooks to your television. You'll have to do the math to see if this will really make sense for you.

> **tip**
>
> Sony recently cut the list price of its PlayStation to $149, with more price cuts rumored before Christmas 1997. Sony has also introduced a budget line of PlayStation game software under $25. Nintendo 64 may be a bit cooler at the moment, but as a Cheapskate you have to set limits!

Buying a Computer for a Writer

What do you write? Novels? Newsletters? Articles? Manuals with lots of cross-references, indexes, and graphics? Let's assume you write fairly complex stuff, and you're making a living at it (or trying to). You need a powerful system—but you *still* don't need to pay an arm and a leg for it.

How about the new Compaq Presario 2200, which uses an inexpensive, new 180-MHz processor from Cyrix, comes with 16-Mb memory, a 2-Gb hard disk, 33.6-Kbps modem, an 8-speed CD-ROM drive, and Windows 95. That's $799 list as I write. Add $300 for a new 15" monitor.

Or, if name brands don't mean much to you, how about the even more powerful P166 system from CompuWorld with 16-Mb RAM, Windows 95 *and* a 14" 0.28-dot-pitch monitor for $919!

Finally, if you need high-end word processing software, add Microsoft Word (or Corel WordPerfect Suite, which combines the latest version of WordPerfect with tons of additional software for roughly the same price). If you've been using a computer, you almost certainly own word processing software which qualifies you for lower upgrade pricing on either of these packages. Standard upgrades are under $100, but if you're one of the millions of people who qualify for academic pricing, you can pay even less. See page 139 for the details.

Buying a Computer for an Internet User

The Web is evolving fast, so it's not easy to make predictions about hardware requirements several years out. Having said that, right now very few Web-related technologies require more than an entry-level Pentium-level system, that is, a Pentium 100. Netscape claims its new Communicator Internet communications suite will run on a 486; Microsoft's current Internet Explorer does as well.

Two significant exceptions are Web-based videoconferencing and document sharing. And as Web sites increasingly use Java and ActiveX—which require your computer to shoulder more of the work—it's likely that faster Pentium systems will begin to make more sense. At the same time, the owners of most Web sites have an interest in setting up as few barriers to access as possible. That means creating sites that can be viewed by virtually any Web user.

One obvious factor in choosing a system for Web use is modem speed. If you're serious about Web access, find a 56-Kbps modem, and an Internet service provider who supports *that specific modem, right now, at no extra charge*, and a modem vendor who guarantees to upgrade your modem to the final 56-Kbps standard at little or no cost.

> *Warning*! Also check with your Internet service provider or telephone company about whether your telephone line will work with 56K modems. In some areas, the local phone companies haven't upgraded the lines to do so.

Buying a Computer for a Nonprofit Organization

Well, there are nonprofits and then there are nonprofits. The Rockefeller Foundation can fend for itself. Let's assume you're a community organization, highly dependent on volunteers, and without much money. Let's say you need to provide workstations for your volunteers to write thank-you letters to contributors, or perhaps to enter data into a database. Nobody expects you to have state-of-the-art equipment, but you do need equipment that *works*.

As always, there are many ways to approach this. How about a Macintosh solution? Older Cheapskate Macs are easier to use and more fool-proof than older Cheapskate PCs, hands down—which is important if you're working with occasional users who might just be trouble prone. Equally nice, they have Appletalk networking built in. It's slow, but it's reliable and easy to use.

How about Macintosh Classic IIs with built-in black-and-white monitors, purchased through the services of the United Computer Exchange clearinghouse for an average price of around $215 apiece, plus keyboard (**www.uce.com**, 800-755-3033)? Or for systems with a little more punch, how about Mac IIci 4/80 bundles with Apple 13" Trinitron and keyboard, cleaned and refurbished by MacResQ and currently $399 each?

If necessary, add one faster Mac to store your centralized database. Tie them all together with standard phone wire and Farallon PhoneNet (or clone) connectors, add an inexpensive laser printer (preferably new, since you'll be using it a lot), and that's about all you'll need.

You won't be able to use the spiffiest new version of Microsoft Word, or create photo separations using Adobe Photoshop and incorporate them in four-color QuarkXpress layouts. But you *will* be able to run Claris Works or any version of Word through 5.1 with no problem, and that should be plenty.

Do You Need Windows 95 (or Windows 98)?

What about Windows 95? Well, if you're buying a new system retail or via mail order, and it's not a Mac, you're *getting* Windows 95—it's not an issue. If you're buying an older system, or if you already have one, *then* it's a question.

So far there aren't a lot of things you can do with Windows 95 or the anticipated Windows 98 that you simply *cannot* do without it. And no matter what anyone tells you, Windows 95 requires more heavy-duty hardware than its predecessors. If your needs aren't too demanding, you can comfortably run Windows 3.1 on an 80386DX/25 system with 8 Mb and a 120-Mb hard drive, and you can get one of those used for $400, *including* a monitor and with Windows 3.1 preloaded.

To get the same performance out of Windows 95, you'd need at least a 486DX/50 with 16 Mb, a lot more storage, and quite possibly, a faster drive. Since most machines of that era *don't* come with Windows 95 preloaded, you'll need the Windows 95 upgrade disk, and possibly a CD-ROM drive to run it on. Now we've spent at least another $300– $400—and we're still talking about used systems that are several years old. To run brand-new applications like Microsoft Office 97, you'll need more memory yet. And when Windows 98 shows up, you'll doubtless need still more.

Having said that, Windows 95 is significantly easier for a novice to learn, it's more reliable than its predecessors and includes a bundle of software that might well save you money in the long run. It's easier to use the Internet and World Wide Web with Windows 95—and the forthcoming Windows 98 has been redesigned to be thoroughly integrated with the Internet.

Since the vast majority of all PCs sold today come with Windows 95 preloaded, most software is now being written for Windows 95 first, and other environments as an afterthought, if at all. This newer software *tends* to do more and do it more easily (though you *will* get some arguments on this). Last but not least, in my opinion, the newer Windows environments are more *fun* than the older ones. Of course, only *you* can evaluate the trade-offs.

Windows or Mac?

As a Cheapskate, I don't want to waste a *whole* lot more ink on this issue than has already been spent. Briefly, if you have a personal preference, go with it. Let's say you just like Macs; you've used them before; you appreciate their simplicity and elegance of design. That's a good reason to stay with Macs. There are Cheapskate solutions for both platforms. (Chapter 9 covers Mac-specific Cheapskate ideas and sources.)

If you're purchasing your first new system, in my humble opinion there's very little ease-of-use difference between Windows 95 and the Mac. Along with a sympathetic guide, sit down in front of a Mac for a half-hour; then do the same with a Windows 95 machine. I'll bet you'll wonder what on Earth people are arguing about.

If you're purchasing an older system, you'll probably find a used Mac easier to learn than an older Windows 3.1 system, and you'll certainly find it easier than a pure MS-DOS PC. Very old Macs like the Macintosh SE and Macintosh Classic came with built-in black-and-white monitors, so it's possible to get a complete Mac solution for $100–$150, plus software. (Make sure you get the original disks, manuals and licenses—and see the detailed tips on buying a used computer in Chapter 3.)

There's been intense competition among PC hardware manufacturers for 15 years, leaving an amazing legacy of choice and price/performance. Traditionally, PC price/performance has been clearly superior to Mac price/performance. Competition is newer on the Mac side, but it's made a huge difference. Even Apple's newest machines are surprisingly cost-effective. The price gap is rapidly disappearing; for many environments, it's completely gone. For three years, Apple has claimed the Mac's PowerPC chip would offer better price/performance than PCs based on Intel-style chips. For three years, this was pure wishful thinking. Now there are early signs it might actually happen.

On the other hand, as Apple's market share has shrunk (down to 5.2 percent, according to Apple's own securities disclosure statements), your choices for add-on software and hardware have shrunk as well. Once, interesting new products appeared on the Mac first. Now they appear for Windows 95 first and may or may not *ever* find their way to the Mac. Also, Cheapskates will find more cheap stuff for PCs than for Macs. The PC market is big enough to have all kinds of segments and niches, including a sizable Cheapskate niche.

Some people try to buy the same type of computer that's in their children's schools. Given that Windows 95 and Macs use pretty much the same visual metaphors and the software for both bears quite a resemblance, I wouldn't worry about it much. Your children are flexible enough to handle whatever decision you make. And for the past several years Macs have read PC disks, so your kids can still bring in their homework on floppy if they want.

If you're doing work for business, it's a little different. File formats can vary between Mac and Windows programs (even when they're not supposed to). While file conversions aren't a major hassle, minor annoyances like font changes can quickly become big problems if you're not careful. So you can make more of a case to own the same type of computer your *clients* do. Typically, that's a Windows PC—but not always.

If you're a graphic designer, or if you're in multimedia, or if you *want* to be, then Macs are still your safest choice. According to a fall 1996 survey by *Web Week*, 64 percent of professional Web site design firms use Macs.[4] That's where the expertise is. That's where the infrastructure is. That's what people *expect* you to have.

A few more points. Windows 95 PCs come with a big batch of free software, none of it top of the line but much of it surprisingly adequate. (See page 120 for more about this.) Macs, except for the recently discontinued Performas, generally haven't.[5]

If you're planning to add hardware to your computer later, that's a lot easier to do on the Mac side. On the other hand, if you're purchasing a complete system that already includes a CD-ROM drive, audio card, and other stuff, it doesn't make much difference.

Unless you've been living in a cave on Mars, you probably know that Apple's had serious financial problems. According to its CEO, it will keep losing money throughout 1997.[6] The current MacOS operating system (currently System 8.0) has millions of passionate admirers, but they've increasingly noticed it's held together with baling wire and Crazy Glue.® The replacement operating system, Rhapsody, is still under development.

If you buy a new Mac today, it will almost certainly run Rhapsody; how fast is anyone's guess. Chances are, most PowerMacs made in the past couple of years will run Rhapsody. Again, if history is any indication, they'll run it more slowly than you might like. Macs older than that definitely *won't* run Rhapsody, though Apple promises to keep upgrading the operating system they use now.

OK? No passionate e-mails on these two pages, please.

▲ ▲ ▲ ▲ ▲ ▲ ▲ ▲ ▲ ▲ ▲ ▲ ▲ ▲ ▲ ▲ ▲ ▲ ▲

4.   *Web Week* Magazine, Volume 2, Issue #15, October 1996, ©Mecklermedia Corp. All rights reserved.
5.   Though there are exceptions, such as Apple's recently introduced Small Business Bundle.
6.   Apple continued losses through 1997, as per 4/16/97 Apple press release.

Buy Now, or Wait?

As you already know, the longer you wait, the better the system you can afford. New systems become more powerful; old systems move down the food chain and become less expensive. On the other hand, you could wait forever, and *never* benefit from the technology. So when is the best time to buy?

1. Don't buy before you've had a chance to shop around. *No* deal is too good to compare with the rest of the marketplace.

2. If you're thinking about buying a computer for Christmas, put a rain check under the tree and wait a month or two. You won't just benefit from the after-Christmas sales; you'll also benefit from Intel's regularly scheduled microprocessor price reductions, which for the past few years have occurred like clockwork in January or February.

3. Be aware of the technologies that are just around the corner but make an intelligent decision about whether you want to wait for them. For example, DVD (Digital Video Disk)—essentially CD-ROMs with ten times the capacity—has been "almost here" for a while now and looks as if it will be almost here for a while yet.[a]

a. Well, you *can* buy DVD today, but the early hardware has problems and there's virtually no software for it. Oh, well.

Other technologies that have been promised for a while but still aren't here include USB, the Universal Serial Bus, which will eventually allow you to connect multiple devices to your PC without opening it. USB is finally beginning to find its way into PCs. Maybe one of these days it will find its way into products you *can connect* to PCs.

Some technologies are already here but won't do you any good until a whole bunch of other things happen. In spring 1997, the best example was Intel's MMX "multimedia extensions," which sound terrific, but are supported by very little software. We'll cover MMX in more detail on page 35.

> **tip** How do you find out what *really* is just around the corner? If you have Web access, my favorite solution is to visit the *Computer Retail News* Web site *(www.crn.com)*, where the *retailers* find out what they'll be selling in a few months.

The Network Computer: For Individuals, a Pig in a Poke?

For the past year, a debate has been raging in the computer industry. In only months, it's become as noisy and acrimonious as the grudge match between Mac and Windows users—and that's been going on for a decade.

The debate is over the *network computer* (NC). This is a device with no floppy disk or hard drive, which is designed to process software and data stored on a network or the Internet. Typically, it will run software written in a new computer language called Java—which doesn't require Microsoft Windows, MS-DOS, or expensive microprocessors from Intel.

It costs a lot for a large business to buy and maintain its PCs, keep all the software running right, and keep all the users happy. (Nope, GM doesn't typically shop where we Cheapskates do.) Moreover, there's a suspicion that people in those large companies are wasting one-third of their time creating fancy documents with too many fonts and too much clip art; wasting the second third visiting the *Playboy* Web site; and spending whatever time is left stealing company secrets on floppy disks.

The network computer is intended as a low-cost solution to all these problems—and not incidentally, as a way of shifting power away from Microsoft and Intel, to other companies like Sun, Oracle, and IBM. It might very well achieve *all* those goals.

How do you fit into this as an individual?

Someone, somewhere, is going to try to sell *you* a network computer. They'll offer to charge you a lot less than your local superstore will charge you for a full-fledged computer… maybe as little as $500–$750. They'll say the low-cost network computer will make the information age accessible to people who couldn't otherwise benefit.

Should you bite? Well, consider.

You'll need to subscribe to a monthly network service which will deliver your programs and data to you—including your personal, private data, which will presumably be encrypted to provide protection. What will that cost? $20 a month? $30? Will you have to rent your software on a per-use basis, like pay-per-view movies?

When the network is down, your network computer will be about as useful as a rock. Will the network be reliable? More reliable than the Internet is today? Will the network be fast enough? Faster than the Internet is today?

On the other hand, since your programs and data are stored centrally, you could theoretically access them from any network computer on Earth, once you properly identify yourself—you wouldn't need a notebook PC.

You wouldn't have to worry about all the routine PC maintenance tasks that slow down computer users nowadays: backups, disk defragmentation, and the like. Presumably, *hopefully*, your network computer service provider would be doing that for you. That's why Sun Microsystems, a leading proponent of the network computer, can advertise it as delivering *freedom* to users.

Suffice to say, others disagree, since network computers are essentially captives of the network, with no independent capabilities. For people who have found PCs empowering, identifying the NC with freedom may be the most Orwellian use of the term since the Cold War ended.

You'll have to decide for yourself, based on your own needs. Right now, as you may already suspect, I think you're better off pursuing a bargain on a *real* PC.

> If NCs start to look viable, you may have another option. JavaSoft, the division of Sun that is promoting Java, says it will deliver software which turns old 486 computers into network computers, and charge roughly $99 for that software when it's introduced. 486s are already cheaper than network computers, and by that time, they'll be *dramatically* cheaper. Plus, they'll still be able to run Windows and DOS software when they're not doing Java stuff.

New, Refurbished, or Used?

Computers are like cars. The instant you drive them out of the showroom, their value plummets. As with cars, some people prefer to let others take the loss; others are uncomfortable with any system that isn't brand new.

Then there are compromise solutions. You can buy a used car from Hertz; you'll know it probably took a good beating for a year, but got every oil change it was supposed to get. Ditto, you can purchase a computer off-lease from a Fortune 500 company like IBM Credit or GE Capital.

You can buy new computers at a department store (shudder), an electronics store, a computer superstore, a warehouse club, by mail, or on the Web. There are manufacturers' outlets and "almost-new" refurbished systems.

Which is best for you? Two rules of thumb: Don't take any risks you're not comfortable with. On the other hand, never pay top dollar for better reliability and support unless you're sure you'll actually get them. Either way, the more questions you ask, the better value you'll get. We'll take a much closer look at these issues in the next two chapters.

Summary

In Chapter 1, I've tried to strip away some of the mystique that goes with buying computers and help you begin to determine what you *really* need. In the next two chapters, I'll get more specific.

Chapter 2 covers buying new computers; Chapter 3 covers buying refurbished and used computers. I'll tell you where to look, what to know, and exactly what questions to ask in order to get the best possible deal.

2

Buying a *New* Computer: Where, When, and How

- Name Brand or Generic

- How Do You Evaluate a Vendor?

- New Systems under $1,000—Finally!

- Where to Buy: A World of Market Channels

- Buying on the Web

- Computer Shows and Swap Meets

- You're Not Finished When You Get the Box Home

- Summary

After considering the issue with utmost care, notwithstanding your Cheapskate nature, you've decided you want a fast, new computer.

Now the question is: *Where* and *how* should you buy it? You have more choices than ever before: not just the traditional computer retailer or department store, but also superstores, warehouse clubs, local clone manufacturers, mail order, manufacturer's outlets, bare-bones systems, even build it yourself. But not all of them are equally well suited to Cheapskates.

Remarkably, nearly 20 years into the personal computer revolution, you still have hundreds of brand names to choose from. Every year there's another industry shakeout among PC manufacturers, and some fall by the wayside. But others shake *in*. While the software industry has undergone a consolidation of nearly black-hole proportions, with Microsoft inhaling one market after another, the same thing hasn't happened in hardware. Yet.

More choices, more power, tougher decisions. Let's get to work.

Name Brand or Generic?

There are two Cheapskate viewpoints about purchasing new computers, each with some merit. One viewpoint holds that you should purchase a computer from a well-known company, thereby making it more likely you will get a quality machine. The consensus list of top-of-the-line vendors currently includes

Compaq
P.O. Box 692000
Houston, TX 77269-2000
1-800-345-1518; 281-370-0670
www.compaq.com
IBM Personal Computer Company
1-800-426-7255 (1-800-426-7235 for Aptiva and Thinkpad 365)
www.pc.ibm.com

Dell Computer Corporation
2214 W. Braker Lane
Austin, TX 78758
1-800-879-8510; 1-800-289-3355
www.dell.com

Micron Electronics
900 E. Karcher Road
Nampa, ID 83687
1-800-347-3490; 1-208-893-3434
www.mei.micron.com

Hewlett-Packard
1-800-472-5277
www.hp.com/PersonalComputing/

Gateway 2000
610 Gateway Drive
North Sioux City, SD 57049-2000
1-800-846-2059; 1-605-232-2000
www.gw2k.com

Another way of defining top vendors is to consider this (partial) list of companies that have achieved ISO 9000 certification for quality, and who happen to sell personal computers:

- ▲ Apple (sells Macintoshes)
- ▲ Canon (no longer sells PCs in the United States)
- ▲ Compaq

▲ Digital Equipment Corp. (no longer sells retail PCs but does sell to corporations; refurbished DEC systems are widely available)
▲ Epson
▲ Hewlett-Packard
▲ IBM
▲ Motorola (sells Macintosh compatibles)
▲ NEC
▲ Sony
▲ Toshiba[1]

Of course, these lists are intended as places to *start*. There are plenty of other high-quality systems out there, and not every system provided by a leading vendor is top quality.

An alternative Cheapskate viewpoint is that your prime concern is to purchase a computer that uses interchangeable, industry-standard parts—the more generic, the better. That way, if something *does* go wrong, the repairs will be much less expensive, and the system will also be much easier to upgrade. Many of the top-tier vendors, especially Compaq and IBM, and to a lesser degree Dell and Gateway, design customized motherboards, making upgrades and repairs more complicated and expensive. The safest way to make sure you get generic parts, they say, is to purchase a generic computer from a generic clone vendor whom you trust to use quality components.

The more comfortable you are around computers, the more sense the second strategy makes. We'll cover both, starting with the brand names.

How Do You Evaluate a Vendor?

Things change fast in the computer business, and even if you're narrowing your list of manufacturers to just a few of the leaders, you'll want to carefully evaluate each vendor's *current* products and performance. Few computer buyers go any further than a little hearsay: "*Uncle Bob has a*

▲ ▲ ▲ ▲ ▲ ▲ ▲ ▲ ▲ ▲ ▲ ▲ ▲ ▲ ▲ ▲ ▲ ▲ ▲

1.   ISO9000 needs to be taken with a small grain of salt, however. In early 1997, as reported in InfoWorld and elsewhere, some Toshiba customers found it so difficult to reach the company for technical support that they swore off Toshiba products indefinitely.

Dell and he's happy with it." As a Cheapskate, you know it's worth invest-ing a little more time upfront to get more reliability, better service, and lower overall life-cycle costs.

There are two ways to dramatically improve your odds. First, see what people are saying about your prospective vendor *now*. There's a rushing river of objective and subjective information out there, much of it avail-able on the Internet for free.

Second, ask the vendor some very pointed questions about product, service, and warranty.

What Are People Saying?

There's a community of millions of PC users, and many of them are eager to share their opinions—usually passionate, often reasoned, sometimes both.

Start with the obvious: the computer magazine reviews, many of which are on-line at the leading publishers' sites (see Chapter 11). But don't stop there.

For a reasonably objective, once-over-lightly treatment of the leading brands and trends, there's the old standby, *Consumer Reports*—to be found in nearly every library on Earth, or on-line through CompuServe. (Surprisingly, there's no *CR* Web site yet.) *CR* reviews personal computers regularly—most recently, in the September and December 1996 issues. *CR's* opinions on computers are sometimes debatable, but then when it comes to computers, what isn't?

For a self-selected, but very large survey of customer satisfaction with various brands' reliability and service (representing nearly 12,000 read-ers), see *PC World* Magazine—most recently the December 1996 issue: **www.pcworld.com/workstyles/athome/articles/dec96/1412p143.html**.

A smaller, family-oriented survey, with just under 1,000 families responding, appeared in *Family PC*, February 1997: **www.zdnet.com/family/pc/content/960916/cover/table.html**.

J.D. Power & Associates, the folks that seem to show up in half the world's automobile ads (best initial satisfaction, and so on) have diversi-fied into rating PCs. You can find summaries of their most recent surveys of customer satisfaction—including separate data for desktop PCs and notebooks—at **www.jdpower.com** (see Figure 2-1).

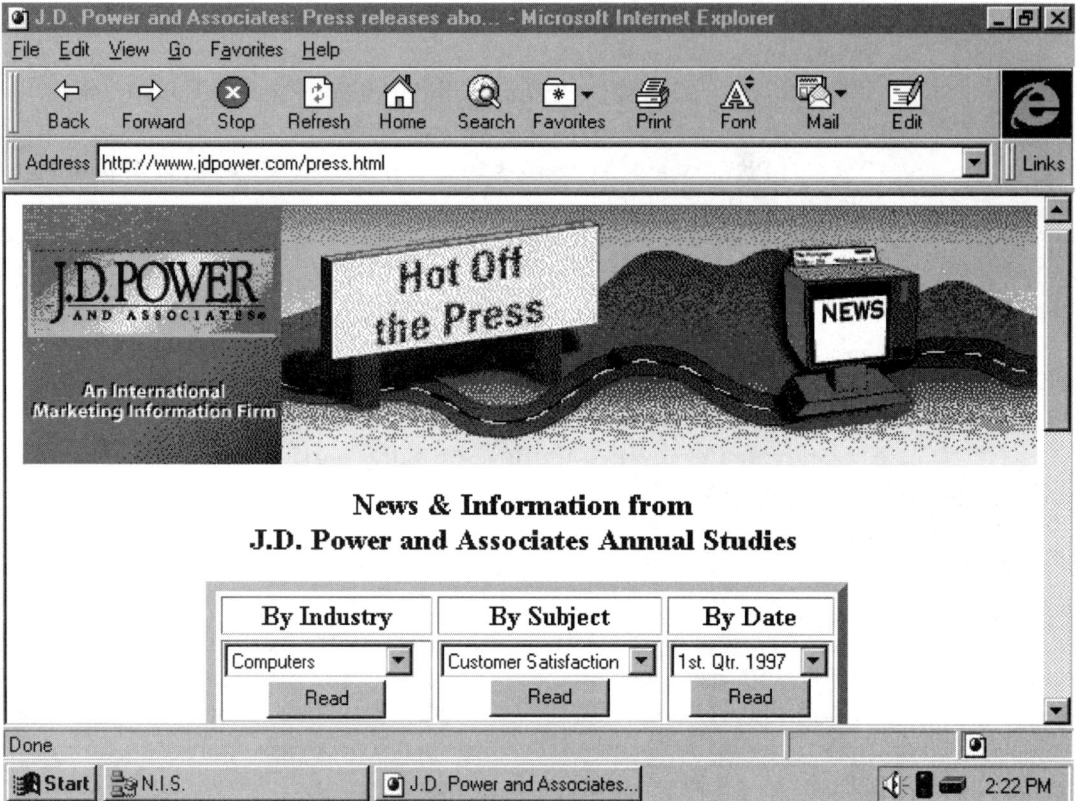

Figure 2–1   J.D. Power: Trying to do for computers what they've done for cars.

At the other end of the spectrum, there's **www.ct.net/~zoo/zoo/**—a Web site that rates users' buying experiences with a wide range of direct channel vendors too small to be caught on the radar screen of those big surveys. The samples are small—and anything but random. But they can be *very* revealing. When all 20 people who report purchasing from a company say the experience was "poor," that tells you something you really ought to know.

Of course, you don't have to rely on surveys. You can ask computer users directly. If you're one of the 1.4 million remaining U.S. CompuServe members, you can post a question on the appropriate forum, or see what people are already saying:

- ▲ IBM, GO IBMPS1 (covers Aptivas and PS/1s)
- ▲ IBM, GO IBMSVR (covers PC servers)
- ▲ IBM, GO IBMPS2 (covers PS/2s)
- ▲ For Dell, GO DELL
- ▲ For Gateway, GO GATEWAY

For those brands that do not maintain a CompuServe forum, such as Compaq, you can ask the sophisticated group of PC experts and consultants who haunt the PC Hardware forum (GO PCHW), or the friendly bunch at the PC New Users forum, (GO PCNEW).

Whether or not you have CompuServe, if you have access to Internet newsgroups, one of the best sources of up-to-date information is **comp.sys.ibm.pc.hardware.systems**.

By the way, the FAQ (Frequently Asked Questions document) associated with this newsgroup is one of the most complete and reliable free sources of information about PCs you'll find anywhere. *Highly* recommended.

One more very good independent source: The Online Computer Buying Guide (**www.cmhc.com/computers/**) is a clearinghouse for personal experiences with several prominent computer vendors—both positive and negative. As of March 1997, four vendors are represented: Dell, Gateway, Comtrade, and Midwest Micro. (Comtrade's report includes an unsatisfactory Better Business Bureau Report dated February 7, 1996.)

Poor Customer Service Reputations

I'll give you one more list: companies that have been getting a lot of bad publicity lately for customer service, either in print or on-line. I'm certainly not saying these are the worst companies in the industry. What's more, things have a way of changing quickly—for worse and for better. Still, you should know whose service and support organizations seemed to be evoking unusual levels of frustration in spring 1997:[2]

- ▲ Iomega (complaints about software and hardware support on Zip and Ditto drives)
- ▲ Midwest Micro (complaints about refunds)
- ▲ Packard Bell (complaints about reliability and access to support)
- ▲ Power Computing (complaints about delivery dates, and occasionally about reliability)
- ▲ Toshiba (complaints about access to support on notebook PCs)
- ▲ U.S. Robotics (complaints about modem firmware and access to support)

Ask the Right Questions

You've narrowed your list down to a few vendors. Now it's time to start asking some tough questions of the *vendor*. By the way, even if you're planning to buy retail, visit the manufacturer's Web site first, or at least call their 800 number. It's the most efficient way to get answers. Your retail salesperson is unlikely to know the answers to all the questions you'd like to ask—and even more unlikely to want to take the trouble.

I've organized the questions you'll want to ask into two categories: questions that can help you compare the real *value* of different products, and questions about support. In each case, you'll find a Cheapskate's comparison chart you can use when you shop—and a discussion of the questions and answers you're looking for.

The System Comparison Checklist in Table 2-1 focuses heavily on system upgrade potential. Even if you have no intention of ever upgrading your computer, these questions are important, because they affect its resale value.

▲ ▲ ▲ ▲ ▲ ▲ ▲ ▲ ▲ ▲ ▲ ▲ ▲ ▲ ▲ ▲ ▲ ▲ ▲ ▲

2.   Based on complaints published in printed trade media and presented in assorted on-line forums.

Table 2–1 System Comparison Checklist (PCs)

	Model #1	Model #2	Model #3	Model #4
Power				
Processor				
Bus speed				
Bus (PCI, ISA, VL-BUS, EISA?)				
Memory (How much?)				
Hard disk [How big (Mb)]?				
Basics				
Floppy drive(s) included? Which?				
Keyboard included?				
Mouse included?				
Operating System included? Win95?				
Useful software?				
Peripherals				
Monitor (How big? Viewable size?)				
Video card (Memory? Brand? Add-in or built-in?)				
CD-ROM (speed?)				
Sound card?				

Table 2–1 System Comparison Checklist (PCs) *(continued)*

	Model #1	Model #2	Model #3	Model #4
Modem? (Speed/brand?)				
Networking (if you care)				
Other features (#1)				
Other features (#2)				
Expandability				
# Serial ports				
# Parallel ports				
Integrated or provided via add-in cards?				
Available **slots?**				
Available **memory slots?**				
Type of memory slots (72-pin, newer DIMM, older 30-pin?)				
Standard Extended Data Out (EDO) or fast-page memory? Speed (ns)?				
Maximum memory?				
Available **Interrupts (IRQs)?**				
BIOS (name)				
Chipset (name)				

Table 2–1 System Comparison Checklist (PCs) *(continued)*

	Model #1	Model #2	Model #3	Model #4
Motherboard form factor (AT, ATX, custom?)				
Functions integrated on motherboard (sound, video, etc.?)				
Service and Support				
Software disks included? (If not, can you create them?)				
Telephone support (days free)				
Warranty (months/years)				
Money				
Price				
Less rebate				
Tax				
Shipping				
Extended warranty				
Installation charges				
Total price				

Processor and Bus Speed

Obviously, processors with "higher numbers" tend to be faster than the processors with "lower numbers." But there's a big catch: At the very top of the new PC spectrum, you almost always pay a lot more for very little more performance. Cheapskates are virtually never found in such rarefied surroundings.

In buying new PCs, the "sweet spot" of the market is always a step or two down. For example, as I write—and this is guaranteed to change—you will pay 15–25 percent more for a Pentium 200 system than you will for a Pentium 166, but you will only get 5–10 percent more performance, all else equal. (To quantify this a little better, see the microprocessor performance table on page 39.)

Expert wisdom holds that systems containing the Pentium 133 and 166 microprocessors are better deals than systems containing the Pentium 120 and 150 microprocessors. That's because the "bus" that controls communications between the microprocessor and everything else is slower in the 120 and 150 systems than in their cousins. The 120s run at 50 MHz and 150s run at 60 MHz—compared with 66 MHz for Pentium 133s and 166s.[3] This is why a Pentium 150 offers very little speed advantage over a 133, even though when these systems were introduced, the 150s cost significantly more.

In any event, as faster processors are introduced, you should ask the *bus speed* of the system you're considering as well as the processor speed.

> tip
>
> In this case, the market has helped compensate for this performance problem: Pentium 120 and 150 systems have become significantly less expensive. What's more, they seem to be much more likely to appear in low-priced closeout deals. In short, even though the 120s and 150s aren't as elegantly engineered, some of them have become very good deals.

• *Pentium Pro and Pentium II*

A word about the Pentium Pro. Ever since IBM introduced the PC AT in 1984, new generations of PCs have always been accompanied by the same mantra: *These are servers. Regular people won't need this much power.*

---

3.   Only PCI cards get the full benefit of PCI bus speeds; older ISA cards still communicate with the processor at roughly 10–16 MHz.

And eventually regular people decide otherwise. But this time around, with the Pentium Pro, it appears it will actually work that way. The Pentium Pro's features have made it especially hard to manufacture inexpensively for the mass market. So Intel has incorporated many of its features in a new microprocessor, Pentium II—adding MMX multimedia extensions, and targeting the new chip specifically for desktop and consumer systems.

If you're considering either a Pentium Pro or a Pentium II, ask about test results on the operating system you intend to run. Pentium Pros were optimized for Windows NT and don't deliver nearly the same bang for the buck on Windows 95. Early reports on Pentium IIs are a bit more promising.

> **tip** If you are purchasing an expensive high-end server system, or if you plan to run Windows NT or UNIX, consider Pentium Pro or Pentium II systems that will support multiple processors —preferably via standard sockets rather than proprietary boards. That will give you relatively inexpensive upgrade options later.

• *MMX: Worth It?*

MMX is a set of new instructions built into microprocessor chips that provide shortcuts for tasks that are most commonly performed by graphics and multimedia software. Therefore, multimedia software designed to work with MMX should run much faster on computers that have MMX.

Which software will take best advantage of MMX? (1) Graphics and design software; (2) games. If those are your priorities, MMX is worth more to you.

The catch is that, as of spring 1997, very few multimedia applications have been rewritten to take advantage of MMX. And it may be 1998 before this changes. To be fair, MMX will also make other applications a little bit faster, but again there may be a catch. Intel's MMX processors contain more internal cache, so some manufacturers (who are paying more for MMX chips) are compensating by cutting back on expensive external memory cache. While the optimal amount of external cache is a matter of some debate, this could lead to systems that may not deliver all the performance benefits MMX can provide.

Sometimes there's a compromise solution: Buy now and upgrade later. But that's not a good option in this case. From a technical standpoint, MMX upgrades are likely to be tricky—unless you use Intel's expensive Overdrive upgrade chips.

So if you're in the market for a new PC in 1997, you can decide with your eyes open whether to pay extra for MMX *now* for results that won't appear until at least next year (and then only if you get the right software). In 1998, of course, this will cease to be an issue: Virtually every Intel-based system will have MMX whether you want it or not.

• *Keeping Intel "Outside"*

One way for Cheapskates to save a bundle is to opt out of paying for Intel's "Intel Inside" advertising campaign by purchasing a system with a competitive processor.

Intel makes very high quality microprocessors, but they aren't the only company that does—and for the most part, competitive manufacturers such as AMD®, Cyrix, IBM Microelectronics, and SGS-Thomson have licked any compatibility issues. (I'll mention a few minor exceptions in a moment.)

As I write, I can purchase an Intel Pentium 166-MHz microprocessor for roughly $209—or a Cyrix 6x86 166+ microprocessor manufactured by IBM that will slightly outperform the Intel chip for just $81.50. At the low end, I can purchase a Pentium 120-MHz microprocessor for $107, or a slightly faster AMD 586 K5 PR-133 for $74.

The differences translate directly into lower system costs. I'm looking at an ad for an Intel Pentium 166 system going for $1,378, and the identical system with the Cyrix 6x86 166+ chip for $1,168.

OK, what's the catch? Very few companies whose names you'll recognize are willing to stray from the comfort of their business relationship with Intel. (Occasionally a non-Intel microprocessor slips quietly into a system made by a second-tier vendor like AST or Packard Bell. And as we'll discuss later, the new Cyrix Media GX processor is at the heart of Compaq's new $999 family PC, but these are exceptions.)

Why are Cyrix and AMD still fighting over 5 percent of the market for Pentium-class chips—and why are their chips scarcer than hen's teeth in top-rank systems? For the most part, Intel has been the only micropro-cessor manufacturer that can supply chips for all parts of the market, from price-sensitive home users to businesses that need top-of-the-line, high-profit servers. Moreover, Intel's vigorous marketing program pays a significant portion of the advertising costs for companies willing to pro-mote Intel Inside.

Companies like Dell, Gateway, and Hewlett-Packard must wonder: Why risk our relationship with Intel, our place in line for the advanced chips we make our biggest profits with, *and* our advertising support—all so we can cut the price of home systems for people who walk into the store asking for "Intel Inside" anyway?

So, who sells systems with "Cyrix" or "AMD" inside? Quite possibly, your local clone dealer. And a bunch of not-quite-household-name national mail-order firms, including

CompuWorld
24441 Miles Road
Cleveland, OH 44128
1-800-6666-CWI; 1-216-595-6500
www.compu-world.com

Technoland
1050 Stewart Drive
Sunnyvale, CA 94086
1-800-292-4500
www.technoland.com

CyberMax
133 N. 5th Street
Allentown, PA 18102
1-800-443-9868; 1-610-770-1808
www.cybmax.com

Yorkshire Computer
11515 W. Carmen Avenue
Milwaukee, WI 53225
1-800-375-1667; 1-414-358-5303
www.yorkshire.com

• *Non-Intel Performance and Compatibility*

Who rates the performance of non-Intel processors? What makes a "166" a 166? For that matter, 166 *what*?

Until recently, there was no easy answer to that question. An AMD chip called the 5x133 *appeared* to compete with a Pentium 133—but in fact it used an older 486-style design, and its performance was roughly comparable to a slower Pentium 75. The 5x133 wasn't a bad chip. It delivers plenty of power for the buck, and it's at the heart of some very good low-cost systems. But a lot of people didn't get what they *imagined* they were paying for.

Now, however, there's an independent performance rating, called the P-Rating, for all Intel-compatible microprocessors. *Micro Design Resources*, the publishers of the respected industry newsletter *Microprocessor Report,* run benchmark tests on real-world Windows 95 applications to determine how new microprocessors compare with existing Intel chips. So when you see a Cyrix chip rated as 166+, you know it was tested to run at least a hair's breadth faster than the Pentium 166. (That's true even though internally the chip runs at only 133 MHz.)

You can see some of the stats in Table 2-2. Note, for instance, that a Cyrix 6x86-PR150+ not only exceeds the performance of a Pentium 150 by 5 percent, it also comes within 0.8 percent of the performance of a Pentium 166.[4] (By the way, these ratings are for non-MMX chips.)

That takes care of *performance*. What about *compatibility*? It's rarely an issue—but I can't quite say it's *never* an issue. With Cyrix chips, make sure your vendor is using a motherboard that has been certified by Cyrix. Early Cyrix chips wouldn't run Windows NT 4.0 or the game Quake, but that's been fixed in more recent versions. Some versions of Windows NT don't recognize AMD's 486 chips (though you'd probably run NT with faster processors anyway).

▲ ▲ ▲ ▲ ▲ ▲ ▲ ▲ ▲ ▲ ▲ ▲ ▲ ▲ ▲ ▲ ▲ ▲ ▲

4.   Table 2-2 also reinforces the point I made earlier about the "sweet spot" of the market, and how Cheapskates should avoid the top of the line. The Pentium 200 offers only 6.4 percent more performance than a Pentium 166 even though it ostensibly runs 20.5 percent faster and as of early 1997, Intel charged about 65 percent more for it.

Table 2–2 Comparing Recent Intel, Cyrix, and AMD Microprocessors[a]

Microprocessor	Benchmark
Cyrix 6x86-PR200+	91.6
Pentium 200	89.0
Cyrix 6x86-PR166+	86.7
Pentium 166	82.7
Cyrix 6x86-PR150+	81.9
Pentium 150	77.6
Cyrix 6x86-PR133+	76.6
Pentium 133	76.6
AMD-K5-PR100	62.0
Pentium 100	60.0
AMD-K5-PR90	58.7
Pentium 90	54.9
AMD-K5-PR75	48.8
Pentium 75	47.4

a. Winstone 96 results measured by MicroDesign Resources (MDR) Laboratories. All chips listed are non-MMX.

A few programs, notably some games, look specifically for a Pentium chip—and since your system will report the Cyrix as either a 486 or a "CyrixInstead," the program won't run. Finally, one area where the Cyrix 6x86 chips are slower than their Intel counterparts is in floating-point calculations. That means engineering and graphics applications won't deliver the same performance as "average" Windows 95 applications.

> You can learn all there is to know about these compatibility and performance issues—and about Cyrix chips in general—at the independent Web site *www.ionet.net/~rbdavis/* and at the official Cyrix site *www.cyrix.com.*

The microprocessor marketplace may finally be getting a little more competitive. Both AMD and Cyrix have just introduced new families of microprocessors to compete with Intel at the high end: the K6 family of processors from AMD and the M2 processors from Cyrix. Both families of chips support MMX, and both companies say they'll maintain pricing significantly lower than Intel's. For more information on who's building systems with Cyrix and AMD chips, you can always contact the chip manufacturers themselves:

> Cyrix Corp.
> 2703 N. Central Expressway
> Richardson, TX 75080-2010
> 1-800-340-7501; 1-972-968-8387
> **www.cyrix.com**

> Advanced Micro Devices, Inc.
> One AMD Place
> P.O. Box 2453
> Sunnyvale, CA 94088-3453
> 1-800-538-8450; 1-408-732-2400
> **www.amd.com**

Memory

If you are purchasing a new system, you're almost certainly purchasing a system with either Windows 95 (or possibly Windows 98, if it's arrived by the time you read this.)[5] That means you're going to need a *lot* of memory.

▲ ▲ ▲ ▲ ▲ ▲ ▲ ▲ ▲ ▲ ▲ ▲ ▲ ▲ ▲ ▲ ▲ ▲ ▲

5.   For Windows NT, add 16–32 megabytes to all estimates here.

Most systems currently ship with 16 Mb. That's fine if you're going to use your system for basic stuff, but it *won't* be enough if you're planning to run industrial-strength software like Microsoft Office 97. Consider at least 24 Mb, and ideally 32 Mb.

Not only will having insufficient memory slow down your computer; it will do so in the most annoying way possible. A computer with a slow processor goes about its business in a slow, methodical way. You know it's slow, but you get used to its rhythms. A computer without enough memory will run beautifully for a couple of minutes, and then suddenly slow to a crawl as it goes searching your hard disk for the code it needs, say, to boldface a block of text. It will be fine when you're adding lists of numbers but slow to a crawl when you decide to multiply them. Every time you get some momentum, zap… you have to stop and wait.

• *How much memory do you really need?*

If you're running Windows 3.1 or Windows for Workgroups, you need a practical minimum of 8 Mb; preferably 16 Mb if you are running serious business applications such as Microsoft Office. If your work is graphics heavy, you may need 24–32 Mb.

If you're running Windows 95, you need a practical minimum of 12–16 Mb, preferably 24–32 Mb if you are running serious business applications. If your work is graphics heavy, you may need 32–48 Mb.

If you're running Windows NT 4.0 Workstation, you need a practical minimum of 24–32 Mb, and you'll be better off with 48–64 Mb.

If you're running Mac OS System 8.0, you need a practical minimum of 16 Mb, preferably 24–32 Mb if you are running serious business applications, and 32–48 Mb or more if your work is graphics heavy.

For a more detailed look at memory requirements for the kind of work you do most, visit **www.kingston.com/srch/srch1.htm**.

As a Cheapskate, you're thinking, "I thought this book was supposed to save me money, not convince me to spend even more." So here's my strategy: Trade down one processor level. That will save you $150–$200. Then add 16 Mb. That will currently cost you less than $75. So, for example, a Pentium 133 with 32 Mb will clearly outperform a Pentium 166 with 16 Mb—at a significantly lower price. Similarly, a Pentium 100 with

16 Mb clearly outperforms a Pentium 133 with 8 Mb, again at a significantly lower price.

See Chapter 5 for more information on buying memory. Here's one tip, however. Two 16-Mb SIMMs currently cost roughly 10-15 percent less than one 32-Mb SIMM. Many new systems are sold with 16 Mb and two empty SIMM sockets. If you're confident that 48 Mb will hold you for a while, purchase two 16-Mb SIMMs, install them yourself, and you've cut your cost significantly.[6]

> *Warning!* If you think you may wish to add memory to an older system that uses 30-pin SIMMs, consider buying sooner rather than later: 30-pin SIMMs are starting to become scarce.

Hard Disks: Know When to Say When

Everyone says the same thing: No matter how big a hard drive you have, in a few months you'll want more.

But who, exactly, *is* "everyone"?

Typically, it's people who write about computers for a living *or* use a lot of different software packages *or* create very large files—typically graphics files, multimedia files, or databases. Since not everyone fits that profile, not everyone needs the largest hard drive on the market.

Let's get out on a limb and see how big a hard drive *you* really need to start with. (In Chapter 5, we'll revisit the subject to discuss hard drive upgrades.)

As of spring 1997, it's very difficult to find a new system from a large manufacturer with a hard drive smaller than 1.2 Gb—that's *1200* megabytes. And the minimum size hard drive is increasing fast, because smaller hard drives are in short supply, as the manufacturers focus on more profitable larger drives. In any event, we'll use 1.2 Gb as our starting point. What can you store on a 1.2-Gb hard drive? Table 2-3 shows you.

---

6.   Make sure to get memory that runs at the same speed (or faster) than the factory-installed memory.

Table 2–3 What's on *Your* Hard Drive?

Contents	Space Needed
Windows 95 (average installation)	100 Mb
Major office suite (full installation, including optional add-ons)	300 Mb
Empty space for Windows swap files	100 Mb
Cache for Web browser	15 Mb
Assorted downloads	100 Mb
5 Additional applications @ 30 Mb	150 Mb
5 Games @ 20 Mb	100 Mb
Assorted utilities	25 Mb
Two book-length manuscripts @ 5 Mb apiece	10 Mb
500 short-to-medium size documents @ 50 Kb apiece	25 Mb
Small business database	25 Mb
Backup copy of your Web site	10 Mb
Total	960 Mb

There are two ways of looking at this information. Some computer users will say, *"Holy cow, my hard drive's almost full, and I've barely started."* OK, *you* need a bigger hard drive. And you're in luck. Right now, systems with 2.5-Gb and 3.1-Gb hard drives are a very good deal.

Others will say: *"Hey, I don't have nearly that much software. I'll have plenty of space."* And they're almost certainly right. But even if events prove them wrong, consider Table 2-4.

Table 2–4 Hard Disk Price Reduction, 1996–1997[a]

	1280 Mb Drive	1620 Mb Drive	2100 Mb Drive
Price Reduction, March 1996–March 1997	20.8 percent	30.0 percent	42.0 percent

a. Western Digital hard drives, bare kits advertised by Insight, the leading mail order hard drive reseller.

When and if they eventually need the extra space, it's likely to cost them a lot less than buying it now.[7] It's a great incentive to be a Cheapskate!

Floppy, Keyboard, Mouse, and Operating System

This is pretty basic stuff. Expect a 3.5" diskette drive, and make sure they're including the keyboard and mouse. If you have clients who expect you to deliver materials on the old-fashioned 5.25" diskettes, get a 5.25" drive as well—but that's increasingly rare.

Make sure the operating system you want is not simply "preloaded:" Make sure they *give you the original disks* you'll need to make adjustments later, or reinstall if your system ever crashes! If you can't get the original disks, make sure the computer gives you an easy way to make your own. (And then *do it!*)

"Useful" Software

Nowadays, many systems come with *huge* software bundles. Ever watch the Home Shopping Network's computer show? Once they start listing that free software, they can go on for five minutes at a clip without catching a breath, and you really think you're getting something.

Spend a few minutes thinking about each individual package. What would you pay for it if it *weren't* bundled? Is it really of any *use* to you? Is it software you'd *want* to use? If it isn't, what's it really worth to you? Not much.

Peripherals

We'll return to peripherals in much more detail in Chapter 5 when we cover upgrades. If you're purchasing at retail, you may have little opportunity to negotiate what comes in the manufacturer's bundle (mail-order suppliers tend to be more flexible). But here are a few quick pointers to help you evaluate what you're getting.

▲ ▲ ▲ ▲ ▲ ▲ ▲ ▲ ▲ ▲ ▲ ▲ ▲ ▲ ▲ ▲ ▲ ▲ ▲ ▲

7.   There's yet another option, which doesn't cost a dime: disk compression. We'll discuss this in Chapter 5.

Warning! Are you getting the *whole* enchilada? Sometimes, trial software is packaged with PCs; it may actually stop working after a period of time. Or you'll sometimes get packages that don't contain all the features you might expect. The tip-off: product titles such as

▲ Special Edition   ▲ SE
▲ Limited Edition   ▲ Trial Version
▲ LE   ▲ Timed Version
▲ Lite   ▲ Evaluation Version

Monitor: No matter what size monitor you've used in the past, if you get a larger one, you'll think you've died and gone to heaven. If this is your first computer, a 14" monitor is probably enough, as long as it's sharp. Since many systems now come with a 15" monitor, trading *down* to 14" is a Cheapskate way to save $50–$75.

You want a dot pitch of 0.28. (For monitors that use Sony Trinitron® tubes, the equivalent is approximately 0.25). Higher numbers are worse. Bottom-of-the-barrel 0.39-dot-pitch monitors had nearly been stamped out, but they've unfortunately made a comeback in the new sub-$1,000 systems that vendors like Packard Bell have begun to offer.

Video card: Video cards have improved so dramatically, you'll be hard pressed to go wrong here. Make sure you get a card with at least 2 Mb memory; 4 Mb is most useful if you plan to do sophisticated graphics or use a 17" or larger monitor, and in *that* case, you may also want memory that's faster than standard DRAMs, such as, "VRAMs." Video card software—that is, drivers—can be as important as hardware. If you can, check Internet newsgroups or CompuServe forums to see if a card's drivers are working smoothly with the operating system you want to use.

CD-ROM: Anything beyond 8X is gravy, unless you're planning heavy-duty on-line database access or gaming. Most CD-ROMs published now are actually optimized for slower 2X or 4X systems.

Sound card: Assuming the system you're considering has sound at all, the issue is: Do you need *wavetable* sound? Essentially, this means the card has a library of real sounds to draw upon, rather than simply manufacturing artificial sounds as needed. Wavetable cards sound better, and cost more. If you don't expect to use your computer's sound capabilities very much, they're a luxury.

Modem: If you're planning to use the Internet, you want all the speed you can get, and these days that's typically 33.6 Kbps. Some systems will be bundled with 56-Kbps modems. Be aware that they'll only go faster than 33.6 Kbps if connected to a device that supports this speed—*and* does it the same way your modem manufacturer does. A 56-Kbps modem does you no good if your Internet service provider can't work with it—or (another problem) if your telephone company's network won't support it, which may be the case for 10–30 percent of all users.

Expandability

Chances are, expandability isn't your number one concern when you're buying a computer. For many people, however, a system with reasonable expandability *could* last a year or two longer. Basic Cheapskate arithmetic shows that will significantly reduce your annual cost of computing. Moreover, expandable systems have better resale value, since they can meet the needs of more buyers.

Most current systems have the basics: two serial ports and one parallel port to connect external devices, such as modems, printers and scanners; and both PCI and ISA expansion slots to support a wide variety of internal add-on boards.

• *The Disappearing Expansion Slots*

Now things get tricky: How many of those expansion slots are actually available? A computer may come with four ISA and three PCI slots, but what if …

One of those ISA slots overlaps a PCI slot, so you can't use both at once?

One of those PCI slots already has a video card in it?

One of those ISA slots already has a modem in it, and another has a sound card?

Suddenly you have a system with only three available slots. Then, when you open the box, you may find that the 16-bit card you want to install won't fit if you have all four SIMM slots filled, and the external serial and parallel port connections block off another slot. So you need to know: *How many slots are really available?*

• *This Will IRQ You*

How does your PC's processor know that another device in your system needs attention? One way is via *interrupts*: The device sends a message to the processor saying, *I need you*. Most devices that require interrupts need one of their very own; if two devices send messages on the same interrupt at the same time, your system will hang.

Therein lies the rub. Interrupts (usually abbreviated as IRQs) are like real estate: They aren't making any more of them. On practically all systems since 1984, there are 16 IRQs. Sounds like a lot, but …

IRQ0 handles internal system timing issues. IRQ1 belongs to the keyboard. IRQ2 and IRQ9 are electrically equivalent, and a few experts even advise leaving one or both of them alone, if possible (though this is a minority viewpoint).

IRQ3 belongs to your second serial port—and if you happen to have four serial (COM) ports, COM4 shares the same IRQ. IRQ4 belongs to your first serial port—and if you have four serial ports, COM3 shares it.

IRQ6 belongs to your floppy drive controller. IRQ7 belongs to your parallel port, IRQ8 to your system clock, and IRQ12 to your mouse port, if your system has one. IRQ13 belongs to the numeric coprocessor that's built into your microprocessor. IRQ14 is your hard disk controller.

And multimedia stuff eats IRQs for breakfast.

In short, if a manufacturer is careless about design, it's possible for them to sell you a system with *no* available IRQs, and hence, virtually *no* expandability.[8] That's not an issue if the system already has everything you'll ever want, built in. But what if it doesn't?

Ideally, you should find out *how many IRQs are available?* I say *ideally*, because this can vary by the specific configuration that's on sale, and not all manufacturers (much less retail salespeople) can easily tell you. But at least ask.

---

8.   It also means you'll have to be careful about managing any IRQs you *do* have.

• *Slots for the Memories*

Next question: How many *available* memory slots do you have?

On most current systems, there are four 72-pin SIMM slots which must be filled in pairs. A system with 16 Mb could have two 8-Mb SIMMs and two empty slots. It could have four 4-Mb SIMMs and no empty slots. (It *can't* have one 16Mb SIMM and three empty slots; that wouldn't be a pair.) Similarly, a system with 32 Mb could have two 16-Mb SIMMs, or four 8-Mb SIMMs, filling every slot.

On some newer, high-end systems, you'll find 168-pin DIMM slots along with (or instead of) SIMM slots. DIMMs change the rules again. In particular, they don't have to be filled in pairs.

If you may want to expand your system later, make sure you have empty memory slots. Otherwise, you'll either have to discard old memory or utilize products that combine two SIMMs in one memory slot. Those won't fit in all systems. Nor are they 100 percent foolproof, because they don't always take into account electrical noise, speed differences, memory interleaving, paging, and other technical issues you probably won't want to be bothered with.

• *Drive Bays: A Big Enough Garage?*

A little while back we implied that you can always buy a second drive if you run out of hard disk storage space. Well, *almost* always. You'll need an open drive bay to put it in. That's rarely an issue on standard tower, mini-tower, or desktop systems, which may come with five or more drive bays. But it's not uncommon on compact systems to get just three: one for your floppy, one for your hard drive, one for your CD-ROM, and *none* to spare. You'd be out of luck if you wanted to add

- ▲ Internal tape drives
- ▲ Second floppy drives
- ▲ Internal ZIP or SCSI drives
- ▲ Second hard drives

Of course, there's a trade-off: Systems with more drive bays are bigger—and they might not fit on your desk, or in your New York City studio apartment.

• *Appropriate Candidate for a Brain Transplant?*

The biggest upgrade of all is a motherboard transplant. You're not only replacing the microprocessor with a faster one; you're also replacing all the surrounding circuitry. Your computer goes to sleep its old slow self—and wakes up a speed demon with a new personality—all for as little as 20 percent of a new system, or less.

Needless to say, this voids your warranty <g>. But in a few years, when that's no longer a concern, you may want the option. If so ask whether the motherboard in the current system is a standard size. Most motherboards are one of two sizes: "Baby AT" or "ATX."[9] If the computer you're purchasing uses either size, chances are you'll be able to swap out the old motherboard and swap in a new one when you want to.

Ask which functions are integrated onto the motherboard: video, audio, networking, and the like. High levels of integration reduce the cost of a PC, which is *good*. But if you ever want or need to replace your motherboard, you'll lose those integrated functions unless you purchase an expensive motherboard from the original source. And *that* could raise your costs enough to make a motherboard upgrade impractical.[10]

Finally, ask whether the system uses standard memory, such as 72-pin EDO or fast page mode SIMMs. Some computers use nonstandard SIMMs that won't necessarily work with your replacement motherboard.

Warranty and Support

Welcome to Wonderland, Alice, where words mean exactly what manufacturers want them to mean—no more, no less. While we're quoting famous people, nobody said it better than Ronald Reagan: "*trust, but verify.*"

▲ ▲ ▲ ▲ ▲ ▲ ▲ ▲ ▲ ▲ ▲ ▲ ▲ ▲ ▲ ▲ ▲ ▲ ▲

9.　　ATX is newer and gradually becoming the standard. For more information about motherboards, see Chapter 8.

10.　　Some functions, like IDE interfaces and serial and parallel ports are integrated on virtually *every* motherboard.

> While it's easy to tell an AT from an ATX motherboard (they're different sizes), sometimes you'll need to find specific answers about a motherboard, and you won't have the documentation—or the motherboard will simply be impossible to identify. A majority of motherboards have an AMI or Award BIOS. These BIOSes are customized to the motherboards they're on and have a specific identifier number. Once you have that number, check it against the motherboard listings at *www.ping.be/bios/index.html*. In many cases, that will help you find out what motherboard you have, and you can *then* get the information you need from the manufacturer.

There's so much fine print in warranties these days, they're worth a Cheapskate table of their own (see Table 2-5).

Again, ask questions—don't assume. Keep in mind that

- Many manufacturers display their current warranties on their Web sites.
- Retailers are required by law to show you copies of warranty terms and conditions—just ask.
- Always keep your receipt.
- Always send in your warranty card.

You want to know *exactly* what will happen if you have a problem. What if it's a software problem? What if it's a hardware problem? What if it happens in the first year? What if it happens instead in the second year of your "three-year" warranty?

If parts are covered, are you expected to install them yourself? If the warranty calls for on-site service, you want to know when a company would *actually* send someone—usually it's entirely up to their discretion. What's not covered?

What happens *after* warranty? How would service be handled *then*?

One more tip: Before you make a major computer purchase of any kind, call the technical support line once or twice. If it's always busy, well, you've been warned.

Table 2–5 Warranty and Support Comparison Checklist (PCs)

	System #1	System #2	System #3	System #4
No-questions-asked, money-back satisfaction guarantee?				
If so, restocking fees?				
Warranty length (parts and labor)				
Warranty length (on-site service?)				
If on-site, is your location covered?				
Who decides if a service person will be sent?				
Warranty length (parts only)				
Can manufacturer replace with used parts?				
If so, length of warranty on used parts				
Warranty length (carry-in or mail-in)				
Who pays shipping?				
All components covered?				
Are network cards covered?				
Cost of telephone support?				
Cost of *out-of-warranty* telephone support?				
Cost of *out-of-warranty* service?				
Do I need to keep the box?				
Do I need to keep the receipt?				
Warranty transferable if I sell?				
What voids the warranty?				

• *Warranties Are Getting Tighter*

For Cheapskates, 1997 has seen an unsettling trend: significantly shorter warranties. Both Compaq and IBM, which pioneered three-year warranties, have shortened warranties on their newest systems to just one year. So have several other manufacturers. Why? Some observers say that retailers prefer to sell high-profit extended warranties, and the longer warranties were cutting into that business. In February, IBM publicly said that since the longer, three-year warranties weren't all inclusive, they were too confusing for salespeople to explain.

You might be forgiven for imagining that the real answer is *money*, pure and simple. The shorter the warranty, the less commitment a manufacturer must make to stock parts on systems that were only manufactured for a few months—and the more service costs can be off-loaded to *you*.

The next trend to watch out for: companies that formerly offered one-year on-site support who are trimming *that* guarantee to 90 days..

Warning! Here's a nasty trick I just found out about: Some manufacturers, like Gateway, include fine print that prevents you from suing them if you have a dispute. You have to go to arbitration. That might not be so bad—arbitration is usually a great Cheapskate alternative to hiring a lawyer. But according to *The New York Times*, Gateway makes you submit to arbitration *in Chicago*, no matter where you live. To me, that's absurd, unreasonable, and just plain wrong. If you agree, and you're considering a Gateway system, you ought to tell them so.

New Systems under $1,000—Finally!

Suddenly, it seems, computer manufacturers are rediscovering the low end of the market—and the 65 percent of American households that don't have PCs. According to International Data Corporation, a leading market researcher, "Most of the consumers who do not currently have a computer do not need cutting-edge performance or the newest toys, and price is a real barrier to lower-income households."

With the high end of the market increasingly penetrated, we're starting to see real new PCs that cost less than $1,000. There's still usually at least one significant compromise, but hey, it's progress.

Some of the systems discussed here may have been replaced or upgraded by the time you read this, but they just may prove to be the harbinger of a new class of PC that really *is* for the rest of us.

The Packard Bell C115

Packard Bell's entry, the C115 (see Figure 2-2), is based on an Intel Pentium 120, comes with 16-Mb RAM, a 1.2-Gb hard drive, 8x CD-ROM, 33.6-Kbps modem, sound, telephone answering system software, Corel WordPerfect Suite, Microsoft Works, and some other stuff, too. Unfortunately, it also comes with a 0.39-dot-pitch monitor—clearly substandard. You can, however, purchase the computer without a monitor and add a monitor separately. But now you're back over a grand.

For more information about the Packard Bell C115—and its descendants—visit Packard Bell's Web site, **www.packardbell.com**.

Figure 2–2   Packard Bell C115.

Everex Explora 995

Leapfrog Labs, which sells systems under the once-famous Everex brand name, now offers the Explora 995, using AMD's K5-PR120 microprocessor, roughly comparable to an Intel Pentium 120. The system comes with a solid 14", 0.28-dot-pitch monitor and a 1.0-Gb hard drive, but only 8-Mb RAM. You need more memory. And now you're back over a grand.

For more information about the Everex Explora 995, visit **www.leapfroglab.com**, or call 1-888-532-7995.

Compaq Presario 2200 with the Cyrix Media GX

If you're interested in a new family system, check out systems based on the new Cyrix Media GX microprocessor, which was designed from the ground up to deliver solid performance at low cost. The chip includes sound, graphics and logic capabilities that computer manufacturers would have had to add separately, and it is priced low enough to permit new name-brand systems well under $1,000. Be aware, though, that in early tests, the Media GX runs more slowly than a Pentium at the same speed.

The first announced system to use the Media GX is Compaq's Presario 2200 (see Figure 2-3), which uses the 133-MHz version of the Media GX, comes with 16-Mb memory, a 2-Gb hard disk, 33.6-Kbps modem, 8-speed CD-ROM drive, and a batch of software. Currently it's $799 *without* a monitor, so you really can have the system complete for around $1,000.

Figure 2–3   Compaq Presario 2200.

If none of these systems grab you, wait a little while. Other major manufacturers are busily making strategies for the sub-$1,000 market. For example, IBM recently partnered with Acer, an internationally respected PC manufacturer based in Taiwan. Together, the two companies are already delivering inexpensive Aptiva systems throughout Europe; expect to see a U.S. product late in 1997 or early in 1998.

Where to Buy: A World of Market Channels

Until now, we've focused on what to buy: how much memory, how many available IRQs, what kind of warranty. Now we'll focus on an equally important question for Cheapskates: *Where* to buy.

According to a variety of surveys, first-time buyers disproportionately buy in consumer electronics and department stores; second-time buyers disproportionately buy in superstores or by mail order. While I have my doubts about superstores, if you're a first time buyer, *at least* learn from the experience of others, and pass up your local department store. You'll rarely find much value or expertise there.

> **tip** And while you're at it, stay away from the home shopping TV channels, too—most of their deals just aren't very good.

Having said that, let's look at the pros and cons of each major channel, from computer superstores to mail order, and even the build-it-yourself option.

Superstores: How Super?

According to *Computer Retail News*, computer superstores "are already operating at margins that are the lowest in the retail market, except for military exchange stores and warehouse clubs. These margins, which are usually only in the mid-teens at their highest and more often are in the mid-single-digit range, virtually require computer superstores to focus on the higher end of the market and the second-time buyer." [11]

What does this mean to you, the Cheapskate? First of all, it *should* mean you'll get reasonably good prices, at least compared with other retailers. It also means that computer superstores are itching to sell you *anything* with a higher margin, which typically includes

▲ Top-of-the-line PCs and notebook systems
▲ Training
▲ Installation and configuration services
▲ 1-900 support services
▲ Consumables

Here are some tips for coping with superstores.

✂ *If you're planning to make a major purchase, do your research before you go to the superstore. In my experience, your odds of finding a salesperson who will have the expertise and patience to answer your questions is roughly one in three. Especially don't expect to find knowledge about technology that's brand new.*

✂ *If a larger item is not on sale, be extra careful to compare prices before buying—especially with mail-order suppliers. Bring a mail-order catalog if you have one.*

✂ *If you're purchasing a computer, think carefully in advance whether you will want an extended warranty. In general, extended warranties are very high profit items. I don't like them, but if you simply never want to worry about a computer repair, you may feel differently. Just don't take the extended warranty on impulse. And make sure you know exactly what it covers.*

✂ *Make sure you know the superstore's policy on matching competitor's prices. Price matching policies aren't always all*

11.   Based on a 1996 survey by MSI Consulting Group, Seattle, Washington.

they seem, though. Superstores often offer unique configurations that aren't available anywhere else.[12] And they won't match memory pricing unless the brand name is identical—which rarely happens, since sale memory is often not branded.

✎ *Like most other retailers, superstores offer* loss leaders—*and those are often quite a good deal. You'll often find those on the back page of their weekly circulars.*

✎ *If you're purchasing a monitor, ask to view it doing the kind of work you do. Monitors are often placed on display in giant Hollywood-Squares style racks, showing video games. It's virtually impossible to judge how they'll perform on your desk running a spreadsheet.*

✎ *Don't purchase anything that's not marked with a price. For some reason—the stores blame unsupervised children, but I have my doubts—many superstore items are not tagged. To find a price, you'll need to find a salesperson. Good luck.*

✎ *Last tip: If you're speaking with a salesperson and you're not confident in the information you're getting, ask questions and look skeptical. You'll often find that another customer will step into the conversation and give you better advice than the store employee.*

▲ ▲ ▲ ▲ ▲ ▲ ▲ ▲ ▲ ▲ ▲ ▲ ▲ ▲ ▲ ▲ ▲ ▲ ▲

12.   Computer City's policy: "We will meet any other local authorized retailer's current advertised prices for any identical item in stock (actual ad required.) If you find a lower advertised price for the identical item in stock, within 30 days after buying from us, bring us the ad and take advantage of our 110 percent Low Price guarantee. Excludes special pricing and finance offers. Other restrictions apply. See store for details."
CompUSA policy: "We'll beat any legitimate price from any local authorized retail store on every product we sell, either at the time of purchase or within the following 30 days. Our low price guarantee pertains to all new, factory sealed products of the same brand and model number that are available and in stock at any local authorized retail store. Our guarantee does not apply to competitors' one-of-a-kind or other limited-quantity offers, special financing, installation, manufacturer's rebate, or when a bonus or free offer is included in the purchase. Some restrictions apply."

Warehouse Clubs

As a Cheapskate, you just might be a member of PriceCostco, B.J.'s Wholesale Club, or some comparable institution. If so, you know they have one of just about everything under those high roofs. One brand of ketchup in 4-gallon size, one Japanese make of tires for your compact car, one generic brand of toilet paper packed in 96-roll boxes.

It's the same with computer stuff. Expect to find one or two systems at each price point, one or two monitors of every size, many of the leading software packages, one sound card, one CD-ROM, one scanner, and one modem, most of them mainstream products if not mainstream brands. Often, you'll find them behind locked glass cabinets. *Don't* expect to find anyone who can answer any questions.

Of course, invisible or untrained salespeople are *not* a warehouse club exclusive. And if the item you happen to want is there, it will often cost significantly less than computer superstores charge—making warehouse clubs the best retail bargain for new software and hardware. Computer books, in particular, are often as much as 40 percent off list price. (Consider that some chain booksellers don't discount most computer books one red cent any more.)

Your odds are best with newer merchandise that hasn't had a chance to sit awhile. Older stuff is more likely to see price cuts at other retailers or mail-order houses than at warehouse stores.

So here's a warehouse club buying strategy:

1. *Decide what you want.* Check all the reviews you're going to check; call the manufacturer's 800 number if you have questions.
2. *Find out if it's there.* Call the warehouse club to see whether they stock the item you want, and what they charge. (Price Costco says in the future it will provide a vendor list at its Web site, **www.pricecostco.com**.) Then see how the price compares with other sources.
3. *Try to see it in action.* Go see a computer system or monitor in person. That may involve a trip to your local computer retailer.
4. *Go get it.* Preferably on a weekday afternoon, when the lines are shorter!

What would it take to make you join a warehouse club if you *weren't* already a member? At $40 per year, this skews the economics more than a little. Just for the sake of argument, if a warehouse club can consistently save you 5 percent over mail order, you'll have to spend $800 before your membership fee is covered. If you're purchasing a complete new computer system, this could be worth it. But $800 is a *lot* of software and accessories.

> **tip** Not sure if a warehouse club is worth it? Ask for a guest pass and case the joint.

The Direct Channel

Every year, more people purchase PCs through the direct channel, via telephone, catalog and now the Web. Manufacturers who focus primarily on direct channel sales range from Fortune 500 firms like Dell and Gateway, to hundreds of smaller companies whose ads make *Computer Shopper* magazine the behemoth it is.

Buying direct has several major advantages. Many manufacturers in the direct channel have learned the art of "build-to-order," so they can keep inventories low, pass along component price reductions more quickly, and deliver more powerful systems at lower prices. According to one survey,[13] the average price of a PC sold through the direct channel was 18.5 percent lower in 1996 than the average PC sold at retail. *Moreover, the price differential nearly doubled in 1996, compared with 1995.*

By making detailed information about each computer available to telephone salespeople through on-line databases, the best direct vendors can be a lot more helpful than mass market computer retailers when it comes to helping you choose the right system. Of course, not all vendors are equal. Nor do all vendors deliver the same level of customer service. Since there's no store to return your computer to, you have to be careful. Start by following these rules.

▲ ▲

13.   Survey by *Value Added Reports;* does not take into account any differences in configuration.

• *Doing Business by Mail: Twelve Cheapskate Rules to Live By*

✍ **Rule 1. Always pay by credit card, no matter what— even if there's a surcharge**. *(There shouldn't be: Most credit card companies require vendors to not surcharge credit card orders. However, enforcement of this restriction seems minimal at best.)*

✍ **Rule 2.** *Get the seller's return policy—in writing. Understand if there's a "restocking fee," and exactly when it is invoked.*

✍ **Rule 3.** *Get detailed written confirmation of your order, including specific parts listings. (If the salesperson said you were getting a U.S. Robotics modem, the written confirmation should specify U.S. Robotics, not simply "33.6 modem."*

✍ **Rule 4.** *Always get the name, title, and telephone extension of the person you are doing business with.*

✍ **Rule 5.** *Check whether the company is a member of the Better Business Bureau (BBB); find out if the BBB has had any complaints about the company and if so, how they were resolved. BBB reports are invaluable, of course, but traditionally, you've had to get those reports from the local BBB where a company is located. Slowly, the BBB is moving to integrate all its reports in a national, computerized database. Reports on companies in the New York metropolitan area, the mid-Hudson Valley, and Long Island are now on-line at* **www.newyork.bbb.org**. *Reports on companies located in Eastern Massachusetts, Vermont, and Maine are on-line at* **www.bosbbb.org**. *(On page 66 you'll learn more about BBB's new program to help police sales on the World Wide Web.) The Better Business Bureau won't have reports on brand-new companies—but you might hesitate to do business with a company that has no track record, anyway. One clue that you might be dealing with a new company is an 888 toll-free number. Most (though not all) established companies have older 800 numbers.*

✍ **Rule 6.** *Check Internet newsgroups (and CompuServe forums if you are a member) to see whether there's any scuttlebutt about the vendor you're planning to use. See page 27 for Web-based compilations of customer experiences with direct vendors.*

✍ **Rule 7.** *Always ask for a precise estimate of shipping costs.*

✍ **Rule 8.** *Find out whether you will be paying sales tax. Depending on where the manufacturer or vendor does business, you may well not be asked to pay sales tax. If you live in a high sales tax area, such as New York City, this could reduce the cost of a computer system by hundreds of dollars. The rule, of course, has been that vendors must charge sales tax to customers who live in states where they have a physical presence.*

Warning! **At the same time, you should be aware (if you aren't already) that many states assess a "use tax," equivalent to the sales tax you would have paid if you had bought in-state. This has been poorly enforced by most state taxing authorities, to say the least. But it's the law, and it's a natural place for states to seek revenue as budgets continue to tighten.**

✍ **Rule 9.** *Use the checklist on page 31 to make sure you're getting all the components you need—and all the ones you* think *you're getting (including keyboards, mice, cables, etc.)*

✍ **Rule 10.** *Make sure that all the components you're purchasing will actually be assembled— and burned in, to make sure they work together.*

✍ **Rule 11.** *Never pay more than the advertised price. There's a term for that:* Bait and switch.

✍ **Rule 12.** *Document everything, and if there's a problem, act on it immediately.*

● *Special Cautions on Notebook PCs*

One thing I *don't* recommend buying by mail is a notebook PC. Every aspect of the way you interact with your notebook PC is very personal and very subjective: the keyboard, the screen, the pointing device. Some people love touchpads; I hate them. Some people find lower-cost dual-scan color screens perfectly acceptable; I don't.

For every one of these factors, you can't tell whether you'll be satisfied until you receive the unit. And the return policies on notebook PCs are tighter than they've ever been.

In typical mail-order transactions, you have a right to expect a 30-day, no-questions-asked money back guarantee. But vendors of notebook PCs have been tightening their return policies, claiming that they've been victims of abusive customers, who purchase notebook PCs for short-term usage and then return them when they're finished. Whether you accept the rationale or not, the fact is you can get stuck big time unless you're careful.

> *Warning!* Another increasingly widespread practice is for vendors to refuse to refund the cost of software bundled with a returned system.

My suggestion: If you are purchasing a new notebook system, visit one or two large retailers first to evaluate the merchandise. Only if you try out a system and like the way it "feels" should you consider purchasing it by mail. The same goes for older, or refurbished notebooks. You may want to investigate local outlets for used systems, such as the Computer Renaissance franchise chain discussed on page 92.

If these are not available, use large, reputable sources of used equipment, such as GE Capital, IBM Credit Corporation, or Sun Remarketing (for Macintosh PowerBooks). You will pay more, but you'll have more peace of mind.

Wherever you buy, and whatever else you do, get the warranty and return policies in writing.

Buying on the Web

There's a whole new way for Cheapskates to buy direct from the manufacturer: buying on the Web. Every leading direct-sales manufacturer—and most second- and third-tier companies—have a Web presence; in many cases, you can actually transact business there.

All the rules about mail order apply to Web transactions as well. Vendors' Web sites are evolving quickly and not all are equally detailed or up to date. Be sure you're getting all the information you need to make a purchase decision, and if you have any doubts, call a live human being.

Comparing Many Sellers at Once

Computer Shopper, the number one print source for computer advertising, is now supplemented by a Web site, **www.netbuyer.com** (see Figure 2-4), which brings together current pricing information on more than 40,000 computer products and over 180 vendors. NetBuyer gives you a quick way to compare prices on computers, peripherals, and software—and it can sometimes even help you find obscure sources for older or more specialized products.

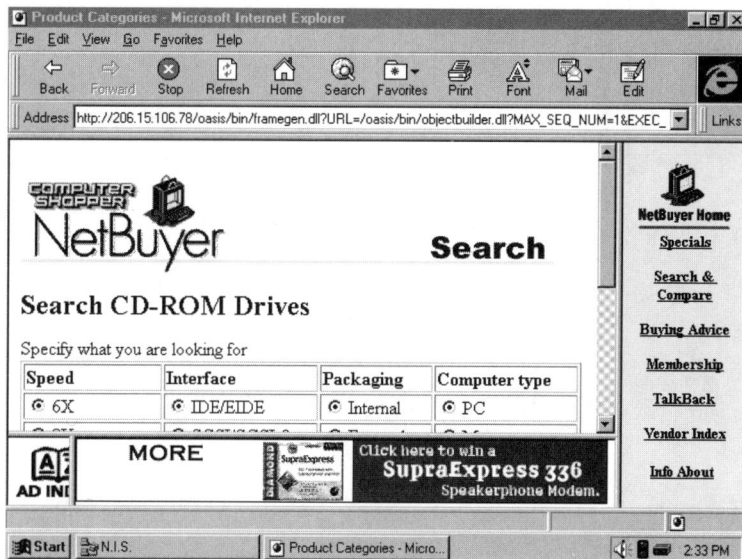

Figure 2–4   Finding older 6x CD-ROMs using NetBuyer.

Targeting an Exact Configuration or Price Point

Dell (**www.dell.com/store/index.htm**), Gateway (**www.gw2k.com**), and Micron (**www.micronpc.com/ showroom.html**) each offer on-line configurators that let you mix and match components to get the specific features or lower price you're looking for. So do a few smaller companies. As we've said, some options may be available by phone that haven't been programmed into the automated configurator yet.

Let's quickly walk through Dell's configurator to see how it's done. Start at the front door to Dell's store and click on the model you're interested in (Figure 2-5).

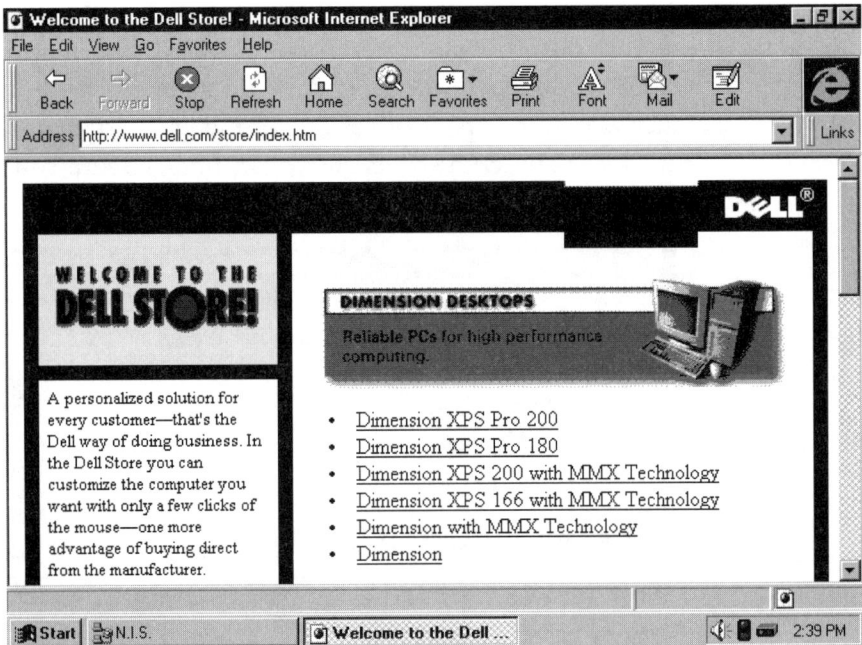

Figure 2–5 The "front entrance" to Dell's configurator.

The configurator opens, with a base price for a "default" system. Walk through this page, changing any options for memory, monitor, video adapter, hard drive, operating system, modem, CD-ROM drive, and service contract. Click 1 to recalculate and see more choices (see Figure 2-6).

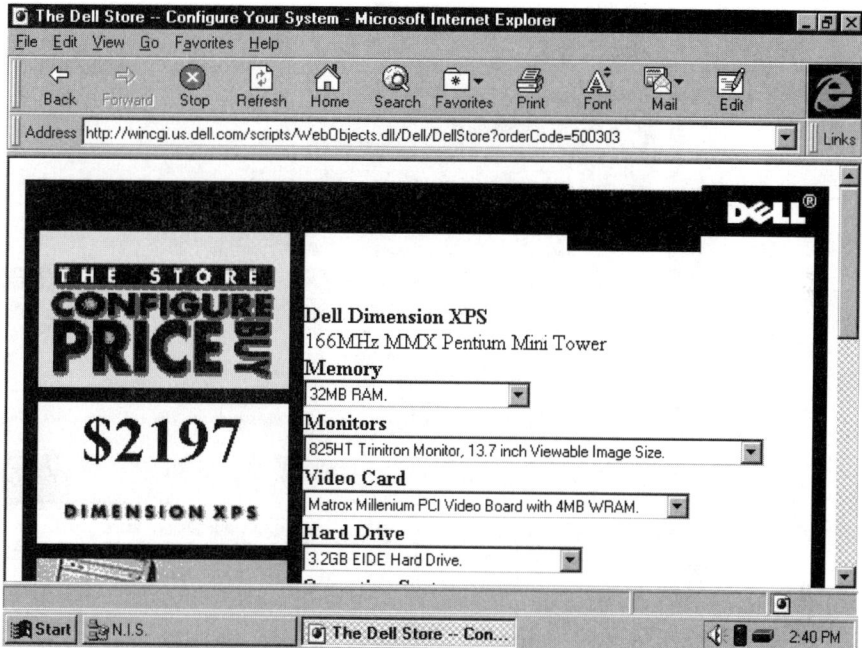

Figure 2–6   Choosing the basic components of your system.

The revised price appears in the lower-left corner of the following page (Figure 2-7). You can now choose options such as keyboards, network cards, tape drives, sound cards, speakers, and bundled software. Click 1 to recalculate again, and you have the final price of the system. You can make more adjustments if you like. You can also click 3 to view and print the configuration you've specified—or click 4 to go ahead and buy it. Why not print your configuration and use it to compare price and configurations with other vendors?

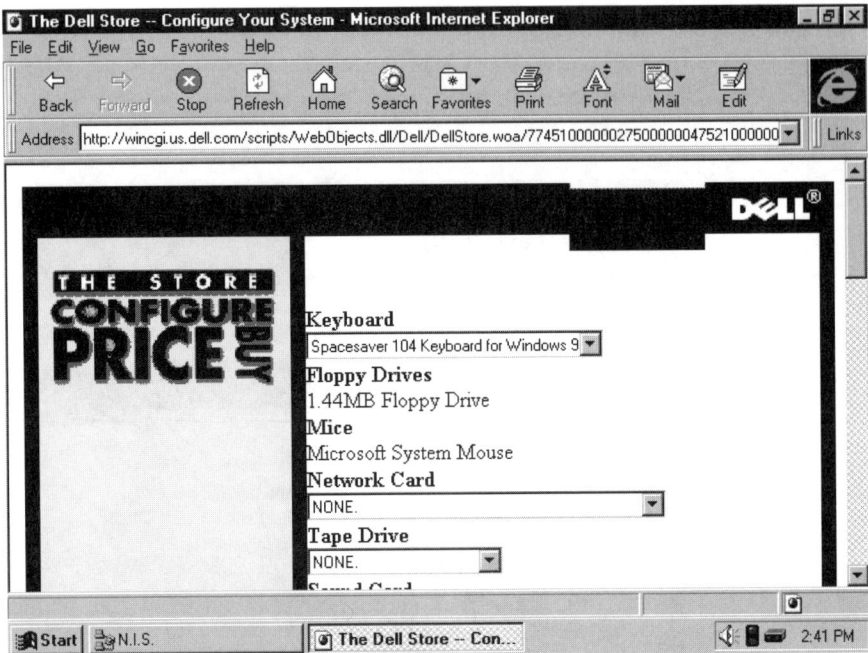

Figure 2–7   Choosing options and arriving at a final system price.

Of course, not everything *is* always equal. Often, the faster systems are outfitted with more memory, larger hard drives, or faster geegaws of one kind or another. This makes comparisons more complex, but when you strip away the differences, the argument still holds.

Hallelujah! The Better Business Bureau Goes On-Line

On the Internet, says the famous cartoon, nobody knows if you're a dog. Unfortunately, nobody knows if you're a thief, either. It's possible to have an awfully good looking site and still be a con man operating out of a boiler room.

The traditional advice has always been to check your suppliers with the Better Business Bureau (BBB). But it can be hard to tell where a virtual vendor is located in so-called meatspace—much less who their local BBB is. That's beginning to change, thanks to BBBOnline, a new program from the Council of Better Business Bureaus. On-line merchants can now display the BBB seal of approval shown in Figure 2-8.

Figure 2–8 Start looking for the BBBOnLine logo when you shop on-line. At some point, it will become a *must*.

That seal should mean at least *this* much:

- No unanswered complaints about the company are on file at the BBB.
- The company has been in business for at least one year.
- The company's management has demonstrated "no significant ethical failures in this or prior businesses."
- Information is on file about who owns and manages the company, and where they are physically located.
- The company has agreed to withdraw advertising the BBB finds to be unsubstantiated.
- The company will handle complaints on-line through the BBB's Web server.
- The company agrees to binding arbitration by the BBB if a customer is dissatisfied after using the company's existing dispute resolution programs.

Here's what's even nicer: If you click on the seal, you'll connect directly to the BBB's report on that company.

It's a little early to expect *all* your on-line vendors to display the BBBOnLine seal—the program was scheduled to kick off in March and roll out throughout 1997. But by early 1998, if you're thinking of doing business with someone on the Net who *doesn't* have the seal, I'd ask why they don't.

Buying Generic PCs

You don't have to buy direct to get a PC nobody's ever heard of. You can easily get one from someone right around the corner.

Nowadays, every town seems to have an independent small business—or several of them—in the business of building generic PCs. In fact, more than one-third of the computer resellers surveyed by *Computer Reseller News*[14] recently said that self-built systems were consistently their top-selling computers.

To a Cheapskate, some of the deals can be *very* competitive—and you may find it alluring to know that your supplier is around the corner. How do you choose a good one? There are few guarantees, but here are some questions to ask.

✎ **How long have they been in business at their current location?** *(Do they even* have *a current location, or are they building systems in their basement?) Many small PC sellers are transient operations—often, purely due to the competitive nature of the business and the narrow margins. It would be nice to find some evidence that they'll be with you for the long haul.*

✎ **What kind of parts do they use?** *Often, motherboards are a giveaway. Top-ranked motherboard companies currently include Intel, Asus, Micronics, Tyan, Supermicro, AMI, and Shuttle. There are other quality manufacturers, but if you hear another name, ask why that motherboard was chosen. If the answer was, because it's cheap, that tells you something.*

✎ **Who are their references?** *I recommend at least* two *local references—ideally including one reference from someone who had trouble with a system, so you can see how the problems were resolved. Business references are often better than consumer*

▲ ▲ ▲ ▲ ▲ ▲ ▲ ▲ ▲ ▲ ▲ ▲ ▲ ▲ ▲ ▲ ▲ ▲

14.   *Computer Reseller News*, The Allure of a Custom-Built PC, May 6, 1996.

references. *Most businesses have little choice but to be tough customers: Their survival depends on the systems they are purchasing. What's more, they usually don't have much time to troubleshoot their own problems, so they can give you real insight into the results the seller delivered when they were in trouble. You can't go on the Web or check* Consumer Reports *to see how a local supplier is viewed in the marketplace, but you can check with local users' groups. See if there's a users' group—or even a PC club—meeting at one of your local schools. (A friend suggests going to a computer show and standing quietly near their booth for awhile: if plenty of unhappy customers show up to complain, that's a clue right there.) Of course, there's always the local BBB as well.*

✐ **Exactly what is their warranty?** *See the warranty checklist on page 51. It's often a challenge to get local suppliers to put their warranty terms in writing. If they wanted to do paperwork all day, they would have kept working for that big corporation instead of going out on their own. Many will simply say: "Don't worry—if you have a problem, I'll handle it." Well, that may be true, but how would you know that in advance? Demand a written warranty—and if you don't like the one they give you, try to negotiate better terms. It's often possible to do so.*

✐ **What kind of testing do they do?** *Do they perform a full 48-hour burn-in on the completed system? Do they install an operating system such as Windows 95, and make sure that's working properly? What responsibility, if any, do they take for the software they install?*

✐ **How many PCs have they built?** *Not to exaggerate the analogy, but heart surgeons who perform more surgeries tend to get better results, and so do PC builders who've been at it a while.*

✐ **How did they get started?** *It would be nice to hear that they had some significant experience with PC hardware before they went into business for themselves.*

✍ *How often do they change suppliers?* One drawback of generic PCs is that no two are alike. The first PC "off the line" may have one generic motherboard from Taiwan, the next PC may have a different one. Companies that consistently use the same manufacturers for video cards, hard drives, CD-ROMs and other components may have an easier time supporting their products, because it's easier for them to get the technical information they need.

If you're comfortable with the answers to these questions—and you can communicate your needs and get answers that make sense—then you've got a pretty safe bet.

Build It Yourself, from Scratch?

Building your own PC is the information-age equivalent of growing your own vegetables, or shooting your own dinner and carrying it home on top of the pickup truck. It carries a certain credibility. With regret, however, I have to take a deep breath and admit: You won't save much money if you build your own PC from scratch.

And who will give you a warranty?

I had to learn this the hard way by trying it myself. The problem was simple: I buy my parts in *ones*, and Dell buys theirs in *thousands*, or *hundreds of thousands*. I may have found a great Cyrix 166+ motherboard, a cool $49 video card from Surplus Direct, and a great package deal on a hard drive and tape drive. But by the time I'd put it all together and worked out the bugs, Christmas was over, and the prices of top-name systems were plummeting. I could have had a system with the same power, for the same price, by making one phone call.

Should You Ride Bare-bones?

There is a Cheapskate compromise, however, and that's the *bare-bones* system. With bare-bones, someone else puts together the motherboard, microprocessor, case, and power supply. They generally (but not always) install a floppy drive and provide a keyboard as well.

The result: You have a system that's much easier to finish building—a system you can test and complain about if it doesn't work properly. Someone else has done many of the toughest tasks, and you at least benefit from *some* economies of scale.

Once you have your bare-bones, you add video, a hard drive, multimedia, memory, and any other options you might want. If you shop carefully, you *can* save some money working from a bare-bones. I'd say about $100, on average.

• *Bare-bones as an Upgrade Strategy*

Bare-bones are often marketed as painless upgrades: You transplant the parts out of your older PC, and *poof*, you have a hot new PC for a fraction of the price. How small a fraction? You can purchase a speed-demon bare-bones for well under $400, or a perfectly respectable bare-bones based on a non-Intel microprocessor for as little as $200.

On first glance, this makes quite a lot of sense. Roughly two-thirds of the home PCs purchased last year were bought by people who already owned a PC. If you were among them, you may have wondered whether you really needed to replace every single component in your PC, when all you really wanted is a system that runs much faster than the one you have.

On second glance, it still makes sense—depending on who you are, and what kind of system you already have.

Are you comfortable with opening your PC, transplanting all of its useful components into a new system, and then troubleshooting loose connections or other potential problems that could (at least temporarily) leave you with no working computer at all?

If you are, then how old is your current computer? Anything older than an 80386-based system won't contain parts worth transplanting to a new bare-bones system. And you might choose not to use some of the components in early 80486 systems, such as the memory in 486SX and 486-25 systems.

On the other hand, if you have a 486-50, 486-66 or newer system, chances are you have a sizable investment in parts that can be reused.

Still with us? Then use the checklist in Table 2-6 to evaluate whether a bare-bones system will be cost effective for you.

Table 2–6 Is a Bare-bones the Right Way for You to Upgrade?

Component	Issues to Consider
Memory	Is your memory 72-pin or the older 30-pin variety? If it is 30-pin, you may need a SIMM converter to use it in a newer motherboard (add $20–$40). Even so, you'll probably find that you'll want to add memory to your newer system in order to run newer software. If you do want to add memory, make sure you don't fill all your memory slots with low-capacity 1-Mb SIMMs from your older computer. Memory prices are volatile, but at press time, adding 16-Mb new memory to a computer should cost less than $75.
Video	As long as you have VGA video or better, you can use it in your new system. Check to make sure that video wasn't built into your original motherboard; if it is, you'll need to purchase a video card for your new system ($50 and up). It will help to have the video card's original driver disks.
Hard Drive	Your biggest issue will be space. Older hard drives are much smaller than newer ones and may not store all the programs you want to use. Disk compression software, which is included free with recent versions of DOS and Windows, can roughly double the size of your existing hard disk. Alternatively, you can purchase a new hard drive for $175–$250.
CD-ROM Drive	This should be no problem, though again it will help to have the original installation disks. Make sure to buy drives with standard IDE (cheaper) or SCSI (more expensive but faster) interfaces.
Sound Card	Same as CD-ROM, except that some off-brand sound cards may have trouble running properly under Windows 95, and you might have to reconfigure your card if you transplant it into a system with new cards that want to use the same resources. (See the discussion of IRQs on page 47.)
Networking Card	Virtually any Ethernet card should work in a newer system.
Operating System	You'll need the disks for whatever operating system you intend to run. If you plan to run a new operating system such as Windows 95, and you don't already own it, you'll have to purchase it.
Diskette Drives	Standard 1.44-Mb 3.5" and 1.2-Mb 5.25" floppy drives should be no problem, assuming you have enough drive bays in your new system. This probably won't be a problem, but double-check with your vendor. Remember that floppy drives, hard drives, CD-ROMs, and internal tape backup systems all require drive bays, and except for hard drives they all require *external* drive bays. Make sure the bare-bones you purchase has enough of them.

Table 2–6 Is a Bare-bones the Right Way for You to Upgrade? *(continued)*

Component	Issues to Consider
Modem	Virtually any internal or external PC modem will transplant into a new PC. Be aware that modems which run at 9600 bps or slower will be too slow to take full advantage of Internet connections. Conversely, even most very old fax modems will send faxes at 9600 bps—the same speed that most of today's fax machines use.
Slots	Currently, most bare-bones have four standard ("ISA") slots and three newer ("PCI") slots. It's conceivable that you may have filled six or seven slots in your older system with ISA boards, some of which won't fit in a newer bare-bones.
Keyboard and Mouse	Assuming your keyboard is from an AT-compatible or newer system, transplanting it should be no problem. Ditto for your mouse. However, check whether your new bare-bones uses the same mouse and keyboard interfaces; if it does not, you may need inexpensive adapters.

Building your bare-bones is beyond the scope of this book, but here are a few pointers to maximize your chance of success.

Make a list of everything you plan to transplant—hardware and software—and collect all the disks you'll need, including driver software.

Before you take apart your older system, inventory what's in it. From a DOS prompt, run MSD and print a detailed listing of IRQs and related information. (For more information on MSD, see page 321.)

Also make backups of all your important data before you begin. Even if you have a tape drive, if a small number of files are especially important to you, back those up on floppies as well.

Take a close look inside your new system and look over the schematic you should have received. Plan for potential bottlenecks. Will the cards you intend to add get in the way of your memory slots? Then plan to add the memory first. Also, choose the right drive bays and card slots to make sure that the connecting cables on your existing drives and sound card can reach where they need to go.

Go slowly. Look closely at each of the connections you are disconnecting. Take notes about everything you disconnect, and everything you reconnect. See page 329 for some tips on making sure you don't foul things up.

If you're not sure what you're doing, try to get help from someone who is—or at least know how to reach them by phone.

With that, here are some sources for bare-bones systems:

CompuWorld
24441 Miles Road
Cleveland, OH 44128
1-800-6666-CWI; 1-216-595-6500
www.compu-world.com

Technoland
1050 Stewart Drive
Sunnyvale, CA 94086
1-800-292-4500
www.technoland.com

StarQuest Computers
4491 Mayfield Road
Cleveland, OH 44121
1-800-945-0202; 1-216-691-9966

Renegade Systems
670 N. Arizona Avenue
Chandler, AZ 85224
1-800-867-4033
www.renegade-systems.com/

Neutron Computers
306 W. College Avenue
State College, PA 16801
800-813-4218; 1-814-237-0902
www.neutronnet.com/shopping_gallery.html

Parts 'n' PCs
9232 West 58th Avenue
Arvada, CO 80002
1-888-727-8767, 1-303-232-2302

Megabyte International
6040-G Northbelt Drive
Norcross, GA 30071
1-800-395-3264; 1-770-449-8630
www.megabyteint.com/sales.html

Smart PC
479 Business Drive, #105
Mount Prospect, IL 60056
1-800-260-1737

KHI
6515 Corporate Drive, Ste. L
Houston, TX 77036
1-800-988-1268

Yorkshire Computers
11515 W. Carmen Avenue
Milwaukee, WI 53225
1-800-375-1667; 1-414-358-5301

Intellysys
3849 Perata Boulevard #H
Fremont, CA 94536
www.svii.com

One larger company that sells bare-bones systems is Tiger Direct, 8700 West Flagler Street, Miami, FL 33174 (1-800-879-1597; 305-229-1119; **www.tigerdirect.com**). They charge significantly more than many of the smaller vendors listed above, however.

> **tip** You can occasionally find bare-bones systems made by major manufacturers, such as AT&T, which originally intended that their resellers complete the systems to the specifications of their customers. Such systems may not even include CPUs. You might, for example, have to choose your own Pentium CPU from 75 MHz to 133 MHz, any of which would fit into the same motherboard.

Computer Shows and Swap Meets

Ahh, the bells, the crowds, the signs proclaiming BARGAINS!!!!! Computer shows are natural magnets for us Cheapskates. And sometimes, it can even work out.

If you know what you are looking for and how much it costs elsewhere, a computer show can be a wonderful place to buy. If you don't, cannot recognize a good product from bad, can be suckered into bargaining, or are a very bad impulse buyer, don't go.

If you have decided to go the route of getting a machine from a local clone builder, a show is a great place to meet one. Don't buy a clone there, but find a local guy with whom you get along who offers decent prices. Do *not*, repeat, do *not*, buy a computer at a show—and if someone tells you he can't make you the same deal at his shop a day later, walk.

> Steve Bass, president of the Pasadena IBM Users Group, suggests using the "5-and-15" rule: Purchase only from retailers who have been in business at least 5 years and are located less than 15 miles from your home.

And, as we've already said, *always* pay by credit card.

There is also a matter of morality at the show. You won't find too much stolen stuff, but you will find "gray market" products the manufacturer did not intend to go where it went, especially when it comes to software, disk drives, small accessories like mice, and books. And when it comes to the hardware, manuals and drivers just may be missing.

Let me give you an idea about my recent show purchases. Two shows ago, I picked up a 2.5-Gb Western Digital drive from a local clone builder, at about 5 percent under the best price in *Computer Shopper* (including sales tax, excluding shipping).

The drive did not come in the classy Western Digital box with installation instructions and warranty card that you would get at Egghead or CompUSA, because the person selling it to me had bought his drives wholesale for integration into his own systems. I wasn't worried, because

I had installed a Western Digital drive before, the man was local, I paid with a credit card, it came with the standard WD driver package, the drive was "fresh," and I knew the company would honor its three-year guarantee at least from date of manufacture if a crisis occurred.

Things I turned down: accessories like disk boxes, floppies, canned air, jewel boxes, mouse pads, and a whole array of stuff CompUSA sells cheaper, and dozens of mail-order houses sell cheaper still. Specialty paper and card stock for turning out everything from birth announcements to business card magnets were there, most significantly overpriced. The suppliers seem to buy large packs, break them up and quadruple the prices. Find out the *real* price before you buy.

All around me at the show were folks pushing, shoving, swapping advice (some of it even accurate), and spending an awful lot of cash on great hardware, dubious hardware, and out-and-out garbage. And oh how exciting it was—a cross between the original Filene's Basement and the Trump Taj Mahal, with just as many winners and losers.

You're Not Finished When You Get the Box Home

You've brought the computer home. You're running it. (Actually, you're running it *hard*. You're going to run it for at least 48 straight hours and test everything there is to test, just in case something's not working. Promise?)

Your job's done. Well, not quite.

Many large retailers (and a few mail-order companies) offer 30-day price protection. If the price of your system goes down within 30 days, you may be able to get a refund for the difference. Ask! Then, keep track of your system after you make your purchase. You *could* save a couple of hundred dollars this way.

Summary

In this chapter, we've focused on the whys and wherefores of buying a new computer. But you may simply *not need* a new computer. As a Cheapskate, you may simply not want to spend that much money. You might be buying a second computer, or a computer for a relative who doesn't need top performance.

For you, there's an extraordinary continuum of used and refurbished equipment out there, from complete IBM PS/2 systems that cost less than $200 with monitor, to almost new refurbished systems comparable to anything in the stores, for 20 percent less. In Chapter 3, we'll check out this fascinating, underpublicized marketplace.

Refurbs, Preowned, and Just Plain Old

As soon as you get a new computer out of the box, it's a used computer. So why not save the trouble and buy a system that's already been around the block once or thrice? You can save a bundle. In this chapter, we'll show you how and where to get reliable used computers that still have plenty of life in them.

We'll start by taking a close look at the exploding marketplace for refurbished computers where you can get discounts of 20 percent or more on systems that are *practically* new.

Big Savings in Refurb Systems

It's remarkable how quickly the refurb market channel is growing. Virtually unheard of a few years ago, according to *Computer Retail Week*,[1] refurbished computers were expected to generate $4 billion in sales in 1997.

That's roughly 10 percent of the overall PC market. That's a *lot* of refurbs. (And even though some refurbs are sold that way only because they didn't match some customer's décor, I wonder what this says about the *quality* of new systems.)

Refurb systems are widely available for $1,000 or less—often, for as little as $600. They're powerful: often no more than a year behind the tech-

▲ ▲ ▲ ▲ ▲ ▲ ▲ ▲ ▲ ▲ ▲ ▲ ▲

1.   *Computer Retail Week,* Rebuilding a market—Refurbished PCs offer independents a niche opportunity, January 6, 1997.

nology curve, and sometimes as up to date as anything you'll find in the stores. And you can get brand names that otherwise might not be worth the premium to you.

What *are* refurbished PCs? Typically, these are units that have been returned to a manufacturer either because they have a problem or because a buyer has changed his or her mind. A refurbished unit should have been serviced, cleaned, and fully tested.

Some companies, such as Packard Bell, use the term *remanufactured*. This means a system has been taken apart, and each part has been tested and replaced if necessary. Then, the system has been reassembled and tested again.

Occasionally, overstocked new units make their way into the refurb channel when a manufacturer incorrectly estimates demand for a product. Technology transitions, such as the transition from 486 systems to Pentiums, are notoriously difficult for PC manufacturers to manage.

Refurbs generally come with at least *some* warranty. Typically, it's 90 days, though some vendors offer less, and a few (IBM and Micron, for example) offer more. Since new computer warranties are getting shorter, you may find there's surprisingly little difference between the warranty on a new system and the one you can get on a refurb.

Refurb Reliability

How reliable are refurbs? In general, they're quite reliable—especially if they are relatively new and have been refurbished or remanufactured by major manufacturers. Of course, there is always a chance that you could get a lemon which slipped through the testing process. Or a computer that was struck by lightning on the road somewhere and hasn't been quite right in the head since.

As we mentioned in Chapter 2, the solution is to set the computer up as soon as you get it home and run it as hard as you can. Leave it on for several days straight. Hook your printer to the parallel port and make sure it works. Run ScanDisk (and Norton Utilities if you have it) to check for serious disk problems. Format some floppies. Hook your speakers to the audio card; make sure they make appropriately joyful noises.

If you're running MS-DOS and Windows 3.1, exit to DOS and run MSD to make sure you're getting what you're supposed to be getting. If you're running Windows 95, click Start, Control Panel, System, and Device Manager and make sure you don't have any unresolved system conflicts or other problems (highlighted by yellow exclamation points).

In short, do all the things you might not normally get around to for weeks or months. If it all works, chances are it will keep working for a good long time. And again: This advice applies to any computer, new, refurb, or used.

Is Your New Computer a Refurb in Disguise?

Speaking of "new, refurbished or used"…

It turns out that many manufacturers include used parts from returned PCs in the *new* systems they sell. This tidbit became public knowledge when Compaq filed suit against competitor Packard Bell, charging that Packard Bell was selling used computers as new. The suit has since been settled, and it's turned out that Packard Bell is not the only computer company using this practice.

Is it terrible? It's probably something consumers can live with, *if* the parts are very recent, and are tested to work. Should they be telling us about it? Without a doubt. Can you find out by asking them? Almost never (though several ongoing state attorney general investigations may change this). Can you do much about it? Probably not.

Then why am I telling you this? Because you should know—and because it *might* make you more comfortable buying a refurb. Heck, you might be getting one anyway.

The Refurb/Used Computer Jargon Hunt

You'll occasionally come across some unfamiliar terms as you prowl the refurbished and used computer marketplace. Here are a few.

A-Goods: A refurbished item of the highest quality, with at least some warranty and no cosmetic imperfections.

B-Goods: A refurbished item with some discoloration, scratches, or other cosmetic problems. The product should not be defective in any way, but if an advertiser calls the product "B"-quality, take that as a warning to ask more questions.

C-Goods: Again, the product should theoretically have been tested to work but may have experienced physical damage such as a cracked case. I would avoid "C"-quality products.

Pulls: These have cards or drives removed from used systems. Make sure to check on the length and nature of the warranty being offered.

New Pulls: These are cards or drives removed from *new* systems, often due to changes in specifications before a computer reached the customer. While these products are usually of high quality, again check the length and nature of the warranty.

Bulk Pack: This is software or hardware that was originally delivered in quantity, without retail packaging. A variation is *Economy Packaging*. Typically this is used in software which was originally intended to be bundled with a system, rather than sold at retail.

DOA Warranty: The item being sold worked when it left the seller's premises and is guaranteed to work when it arrives at yours—but not one day more.

What Brands Show Up as Refurb?

Many brands do—but some more than others. Lately, you'll find the refurb channel chock-full of products from

- AST
- AT&T
- Compaq
- Digital
- Hewlett-Packard
- IBM
- Packard Bell
- Toshiba

You should know that AT&T has left the PC business and spun off the rest of its computer business as NCR; Digital now only markets its new PCs to businesses. AST has had serious financial trouble and is now owned by Samsung; Packard Bell sales dropped significantly last year. However, companies like Compaq, Hewlett-Packard, and IBM are on nearly everyone's short list of top manufacturers.

Where to Get Refurbs

When it comes to buying refurbs, you have a continuum of choices, from manufacturer outlets to a wide variety of small, independent distributors and resellers, who may purchase their systems at auctions or directly from the manufacturer.

Manufacturer Outlets

What do major computer manufacturers do with systems that have been returned to them, or overstocks and closeouts? Often, they sell those systems themselves, through outlet stores or by mail order. Not surprisingly, the manufacturers tend to lay low when it comes to promoting these venues: Supplies are limited, manufacturers don't want to undercut sales of full-priced merchandise, and who wants to admit you have that many leftover or returned systems?

In this section, we'll describe manufacturer outlets from several leading PC suppliers. You may be surprised to discover how recent the merchandise sold in these outlets can be. There is a trade-off, though: The manufacturer outlets often try to squeeze a few more bucks out of each system than third-party distributors do.

IBM PC Factory Outlet
1-800-426-7015

Until recently, IBM had a retail outlet store near its offices in Research Triangle, North Carolina, but the company now sells refurbs only by mail. The IBM PC Factory Outlet offers a 15-day money-back guarantee on all systems, and warranties ranging from one to five years. Merchandise includes desktop systems, a wide range of IBM ThinkPad notebooks, and a smaller selection of monitors. For a fax of all current inventory, call 1-800-426-3395 and request document 3001.

Packard Bell Factory Outlet
1-888-474-6772
www.pbfactoryoutlet.com

Packard Bell's Factory Outlet is one of the few authorized manufacturer outlets on the Web, and the only one I've found that links directly from the company's main Web site. Check the specials page; Packard Bell occasionally bundles high-end refurb systems with a monitor for under $1,000. Check the specs on those monitors, though. Packard Bell often packages 0.39-dot-pitch monitors with their low-end systems, and these are unacceptable for serious work.

> **tip** Packard Bell merged recently with NEC, the major Japanese technology firm. As NEC also owns Zenith Data Systems—one of the leading suppliers of PCs to government agencies—you'll also find ZDS systems at Packard Bell's Factory Outlet on the Web.

Acer Outlet
520 Brennan Street
San Jose, CA 95131
408-433-4903

The Acer Outlet sells a wide range of remanufactured computer systems, notebooks, monitors, and accessories. Most items carry a limited 90-day depot warranty, but some have a full year warranty. Acer also offers a limited selection of refurbished Aspire systems on its Acer Direct Web site at **www.acer.com/aac/direct/weborder.htm**. You fill out a form to indicate which products you're interested in purchasing, and an Acer sales agent calls you back to review your order and take purchase information by phone.

Compaq Works
1-800-318-6919

Compaq Works is a mail-order source for a wide variety of customer return units, cosmetically blemished products, older discontinued products, and excess inventory. All products carry a 90-day limited warranty and must be returned to Compaq for service. Recent deals include a refurbished Compaq Presario 4402, 133 MHz Pentium processor, 16-Mb RAM and built-in 15" monitor for $1099.

NEC LikeNew
1-800-NEC-INFO

NEC LikeNew offers products that don't meet NEC's specifications due to a minor blemish or other imperfections but have been examined and tested to meet NEC's performance standards and are backed by a 30-day no risk guarantee and, in most cases, a one-year limited warranty. LikeNew sells both NEC's Ready brand of PCs and its well-respected MultiSync monitors. For more information on products currently available, call NEC FastFacts at 1-800-366-0476 and request catalog 5 for a list of LikeNew document numbers.

Dell Factory Outlet
1-800-336-2891

Dell Factory Outlet sells a wide range of desktop, minitower, and notebook PCs. To have this week's specials faxed to you, call Dell TechFax at 1-800-950-1329 and enter document number 10002.

Tandy Outlet Store
812 E. Northside Drive
Fort Worth, TX 76102
817-870-5709

From the people behind your local Radio Shack, the Tandy Outlet Store sells computers from 486SX/25 to Pentium systems, all loaded with Windows and DOS. You can call for a quote, or visit their store. And if you happen to be in the neighborhood, they hold a sidewalk sale from 6 A.M. to 11 A.M. on the third Saturday of every month.

Gateway 2000 Factory Outlet

Gateway runs several factory outlet stores selling a wide variety of remanufactured computer systems; prices run roughly 15 percent below new systems. If none of the stores are accessible, you can phone to receive a current price list by fax. Call the North Sioux City store; they're the one with the 800 number!

745 North Derby Lane
North Sioux City, SD 57049
1-800-846-3614

3109 West 41st Street
Sioux Falls, SD 57105
1-605-357-1001

10129 State Line Road
Kansas City, MO 64114
1-816-545-3699

Gateway 2000 Country Stores
507 Boston Post Road
Orange, CT 06477
1-203-795-4925

9603 East Independence
Matthews, NC 28105
1-704-844-2000

> By the way, if you happen to be in Dublin, Ireland, they've got a factory outlet there, too. (Per the discussion of Gateway's unfortunate warranty small print on page 52, I don't know whether you'll have to submit to arbitration in Chicago if you have a dispute over a system you buy in Dublin.)

Micron Factory Outlet
1-208-893-7600

Micron sells refurbished systems at an outlet store in Boise, Idaho. Micron's refurbs are covered by a one-year depot (not on-site) warranty; all refurb sales are final. For more information about refurbished Micron systems, fill out Micron's form at **www.mei.micron.com/sales/mrd-sales.html**, and a Micron salesperson will contact you.

Systems Coming Off Lease

Many major corporations lease their computers instead of buying them; when the leases are over, the computers are returned to the leasing company. Those computers are rarely leased again; rather they are tested, cleaned up, and sold. It's a cost-effective way for Cheapskates to get a brand-name system that's a few years old but backed by a brand-name company.

IBM Credit Corporation

IBM Credit Corporation is my favorite source for refurbished PCs coming off lease. IBM Credit offers a wide selection of 486s, Pentiums, and notebook PCs, backed by a 7-day money-back guarantee and 90-day quality warranty, and generally available for shipping within 48 hours. They also accept MasterCard, Visa, American Express and Discover. You can reach IBM Credit on-line at **http://mer.shop.ibm.com/shopping/ibmcredit** (see Figure 3-1), or by phone at 1-800-IBM-5440.

GE Capital

GE Capital is not the cheapest source of used PCs, but it does offer a wide selection of well-maintained Compaq, IBM, Apple, AST, Toshiba, and Digital equipment. They're also a source for high-powered used workstations from Sun, Hewlett-Packard, and Silicon Graphics. To contact GE Capital, call 1-800-431-7713.

Rentex

Rentex specializes in short-term rentals of Compaq, IBM, NEC, and other PCs; Macs; and Sun workstations. Once the equipment can no longer be rented, Rentex sells it. Currently, the Rentex for sale list includes a wide variety of brand-name 486s, 386s, and laptops, as well as Macintoshes ranging from Classics to Quadra 950s.

Rentex Computer Rentals
337 Summer Street
Boston, MA 02210
1-800-545-2313
www.rentex.com

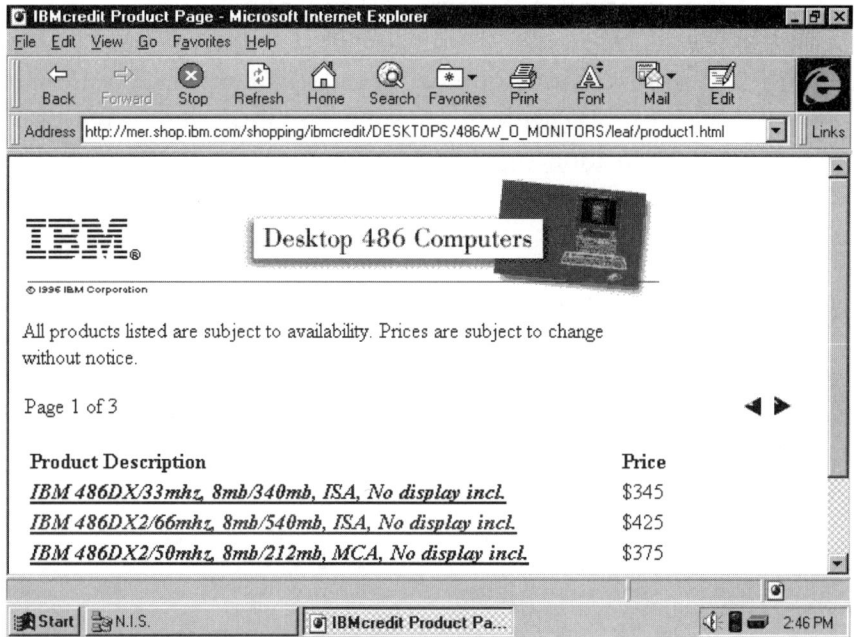

Figure 3–1 Good deals on systems coming off lease—and good warranties, too—from IBM Credit Corporation's Web Site.

What about *your* company? Some companies that don't lease, scrap their old systems for little or no money—perhaps ten cents on the dollar. Ask your company's IS (Information Systems, sometimes called "MIS" for Management Information Systems) department what they might be getting rid of. The closest bargains might be closest to home.

Retail Refurbished Computer Outlets

An increasing number of independent resellers are specializing in selling refurbished systems in storefront locations, by mail, or both. These resellers include

Tredex
5306 Beethoven Avenue
Los Angeles, CA 90066
1-800-899-6800
www.tredex.com; www.auctionx.com

True Data Products
775 Quaker Highway, Route 146A
Uxbridge, MA 01569
1-800-635-0300; 1-508-278-6555
www.truedataproducts.com

Micro Exchange
Nutley, NJ
1-800-284-9296
www.microexch.com

Capital Resource Recovery
200 N. 2nd Street, Suite 300
Minneapolis, MN 55401
1-800-452-6670
www.remarketing.com/broker/crr/

Delaware Computer Center, Inc.
621 West Newport Pike
Wilmington, DE 19804
1-800-668-3270; 1-302-633-1500

International Marketing Associates
1-301-299-7821
www.netm.com/ima

Image Microsystems
4929 Wilshire Boulevard
Los Angeles, CA 90010
1-800-800-4142; 1-310-815-1000
www.imagemicro.com

Dollar Computer Corporation
1809 E. Dyer Road, #304
Santa Ana, CA 92705
1-800-910-0085; 1-714-975-0542
www.earthlink.net/~dollar/

Maxim Technology
3930 West 29th Street South
Wichita, KS 67217
1-800-755-1008; 1-316-941-0799

Data Path Technologies, Inc
220 Tompkins Avenue
Pleasantville, NY 10570
1-914-769-1999
www.data-path.com

Electrified Discounters
110 Webb Street
Hamden, CT 06517
1-800-678-8585; 203-787-4246
www.electrified.com
Specializes in used notebooks and laptops.

> When you purchase a used system from an independent reseller, check whether it will come with a copy of DOS and/or Windows. If not, factor in the cost of purchasing one.

Computer Renaissance

Computer Renaissance is a national franchise chain of retailers specializing in brand-name used, refurbished, and closeout computer equipment. I was pleasantly surprised by the selection and expertise at the Computer Renaissance I visited recently in Paramus, NJ: a wide variety of solid 486 systems in the $400–$600 range, quality refurbished monitors for around $200, as well as a few notebook systems under $1,000.

You can probably get these systems for a *little* less by mail, but not for dramatically less. And, at least at the store I visited, the staff seemed to know something about computers. In retail establishments, that's rarer than it ought to be.

You can also trade in your current system at Computer Renaissance—though you could probably make a better deal selling privately, if you have the time and patience.

If you're interested, you can find your nearest Computer Renaissance on the Web at **www.computerrenaissance.com** (see Figure 3-2).

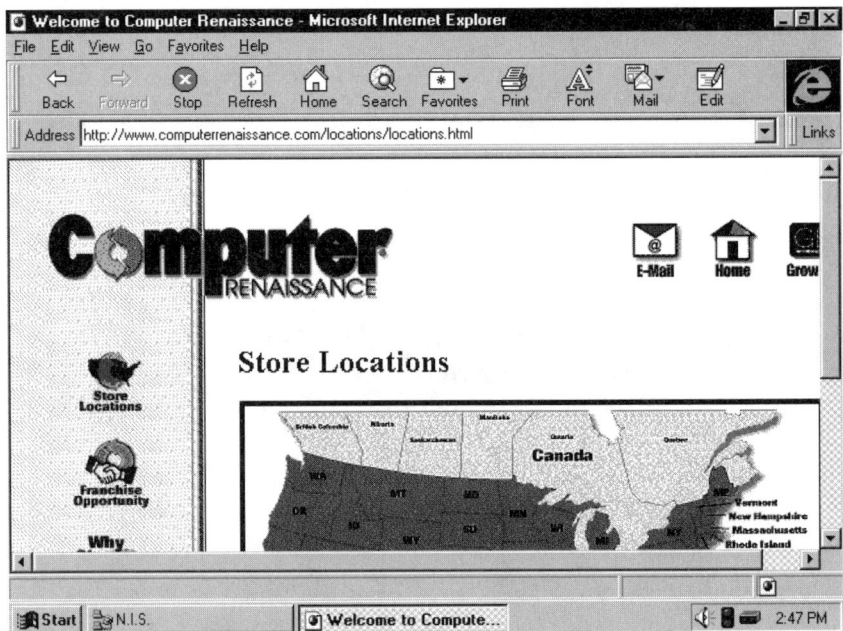

Figure 3–2   Finding your nearest Computer Renaissance used computer store at **www.computerrenaissance.com**.

By the way, Computer Renaissance is a division of a larger company, GrowBiz International, which specializes in franchise concepts based on used and refurbished items. Among their other franchises are stores for used children's clothing and sporting equipment.

Where the Refurb Vendors Get *Their* Stuff

If you're wondering where the refurb distributors and retailers get their systems, one major source is auctions. If you're careful, you may be able to cut out the middleman and save money by purchasing a refurb system at an auction yourself. Some auctions only offer systems in large quantities, but others sell the "onesies" and "twosies" you're probably interested in.

You can typically learn about computer auctions in the business or classifieds section of any major city's Sunday newspaper. You may also want to check Web sites such as the Internet Auction List, **www.usaweb.com/auction.html,** or sites operated by major auctioneers such as Koll-Dove.

As with any auction, it's critical to be prepared.

✍ *Know what a product is worth. Get a catalog in advance, if possible, and check the going rate for similar products elsewhere. Then have the discipline not to bid on it if the price is too high.*

✍ *Take advantage of opportunities to preview the product and ask questions.*

✍ *For all-day auctions, consider bidding only in the afternoon, when many of the amateur bidders will have left. These bidders tend to drive up prices, because they don't know what equipment is really worth.*

✍ *Make sure you know what warranty, if any, is offered on the equipment you're purchasing. In some cases, you will be offered an opportunity to purchase an extended warranty. Consider in advance whether you will want such a warranty and take its cost into account when you plan your bids.*

✍ *Be aware of buyer's premiums, which are surcharges added to winning bids by the auction house. For example, Remington York applies a 13 percent buyer's premium, discounted to 10 percent for payment made with cash, cashier's checks, or checks accompanied by a bank letter of guaranty.*

✍ *If several identical items are being offered, consider* not *bidding. Often, a high bidder will only be interested in purchasing one item, and after he or she wins the bidding war, you may be given an opportunity to purchase additional items at the same price. Of course, if you* had *been bidding, you would have had to bid against the winner and driven the price up.*

• *Koll-Dove National Computer Auction Exchanges*

Koll-Dove, one of the nation's leading auction houses, runs a series of National Computer Auction Exchanges—public auctions of new or factory refurbished, advanced desktop, notebook, multimedia systems, and peripherals. Many of Koll-Dove's auctions are held at the Meydenbauer Center in Bellevue, Washington; advance previews are at Koll-Dove's warehouse facility on 24100 Woodinville/Snohomish Road, also in Bellevue.

Koll-Dove auctions systems from a variety of first- and second-rank manufacturers, recently including Apple Computer, AST, Canon, Epson, IBM, and Texas Instruments. Koll-Dove welcomes both individual and business buyers; all items are individually tagged so buyers can choose how many units they wish to purchase, and if you buy fewer than ten items, they may be picked up at the auction site on the same day.

Koll-Dove
1241 East Hillsdale Boulevard
Foster City, CA
415-571-7400
www.koll-dove.com
acpccyberswap.com

- *Remington York Computer Auctions*

Remington York runs computer auctions and tag sales, typically from its showroom in Irving, Texas, but also at other sites around the country. Remington York sells new, factory refurbished units, units returned to manufacturers by consumers, overstocks, liquidations, and used equipment. According to Remington York, most merchandise is available in both single-item lots and larger quantity dealer lots.

For more information, or to download catalogs for auctions and tag sales, visit Remington York's Web page at **www.remingtonyork.com**, or call 972-438-1737.

Remington York
2010 Century Center Boulevard, Suite R
Irving, TX 75062
972-438-1737
www.remingtonyork.com

Government Surplus

Anyone who buys a lot of stuff eventually holds a garage sale to get rid of some of it—and gives or throws away the rest. That includes your governments—all of them, from the feds to your local school system. And some of the stuff at said garage sales is, not surprisingly, computer hardware. Here are Cheapskate ideas for finding some of the government's bigger "garage sales."

Defense Reutilization and Marketing Service

To start with the government with the biggest budget—and a good source of cheap computers—there's the military, specifically the Defense Reutilization and Marketing Service (DRMS). The Department of Defense disposes of stuff in two ways. The first is by auction—and forget about DoD auctions unless you want to bid on 100+ used PCs in unknown condition or 5,000 keyboards, usually 2,500 miles away.

Rather, you want to find your nearest DRMS retail store and check out whether they're one of the DRMS retail stores that sell computers. A visit to a DRMS store is a wondrous thing. In addition to the stuff you're after, you're liable to find anything from old elementary school texts from base schools to Size XXL arctic camouflage gear. Or how about stacks of hermetically-sealed gauze pads at $2 per thousand, or boxes capable of keeping anything you own dry underwater?

Like almost everyone else these days, the DRMS has a Web site and an 800 number. Try 1-800-468-8289 or **http://www.drms.dla.mil** for information (see Figure 3-3).

Some DRMS retail stores are great for Cheapskate computer shopping, and some are horrors. It depends on the local manager and the manager's boss. At one Navy shop, you used to be able to walk in, try out a Zenith Flat Screen VGA monitor, and, if you liked what you saw, walk out with it for $50. Then some clone builders got on the back of the man-

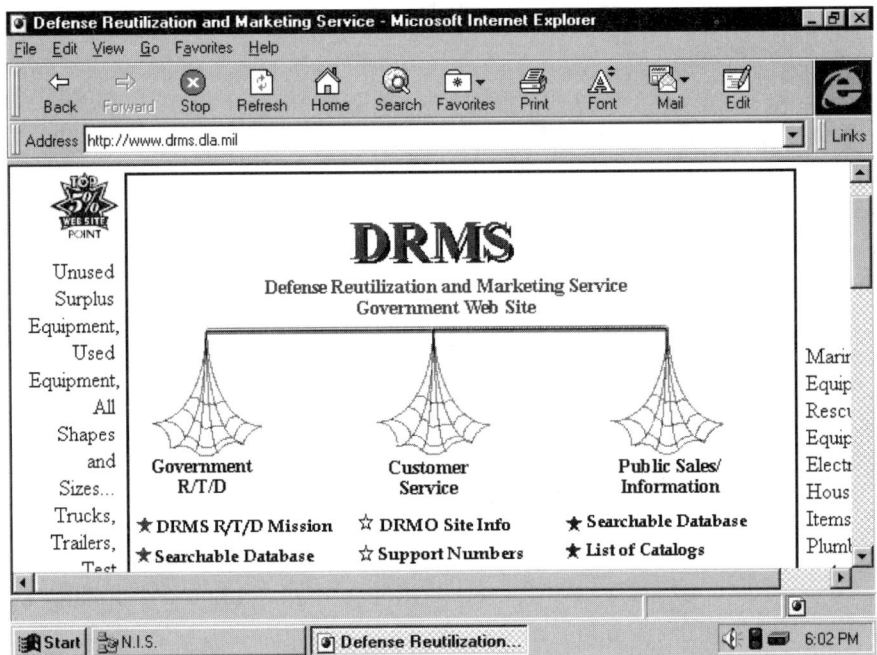

Figure 3–3 Locating your nearest Defense Reutilization and Marketing Service on-line.

ager's boss, and, at least according to the manager, demanded the monitors be sold in big lots so they weren't being undercut on their used gear sales. The dealers would then buy the same equipment, a dozen monitors at a time, jack up the price, and sell them used—at less profit to the government.

DRMS folks who learned about this deal promised that wouldn't be the case anymore, and anyplace where DRMS sold computers retail the consumer would be able to buy one or two boxes and not be forced into buying a thousand. We'll see.

The same shop sold PCs in various states of repair, ranging from full 80386 and 80286 systems, up for testing before sale at $250–$350 to $5 special DECmates, CPU box only. The best deals at this shop were monitors, and big old untested cases—ready for your motherboard and peripherals. Sometimes the power supplies worked; that was a bonus. Otherwise, you got a big metal last-forever computer case for about $5, with whatever hadn't been gutted thrown in as a bonus for either building your system or for your spare parts collection.

> **Despite their best efforts to advertise, the DRMS staff doesn't even have every retail store on their list. The best bet to find prime locations is probably to ask a soldier/reservist who's into computers.**

Say Uncle: U.S. Customs Auctions

The U.S. Customs Service holds regular auctions in several regional locations, selling a wide variety of merchandise that was confiscated upon entry into the country. These events cover the waterfront: computer equipment, electronics, clothing, jewelry, cars, oriental carpets. Often, equipment is auctioned in large, commercial lots. However, consumer quantities of some items are also available, and there are occasionally some very good deals.

In general, you can view the merchandise you're bidding on the day before the auction, or early on the morning of the auction. That's your *only* chance to evaluate what you're buying—take it!

Before bidding, you must obtain, fill out, and turn in a bidder registration card at the sale site; you'll need a photo ID to register. You'll get a bidder number and sales catalog. Forms of payment are generally cash, cashier's check, or Visa or MasterCard subject to verification. Cashier's checks should be made payable to the U.S. Customs Service, and cashiers cannot make change for more than 10 percent of the value of the check. Personal or business checks, bank letters, or letters of credit are not acceptable. Purchases under $5,000 must generally be paid for on the sale day.

U.S. Customs auction sites include

> 60 Distribution Boulevard
> Edison, N.J.

> Broward County/Greater Ft. Lauderdale Convention Center
> 1950 Eisenhower Boulevard
> Port Everglades, FL

> 5900 Luckett Court
> El Paso, TX

> 2332 East Pacifica Drive
> Rancho Dominguez, CA
> (Los Angeles-Compton Area)

> 55 Bodega Drive
> Nogales, AZ

You can get regular advance notification of lots to be auctioned by calling the Public Auction Line at 703-273-7373; some of the items to be offered are posted in advance on the U.S. Customs Service Web site at **www.ustreas.gov/treasury/ bureaus/customs/** .

The auctions are run by EG&G Dynatrend. Employees of the Department of the Treasury, EG&G Dynatrend, or its subcontractors, or their immediate families, are prohibited from bidding.

Other Government Sources

All other federal agencies are supposed to reuse everything they can and then sell the rest for the best bucks they can get. They don't. There is at least one Southern New Jersey civilian federal facility where I have seen thousands of dollars of electronics hardware tossed out of a garage, left to bake and soak for six months in a sandy yard, and then sold as metal scrap, because management couldn't be bothered. It makes a hacker cry to see a relatively new Tektronix top-of-the-line oscilloscope bleached to a bone and rusted out, to be sold for a few cents when the guy could have gotten $100 to $1,000 for it, depending on how much of it still worked.

If you're near a federal government facility, stop by and ask about how they get rid of surplus property. If you spot serious abuses, call your local newspaper and your local member of Congress. The end result will be lower taxes for all of us and cheap computers for you.

State and local governments have their own rules for disposing of the goods when they are no longer needed. So do colleges and universities. At some, the computer science department handles disposal of old systems; at others it's handled on a campus wide basis. Ask.

Many local governments hold annual auctions of surplus stuff and inventory seized from ne'er-do-wells, or stolen and never claimed.

Generally the lots are small at these auctions and you can buy a computer. You face two problems: The first is that you may not have adequate time to properly inspect what you are bidding on. The second, as usual, is auction fever.

Then again, sometimes you'll get a chance to bid on some prime stolen laptop or a bookie's server system, and it will be a rainy weekday when no one shows up to bid against you. Bring someone who knows the stuff if you don't know it yourself and don't bid more than you can afford to lose should the item turn out to have been trashed while in an evidence garage.

On-line Auctions

You don't have to go to an auction site to find an auction anymore. You can bid on-line, at one of the on-line computer auctions that are springing up like weeds all over the Internet.

As a Cheapskate, you have to be just as careful at Internet auctions as you would in person. Never forget that Internet auctioneers are counting on auction fever to drive prices beyond where they ought to be. It's part of their business model. Don't get your heart set on winning a particular item; if you lose, there will almost certainly be another item like it available at another auction, or through some other channel, some time soon. These are not one-of-a-kind antiques we're talking about; they are items that were mass produced in the thousands.

If you are careful and you understand the value of the products you're bidding on, there are some very good deals to be had. Here are a few *winning* bids I've seen recently:

- ▲ Mac Classic, Rasterops Clearvue Classic and Rasterops 15" Portrait Display: $175
- ▲ Allied Telesis 16-bit Shared Memory Ethernet Adapter Card: $9.00
- ▲ IBM PS/2 Model 56—386SLC20 with 8-Mb RAM, 80-Mb hard drive and Token Ring adapter: $59.00
- ▲ Zenith Pentium 75 PC: $380
- ▲ MS-DOS 6.0: $9.00

In many cases, Internet auctioneers auction products that come from other sources: small resellers, distributors, and liquidators, for example. In some cases, however, they auction their own products. That's the case at the **www.auctionx.com** site, which is operated by Tredex, a company that has sold closeout and refurbished computers and printers for several years.

Before you place a bid at AuctionX, check **www.tredex.com** or call 1-800-899-6800 to make sure Tredex isn't selling the same system there for less money.

No matter where you bid, you should expect to find detailed descriptions of the products you're thinking of bidding on, as well as information about the company that will actually be delivering the product, its warranty policies and shipping costs. Don't bid if you're not satisfied with this information.

Most on-line auction sites also provide a page with all the rules of the auction. Read the rules carefully before bidding. There are different kinds of auctions, even within a single site. For example, some auctions are Yankee auctions, where multiple identical items are offered for sale at the same price, and the highest bidders win the available inventory at their actual bid price. Others may be Dutch auctions, where the highest bidders win at the lowest successful bidder's price. A few auction houses may add buyer's premiums to winning bids.

One other pointer: With some Web browsers, when you return to a site, you may inadvertently see the same data (and prices) that were there when you first placed your bid, because your browser displays information stored in your cache. If you find yourself having this problem, clear your cache.

Typically, before you place any bids, you are asked to register for an account, using your credit card number. Once you've done so, you're assigned a password you can use to place a bid. Most auction houses use Internet security techniques that incorporate encryption while you are transmitting credit card information; a few sites secure *all* their pages.

Once you place a bid, there's no withdrawing it—so once again, be careful. Some auction houses will notify you by e-mail when your bid is surpassed—encouraging you not so subtly to rebid higher.

On-Line Auction Tips and Tricks

How do you get good deals at an on-line auction?

One trick is to bid only on items the auctioneers are selling in quantity. Let's say they're auctioning 20 identical computers, or 50 copies of a software package. You're still bidding against the same number of people, but unless someone bids on the entire lot, many more people will win—including many people with bids that are significantly lower than the top bid.

In such a situation, be careful not to bid higher than you have to. Let's say an auction house is auctioning 20 computers; the current top bidder has bid $800; 6 more bidders have bid $750; 13 more bidders have bid $700. If *you* bid $750, you sneak in ahead of all 13 $700 bidders.

In general, you'll face less competition bidding for older computers than newer ones. I saw the same Compaq 386SX/20s going for $85 at Auction Board for six consecutive weeks. You may also face less competition for software packages, especially since they are often sold in large quantities. It's common to find CD-ROMs going for $10 or less. (Often, these CD-ROMs will have been unbundled from CD-ROM and multimedia kits, without the approval of the manufacturer.)

> Consider "lurking" on an on-line auction site for a few weeks, to get a feel for the dynamics of the bidding: How quickly do bids rise? How much bidding takes place at the last minute? Which items are generating the most excitement?

When you're ready to bid, set yourself a target price, taking into account extra costs such as shipping (typically around $30–$40 for a complete computer system). Decide in advance that you won't place any bids unless they'll save you at least 10 percent compared with purchasing the same product elsewhere.

Typically, a site will hold between one and three auctions per week. At many auctions, there's an advantage in bidding near the bidding deadline. You won't have helped to drive the price up any more than necessary—and you won't give other casual bidders as much time to top *your* bid.[2]

Of course, you won't be the only person with this idea, and it's possible that more serious, last-minute bidders will top you, without your ever getting a chance to respond. Many sites will allow live bidding to continue past the timed deadline. Nevertheless, it's usually a chance worth taking.

Here are several of the most well known on-line auction sites:

ONSALE
www.onsale.com
In less than two years, ONSALE (see Figure 3-4) has become a $50 million business. It purchases large lots of goods from Apple, Canon, Lexmark, NEC, Hewlett-Packard, Toshiba, and other major companies but also serves as an on-line opportunity for distributors and liquidators to move products, in exchange for a cut of 10–20 percent.

Worldport Auction Board
www.worldport.com/auction/
Associated with Creative Computers, owners of the PC Mall and Mac Mall mail-order firms.
www.zauction.com
www.auctionpc.com
www.auctionx.com
Associated with Tredex, the closeout systems dealer.

▲ ▲ ▲ ▲ ▲ ▲ ▲ ▲ ▲ ▲ ▲ ▲ ▲ ▲ ▲ ▲ ▲ ▲ ▲

2.   On a few sites, if two bidders end up with the same bid, preference is given to the one who placed a bid – any bid – first. On those sites, consider placing a very low "placeholder" bid early in the auction, simply to establish your priority.

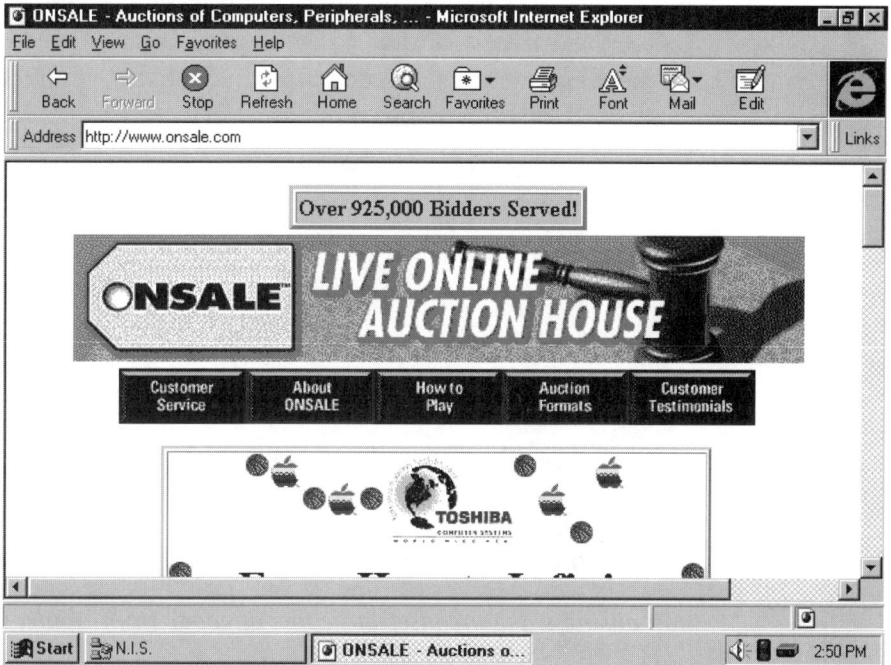

Figure 3–4 The **www.onsale.com** on-line auction site is one of the larger ones—and it's one of the few to auction noncomputer-related electronics, such as audio equipment and cameras.

Buying Used

Many of the buying sources we've talked about provide both recent refurbished computers *and* older used computers. In the next few pages, we'll focus specifically on purchasing older, used computers from both commercial and private sources: where to look, and what to know. But first, what to *watch out for.*

The Late, Lamented

All things equal, you'd like to buy a used system from a vendor that's still in the business, so you'll at least have a prayer of getting information, parts, and system updates. (Failing that, as we've said before, you'd like to buy a system that's reasonably generic, with parts that are interchangeable.)

There's a long, pitiful list of companies that once sold IBM-compatible PCs to U.S. consumers but don't any longer. It includes

- Ambra (former discount division of IBM)
- Amstrad
- AT&T
- Canon
- CLUB American
- Columbia
- Commodore
- CompuAdd
- Digital (still sells to corporate market)
- Eagle
- Franklin
- Grid
- Hyundai
- Kaypro
- Leading Edge
- Northgate
- Sanyo (early Sanyo "MS-DOS" machines weren't truly PC compatible)
- Tandon
- Tandy (Radio Shack now resells IBM systems)
- Zeos (purchased by Micron)

Just Too Old

Unless you're a collector, or running a museum, *some* computers are just too old to bother with:

- Apple II systems of any stripe
- Atari 400/800, TI 99/4A, Timex/Sinclairs, and others of their era
- Commodore 64s (128s, PETs, VIC-20s, Plus-4s, you name it)
- Original Macintosh 128, 512, XL, or Macintosh Plus models
- First-generation IBM PCs or clone systems without hard drives

Evolutionary Dead Ends

Some technologies just never made it—and the systems that used those technologies are harder to upgrade, harder to use, just plain not worth it. Examples include

- ▲ Pen-based Windows systems
- ▲ 2.5" floppy diskettes (seen on certain Zenith laptops)
- ▲ Amigas (terrific computer in its day, but now purely for cultists)
- ▲ Systems with "passive backplane" designs, in which the case contains nothing but what look like add-on cards—one of which is what every other computer maker calls a "motherboard."

IBM's Micro Channel Architecture is probably the best example of a technology that was intended to be an advance and turned into an obstacle. Micro Channel Architecture, introduced with IBM's PS/2 line of computers in 1987, was intended to be a better way to connect internal boards, and purely from a technical standpoint, it was.

However, few clone vendors chose to license (and pay) IBM for the rights to use Micro Channel Architecture, so few companies designed internal boards for it, making it more expensive and more difficult to expand Micro Channel Architecture computers.

I'll discuss PS/2s in more detail in Chapter 8. Suffice it to say that since Micro Channel Architecture-based PS/2s are in low demand, determined Cheapskates can get some remarkable bargains on them—as long as you're not planning to add internal boards. The following companies sell dirt-cheap, used PS/2s:

Alternative Computer Products Corporation
1120 Holland Drive Suite 5
Boca Raton, FL 33487
561-994-9899

Computer Service Point, Inc.
69 Bloomingdale Road
Hicksville, NY 11801
516-937-3800

105

NEI Computer Products
Hicksville, NY 11801
516-231-5845

Universal Sales Agency, Inc.
230 Duffy Avenue, Unit R-1
Hicksville, NY 11801
516-932-1400

Commercial Sources for Older Used PCs

The companies mentioned in the previous section sell not only IBM
PS/2s but systems from other major manufacturers as well. Other companies that resell older systems include

Image Microsystems
4929 Wilshire Boulevard
Los Angeles, CA 90010
1-800-800-4142; 1-310-815-1000
www.imagemicro.com

TII
26 Main Street
East Haven, CT 06512
1-203-466-1644

Maxim Technology
3930 West 29th Street South
Wichita, KS 67217
1-800-755-1008; 1-316-941-0799

Global Computer Concepts, Inc.
5100 La Palma Avenue, Suite 114
Anaheim Hills, CA 92807
1-800-411-1150

Breakaway Technologies, Inc.
847-265-6890

The World Wide Web is also becoming an excellent source for used equipment. For example, The Used Computer Mall (**www.usedcomputer.com**) is a clearinghouse of used computer dealers, organized by brand name or type of stuff sold. The same site also maintains a list of computer shows and swap meets (**www.usedcomputer.com/show.html**).

The Internet Clearinghouse

If you're worried about whether a seller will abscond with your money without delivering the goods as promised, the Internet Clearinghouse (**www.internetclearinghouse.com**) offers a possible solution.

The Internet Clearinghouse is a bonded and licensed computer broker that lists new and used items available from sellers nationwide. When a buyer wants to purchase merchandise on the site, payment is sent to Internet Clearinghouse, which accepts major credit cards.

When the funds clear, the seller is notified that he or she can safely deliver the equipment. Then, when the equipment arrives at the buyer's location, the buyer has an opportunity to inspect it. When the buyer is satisfied, he or she calls Internet Clearinghouse and the money is released. If the buyer is not satisfied, he or she returns the system, and once it arrives safely, the original payment is returned to the buyer.

Finding Private Sellers

You can find private sellers just about anywhere, especially in local newspaper classified ads. These days, an increasing number of used computers are showing up at yard sales. If you haven't found what you want locally, there are many other options.

On-Line Classifieds

CompuServe, America OnLine (AOL), and the Microsoft Network each have classifieds areas for private sellers; CompuServe and AOL allow companies to advertise as well. You can often find excellent deals on refurbished systems, peripherals, memory, and software on these sites. Figure 3-5 shows CompuServe's classified area, accessible via GO CLASSIFIEDS:

```
Browse of IBM-CLONE Desktop Computers : 41 ads

    486-$379, Pentiums-$699 New Systems      CA
    IBM 486/25 $325                          MA
    Cheapest Memory/CPU/Motherboard          NY
    IBM 486/33 $350                          MA
    Grid 486 DX/50 Mid Tower $345.00         TX
    486 DX2/66 Mid Tower $395                TX
    SYSTEM OF THE WEEK                       OH
    COMPAQ 386/35 $179                       MA
    Pentium 133 Mhz MultiMedia Tower $965    TX
    New 486 DX4/100 Mini Tower $425.00       TX
    New 5X86-DX4-133 Multimedia Tower $825   TX


              [ Read ]              [ Cancel ]
```

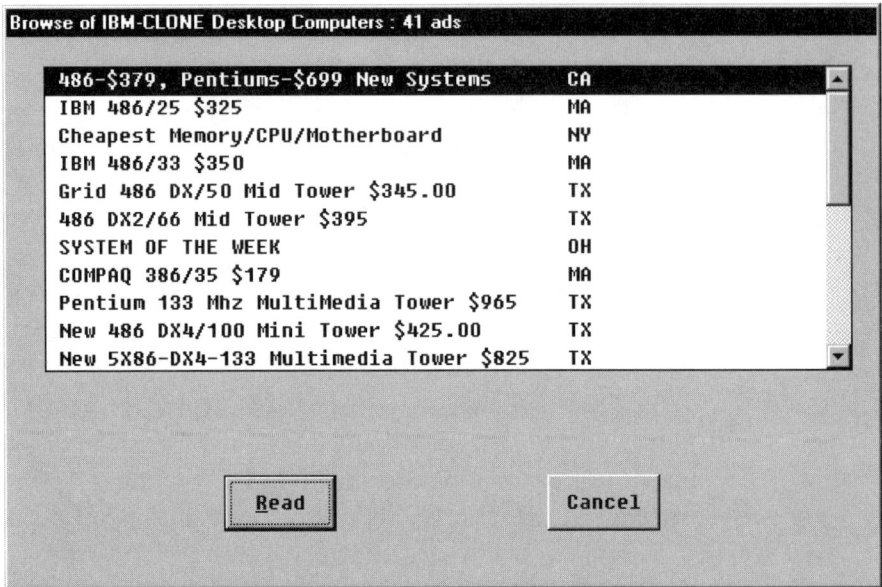

Figure 3–5   CompuServe's on-line classified area is home to many small resellers of used computer equipment and software.

Not surprisingly, more and more classified opportunities are appearing on the World Wide Web. For example, traditional automobile classifieds publications are promoting advertising of used PCs, and in the New York/New Jersey/Connecticut area, for example, hundreds of used PC listings can be found at **www.carbuyers.com**, the on-line site of the *Car Buyers Market* weekly newspaper.

Meanwhile, the search engine Yahoo! (**www.yahoo.com**) has introduced both nationwide and local free classifieds, and is beginning to attract a significant number of advertisers. And there is also a family of Usenet newsgroups where anyone can post computer equipment for sale, including

misc.comp.forsale
misc.forsale.computers.discussion
misc.forsale.computers.mac-specific.cards.misc
misc.forsale.computers.mac-specific.cards.video
misc.forsale.computers.mac-specific.misc

misc.forsale.computers.mac-specific.portables
misc.forsale.computers.mac-specific.software
misc.forsale.computers.mac-specific.systems
misc.forsale.computers.memory
misc.forsale.computers.modems
misc.forsale.computers.monitors
misc.forsale.computers.net-hardware
misc.forsale.computers.other.misc
misc.forsale.computers.other.software
misc.forsale.computers.other.systems
misc.forsale.computers.pc-specific.audio
misc.forsale.computers.pc-specific.cards.misc
misc.forsale.computers.pc-specific.cards.video
misc.forsale.computers.pc-specific.misc
misc.forsale.computers.pc-specific.motherboards
misc.forsale.computers.pc-specific.portables
misc.forsale.computers.pc-specific.software
misc.forsale.computers.pc-specific.systems
misc.forsale.computers.printers
misc.forsale.computers.storage
misc.forsale.computers.workstation

Buying Used Computers from a Private Seller

So you've seen a deal in the local weekly newspaper—or on the Web—that looks too good to pass up. Before you trundle over to some stranger's house, carrying a wad of twenties, what should you know? You'll probably be called on to make a decision in someone's den, with the seller's spouse and kids looking on. The more detailed an inspection you can make, the better your chances of staying happy once you get the system home. Hence . . .

The Cheapskate's Twelve-Step Program for Evaluating a Used PC

1. Give some thought to the price in the ad. Review the general pricing guidelines for each generation of PC on page 7. (Or the Mac pricing guidelines in Chapter 9.) Does the seller seem to be in line with those? Low-end rule of thumb: You can get a very low-end Windows 3.1 machine (say, a 386/16SX or 386/20SX with 4 Mb) mail order for $125 these days—though you'll have to add a monitor and, most likely, a copy of Windows. High-end rule of thumb 2: You can get a complete, reasonably quick system, with monitor and Windows 95, for well under $1,000. Is the seller in the same ballpark?

You can get up-to-the minute pricing for used computers at the Used Computer Mall Web Site, where the MicroPricer^{TM} page compiles current asking prices for thousands of used systems and peripherals. If you're considering purchasing a Mac, also visit the United Computer Exchange (**www.uce.com**) to view their price guide, updated weekly (see Figure 3-6).

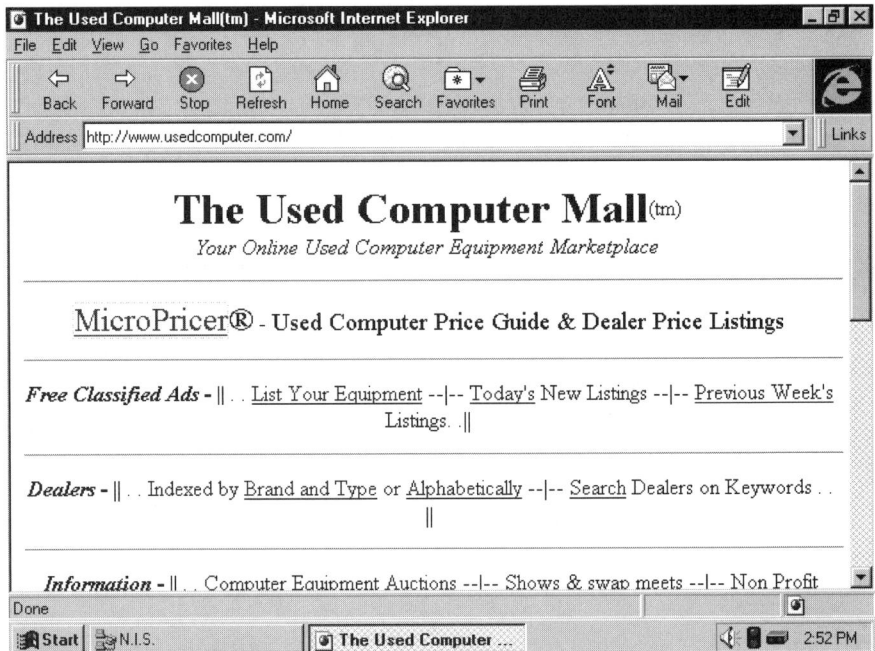

Figure 3–6 The MicroPricer^{TM} page at the Used Computer Mall Web site.

> At United Computer Exchange's Web site (see Figure 3-7), you can even download a copy of UCE's MacAppraiser software—with current prices built in. Load it on the seller's Mac and *show* them how much their machine is worth!

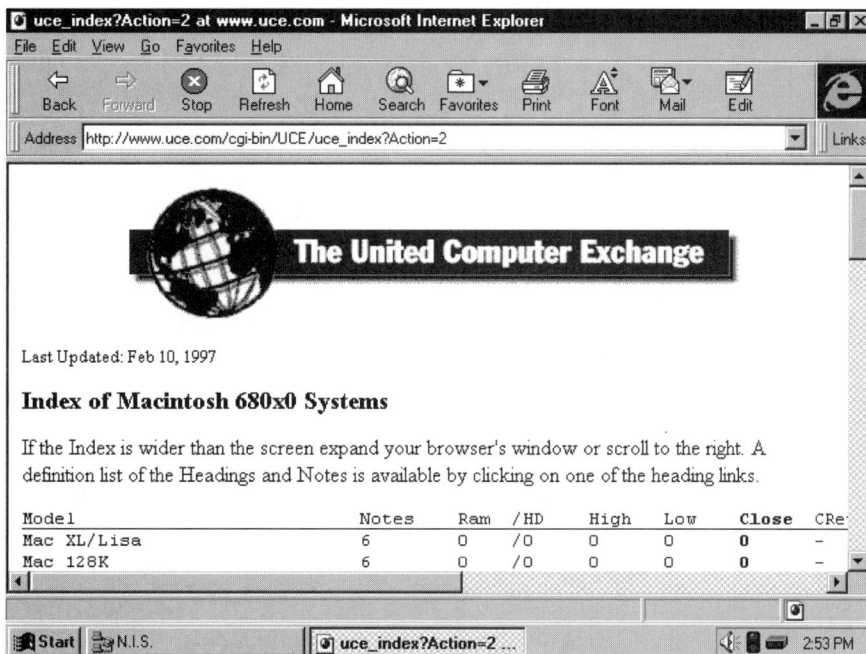

Model	Notes	Ram	/HD	High	Low	Close	CRe
Mac XL/Lisa	6	0	/0	0	0	0	–
Mac 128K	6	0	/0	0	0	0	–

Figure 3–7   Pricing used Macs at the United Computer Exchange.

Private sellers sometimes value their computers a bit too optimistically. "Let's see, I paid $2,500 for this system just five years ago, and I didn't really use it all that much—$1,600 should be fair, wouldn't you say?" Try $500—*maybe*! If your idea of a great shopping experience is a Middle Eastern bazaar, go ahead and disregard this advice, but it's usually a waste of time to negotiate buying a computer with someone whose precon-

111

ceived pricing is that far off. Hey, who knows? They just *might* find someone willing to pay that much. Just as long as it isn't you!

2. When you arrive, talk to the seller for a few minutes about how he or she used the computer. Have the kids been banging on it every night for the last few years? Does it seem well cared for?

Wipe the monitor and keyboard, ideally with some gauze or a soft towel moistened with rubbing alcohol. Also bring a small bottle of rubbing alcohol and some gauze or a soft towel. Wipe the face of a used monitor. If it comes away orange, the computer was used by a smoker—and smoke is as bad for the health of electronics as it is for humanity. Keyboards, monitors, and floppy drives can be expected to live a shorter life if kept in smoke-filled rooms. Dirty and dusty manufacturing environments also kill equipment fast. (See Chapter 8 for more pointers on well-maintained PCs.)

3. Next, start evaluating the hardware itself. Start with the easy stuff: Do all the keys on the keyboard work? Begin with the ~ character at the top left of the keyboard and work your way across and down. I don't care how little typing you do; sooner or later you're going to need all 26 letters of the alphabet, both lowercase and caps, as well as all 10 numbers!

If you find a key that sticks, try gently removing the key cap, cleaning it, and replacing it. If the key *still* doesn't type smoothly, assume you'll have to replace the keyboard. Cheapskate-level PC keyboards can be had for less than $20 (Mac keyboards generally cost at least twice as much), but at minimum, that's $20 *less* you should pay for the system being offered.

4. Take inventory, and take notes. What does the system *contain*? Look at the back of the computer to note any ports. Figure 3-8 shows the front and back of a fairly recent, well-configured PC. Note the internal modem, sound card, two serial ports, and parallel port.

5. Turn the computer and monitor on, and watch for any error messages that appear as the computer starts up. (These messages may fly by too quickly for you to see, but at least give it a try.) Generally, these are software related and fixable, but some messages may indicate that the computer can't recognize hardware that it *should* recognize, such as a CD-ROM or sound board. Was the seller unable to configure the equipment properly? (If so, can you expect to have better luck?) Or is the component simply not working?

Front View (Locations may vary)   Back View (Locations may vary)

Empty 5.25" Drive Bay

Inside (Cutaway View): Power Supply

CD-ROM Drive in 5.25" Drive Bay

Inside (Cutaway View): Motherboard

Power

3.5" Floppy Drive in 3.5" Drive Bay

3.5" Drive Bay, Probably Containing Hard Drive

Inside (Cutaway view): Add-on boards (video, sound, etc.)

Power Plugs

Fan

Keyboard Connector

9-pin (male) serial port

Empty slot (usually)

15-pin game port

25-pin (female) parallel printer port

25-pin (male) serial port

15-pin VGA video adapter

Modem

Sound Card (Inputs & Outputs)

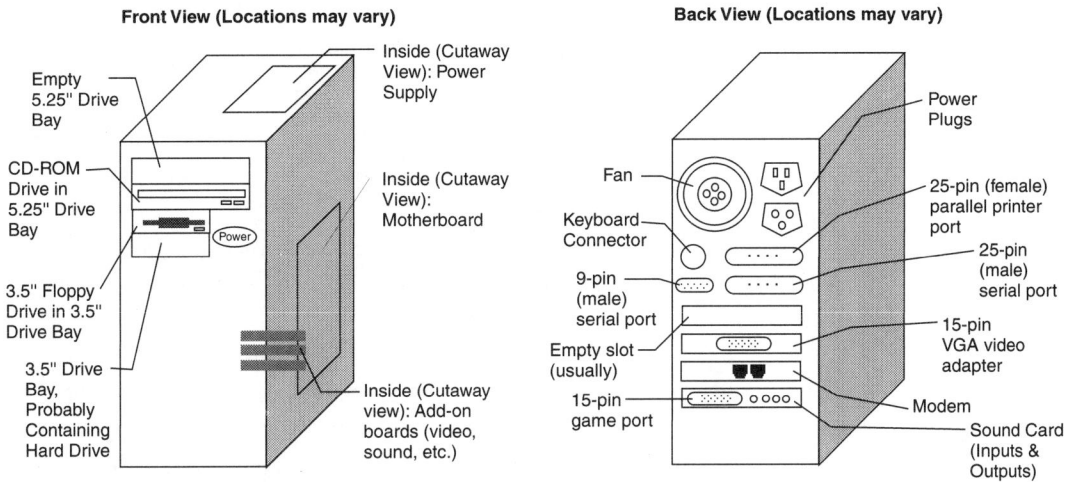

Figure 3–8   Front and back of a recent-vintage PC.

6. Put your hand on the power supply fan at the back of the computer—near the power plugs. If it is dead, question the value of the system. If it has been dead long, the components in the box have baked and may die a lot sooner.

If you see a lot of dust or animal hair around the fan or inside the box, it indicates someone did not take proper care of their machine—which requires regularly opening up and gently vacuuming out the power supply fan and, less often, the inside of the box itself. Few computer users take the trouble, or know they should. Many have never opened the box. Plan on doing a thorough vacuuming yourself if you purchase the system—and take into account any allergies you may have!

7. If the system is DOS-based, type **dir** at the C: prompt to see what software is present on the computer. If the system is Windows 3.x-based, open File Manager. If the system is Windows 95-based, click Start, Programs, Windows Explorer. If it's a Mac, double-click on the hard drive icon.

If you're not sure how to run the software on the system, ask the seller to show you how. Spend a few minutes working with any software you might be interested in using. See if the software seems to run properly, or if it returns error messages that indicate important files are missing or damaged.

Does the computer come with software you would actually *use*? (If not, the software isn't worth anything to you—which may be the most self-evident, universally ignored rule in computing. Everyone thinks, well it *would be nice* to have crossword-puzzle software, but unless you already do crossword puzzles, you're not about to start just because you own the software.)

8. While you're working with the software, keep an eye on the monitor. Yes, I realize it would be difficult to do otherwise, but I want you to think about the *experience* of working with the monitor. Is it blurry or fuzzy? Does it give you eyestrain? If so, you don't want it—and if you are buying a computer for your children, you don't want to impose it on them either. (See Chapter 5 for more information on used and new monitors.)

9. Speaking of software, is the seller providing the original diskettes, or simply leaving the software on the hard drive? Without them, you won't be able to reinstall the software, you may not be able to move it reliably to another computer if you upgrade later, and you won't be able to add optional features that aren't already installed.

Assuming the software is legally registered, would the seller sign a piece of paper listing the software and transferring rights to you? (That's usually an easy request, and it's the last question to ask, after you've decided to make an offer.)

If there isn't any applications software, is the seller at least including the operating system disks? This is critical. If you ever have a system problem that requires you to reinstall your operating system, it will help if you *have* one.

Of course, original manuals should go with original disks. And it doesn't hurt to ask if the seller has any third-party books they'd be willing to throw into the deal.

10. You may want to check whether the hard drive is compressed. Some people (and some companies) selling 110-Mb hard drives will compress them and tell you the computer has a 220-Mb hard drive. I'm not against disk compression (see Chapter 5 for a much more detailed

discussion of this), but you should know what you're getting. Hey, you may be planning to compress the drive yourself, with the idea you could get 440 Mb—if it's already compressed, you'll get a rude surprise.

You don't want a drive compressed with an off-brand compression program. Personally, I'd only accept a drive compressed with Microsoft DriveSpace, Microsoft DoubleSpace, or a later version of Stacker. DoubleSpace was available with MS-DOS 6.0 and 6.20; the 6.20 version includes some safeguards that make it more reliable than the 6.0 version.

How can you tell if a drive is compressed—and if so, with what software? The DOS 6.x Scandisk program will tell you whether DriveSpace or DoubleSpace is in use. To find out whether Stacker's on a drive, run the following command:

```
DIR C:\STAC*.* /S
```

Of course, you could just *ask*.

11. Ask the seller to help you test any devices that are included with the system. You want to watch modems establish connections, you want to see printers print, and you want to hear sound boards make noise. Don't assume!

12. Last but not least, if you're willing to be especially forward, consider running diagnostic software on the system right then and there (See Chapter 8 for information on diagnostics software.) Needless to say, not every seller will be comfortable with your running any software on their system—it's up to you whether to even try.

> If you're really concerned about performance, you could request Ziff-Davis' free Winstone 97 benchmark software at *www.zdnet.com/zdbop/ winstone/winstone.html* and run that, too. (It's too big to download. ZD sends it to you on CD-ROM, so it's only useful for testing CD-ROM based systems.) If you find, for example, that a Pentium 90 system actually performs more like an average Pentium 75 system, that might give you a little bargaining leverage to shave a few bucks off the price.

Finally, it's common when you buy a used car to make a deal with the seller that if your mechanic says it's bad you can return it. Consider requesting the same deal with a private seller. If you don't know anyone who really knows machines and will do it for nothing, in many areas you may be able to hire a qualified computer repair person for around $30–$40 to pop the hood and take a look, assuming you bring the machine in. I'd expect to pay more in areas like the Northeast, where *everything* costs more.

Nonprofit Computer Recycling Programs

We Cheapskates should never forget to count our blessings—or to share them. If you've decided to give your old computer a new home, you might considering donating it to a non-profit organization that will use that hardware to benefit schools or community groups. And if you represent a nonprofit organization that needs equipment, one of these agencies may be able to help you.

Computer Recycling Programs exist on five continents and in at least 28 states. Some organizations can offer you a tax deduction; others can't.

You can find out about the program nearest you by visiting the PEP National Directory of Computer Recycling Programs at **www.microweb.com/pepsite/Recycle/ recycle_index.html**.

If you can't find a local organization that will make good use of your old system, consider these national organizations. Of course, get in touch with them *first*, before you box up that old XT and call UPS!

The East-West Education Development Foundation
23 Dry Dock Avenue
Boston, MA 02110
617-261-6699

Founded in 1990 to provide computers for journalists in the former Soviet Union, the foundation now remanufactures and donates computers to nonprofit organizations in the United States and worldwide—so far, they've donated more than 6,000 systems.

Educational Institutions Partnership Program (EIPP)
c/o Defense Information Systems Agency
701 S. Courthouse Road
Arlington, VA 22204-2199

A program of the Department of Defense, EIPP provides used equipment to eligible schools, including K–12 institutions, colleges, and certain nonprofit organizations.

National Cristina Foundation
591 West Putnam Avenue
Greenwich, CT 06830
203-622-6000; 1-800-274-7876

The Foundation matches companies and individuals who have computers to donate with nonprofit organizations and schools that serve individuals with disabilities. When a match is found, you send your equipment directly to the beneficiary.

Non-Profit Computing Inc.
40 Wall Street, Suite 2124
New York, NY 10005-1301
212-759-2368

This organization donates computers, peripherals, and software to nonprofit organizations, schools, and government agencies. Non-Profit Computing Inc. works primarily in New York City but will donate equipment to agencies elsewhere if they can arrange for delivery.

Summary

Hidden away, without the glitz of the four-color circulars and TV advertisements, there's a thriving market in used and refurbished PCs. For many computer buyers, these systems offer much better price/performance than any new computer could, and for some they're the only financial option that makes sense.

In this chapter, we've reviewed several ways to purchase used and refurbished systems. But no matter what kind of computer you purchase, you'll need software to run on it—and that's where we'll focus our attention next.

Software "On the Cheap"

Without software, your computer may as well be a rock. But that doesn't mean you need to invest a fortune in software. You may already own a good deal of the software you need. In this chapter, I'll help you take stock. I'll also show you some great sources for new, old, used, and free software.

Combine that with the contents of the Cheapskate's CD-ROM (covered in Chapter 12), and you may never pay full price for software again.

What Do You Already Have?

If you've purchased a new PC any time in the past several years, you may have more software than you realize. Both Windows 3.x and Windows 95 come with bundles of miniature applications, called "applets," which may be all you need to perform many of the tasks you bought a computer for. (If you've installed Windows 95 *over* Windows 3.x, you probably have *both* sets of applets.)

In the next few pages, we'll look at both Windows 95 and Windows 3.1, to show you what Microsoft has given you, what you can reasonably expect to do with it, and what you still might need to pay extra for.[1]

▲ ▲ ▲ ▲ ▲ ▲ ▲ ▲ ▲ ▲ ▲ ▲ ▲

1.   Microsoft's free disk utilities are covered in Chapter 8, and direct cable connection is covered in Chapter 9.

Windows 95 Applets: A Gold Mine

I hope you know by now that I'm *not* trying to talk you into buying a Windows 95 system. There is a ton of useful computing you can do with Windows 3.1 or even MS-DOS, using older computers that will typically cost you a lot less than Windows 95 systems will. And of course, there's the Macintosh, which gets an entire chapter later in this book.

But if you *have* decided to go the Windows 95 route, why not squeeze every dime's worth of value out of your investment? That means making the most of the software that Microsoft has generously[2] bundled with Windows 95.

> If you can't find any of these programs, you may not have installed them when you installed Windows 95. Choose Start, Settings, Control Panel, Add/Remove Programs, Windows Setup, and check the boxes for the Windows 95 components you wish to add. Of course, you'll need your original CD-ROM or floppy diskettes.

The WordPad Word Processor

WordPad (see Figure 4-1) is a surprisingly capable, downsized version of Microsoft Word which includes nearly all the features a casual writer might want, including a wide variety of text formatting options, tabs, bullets, left, center and right-alignment, page preview—and even the ability to insert images, or current date/time information.

If you primarily use a word processor to write letters, notes, informal memos, or short (say, high-school-level) term papers, WordPad might be all you need. And since it will save files in Word 6 format—the lingua franca of corporate America these days—you can send WordPad files to

---

2. Perhaps the word generous is inappropriate. Microsoft reportedly provides little or no compensation to many of the companies that write these accompanying applications. The idea is that they will benefit by being associated with Microsoft's products—and that customers who like these applets will be more likely to invest in the companies' full-featured versions. You might find this business practice debatable; the software industry certainly does. While you're debating it, however, nothing's stopping you from *using* all the free software Microsoft has sent your way.

practically anyone you like, whether or not they use Windows 95. (Things can get dicey, however, if you use WordPad to open Word 6 files containing features that WordPad doesn't support.)

What's *not* included in WordPad? A spell-checker, footnotes, borders and shading, multiple columns, tables, or any of the fancy stuff that shows up in the word processor ads these days. It's probably *not* enough if you're writing more complex documents. For that, Microsoft will be pleased to sell you Microsoft Word. (And if you don't want to spring for Word, or don't have industrial-strength hardware to run it, they'll sell you Microsoft Works, a lower-cost integrated package with word processing capabilities roughly halfway between WordPad and Word.)

Word is an amazing program which will do everything but wash your dishes for you. But there are Cheapskate alternatives. Later in this chapter, I'll tell you about them—and I'll show you the cheapest ways to get Word if you want it. And of course, also see Chapter 12 where we cover word processors of varying sophistication and cost that are included on the Cheapskate's CD-ROM.

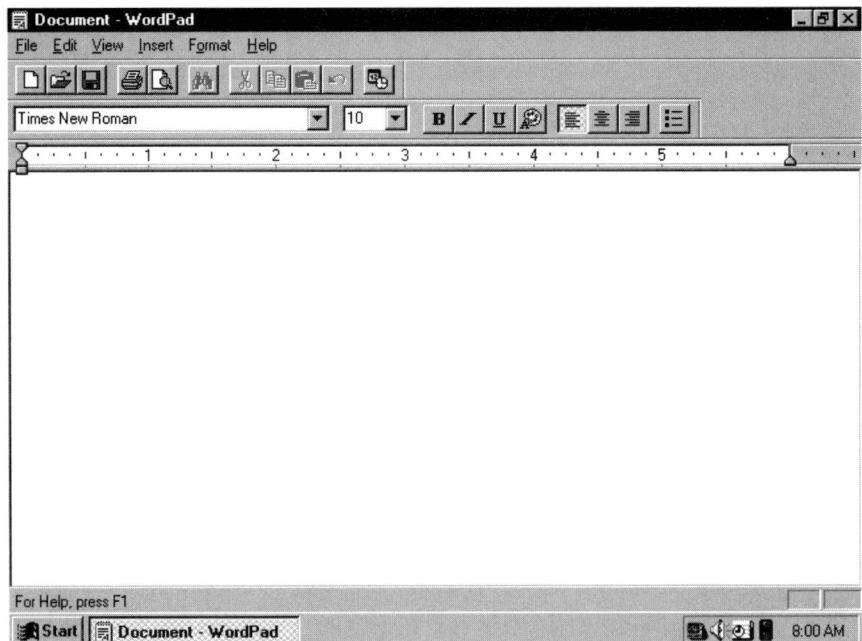

Figure 4–1 WordPad for Windows 95.

The HyperTerminal Communications Program

Say you want to transfer a file to a friend, and you don't want to be bothered with the delay or potential incompatibility problems that can arise from using an on-line service or the Internet. Or you want to connect directly to a Bulletin Board Service (BBS), perhaps to download a driver for that recalcitrant CD-ROM drive, or for whatever reason you choose.

You need an old-fashioned general-purpose communications program, the kind that got more publicity before anyone heard of Web browsers. Windows 95 gives you a very solid program, HyperTerminal. It has built-in, down-and-dirty text-only connections to AT&T Mail, MCI Mail and CompuServe and can connect you to any other computer or BBS, using any of the five leading file transfer protocols: Zmodem, Ymodem, Ymodem-G, Xmodem, or Kermit.

It can't script an automatic connection, however—for that, you'll need to spend money. It will, however, automatically recognize and set parameters such as parity, stop bits, and data bits for you. That's three less things to worry about.

> Hilgraeve, the company that wrote HyperTerminal for Microsoft, offers HyperTerminal Private Edition 3.0, a free upgrade, on its Web site: *www.hilgraeve.com/htpe.html*. You won't notice dramatic changes right away when you open HyperTerminal PE, but under the surface there are a lot of improvements, including
>
> ▲ Autoredial
> ▲ Support for TCP/IP Telnet sessions
> ▲ "Crash recovery" that allows you to resume interrupted Zmodem file transfers safely

Microsoft Fax Software

If you have a faxmodem, Windows 95 gives you all the software you need to send faxes to just about any fax machine or computer, anywhere. Assuming you've installed it (it's part of Microsoft Exchange or Windows Messaging during the install process), all you need to do is choose

Microsoft Fax as your printer in the Print dialog box of any Windows 95 application. Microsoft Fax (see Figure 4-2) includes fax cover sheets and an address book where you can place fax numbers you use repeatedly. You can even send faxes to several people at once. Best of all, Microsoft Fax walks you step by step through the faxing process, so once you've got it up and running, it's very easy to use.

You don't have to have a fast faxmodem. With a few exceptions, even an ancient modem that transmits data at only 2400 bps will send faxes at the industry-standard rate of 9600 bps. If you have a PC that won't need Internet access, this means you can add send-and-receive fax for just $15 or $20 in old faxmodem hardware. (Ask around. Chances are you'll find a computer user who has replaced their old modem with a faster model and has it sitting in a closet somewhere. Or you might try NEI Computer Products, 516-231-5845; they often stock low-speed bps faxmodems.)[3]

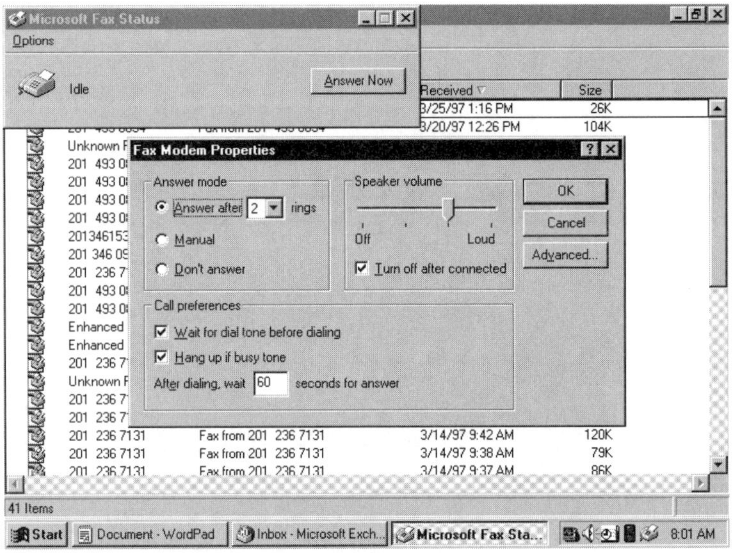

Figure 4–2   Microsoft Fax: All the fax software a lot of people will ever need.

▲ ▲ ▲ ▲ ▲ ▲ ▲ ▲ ▲ ▲ ▲ ▲ ▲ ▲ ▲ ▲ ▲ ▲ ▲ ▲

3.   A few nonstandard faxmodems aren't compatible with Microsoft Fax. According to Microsoft, these include faxmodems that use Rockwell Protocol Interface compression at speeds greater than 9600 bps, such as the Zoom 14.4 PC Model 110. Other faxmodems that Microsoft Fax may be incompatible with include the U.S. Robotics Sportster 28.8 V.FC and the Gateway Telepath PM144.

Microsoft Exchange

Microsoft Fax can retrieve addresses from a centralized Windows 95 address book built into Microsoft Exchange, which as we've said, also comes free with Windows 95. Exchange is an odd duck, clumsy but capable of doing quite a lot if you have the patience.

To open Exchange, you have to double-click on *Inbox*. Right away you can see how intuitive this is going to be! I confess it took me months to realize that for all practical purposes, Exchange was Inbox and Inbox was Exchange.[4]

Figure 4-3 shows Exchange's central storehouse for messages of all kinds: incoming faxes, incoming and outgoing e-mail, you name it.

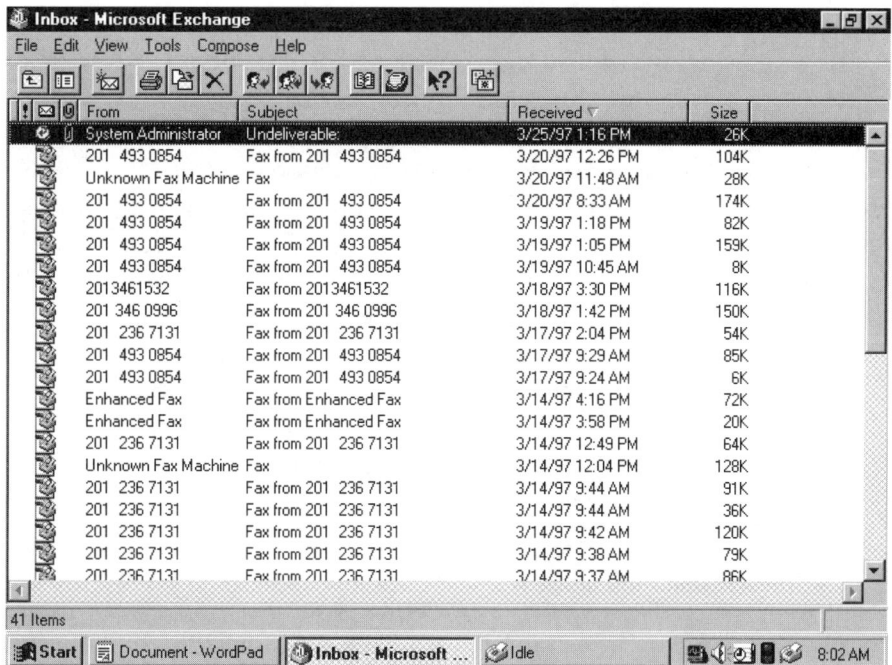

Figure 4–3   Microsoft Exchange's Inbox window.

▲ ▲

4.   If I had a major corporate network in my bedroom, I could get Microsoft Exchange Server, which makes Exchange more than just a glorified mailbox. But whatever.

125

To enter names in the Address Book, choose Address Book from the Tools menu. From here, you can add Fax, e-mail, and snail mail addresses, as well as other basic business information and free-form notes. The idea of Address Book was to provide a central repository all Windows 95 programs could use to get personal information. It hasn't quite worked out that way yet, but if you happen to own Word 95 or Word 97, you can use this information in mail merges, to generate labels, or to help automate the process of writing letters. And Address Book is a perfectly adequate stand-alone address book.

Microsoft Paint

I look at Microsoft Paint (and its Windows 3.1 sibling, Paintbrush) as an ideal children's program. It's not a precision tool (try signing your name with a mouse and you'll see what I'm talking about). But it's plenty of fun for doodling—and thoroughly harmless, to boot.

You get all the basic computer painting tools: paintbrush, roller, spray can, pencils, basic shapes, and 28 colors—the built-in pastels, or any 28 colors you choose. Unless you're feeling awfully nostalgic, don't buy an Etch-a-Sketch® for your child until you've checked out Paint's pencil tool.

Paint (see Figure 4-4) adds a few tricks that aren't in Paintbrush: It can flip, rotate, and skew images, for example. Otherwise, they're surprisingly similar. They both work with standard Windows bitmaps. Paintbrush can also support PCX files, but Paint can't. Neither can work with JPEG or GIF—the two file formats recognized on the Web. That means you'll need software to convert your "paintings" to JPEG or GIF. But that software is widely available for little or no cost.

Microsoft Phone Dialer

If you have a modem and you've connected it to your telephone, you can use Phone Dialer (see Figure 4-5) to dial your phone for you. It even has speed-dial numbers. Then, when the phone at the other end rings, just pick up.

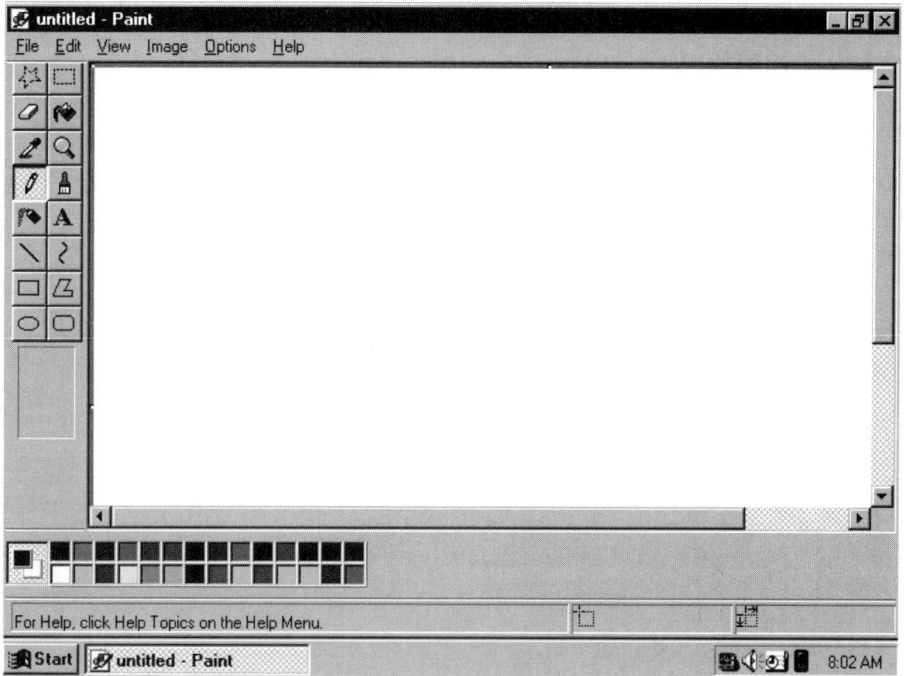

Figure 4–4   Microsoft Paint.

Figure 4–5   Phone Dialer for Windows 95.

127

Calculator

This perfectly serviceable Calculator (see Figure 4-6) would cost you five bucks if you bought it in Wal-Mart.

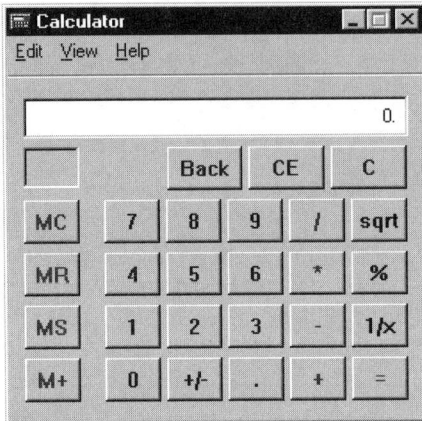

Figure 4–6   Calculator for Windows 3.1.

Microsoft Games

Windows 95 comes with four games: FreeCell, Hearts, Solitaire and Minesweeper (see Figure 4-7 & 4-8). Hearts and Solitaire are just what they sound like: computerized versions of the classic card games. Solitaire is arguably the one program that has done the most to *reduce* productivity since the PC has been invented. You can bet the manufacturers of network computers won't include anything like *that*!

FreeCell is another card game. The goal is to move all cards to "home cells," using free cells as placeholders. You win by making four stacks of cards, one for each home cell, each stacked in order of rank.

In the especially addictive Minesweeper, you attempt to locate all the mines on a playing field of varying sizes—without getting blown up by any of them. You do so by uncovering squares, one at a time. Each square that does not cover a mine gives you a clue about how many mines are nearby—but *not* which cells contain the mines.

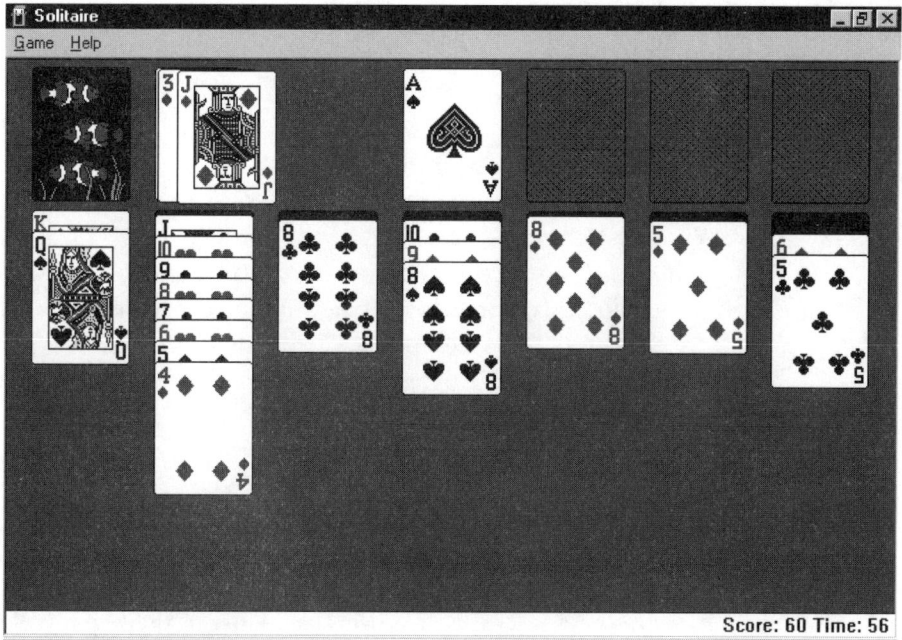

Figure 4–7   Solitaire for Windows 95.

Figure 4–8   Minesweeper.

129

Windows 3.1 Applets: An... Umm... *Silver* Mine

Windows 3.1 isn't as well endowed with free software as Windows 95. But it does come with

Write, a basic word processor

Paintbrush, a simple painting program similar to Microsoft Paint for Windows 95

Terminal, a functional communications program

Cardfile, a stripped-down personal information manager

Calculator, the same one we've already discussed in Windows 95

Macro Recorder, a program that can help you automate many of the tasks you perform in Windows 3.1

And, of course, the obligatory *Solitaire*.

> **tip**
>
> If you upgrade to Windows 95, you can keep your Windows 3.1 applets by installing Windows 95 in a different directory. Most of them will still work (Windows Terminal and Macro Recorder are two exceptions). Hidden away on your Windows 95 upgrade CD-ROM, you'll also find the old DOS 6.x applets you might occasionally have use for. They're in the OTHER\OLDMSDOS folder.

Let's take a closer look at some of these applets.

Windows Write

Many linguists delight in trying to identify words and basic features from the proto-languages used by our Iron Age ancestors. But there's no need to guess the ancient origins of today's Windows word *processors*. All you have to do is look at Write (see Figure 4-9). It can do everything you'd expect from an ancestral word processor: cut, copy, paste, format text in multiple fonts and sizes; align, center, or justify text.

It also has a few pleasant surprises, too: underlining, superscript, subscript, double-spacing, indents, tabs, margin settings, even headers and footers.

In short, if you're a professional writer, or a college student working on heavily footnoted and annotated reports, you'll probably want to look elsewhere. But if you need a word processor for casual correspondence, or for schoolwork short of college, try out Write before you write any checks.

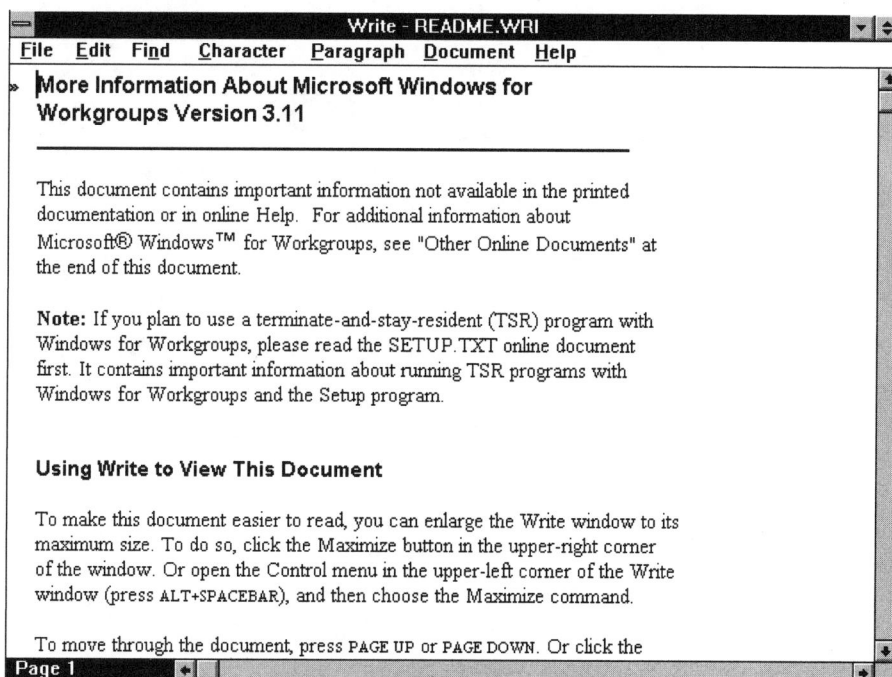

Figure 4–9   Windows Write for Windows 3.1 and beyond.

Windows Paintbrush

Like Microsoft Paint, Paintbrush (see Figure 4-10) is a nearly ideal children's painting program, with rollers, spray cans, paintbrushes, pencils, basic shapes, and your choice of 28 colors.

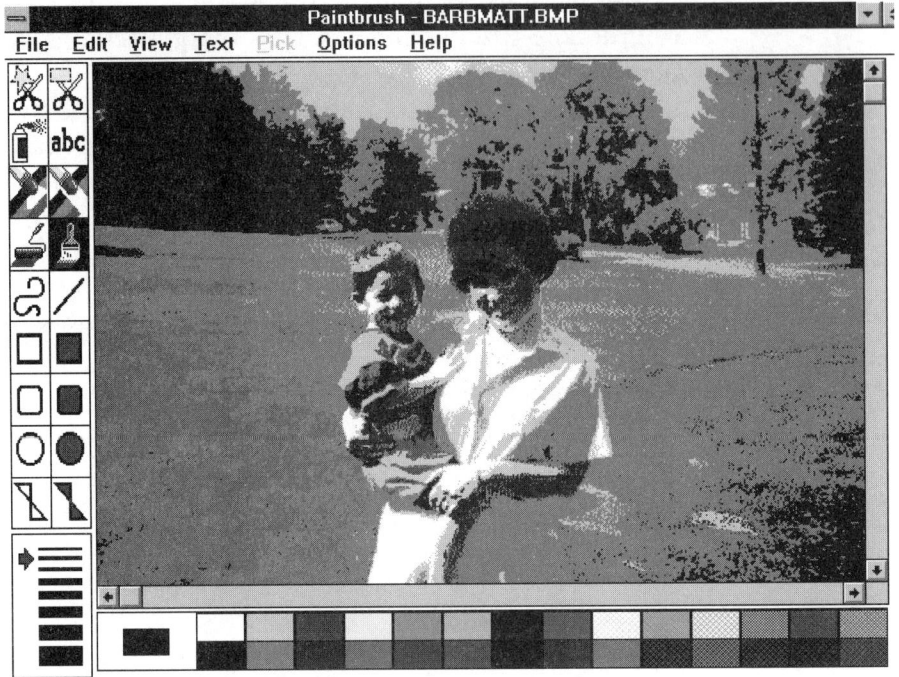

Figure 4–10   Microsoft Paintbrush for Windows 3.1 and beyond.

Windows Terminal

If you need to connect with a bulletin board, or send a file directly to a friend via modem, you need a communications program, and Windows 3.1 gives you one: Terminal (see Figure 4-11). It's basic, but it does the job. You can use Terminal to establish connections, and send and receive both binary and text files. You are, however, limited to two binary file-transfer protocols, Kermit and Xmodem. (Nowadays, Zmodem is more fashionable, but the old protocols still do the job fairly well. You'll just have to make sure the computer on the other end is set up for them.)

Terminal doesn't do scripts, so, for example, you can't use it to automate sign-ons to a bulletin board—you'll have to manually enter your ID and password every time. However, it *will* store settings, so you can create separate terminal files that specify phone numbers, preferences, protocols, and other details associated with specific computers you connect with.

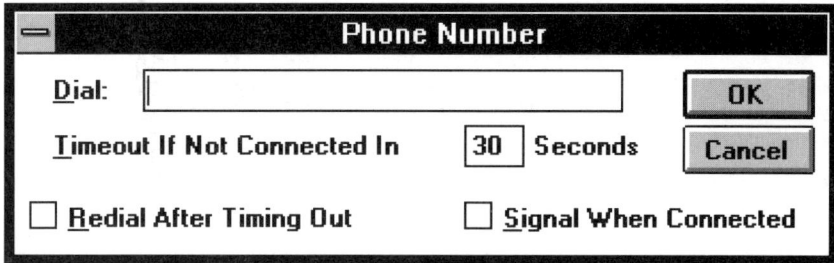

Figure 4–11   Microsoft Terminal for Windows 3.1

Windows Cardfile

This is a skeletal personal information manager that's slipped below the radar of virtually every Windows user. But if all you need is to keep track of a few dozen names and addresses—or a hundred—it may be all you need.

You won't be surprised that Cardfile (see Figure 4-12) uses the card file metaphor. Think of a stack of searchable 3" x 5" cards, each with whatever information you choose to add. Each card has an index line; if you enter an individual's name in the index line, last name first, Cardfile will keep all your cards alphabetized for you.

You can enter any information you want on a card; they're completely free-form. You can even insert pictures, if you like, which means you can use Cardfile as a basic "family tree" program—minus the parent/child/sibling links a true genealogy program would provide.

You can search your entire Rolodex for any information that's in the form of text—names, phone numbers, birthdays, and the like. You can even use Cardfile as a Windows 3.1 autodialer, if you set up your cards so that the first lengthy number in each card is a telephone number. (Tricky, since Cardfile gets hung up on Zip codes.)

So why isn't *everyone* using Cardfile? (1) It will do everything I've described—but not one thing more. (2) Cardfile is the Roach Motel of data: Once you enter it, there is no convenient electronic way to get information out of Cardfile. You can print, but you can't create labels, run mail merges with letters, save tab-delimited files for export—*nothing.*[5]

▲ ▲

5.   OK, you *could* open it in a text editor and manually clean out all the formatting Cardfile adds.

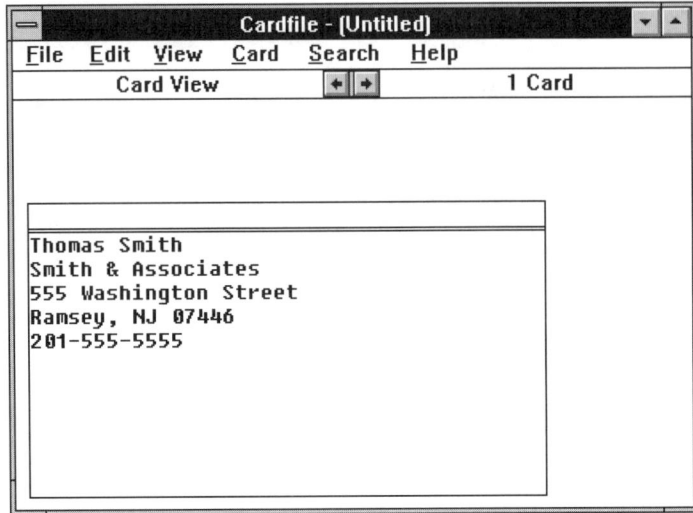

Figure 4–12   Cardfile for Windows 3.1

Macro Recorder

In Windows 3.1, Macro Recorder (see Figure 4-13) allows you to record a series of mouse movements and keystrokes and then play them back whenever you want. Let's say you use Windows Write; when you finish working on a document, you always select all the text and follow the same several steps to reformat it. Macro Recorder could automate that.

Of course, you'll have to record the mouse movements and keystrokes exactly as you plan to use them, in exactly the same locations. (If you're going to use Write as a full-screen application, make sure it's full-screen when you record the macro, or Recorder may click in the wrong place.) And unlike true macro languages, you can't edit or script your macros. But then again, who ever heard of a Windows 3.1 macro recorder virus?

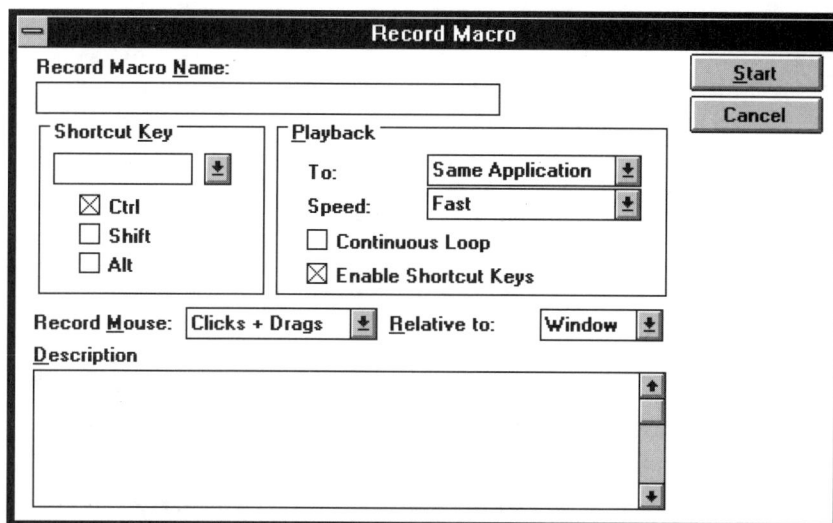

Figure 4–13   Macro Recorder for Windows 3.1

Freebies That Come with Dos 6.x

Even if you're running MS-DOS 6.x *without* Windows, you own a few goodies that you might not have noticed:

- ▲ A basic text editor, called EDIT.
- ▲ Disk utilities, including basic backup (MSBACKUP), antivirus (MSAV), disk checking (SCANDISK), and defragmentation (DEFRAG) software. These programs are covered in more detail in Chapter 8.
- ▲ Memory optimization software (MEMMAKER) to help you get the most out of your critical 640K "base" memory, and disk cache software (SMARTDRV) to help you get the best performance out of 80286 and higher systems.
- ▲ Disk compression software (DBLSPACE or DRVSPACE) to nearly double the amount of information your disks can store. Disk compression is covered in more detail in Chapter 5.

Big News: DOS Is Now Free

You may be surprised to learn that DOS is now free.

Not MS-DOS. Microsoft is giving away quite a few things nowadays, as we'll discuss later in this chapter, but DOS certainly isn't one of them.

I'm talking about OpenDOS, from Caldera Inc.

OpenDOS is the descendant of Novell DOS 7, which in turn is the descendant of DR-DOS, both of which were relatively unnecessarily competitors to MS-DOS several years ago. In September 1996, Caldera purchased the rights to these products from Novell. Since then, Caldera has buffed them up a bit, added some new features, and made the whole shebang available at no charge to individual users,[6] via the Internet at **www.caldera.com** (see Figure 4-14).

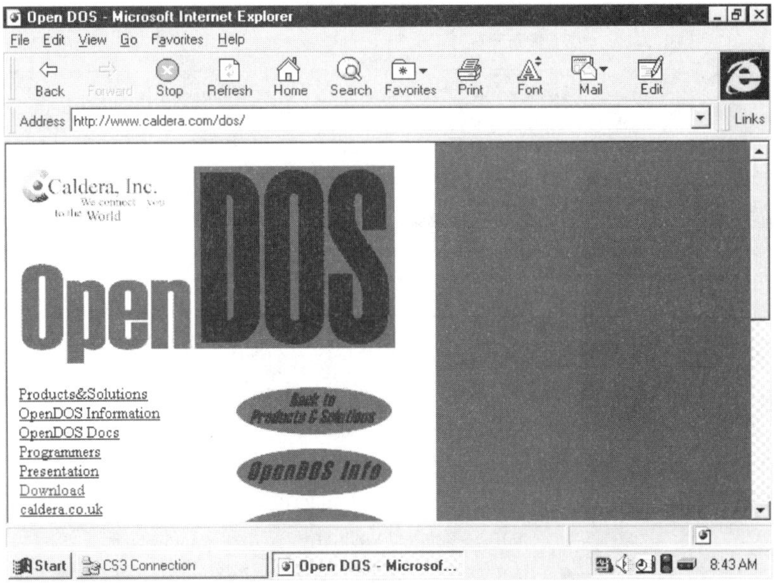

Figure 4–14   Extra! DOS liberated, at **www.caldera.com**.

▲ ▲ ▲ ▲ ▲ ▲ ▲ ▲ ▲ ▲ ▲ ▲ ▲ ▲ ▲ ▲ ▲ ▲ ▲ ▲

6.   Technically, the license agreement runs as follows: students, faculty or staff members at educational institutions, and staff members at religious and most charitable non-profit organizations get a free license to use OpenDOS. Other individuals may evaluate the software for an indefinite period. Companies considering OpenDOS for commercial use are limited to a 90-day evaluation period.

OpenDOS is quite MS-DOS-compatible—though probably not *perfectly* DOS-compatible. For example, I wouldn't encourage you to install Windows 3.1 over it, if for no other reason than that Microsoft won't support that setup.

It does, however, come with a full range of utilities, including Stacker®-compatible disk compression; basic networking that includes the Personal NetWare server and NetWare compatible client software; drivers for a wide range of hardware, especially CD-ROM drives; and the Advanced NetWars 2.0 network-based game.

So if you're perfectly happy with your old copy of WordPerfect 5.1 for DOS (another former Novell product), you see no reason to upgrade to Windows but you *would* like a more modern version of DOS, scoot on over to Caldera's Web site and see if OpenDOS might be for you.

GEOS: Faux "Windows" on Your Ancient XT

So you have a very old PC, and you have Windows envy.

Once upon a time, there was a company named Geoworks which created an operating system called GEOS that looked an awful lot like Windows—except that it could run on virtually any PC, even (in its first incarnation) XTs and (in all versions) 286s. See for yourself in Figure 4-15.

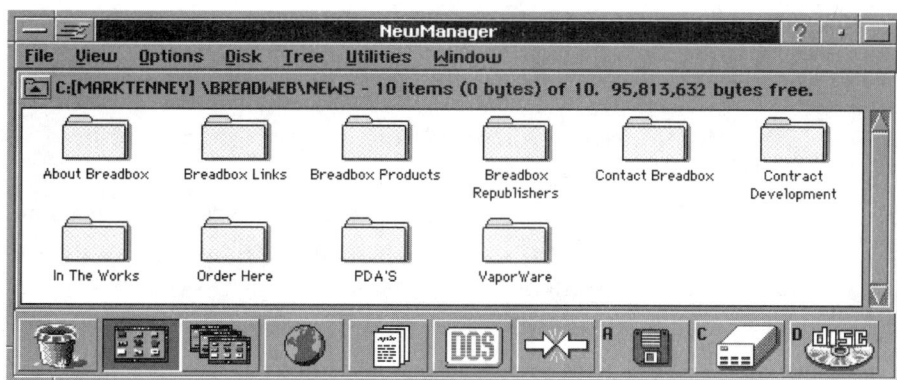

Figure 4–15 GEOS: Faux Windows on a pre-Windows system.

GEOS never really caught on. Geoworks has moved on to other things: operating systems for cellular phones, handheld devices like the Sharp Zoomer, and other devices that don't have much computer power. But the GEOS operating system is still hanging in there, with the support of a small cult of computer users worldwide who swear by it. No wonder; it's really quite a technical tour de force.

You can get a demo copy of GEOS that includes a working copy of the GeoWrite word processor at **ftp://ftp.argo-navis.com/ensemble/Geo-Publish** or at **www.coast.net/SimTel/msdos/geos2x.html**. If you like it, the best U.S. source for a full working copy of GEOS and GEOS-related software is

> Breadbox Computer
>
> P.O. Box 808
>
> Port Richey, FL 34673
>
> (813) 847-6996
>
> **www.breadbox.com**

You can also call New Deal Inc., the company Geoworks has out-sourced GEOS marketing to, at 1-800-985-4263.

Cheap Commercial Software

OK, you have to create a database with thousands of records, and Cardfile obviously won't cut it. You're writing a book, and WordPad can't handle footnotes. Or you're starting a business, and you need spreadsheet software to project your cash flow.

In short, you know what your needs are, and you know you need commercial software to meet those needs. How can you get the software you need, and still be a Cheapskate?

There's shareware, of course—software you're allowed to try out for a limited time and then pay the author directly if you like it. We'll discuss shareware in greater detail in Chapter 12; the Cheapskate's CD-ROM is chock full of it.

In this section, however, we'll focus on commercial software. You have tons of options, and we'll cover them all, including

- ▲ Academic software
- ▲ Low-cost integrated packages
- ▲ Orphan software
- ▲ Used software
- ▲ Previous version software

Academic Software: Brilliant, If You Qualify

With 35.5 percent of the U.S. population younger than 25, the odds are pretty good that there's a college student, teacher, or college faculty member in your household someplace. Check under the carpets and behind the sofa if you're not sure. It's worth it. That person may be eligible for amazing academic discounts on a wide variety of business and graphics software.

If you are a current-term college, trade, or vocational school student, or if you are a faculty member at any accredited school, including K–12, you may be eligible for large discounts on many of the world's leading software packages. These discounts are often 50 percent or greater. They can be so large you might decide that now would be a good time to take that course you've been thinking about.

Table 4-1 gives a few recent examples.

Table 4–1 Academic versus Regular Software Prices

Package	Standard Mail Order	Academic Mail Order
Adobe Photoshop	$546	$260
Adobe PageMaker	$546	$180
Corel WordPerfect Suite (Upgrade)	$ 90	$ 37
Macromedia Director	$850	$300
Microsoft Office 97 Standard (Full Product, not upgrade)	$454	$150

In nearly all cases, you get the same product and documentation as other purchasers. Occasionally, however, the software manufacturer may limit your access to technical support or deprive you of the spiffy, four-color packaging.

So how do you qualify for these great deals? If you're ordering by mail, you'll typically need to fax the supplier a copy of your student, faculty, or staff ID which has been validated for the current semester. If you are a member of the faculty or staff, and you do not have an ID, some suppliers will accept a current pay stub or a copy of a teaching contract recognized by the U.S. Department of Education. The Software Source, a leading supplier of academic discount software, accepts any of the following:

- ▲ A valid student ID card
- ▲ A current class schedule
- ▲ A current registration form or tuition bill
- ▲ A valid teacher/faculty ID card
- ▲ A recent faculty pay stub
- ▲ A valid teacher's contract/certificate
- ▲ A letter from the school verifying enrollment or employment
- ▲ A school purchase order

Some academic software manufacturers or resellers will even sell to home-schoolers who can show some kind of official credential.

Who sells academic software? Here are a few of the leading vendors:

The Software Source
1750 Brielle Avenue, Unit A-2
Ocean, NJ 07712
1-800-289-3275; 1-908-695-2100
www.iaswww.com/source.html
Surplus Direct
P.O. Box 2000
Hood River, OR 97031-2000
1-800-753-7877
www.surplusdirect.com

Peripherals Plus
485 Wright Debow Road
Jackson, NJ 08527
800-444-7369, 908-928-9600

Software Plus Academic, Inc.
377 Route 17 South, Suite #116
Hasbrouck Heights, NJ 07604
800-377-9943; 201-288-7441
www.spainj.com

PC People, Inc.
6300 Richmond, Suite 100
Houston, TX 77057
1-800-877-9761; 1-713-789-6300
www.pcpeople.com

Premier Technology Group
2838-C South I-85 Service Road
Charlotte, NC 28208
704-391-9947
www.premiertechgroup.com/aer.html

Campus Connection
761-B Lighthouse Road
Monterey, CA 93940
408-373-0323

Focus Computer Center
1303 46th Street
Brooklyn, NY 11219
1-800-223-3411; 1-718-871-7600

If you want to know whether a product is available at educational discount, the *Syllabus* Magazine Web site lists a wide range of programs, along with selected manufacturers' and distributors' phone numbers. You'll find *Syllabus'* list at **www.syllabus.com/ed.discount.html**.

• *Limited Academic Versions*

Some programs are also available in limited academic versions for even more dramatic discounts. These products are ideal if your primary goal is to learn the software. For example, Macromedia and Prentice Hall PTR together distribute Director Academic and Authorware Academic, multimedia authoring environments that are complete in every way except that they limit the size and complexity of the multimedia programs you can develop with them. Director Academic retails for $99, roughly one-eighth the price of the full product.

Dirt-Cheap Business Applications

For years the streets have been littered with the remains of companies that have tried to compete with Microsoft and failed. The carnage has subsided a bit of late: There just aren't as many of these software companies left. Still, if you tiptoe through the wreckage carefully, you can pick up some great deals—even on industrial-strength software that "coulda been a contender."

> **tip**
>
> Like GM and Toyota, software companies regularly introduce new models—and sometimes offer clearances on the "old model year" just before the new models arrive. Word 95 suddenly dropped in price from around $90 to $60 just before Word 97 was released. If you're interested in purchasing a major software package, check the trade publications to see whether a new version is on the horizon.

• *When to Bite the Bullet*

For the Cheapskate, the off-brands we'll discuss are awfully tempting. But when should you just bite the bullet and get the premium-priced spread from Microsoft or whomever?

▲ When you expect to need extensive support, either from the software company, or from friends who are familiar with the same package.

▲ When you simply can't afford to take a risk of winding up with an inferior product (not that the leading products are always superior, but "you can't get fired for choosing Microsoft").

▲ When you're working in an environment where everyone has standardized on the same package.

▲ When you need to deliver files in a specific file format, such as Word 6 format, that the package you're considering won't support.

● *The "Big Three": Word Processors, Spreadsheets, Databases*

Here's a list of capable word processors that have fallen by the way-side over the past few years, and are available dirt-cheap when you can find them:

▲ WordStar for Windows. This is a reasonably full-featured package, the distant descendant of the original WordStar from the days before the IBM PC. It's available from the Learning Company (formerly Softkey). WordStar lists for $49.95, but you may be able to find it for significantly less. For Windows 3.1 only.

▲ Lotus AmiPro 3.1 (the predecessor of Lotus WordPro, this is sometimes found stand-alone, but more often as part of an older version of SmartSuite).

▲ Professional Write Plus

For spreadsheets, a good cheap choice is

▲ Quattro Pro, developed by Borland but now sold by Corel. You can find older Borland versions, which are quite powerful, and very inexpensive.

And for databases:

▲ AceFile, a relatively simple, straightforward flat file database that never caught on, despite good reviews

▲ Paradox, for more sophisticated users—again formerly by Borland

You can sometimes find a great deal on a combination package that contains the Lotus 1-2-3 for Windows spreadsheet and the Lotus

Approach database. By the way, I recommend Approach highly. It is simply the easiest database for mere mortals to do anything useful with.[7]

> *Warning!* Companies like Lotus and Corel look as if they'll be around for awhile. Lotus, in fact, is now a division of IBM. In any event, they have user communities large enough that you'll be able to get help even if they suddenly fold. But if you anticipate needing help, be cautious about buying software developed by a smaller company that's gone out of business. In particular, if you want to run Windows 3.1 software under Windows 95, make sure it's compatible before you buy.

• *Graphics*

In graphics programs, there hasn't been any significant competition from Microsoft, so a number of solid low-cost programs are hanging on, sharing the low-end of the market:

- ▲ PC Paintbrush
- ▲ PhotoFinish (see Figure 4-16)
- ▲ Windows Draw
- ▲ Serif Draw Plus

There's also the close-out MicroGrafx ABC Graphics Suite 1.0 for Windows 95, a complete graphics suite that includes business diagramming, flowcharting, image editing, illustration, 20,000 pieces of clip art, and 7,500 photos. This package has been superseded by Release 2.0, so it's currently available from Surplus Direct for $49.99.

Finally, I can't resist mentioning Jasc's PaintShop Pro (see Figure 4-17), which is sold in both shareware and retail versions, and offers enormous value for the money. This program is competitive in many respects with Adobe's $600 PhotoShop software, for $69. You'll find the shareware version on the Cheapskate's CD-ROM.

▲ ▲ ▲ ▲ ▲ ▲ ▲ ▲ ▲ ▲ ▲ ▲ ▲ ▲ ▲ ▲ ▲ ▲ ▲ ▲

7.   Claris FileMaker Pro is a close second, but Approach can do more.

Figure 4–16   PhotoFinish: Quite a bit of image processing power for not so many bucks.

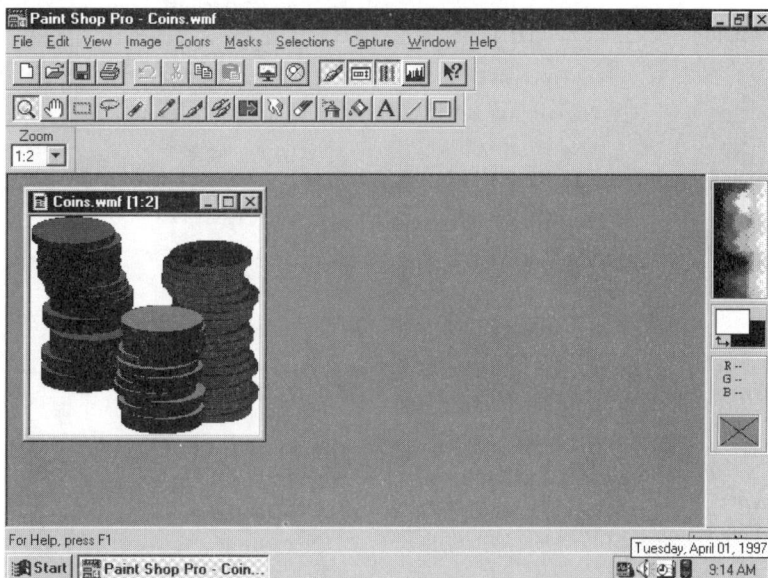

Figure 4–17   PaintShop Pro, the world's leading graphics shareware—for good reason.

> If you do need a high-end graphics program, such as Adobe PhotoShop or Illustrator, check the on-line classifieds before paying full price. It's common for packages like these to be bundled with high-end scanners. In many cases, the purchasers don't need the software; they already have it. They often resell it for half the usual retail price, or even less. Before buying, though, make sure the software hasn't already been registered; you'll want to register it to qualify for low-cost upgrades in the future.

• *Desktop Publishing*

Finally, we come to desktop publishing. Unless you are a professional designer using a service bureau that demands Quark XPress (or possibly Adobe PageMaker) files—or you are doing sophisticated four-color work—you should never pay more than $75 for a desktop publishing program. *Don't be seduced!*

But the first question is: Do you really need a desktop publishing program at all?

If you own an industrial-strength word processor—any version of Microsoft Word for Windows since release 6, or any version of WordPerfect for Windows will do—you already have built-in newsletter templates. You also have many of the features you need to create a surprisingly wide range of documents, including multiple columns, frames for pictures, borders, and utilities that let you manipulate type into all manner of strange and fanciful forms.

For around $59.95, Serif PagePlus Home/Office Edition includes more than 100 design wizards and templates to create fliers, banners, reports, calendars, brochures, invitations, newsletters, greeting cards and more. To try it out, you can currently download a stripped down version called PagePlus Intro, available from a variety of Internet ftp sites you can connect to through **www.shareware.com**.

For around $70–75, Microsoft Publisher 97 for Windows 95 (see Figure 4-18) will do all that, and also create Web pages at the same time. You can currently download a 60-day trial version of Publisher 97 on

Microsoft's Web site, **www.microsoft.com/publisher/trialreg.htm**. To avoid the long download, call Microsoft at 1-800-370-9272. Shipping and handling is free.

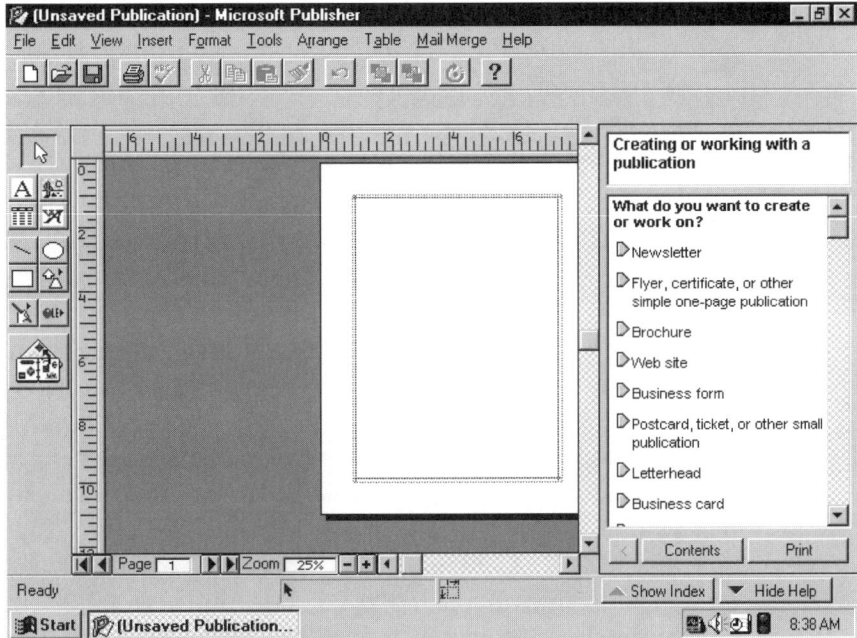

Figure 4–18   Microsoft Publisher 97 for Windows 95.

> If you've invested in Microsoft Office 97, you already have the trial version of Publisher. Look for it in the VALUPACK/PUBTRIAL folder.

PagePlus and Publisher are both very good. I personally think Publisher is the class of the field. In one major respect, these programs are much better than the $600 programs: They offer you much more help.

With Quark XPress in particular, you sink or you swim—once they have your $600, you're of no particular concern to them.

If you choose Publisher and you have a CD-ROM drive, make sure to get the CD-ROM version. It comes with tons more clip art and utilities, for just about the same price, take or leave a buck.

One more point. If you do fewer publications and more banners and posters, consider PrintMaster Gold from Mindscape for around $39.95, or one of the many versions of the venerable Print Shop, from Broderbund, ranging from around $30 to $75.

• *Cheap and Free Clip Art*

When I worked for a weekly newspaper, clip art was expensive and terrible. There were only a couple of clip art companies. You subscribed to their overpriced, oversized books of images, which would show up every month, overflowing end to end with cliched images. It was still cheaper than drawing the stuff yourself, or hiring someone to do it for you.

Computers changed everything. The first generation of commercial clip art collections were still expensive and cliched—but they were a whole lot cheaper than what was out there before. Then, with the advent of CD-ROMs, there was an implosion of clip art pricing. Collections appeared including 10,000, 25,000, now even 100,000 images—all for $75 or much less. Some of it is *still* cliched junk—but at that price it hurts a lot less.

Bottom line: Unless you are a professional designer, or your needs are specialized, you shouldn't pay much more than a tenth of a penny per image today.

Here are some of the better current deals on commercial clip art:

- ▲ *Corel MEGA GALLERY for Windows:* 50,000 vector clip art images, 60,000 Internet-ready (relatively low-resolution) photos. Street price, around $65.00
- ▲ *ClickArt Incredible Image Pak 65,000:* 60,000 clip art images, 2,000 fonts, and 5,000 royalty-free photos. Street price, around $60.00 (see Figure 4-19)
- ▲ *IMSI MasterClips 101,000:* Over 33,000 vector and 40,000 TIFF images, plus 26,000 photos and special effects, and a library of Web graphics, sounds, fonts, and video clips. Street price, around $60.00

Figure 4–19 ClickArt 65,000 image package on five CD-ROMs.

• *Free Clip Art on the Web*

Of course, you might not have to pay a nickel. If CD-ROMs revolutionized clip art once, the Internet is revolutionizing it again. There is an extraordinary variety of free clip art on the Web. In some cases, commercial clip art publishers post samplers to encourage you to purchase their products. In other cases, individuals simply create their own clip art and make it available to the world. The rules they set for usage may vary. In some cases, you'll be allowed to do anything you want with the clip art they post; in other cases, commercial usage may be limited or prohibited.

Web clip art ranges from the usual mundane stuff to samples of clip art with a whole lot more personality and distinctiveness—typically from individual artists or small firms who want you to start using (and paying for) their work regularly.

Here's a sampler of clip art sources. Explore. There are tons more where these come from.

▲ Caboodles of Clip Art (**www.caboodles.com/clipart/**) hosts roughly 100 themed clip art collections covering everything from birds to bowling, Christianity to crafts—all of them free for download, and many of them free for unlimited use. Make sure to read the associated copyright/credit information associated with each collection (see Figure 4-20).

▲ The Clip Art Connection also includes extensive theme-specific clip art collections, as well as commercial samplers and an archive of over 1,000 free Web page images—custom backgrounds, horizontal rules, animated globes, decorative lettering, you name it (**www.ist.net/clipart/**).

149

▲ Psyched Up Graphics stocks more than 2,000 images, many Web-oriented, at **www.econ.cbs.dk/~gemal/psychedupgraphics/**.

▲ Randy's Icon and Image Bazaar (**www.iconbazaar.com**) stocks nearly 30 ZIPped file archives (and also links to a sibling sound site, **www.wavbazaar.com**, with more than 30 categories of sound clips. Some of those are copyrighted, though, so be careful how you use them.

▲ TASK FORCE Clip Art, The FREE Edition, from NVTech: 200 WMF and CGM images for Windows and DOS, plus Task Force Commander, which allows you to search, rescale, rotate, and flip images in any of their collections. The site also includes TASK FORCE Web Art LITE, a free collection of 140 GIF icons, bullets, buttons, bars, icons and backgrounds designed for Web sites, and TASK FORCE Clip Art for Macintosh LITE, 40 vector-based EPS images in color. Get it all at **http://fox.nstn.ca/~clipart/fre00.html** (see Figure 4-21).

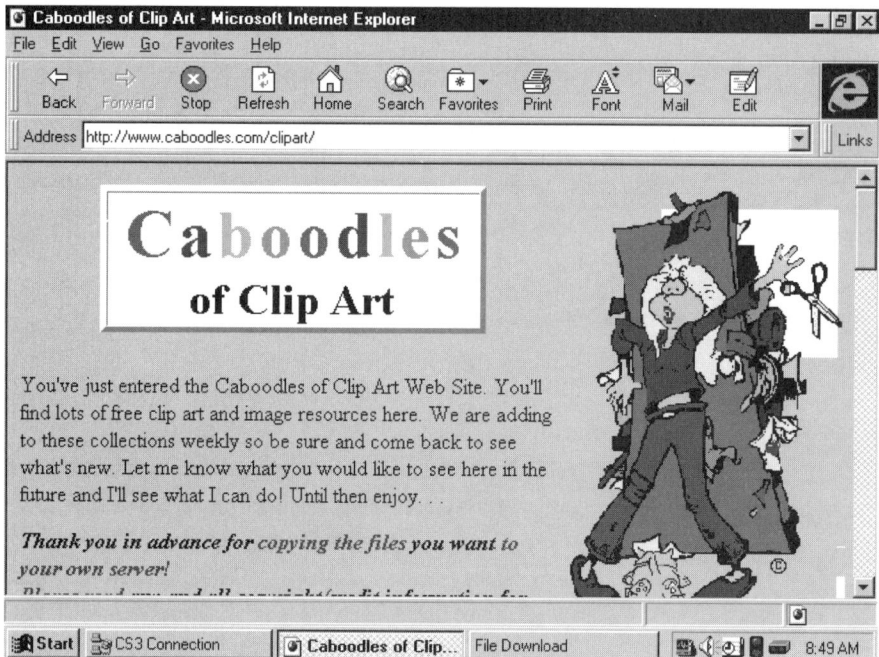

Figure 4–20   Caboodles of clip art: They're not kidding.

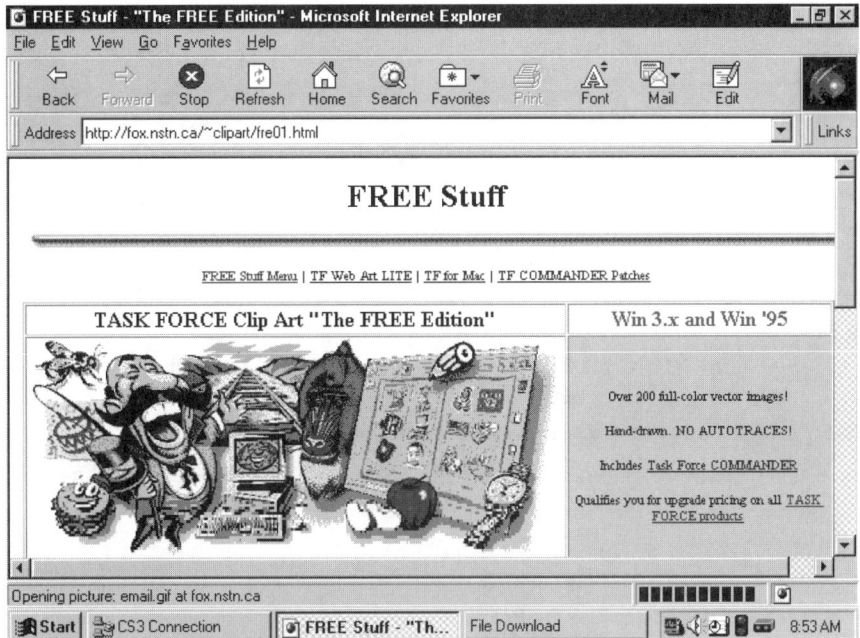

Figure 4–21   Downloading TASK FORCE Clip Art, The Free Edition.

And a few more specialized freebies—again, seek and ye shall find plenty more:

- ▲ Raw Graphics: Five free, angst-ridden images from Quigman's Raw Graphics CD-ROM—clip art with an attitude. (**www.quigmans.com**). One of them might be just right for that 'zine you publish in your bedroom.
- ▲ Free Science-Related ClipArt: GIFs from SoftShell Online related to science, scientists and computers (**www.softshell.com**).
- ▲ The Ventana site, **www.vmedia.com**, also includes free sound clips and backgrounds for building Web sites, not to mention 100 great black-and-white drawings of deranged animals by well-known Chapel Hill, North Carolina artist EFF. You'll find *his* inEFFable work at **www.vmedia.com/commodity/clipart/eff/art.html.**

> Fonts are a dime a dozen nowadays, but they're not all of equal quality. For Windows, my favorite deal—not easy to find these days—is Bitstream's 500 Font CD, a very solid font library in both TrueType and PostScript formats, for under $40.

Get the "Works": Integrated Software

Many Cheapskates simply don't need an expensive, industrial-strength "office" package. For less than $50, you can very likely get all the power you need in an integrated software package.

Integrated software has been around for years, and it's always been viewed as the "poor relation" of commercial software. But today's leading packages, Microsoft Works and ClarisWorks, pack quite a punch.

For under $50, both of these packages include

- ▲ Word processors
- ▲ Flat file databases
- ▲ Spreadsheets
- ▲ Drawing
- ▲ Communications

Microsoft Works also includes an address book; ClarisWorks adds a painting program. Microsoft Works comes with tons of help: It offers to show you how to do just about everything, making it great for beginners. Those who are more experienced may find the help annoying; it can be turned off. ClarisWorks comes with Assistants and 150 "Shortcuts" that guide you through complex tasks and provide expert advice.

> If you're one of the millions of people who have fairly heavy-duty requirements in a word processor but lightweight requirements for everything else, you might consider Microsoft Home Essentials 97 for Windows 95, which for under $100 includes Word 97, Works 4.0, the Encarta 97 encyclopedia, Microsoft Greetings Workshop to make your own Hallmark® greeting cards, and a few classic games.

Both Microsoft Works and ClarisWorks offer plenty of extra support as well. Works for Windows 95 has a Web site of its own, **www.microsoft. com/works/html/Templates/temp.htm**—where you can get extra templates. Nearby, there's free clip art and practical advice from experts such as top designer Roger Parker.

ClarisWorks is supported by the ClarisWorks User Group, which offers a Public Domain Library with more than 500 megabytes of ClarisWorks-compatible templates, fonts, graphics, utilities, and system software for both Macintosh and Windows. Membership in CWUG is $39 a year, but you don't have to join to purchase the CD-ROM.

For information on CWUG, write

ClarisWorks User Group
Box 701010
Plymouth, MI 48170
1-313-454-1969
E-mail: cathy@cwug.org

You may save $150 or more by purchasing an integrated package instead of a full-fledged Office package, but that's nothing compared with your hardware savings. "Works" programs don't gobble hard drive space, memory, or processor power the way "Office" programs do. It could easily cost you $500–$1,000 more to get the same performance running Microsoft Office 97 that you can get from Microsoft Works 4.0 for Windows 95. And Microsoft Works 3.0 for Windows 3.1 will run very nicely on a fast 386 with 8-Mb RAM. Nowadays, that's a $300 computer!

> **tip**
>
> Microsoft Works and ClarisWorks are available for both Windows and the Macintosh. However, ClarisWorks, manufactured by Apple's software division, is a bit more faithful about working the same way on both platforms.
>
> Ironically, Claris charges more for ClarisWorks on the Mac platform than it does for the Windows version. On the Mac side, they own the market. On the Windows side, they're hungry. It's the free market at work. But it sure doesn't help with the market perception that Apple computing is more expensive.

> Before you purchase Microsoft Works, check to see whether it came with your computer. Works has been packaged with a wide variety of so-called "family" computers in lieu of more expensive packages. Among the many companies that have included Works with their systems at one time or another are Compaq, Gateway 2000, Micron, NEC, Packard Bell, Acer, AST, ACMA, Leading Edge, Blackship, Atlantis, CompuAdd, and USA Flex.

• *Not Cheap Enough? Try the Competition*

Microsoft Works and ClarisWorks are the market leaders in integrated software, and they're cheap enough that I advise sticking with them. But there are some even less expensive choices.

PFS: WindowWorks Plus, recently discontinued by the Learning Company, brings together many of the same modules as Microsoft Works, though they're a little less sophisticated. WindowWorks is regularly auctioned at **www.onsale.com** and rarely brings more than $10 plus $5 shipping. Push Button Works, currently available from Surplus Direct, is an imported low-end package revamped for U.S. distribution. It, too, has been discontinued and is available for under $10.

> If, after rummaging through the Cheapskate's CD-ROM, you *still* don't have enough Windows 95 software, consider the *CD Sampler for Windows 95* from WUGNET, the Windows User Group. For $19.95, you can get a two-CD-ROM collection with 70 high-quality shareware applications. You also get more than a gigabyte of tryout commercial software. Most of the commercial software is full-featured, or close to full-featured. The catch is that it stops working after a period of time, typically 30 days. In a few cases, however, the software works permanently. For example, Hilgraeve's HyperTerminal Private Edition is included—the same free upgrade to Windows 95 HyperTerminal that we discussed earlier.

The Cheapskate's List of Useless Software

Some programs aren't worth the disks they're printed on. In fact, some entire categories of software should never have been created. Keep your pocketbook snapped shut when you encounter anything on this Cheapskate's list of useless software.

1. Screen savers. Unless they deliver useful information, like PointCast (see Chapter 7). Maybe I'm being too puritanical here, but most screen savers do nothing but waste your computer's processing power and destabilize your system. (I knew this intellectually, but I realized it *emotionally* a few years ago, when the Energizer Bunny marched across my screen, crashing my computer while I was sending an urgent fax to my most important client.)

   Moreover, screen savers certainly don't "save your screen." It's been many years since monitors were susceptible to the "burn-in" that screen savers are supposed to prevent.

   Sorry, no bunnies. Or flying toasters.

   Well, if you *must*, Windows 95 comes with a few built-in screen savers that don't do too much damage. And you can get tons of free screen savers on the Web, at **www.bonanzas.com/ssavers/.** There's even inexpensive shareware you can use to make your own. But for goodness sakes, don't spend hard earned money on someone else's.

2. PC memory enhancers. These are supposed to increase the amount of memory available to Windows through assorted sleight of hand techniques, such as compressing the contents of your memory. There's a product for the Macintosh, RAM Doubler from Connectix, that actually works. There are now a horde of products for Windows that barely work, or rarely work, or never work, and one—SoftRAM 95 for Windows 95—which was so thoroughly worthless that many experts doubted it was even *trying* to do anything useful.[8]

---

8.   SoftRAM's publisher, Syncronys Softcorp., is still in business and apparently on the rebound. In Germany, nearly three-fourths of SoftRAM's customers returned the product for a refund. In the United States, most customers decided to hold on for a promised upgrade, which finally showed up early this year, several months late. According to *Computer Reseller News,* many leading stores, including a number of Computer City outlets, continued to stock the worthless product for months after it was savaged by the trade press. (Egghead, on the other hand, pulled it right away.) Slowly Syncronys, with the same leadership, is building and licensing a new product line. They have a lot to offer their business partners: an extraordinarily strong marketing and distribution apparatus. You can decide for yourself whether they're a company *you* would like to do business with.

3. Hard drive accelerators. They *do* seem to help a little—but not nearly as much as advertised. (One possible exception: OnTrack's Drive Rocket, which can provide support for IDE drive block mode and ATA Modes 3 and 4 if your system's BIOS doesn't already have it. If your drive supports these technologies, this can significantly improve performance.)

> CD-ROM accelerators, which copy CD data onto your hard drive where it can be accessed much more quickly, *are* effective enough to be worth considering—if you have enough spare hard drive space.

4. Microsoft software add-ons. I have in mind products like Microsoft's Word Assistant for Word 6 and Microsoft Plus for Windows 95—both costing at least half as much as the software they're intended to supplement, yet offering only a tiny fraction of the value.
5. Notoriously buggy versions of software. Some software packages were so buggy that they were quickly replaced by newer versions. Two that come to mind are WordPerfect 6.0 (look for 6.1 instead), and Packrat 5.0 (a personal information manager that was so buggy, most of its devoted admirers finally gave up and went elsewhere).

The Learning Company (Formerly Softkey)

No discussion of Cheapskate software could be complete without a discussion of companies that market very inexpensive software, often in nontraditional venues such as supermarkets. In 1995, so-called "budget software" accounted for 10 percent of all retail software sales—and roughly 25 percent of all purchases made.

The leader in this market is the Learning Company, known until recently as Softkey. Softkey's pioneers believed that software could be marketed just like soap: You segmented the market, and came up with products for every niche. Softkey learned to repackage multiple versions of the same, or similar software, at very different "price points." Depending on where you ran into the software, you might pay half as much—or twice as much.

Two years ago, I would have told you to stay away from all Softkey software. Most of it was out-and-out junk. Softkey's *Key Home Gourmet* was the single worst package I was ever dumb enough to pay for—not worth using as a coaster.

Things have become more complex, however. Softkey purchased Compton's, as well as two well respected educational software publishers, MECC, and the Learning Company—from whence came its new name. Each of these companies had a reputation for publishing quality titles. And the new Learning Company has repriced some of these titles at $12.95. At that price, they're an excellent value. Titles available for $12.95 currently include the following.

From MECC:

- ▲ Dinopark Tycoon
- ▲ Museum Madness
- ▲ Odell Down Under (Win 3.1)
- ▲ Snap Dragon
- ▲ Super Munchers
- ▲ Troggle Trouble Math

From Softkey/The Learning Company:

- ▲ PC Paintbrush Designer
- ▲ CAD Creations (imports and exports DXF files)
- ▲ 20,000 Leagues under the Sea
- ▲ Storybook Weaver
- ▲ The Oregon Trail
- ▲ Word Munchers
- ▲ WillMaker 5[9]
- ▲ BodyWorks Classic Edition
- ▲ Compton's Interactive Encyclopedia
- ▲ Consumer Reports Cars 1996 Edition
- ▲ The Family Doctor
- ▲ The American Heritage Dictionary

By the way, some of these titles can be purchased on the Web at the Learning Company's on-line store, **www.learningco.com**.

▲ ▲ ▲ ▲ ▲ ▲ ▲ ▲ ▲ ▲ ▲ ▲ ▲ ▲ ▲ ▲ ▲ ▲ ▲

9.   WillMaker 5 is one version behind the current version, WillMaker 6, available from Nolo Press for $29.97. Nolo Press is the nation's best legal information resource for nonlawyers, so I'm loathe to recommend buying Will-Maker 5 from SoftKey instead. But WillMaker 5 is so complete, it will almost certainly be all you need. According to Nolo, here's some of what you *won't* get if you purchase the older version: the ability to choose different guardians for different children; create a "pot trust" for all your children; make an unlimited number of bequests; name co-executors, or write a "Letter to the Executor."

> *Warning!* The Learning Company is still selling some of the old Softkey junk, though. It's tough to give hard-and-fast advice about which Softkey products are worth buying, but in general, I suggest staying away from any product that has "Key" in the name, for example, "Key Publisher."

Essex Interactive

These folks are trying to go Softkey one better: They've purchased rights to a line of reference and productivity software on CD-ROM, and they're selling these packages for $9.99.

I'm not especially enthusiastic about most of the productivity packages, but the reference line includes three very good disks. They're a few years old at this point, but they still offer an enormous amount of useful information for the price.

Business Library includes the complete text of 12 popular business books, covering market research, product development, finance and accounting, global strategy, direct marketing, career development, and more. It's the best of the bunch.

Business 500 includes comprehensive information on over 500 major U.S. companies, public and private, including ten years of stock and financial information, executive names, addresses, and phone numbers.

Finally, *PC Library* includes 46 computer reference books, tutorials, and manuals, covering a wide variety of Windows 3.x and DOS topics, as well as hardware repair and upgrades.

Two other Essex Interactive titles that are easily worth $9.99 include

Arts & Letters Draw, a complete drawing program

Simply Money, financial management software formerly sold by Computer Associates

You can order any of these CD-ROMs at **www.essexinteractive.com**.

Software Upgrades: When Are They Worth It?

You'll see it yourself if you're ever in a computer store after a major software upgrade is announced—especially an upgrade from Microsoft. People come in, *looking for reasons to buy it.* "I know I *should* need this," you can almost hear them saying. "Tell me *why* I do."

Boy, that's effective marketing. But as I said at the beginning of this book, we Cheapskates want to make purchasing decisions based on a clear understanding of what we really *need*. How can you tell if you need a software upgrade?

1. Are there things your current software version doesn't do that you already know you need to do? (For example, if you use a small-business accounting program, do you need more control over how your invoices appear, or reports that the software can't seem to provide?) Does the upgraded package have those features?

2. Are there features in the upgraded package that would make you significantly more effective, or save you a significant amount of time? Would you actually use those features if you had them?

3. If the answer to either of the first two questions is yes, then is the upgrade worth the money—compared with other expenditures you might make, or better yet, with socking those bucks away? (Don't forget to consider whether you'll have to upgrade your hardware to run the new software at the speed you're accustomed to. Along the same lines, will the upgrade take away anything you've come to depend on?)

   If you decide an upgrade is worth it, keep the old programs on your hard disk, in case you find the newer ones aren't all they're cracked up to be. Usually you can do that by choosing to install the new software in a different directory or folder—and by refusing to delete old files if the installation program offers to do so. Also make sure to read any on-line notes, such as readme.txt files, which cover problems or compatibility issues that may have been uncovered at the last minute. Somehow, they have a sneaky way of applying to you.

● *Applying the Rules: What about Office 97?*

These rules aren't so unreasonable, are they? Now, let's apply them to one of this year's most widely promoted, enthusiastically reviewed upgrades, Microsoft Office 97. I should tell you up front: I really *like* Office 97. I wrote a book about Word 97, the word processing component of Office.[10] But whether *you* need Office 97 is an entirely separate issue.

Let's assume you already own a copy of Microsoft Office 4.x or Microsoft Office 95. Microsoft is asking roughly $180—after rebate—for the basic upgrade; about $250 if you want the "Professional" version.

What will this money buy you?

▲ Many new ways to create and publish Web pages easily. *So, are you planning to create Web pages? And if so, do you already have a convenient way to get the job done?*

▲ A new programming language, Visual Basic for Applications, which lets you write custom programs to make Word, Excel, and PowerPoint do things they can't do on their own. *So, are you planning to write custom Word, Excel or PowerPoint applications—beyond simple shortcut macros that you could just as well create with the older versions of these programs?*

▲ A powerful new program, Microsoft Outlook, designed to help you manage your contacts, calendars, and e-mail. *Are you in the market for a personal information manager? Are you the kind of person who will really use one? Do you already have one you're comfortable with?*

▲ A few new smaller programs that may be all you need to perform certain tasks. For example, there's Microsoft Photo Editor, a basic photo manipulation program. Office 97 contains better drawing tools than its predecessors, so it's conceivable you wouldn't need to buy a separate drawing program. *Are these tools you'll use? How much are they worth to you?*

▲ *Quite a few smaller improvements you may not notice at first, which might come in handy once you have them.* For example, in Word, you can now add hyperlinks that make it easy for on-line readers to skip between locations; you can automatically summarize a document; features like Word Count provide more accurate results. In PowerPoint, you have more sophisticated control over presentations you deliver with the computer, as well as a larger library of prefabricated, prestructured presentation skeletons to build from. In Excel, you can share a worksheet with other users, allow both users to make changes at once, and track and resolve the results.

▲ ▲ ▲ ▲ ▲ ▲ ▲ ▲ ▲ ▲ ▲ ▲ ▲ ▲ ▲ ▲ ▲ ▲ ▲

10. *The Windows Sources Microsoft Word 97 for Windows SuperGuide* (if you'll pardon the shameless plug), Ziff-Davis Press, December 1996, ISBN: 156276506-X.

Office 97 may also complicate your life in two ways. First, it introduces new file formats, so you'll have to be extremely careful about how you share files with others who don't have it.

> **Microsoft has recently introduced a "Service Release" that should make sharing files with others who don't have Office 97 a little less painful.**

Second, you'll find that Office 97 will run *much* more quickly with 24-Mb or 32-Mb memory than it will with 8 Mb or 16 Mb.

OK. Now that you know what's in Office 97, will you *use* those new goodies enough to justify what they'll cost you? If so, buy it. If not, don't.

• *Upgrades versus Full Licenses*

Now I have something *nice* to say about upgrades.

There must be someone, somewhere, who has paid full price for an office suite or major business application package lately.

I hope it wasn't *you*.

Even though the software business has rapidly consolidated over the last few years—stalwarts like WordPerfect Corporation, Lotus, and Software Publishing Corporation have all been absorbed, with varying degrees of indigestion—the remaining companies are still fighting tooth and nail for market share, which means you can usually count on great upgrade deals—not just for upgrades of a company's own product, but upgrades "away" from a competitor's product, too.

To purchase a "full" version of Microsoft Office 97 Standard costs roughly $459 mail order, but as we've said, if you have an earlier version of Word, Excel, or PowerPoint, it will only cost around $220, less a $40 rebate. Any version of Word, Excel, or PowerPoint will qualify, no matter how old. *So will competitors' products*. If you don't have one around, you can probably get one dirt cheap, and save most of the difference.

Table 4-2 covers current upgrade eligibility for each version of Microsoft Office. Corel is equally liberal in its WordPerfect Suite upgrades, if not more so.

Table 4–2 Software That Qualifies You for Microsoft Office "Upgrade" Pricing

	Office 97 Standard or Professional Edition	Office 97 Small Business Edition	Home Essentials 97
Office Suites			
Microsoft Office (all versions for Windows and Windows NT)	X	X	
Microsoft Works (all versions for Windows)	X	X	
Borland® Office (2.0)	X	X	
Lotus® Smartsuite (2.0 or later)	X	X	
Novell® Perfect Office (3.0 or later)	X	X	
Corel® WordPerfect Suite 7	X	X	
Corel® Office Professional	X	X	
Word Processors			
Microsoft Word for MS-DOS (2.0 or later)	X	X	X
Microsoft Word (all versions for Windows and Windows NT Workstation)	X	X	X
WordPerfect for MS-DOS (4.0 or later)	X	X	X
WordPerfect for Windows (5.1 or later)	X	X	X
WordStar 2000 for MS-DOS (3.0 or later)	X	X	X
Ami Pro for Windows	X	X	X
WordStar 1.0 for Windows	X	X	
DisplayWrite			X
First Choice			X
Lotus Manuscript			X
MultiMate			X
Professional Write Plus			X
Q&A for DOS			X

Table 4–2 Software That Qualifies You for Microsoft Office "Upgrade" Pricing *(continued)*

	Office 97 Standard or Professional Edition	Office 97 Small Business Edition	Home Essentials 97
Samna Word IV for DOS			X
Sprint			X
Volkswriter			X
Word Pro			X
WordStar Pro for MS-DOS	X	X	X
XyWrite			X
Desktop Publishing			
Microsoft Greetings Workshop			X
All versions of Microsoft Publisher			X
Aldus Home Publisher			X
Micrografx American Greetings CreataCard Plus			X
Micrografx Hallmark Connections Card Studio			X
PageMaker			X
PagePlus			X
Print Artist			X
Print House			X
The PrintShop			X
Printmaster Gold			X
Publish It! Quark Xpress			X
Spreadsheets			
Microsoft Excel (all versions for Windows and Windows NT Workstation)	X	X	X
Microsoft Multiplan (all versions)	X	X	X
Borland Quattro Pro Special Edition (1.0)	X	X	X
Lotus 1-2-3 for MS-DOS (2.01 or later)	X	X	X

Table 4–2 Software That Qualifies You for Microsoft Office "Upgrade" Pricing *(continued)*

	Office 97 Standard or Professional Edition	Office 97 Small Business Edition	Home Essentials 97
SuperCalc for MS-DOS (3.1 or later)	X	X	X
Borland Quattro Pro for MS-DOS	X	X	X
Borland Quattro Pro for Windows	X	X	X
Lotus 1-2-3 for Windows	X	X	X
Presentation Graphics			
PowerPoint for Windows (2.0 or later)	X		
Harvard Graphics for MS-DOS (2.3 or later)	X		
Harvard Graphics for Windows (1.0 or later)	X		
Lotus Freelance for MS-DOS (4.0)	X		
Lotus Freelance for Windows (1.0 or later)	X		
WordPerfect Presentations for MS-DOS 2.0	X		
WordPerfect Presentations for Windows (2.0 or later)	X		
Aldus Persuasion for Windows (2.0 or later)	X		
ASAP® Version 1.0 or later	X		
ASAP® WordPower 1.02 or later	X		
Databases			
Lotus® Approach for Windows (1.0 or later)	X		
Borland® dBase 5.0 for MS-DOS	X		
Borland® dBase 5.0 for Windows	X		
Borland® dBase IV MS-DOS (1.0 or later)	X		

Table 4–2 Software That Qualifies You for Microsoft Office "Upgrade" Pricing *(continued)*

	Office 97 Standard or Professional Edition	Office 97 Small Business Edition	Home Essentials 97
Borland® Paradox for MS-DOS (4.5 or later)	X		
Borland® Paradox for Windows (1.0 or later)	X		
Claris® FileMaker Pro for Windows (2.0 or later)	X		
DataEase 5.0 for Windows Microsoft Access (1.0 or later)	X		
Microsoft FoxPro for MS-DOS (2.0 or later)	X		
Microsoft FoxPro for Windows (2.5 or later)	X		
Microsoft Visual FoxPro for Windows (3.0)	X		
Personal Oracle® 7 for Windows	X		
Superbase® for Windows (1.2 or later)	X		
Superbase® for Windows 95 (3.0)	X		
Symantec® Q&A for MS-DOS (4.0)	X		
Symantec® Q&A for Windows (4.0)	X		
Scheduling			
Microsoft Schedule+ (7.0)	X	X	
Project Management			
Microsoft Project (1.0 or later)	X	X	
Multimedia Encyclopedias			
Microsoft Encarta Encyclopedia			X
Compton's Interactive Encyclopedia			X
Grolier Multimedia Encyclopedia			X

Table 4–2 Software That Qualifies You for Microsoft Office "Upgrade" Pricing *(continued)*

	Office 97 Standard or Professional Edition	Office 97 Small Business Edition	Home Essentials 97
Desktop Publishing			
Microsoft Publisher (all versions for Windows & Windows NT Workstation)		X	X
Microsoft Greetings Workshop			X
Micrografx® Hallmark Card Studio		X	X
Micrografx® American Greetings CreataCard		X	X
Adobe® HomePublisher™		X	X
Adobe® PageMaker®		X	X
Serif® PagePlus		X	X
Sierra On-Line® Print Artist		X	X
Claris® Print House		X	X
Broderbund® The PrintShop		X	X
Micrologic® Software Print Master Gold		X	X
Publish It!		X	X
Quark® Quark XPress®		X	X
Other programs			
Microsoft Arcade			X
Microsoft Works			X
AppleWorks (Apple II)			X
Claris Works			X
GreatWorks			X
PerfectWorks			X
Microsoft AutoMap Streets		X	
Microsoft Trip Planner		X	
America Online 3.0	X		
Compuserve 2.01	X		

Check out the last two programs on the list: AOL 3.0 and CompuServe 2.01. Millions of these disks have been distributed free. If you don't have any of the other programs on the list, you might just have one of those around!

Rebates: How Manufacturers Have Their Cake and Eat It, Too

As we mentioned, Office 97 currently offers a $40 rebate, which brings us to the topic of rebates in general.

If the price in that catalog looks too good to be true, look for the asterisk: that price may be "after rebate." Recently, rebates for computer software (and hardware) have proliferated like Canada geese or kudzu, depending on where you're from.

Are they a good deal? Only if you mail in the paperwork to get them. *Will* you? Really? Well, consider. Software Publishing Corporation recently offered a $50. rebate to individuals purchasing their new Active-Office product with Microsoft Office 97. The price of ActiveOffice? $49.99. How many people do *you* think they expect to request the rebate?

Let's look a little closer. Microsoft Office also offered a $40 rebate at the same time. *But both rebates required an original receipt.* You would have to realize this before you arrived at the checkout counter—and ask for a duplicate receipt—or else you would lose out on one of the rebates. (And even then, you would probably have to clip the word "Duplicate" or "Reprint" off the receipt, or risk not having your application accepted.)

They don't make it easy. No wonder the majority of rebates are never collected.

Why Does This Rebate Exist?

As a Cheapskate trying to sniff out a bargain, you should consider the presence of a rebate to be a significant clue. Why is this rebate being offered? Chances are, one of the following situations applies:

▲ The manufacturer is being forced to compete with a lower-priced supplier and is trying desperately to avoid lowering prices. *You* should ask: Who is the lower cost supplier? Should I be considering *their* product instead?

▲ The manufacturer is getting ready to introduce a new version of a product and wants to clear out old inventory. *You* should ask: What's the scuttlebutt on this new product? Should I wait until it comes out?

▲ The manufacturer is overstocked, plain and simple. *You* should ask: Why isn't this product selling? Should I read a few more reviews before I plunk down my hard-earned money?

▲ The retailer needs to get you into the store. Rebates are one of the most painless ways to offer a loss leader. Check the back of your next Computer City or CompUSA catalog, and you'll see. OK, everyone loves free diskettes (see Chapter 6). But when you get into the store, keep your wits about you and try to avoid handing back your rebate savings on some full-price item you could have purchased for less by mail or done without altogether.

How do you decide if a rebate is worth your time? Well, obviously, if the rebate is too small to bother with, forget it. Will you really spend the time (and 32 cent stamp) required to get a $1.50 rebate on a ten-pack of diskettes?

Do you need to fill out a separate form to get the rebate? I recently placed a mail order with 1-800-EGGHEAD; the purchase had rebates; the forms didn't come; and when I called the special "rebate department," I got a recording saying they were so backed up, they couldn't answer my phone call for three days.

Does the rebate expire too quickly for you to get the paperwork done? (Check the packaging: It may have expired before you even make the purchase.)

Buying Software by Mail

Now that we've discussed at length what to buy—and what not to buy—the next question is: *Where do you buy it?*

For new software, the easiest way to get a good deal is typically by mail from one of the leading direct resellers. Retailers are rarely competitive with mail-order software suppliers, *except* on sale items.

In general, you'll find that prices on high-volume items are almost identical among the top mail-order sources, though prices can vary significantly on lower-volume items. Shop around—or check a couple of Web sites. Table 4-3 compares some of the top national mail-order sources.

> This tip was suggested by a former editor of *The Penny Pincher's Almanac*; I haven't tried it. He suggests calling a computer store in New York City for a price, and then using that price as leverage to get a lower price from a mail-order warehouse.
>
> The theory: New York City retailers may sometimes offer lower prices to compensate for New York's 8.25 percent sales tax rate. If you can get the same low price from a top mail-order warehouse with better delivery and service policies, you'll have the best of both worlds.
>
> You might try CDW. Their catalogs say: "We encourage you to call if you find a better price elsewhere—we will do our best to match or beat a competitor's price whenever possible."

You may find the biggest cost difference between one mail order house and another will be sales tax. Depending on where they're located, one mail-order company may be required to charge you sales tax, whereas another won't. (For a more detailed discussion of sales taxes and use taxes, see the *Doing Business By Mail* section in Chapter 2.)

Table 4–3 The Leading Mail-Order Firms

	PC/Mac Connection	Computer Discount Warehouse	PC/Mac Mall	Insight	PC/Mac Warehouse	Computability
Sales	PCs: 1-800-800-5555 Macs: 1-800-800-0009	PCs: 1-800-471-4239 Macs: 1-800-622-4239 local: 1-847-465-6000	1-800-328-2790 PCs: 1-800-863-3282; Macs: 1-800-328;2790	1-800-INSIGHT; 1-800-488-0002	PCs: Macs: 1-800-255-6227	Hardware/Software: 1-800-554-9925 Computers/Notebooks: 1-800-896-1342 Networking: 1-800-741-9169
Customer service	1-800-800-0018	Same as above	1-800-222-2808	1-800-377-3000	Macs: 1-800-925-6227 PCs: 1-800-285-7080 Datacomm: 1-800-328-2261	Same as above
Return Merchandise Authorizations (RMA's)	1-800-800-0018	Same as above	1-800-555-3613	Same as above	Same as above	Same as above
Address	6 Mill Street Marlow, NH 03456	CDW Computer Centers 1020 E. Lake Cook Road Buffalo Grove, IL 60089	2645 Maricopa Street, Torrance, CA 90503-5144	6820 South Harl Street, Tempe, AZ 85281	1720 Oak Street P.O. Box 3013 Lakewood, NJ 08701-5926	P.O. Box 17882 Milwaukee, WI 53217
Web site	www.pcconnection.com	www.cdw.com	www.cc.inc.com/cfm/tables/cchomepage.cfm	www.insight.com	www.warehouse.com	www.compatibility.com
Sales taxes where?	Ohio	Illinois	California Tennessee	Arizona	Connecticut, New Jersey, Ohio, Illinois	Wisconsin

Table 4–3 The Leading Mail-Order Firms *(continued)*

	PC/Mac Connection	Computer Discount Warehouse	PC/Mac Mall	Insight	PC/Mac Warehouse	Computability
Shipping	$5 for first 10 lbs; $1 per additional pound. Airborne Express generally used; in-stock products can be ordered as late as 3 A.M. for next-day delivery	97% of orders shipped same day if ordered by 6:30 p.m. CST. UPS and FedEx shipping avail. Orders under $200 can be shipped UPS ground for $2.99; for others, CDW charges actual freight, ins. and packaging costs.	FedEx $3 for first 5 lbs; $1 per add'l lb; if credit confirmed by 11 P.M. weekdays, can deliver items in stock by 10:30 A.M. UPS ground shipping avail. COD orders, $6 extra.	FedEx shipping; same-day delivery available in some locations.	Overnight delivery $3 per order up to 5 lbs., $1 per add'l. lb. Airborne Express used unless UPS Ground offers overnight delivery. Sat. delivery avail. in most areas at no extra charge. U.S. shipments insured at no extra charge. COD orders, $10 extra.	Orders under 15 lbs. generally shipped by UPS 2-Day Air. Software shipping $7 per order; call for specific charges for hardware shipping. Most orders shipped within 48 hours.
Returns	All sales final; no refunds after 30 days. Ask sales consultant if product covered by a money-back guarantee. Other products are returnable for repair only as per terms of product warranty. Incomplete or unauthorized returns may be refused or subject to a 15% restocking fee	All nondefective returns for credit or exchange subject to a 15% restock. fee & must be completed within 30 days of inv. All defective products except computers & printers accept. by CDW for credit, exchg, or repair, at CDW's discretion, within 30 days of inv. date. AST, Apple, Compaq, H-P, and IBM products may only be returned for repairs. CDW reserves the right to author. product returns beyond 30 days, but only for credit toward future purchase	All merchandise sold "as-is." Money-back guarantee only on products designated by an MBG logo. All other purchases final unless product is defective. All nondefective product returns for credit or exchange subject to a minimum 15% restocking fee and must be completed within 30 days. RMAs: 800-555-3613.	Many unopened products may be returned for a full credit, excluding shipping charges, within 30 days. No refunds after 30 days. Return of opened product, computers, notebooks, scanners, and printers subject to 15% restocking fee. Hardware returns must be received by Insight unopened within 15 days of purchase. RMAs: 1-800-800-0018.	Call 1-800-925-6227 to find out if a specific product comes with a money-back guarantee. All products come with a 30-day guarantee against defects.	All returns subject to a restocking fee.

What *about* those midtown Manhattan storefront retailers previously referred to—the ones who attract customers from all over the world? In general, I'm *not* impressed. You'll often find a mish-mosh of merchandise, some very competitively priced, but much priced significantly higher than mail order. And you have to be very careful about warranties and customer service. Don't purchase from one of these stores if you're in New York only for a short time; you could easily get stuck.

If you're a native, you might also want to check with the New York City Department of Consumer Affairs, which can tell you about a store's record in complying with New York's relatively tough consumer rules.

There is *one* New York retailer I really like: J&R Computer World (1-800-221-8180), which also sells by mail order. In my experience, they deliver what they say they will, when they say they will, usually at a reasonable price.

On the Left Coast, there's Fry's Electronics, the "geek emporium" Silicon Valley computer people love to hate—and keep going back to. No doubt about it: You can get a bargain at Fry's. Of course you can also get in trouble. Keep an eye out for returned merchandise which may or may not have been retested properly (you'll recognize it by the poor shrinkwrapping and Fry's QA sticker). Was it defective, or just too hard to configure? You won't get a convincing answer from the floor help. Fry's is noisy, full of mismarked merchandise, but still often the best bargain around. If you're from the area, you have to go at least once. If you're a tourist, it deserves a spot on your must-see list alongside the Marin County wineries, the City Lights bookstore, and Alcatraz.

Alternate Sources

Two more great ways to get software dirt cheap are to buy *old* and buy *used*. By buying "old," I mean purchasing previous-version software. You can often get versions of major market software that are a couple of years old—but still new and shrinkwrapped—for one-third of what the new software would cost. And once you own the older version, you can generally qualify for lower upgrade pricing if you want it.

Buying "used" means just what it says. Used software is controversial, because many "used software" ventures have reeked of piracy. But not all used software is pirated. You *can* get great deals—honorably.

> *Warning?* Here's a flea market scam to watch out for: OEM-version Windows 95 CD-ROMs selling for $15–$20. Why a scam? First of all, Microsoft makes computer makers promise not to sell Windows 95 CD-ROMs separately from new computers, so the software's not licensed—and you may not get documentation. Aside from being illegal, unlicensed, and undocumented, however, most of these CD-ROMs *won't install* on any system that already has an operating system. Unless you're an expert on Microsoft's installation scripting language, you'll have to completely wipe out everything on your hard drive to make them work.

Buying "Previous Version" Software

A year ago, I would have said that the best source for previous version software was Surplus Direct—hands-down. They're still good, but they've refocused their business to offer more hardware and less software. They're also getting a little trendy, and they're not the big secret they used to be—their recent giveaway of a Hummer on the Web saw to that.

So it's a more competitive ballgame now. I'd still start with Surplus Direct, though. Some of their best recent software deals have included

▲ Lotus SmartSuite 2.1 for Windows, $44.99

▲ PhoneDisc PowerFinder complete U.S. business and residential phone listings, September 1995, $19.99

- ▲ Rand McNally TripMaker 1996 (highways maps and trip planning) and StreetFinder 1996 (street maps); $19.99 each
- ▲ Now Up-to-Date Personal Information Manager for Windows 95, $18.99
- ▲ Serif PagePlus 3.0 CD-ROM for Windows 95, $24.99
- ▲ Micrografx Windows Draw 4.0 CD-ROM for Windows 95 CD-ROM, $19.99
- ▲ Harvard Graphics 2.0 CD-ROM for Windows, $18.99
- ▲ Maps and Data for Microsoft Office 95 (detailed demographics information for marketing) $24.99
- ▲ Maplinx 3.0 for Windows 95 (professional mapping software), $29.99
- ▲ Borland Paradox 5.0 database for Windows, $49.99

You can get a catalog or visit Surplus Direct on the Web.

Surplus Direct
P.O. Box 2000
Hood River, OR 97031-2000
1-800-753-7877
www.surplusdirect.com

If Surplus Direct doesn't have what you're looking for, I'd hop over to Software Clearance Outlet. Some of *their* best recent deals include

- ▲ DeLorme Map'N'Go travel planning software, $10.00
- ▲ Infopedia multimedia reference tool, $5.00
- ▲ FaxWorks Pro 3.0, $19.95
- ▲ Janna Contact 95 personal information manager, $10.00
- ▲ MS-DOS 6.22 upgrade, $29.95
- ▲ QuickBooks 3.1 CD, $39.95
- ▲ Quicken 8 for DOS, $19.95
- ▲ Select Phone 96 U.S. business and residential telephone directory, $29.95
- ▲ Family Tree Maker 2.0 for Windows, $19.95
- ▲ Grolier's Multimedia Encyclopedia, $10.00

And unlike Surplus Direct, they also stock Mac software, including

- ▲ System 7.5 CD, $10.00
- ▲ Dabbler 2 CD painting program, $10.00
- ▲ Kai's power tools graphics filters, $19.95
- ▲ Macromedia Director 3.1, $199.95
- ▲ Quicken Deluxe, $29.95

You can reach Software Clearance Outlet at
> Software Clearance Outlet
> 3501 West Moore #C
> Santa Ana, CA 92704
> 1-800-230-SOFT
> **www.softwareoutlet.com**

Software Clearance Outlet also has a retail store in Orange County, California:

> Softwarehouse
> 17850 Newhope Street, Unit #101
> Fountain Valley, CA 92708
> (714) 434-4797
> **www.softwareoutlet.com/s-house.htm**

Lately another source has turned up: the National Computer Clearinghouse. Like Surplus Direct, they sell more hardware than software, but when they do offer software, it's usually a very good deal—and they sometimes offer packages that are virtually impossible to find elsewhere.

> National Computer Clearinghouse
> 316-681-0555
> 830 S. Woodlawn
> Wichita, KS 67218
> **www.ncc-pc.com**

And if you're in California, Software Outlet (not to be confused with Software Clearance Outlet) offers a wide variety of closeout game software for Windows, the Macintosh, and older systems such as Atari and Commodore. Software Outlet's stores are at

> 2146 Parker Street
> San Luis Obispo, CA 93401
> (805) 544-6616
> **www.greatbuy.com**
> 3614 Ming Avenue
> Bakersfield, CA 93309
> (805) 837-1469

Clearance center:
330 Nut Tree Road
Vacaville, CA 95687
(707) 451-4149

There's also Cyber Exchange, a chain of more than 40 stores specializing in buying, selling, and trading new and used software of all sorts, from games to utilities to professional business tools. You can find out more at **www.cyberexchange.com.**

One last source for old software is

Computer Reset
P.O. Box 461782
Garland, TX 75046
214-276-8072
wwwipp.unicomp.net/c-reset/

Few sources offer as much commercial DOS software; they even have GEOS and IBM "PCjr" software.

USoX

USoX (**www.midwinter.com/usox/**) is an Internet clearinghouse for individuals who wish to buy and sell used software. It offers a convenient search engine, so you can ask USoX: "Show me all the databases for Windows 95 being sold for less than $100." UsoX asks sellers not to use it as a vehicle for software piracy and asks that sellers honor license agreements. As a buyer, you'll want to make sure you are receiving all original diskettes and licenses, and (as discussed earlier) you may wish to request a letter certifying transfer of the software to you.

USoX (see Figure 4-22) doesn't vouch for the honesty of either sellers or buyers, but most are OK folks. USoX makes several suggestions about protecting yourself in private transactions with strangers—ideas that are worth following no matter how you encounter those strangers:

▲ To verify that the seller actual has the software, ask for the software's serial number and manufacturer's phone number.

▲ Ship (or request shipping) via COD.

Having offered those cautions, the prices offered by sellers are often excellent. Recent seller's prices have included

- ▲ Windows 95 Upgrade CD-ROM, $35.00
- ▲ MS Works Release 4 for Windows 95, $15.00
- ▲ Lotus WordPro 96 for Windows 3.1, $20.00
- ▲ Microsoft Office 95 Professional, $125.00
- ▲ Word 6 for Windows, $25.00
- ▲ Serif PagePlus 3.0 CD-ROM, $7.00
- ▲ Windows 95 upgrade CD-ROM, $37.00
- ▲ Freehand 5.5 for the Macintosh, $60.00
- ▲ PhotoShop 4.0 for the Macintosh, $150.00

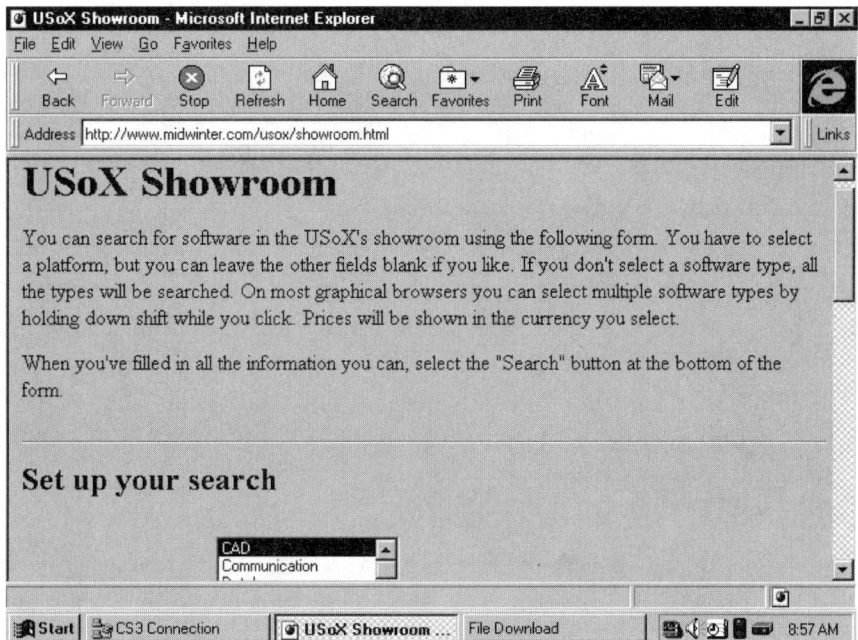

Figure 4–22 USoX, one of the few legitimate places to buy and sell used software.

Seven Pointers for Buying Used Software

When buying used software *anywhere*, make sure you:

1. Get the manual (or at least make sure you can get a third-party book inexpensively).
2. Get *all* the disks (count them—make sure no disks "in the middle" are missing). There can be 40 or more diskettes in recent office suites, and if *one's* missing, you may not be able to install the package.
3. If the software is on CD-ROM, make sure the disk is in good condition; scratches and gashes could make the software uninstallable.
4. If the software is on floppy diskette, make sure it's in a format you can use. For example, most recent computers come with 3.5" drives, but much older software came on 5.25" disks.
5. Get the software's serial number. You may not be able to install the software without it.
6. Get the license card if possible—and get a signed note from the seller transferring the license to you.
7. If the software is an upgrade, make sure you get (or already have) the older disks you may need for the software to install properly. For example, Norton Utilities 2.0 for Windows 95 upgrade CD-ROMs expect you either to have installed Norton Utilities 1.0 or to have the original 1.0 floppies available while you're installing 2.0.

Free Software on the Web

In the wake of Netscape's discovery that you can get very rich giving away your software, there's been an explosion of commercial software available for download on the Web:

▲ Low-end versions of expensive high-end software
▲ Trial software that expires after a certain period of time
▲ Full-featured beta software
▲ In a few cases, software that's just plain free

> *Warning!* It was bound to happen: counterfeit CD-ROMs. How can you tell when you're getting one? You can't always tell, but according to the Business Software Alliance, some of the sloppier counterfeits are printed poorly, contain misspellings, or off-center artwork on the packaging. These show up some times at computer fairs and occasionally in "mom-and-pop" retailers desperately looking for ways to compete with the superstores on price.
>
> Why do you care? Aside from the fact that counterfeits rip off legitimate software companies, they may not include the documentation you need, and they certainly won't include the support you need—assuming, for the sake of argument, that the *legitimate* version came with support!

In this section, we'll show you a few of the best sites for free commercial downloads.

The Microsoft Web Site

Microsoft may be the world's best source of free software. These folks obviously have money to throw around—and plenty of motivation to stay on top, by any means available. Go to **www.microsoft.com/ msdownload/** to see what's on their plate now (see Figure 4-23).

As I write, the list includes betas of some of Microsoft's most interesting new software, including

Microsoft Music Producer, which lets you create royalty-free music based on one of over 100 professionally prepared music styles, each of which you can vary by customizing instruments, tempo, volume, length, and other elements.

Microsoft Image Composer, which lets you create and modify composite images, and save them in a wide range of formats for use on the World Wide Web or elsewhere.

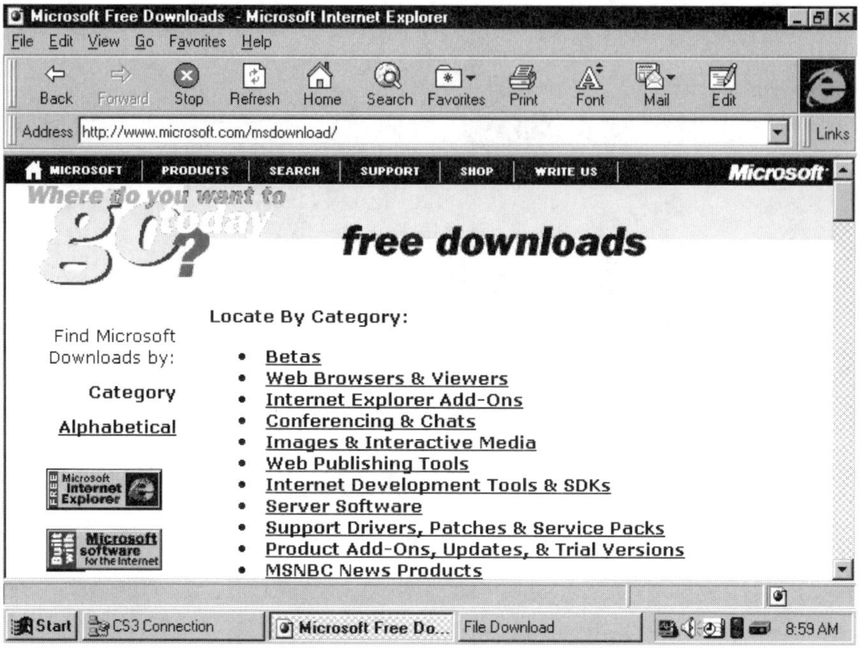

Figure 4–23   Microsoft's free download area: Always something new here.

Microsoft Media Manager, which helps you organize and easily locate multimedia files.

These programs will soon become retail products, no longer available for free. And the betas will stop working at some point in the future. But in the meantime, users who download them can use them with no restrictions. And the site is also full of stuff that's out-and-out free, indefinitely,[11] including

- ▲ The latest version of Microsoft Internet Explorer,[12] the full-featured Web browser, currently number 2 in the marketplace and closing in on Netscape.
- ▲ *NetMeeting* conference software that works with Microsoft's Internet Explorer Web browser, allowing you to talk, share documents and applications over the Internet—all at the same time.

▲ ▲

11.   Of course, Microsoft reserves the right to change their mind or remove software from their site.

12.   You'll find a copy of Internet Explorer on the Cheapskate's CD-ROM, but *this* is the place to go for updates.

▲ Add-ons and free templates for Microsoft Word, Excel, and Office.

▲ Free TrueType fonts for both Windows and the Macintosh, intended for display on computer screens and the World Wide Web, but attractive enough to use anywhere.

▲ Trial versions of Microsoft games for grown-ups and kids; these games will work indefinitely but have fewer levels or less complexity than the commercial products.

▲ PowerToys that add convenience and flexibility to Windows 95; for example, allowing you to change screen resolution without rebooting your computer.

▲ Programming tools that help you automate Web sites using Microsoft's ActiveX technologies and more.

▲ Imaging for Windows 95 (see Figure 4-24), a basic set of tools for managing and manipulating scanned images or incoming faxes.

▲ Windows 95 Support Assistant: This Help File includes more than 100 articles on the most common Windows 95 problems and setup issues, plus interactive troubleshooters that walk you through solving these problems.

▲ Sample games like Chess (see Figure 4-25), Rattler Race, and Rodent's Revenge which are available free even though they are part of Microsoft Entertainment Pack products.

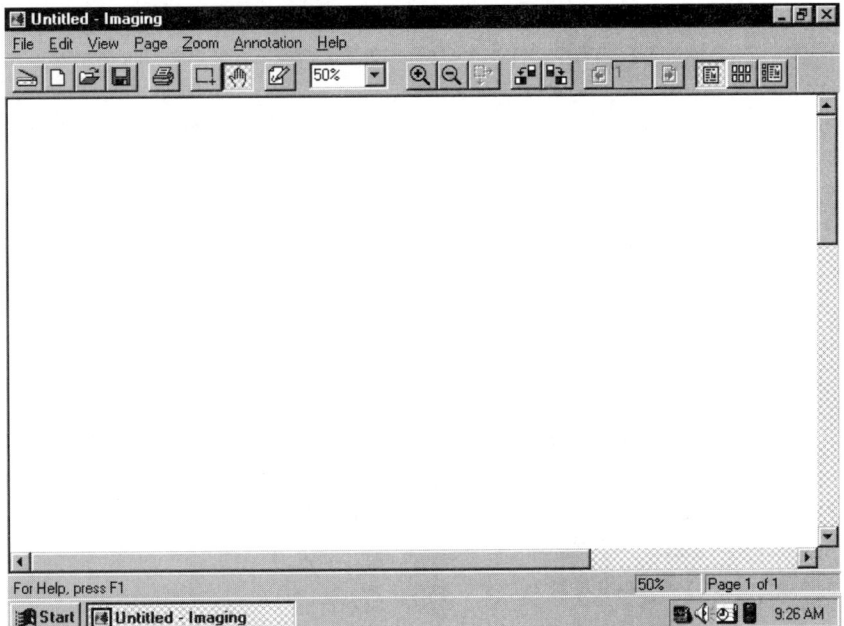

Figure 4–24   Imaging for Windows 95, another freebie that's great for folks with recent-vintage scanners.

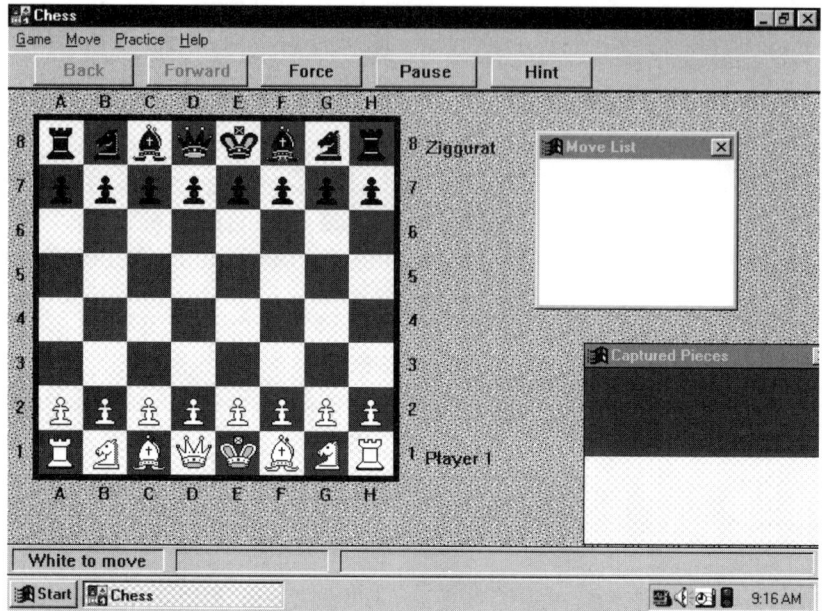

Figure 4–25   Microsoft Chess, currently free on Microsoft's Web site.

Of course, the list will change over time, but this is a representative sample of what to expect.

Symantec: It's Always Something

While you're on the Web, visit Symantec to see what *they've* got available for downloading. For several months, it was Norton CrashGuard for Windows 95, software designed to intercept and repair many Windows 95 application crashes long enough for users to save their work. Now that's gone—transformed into a paying product—but Norton Secret Stuff for Windows 95/NT has taken its place.

Norton Secret Stuff (see Figure 4-26) allows you to create self-decrypting files you can send to anyone, whether or not they have the same software. You tell your recipient the password, and they can decrypt the file; nobody else can. (No *regular* people, anyway. Since the software's approved for export, you have to assume it can be defeated by expert cryptographers.)

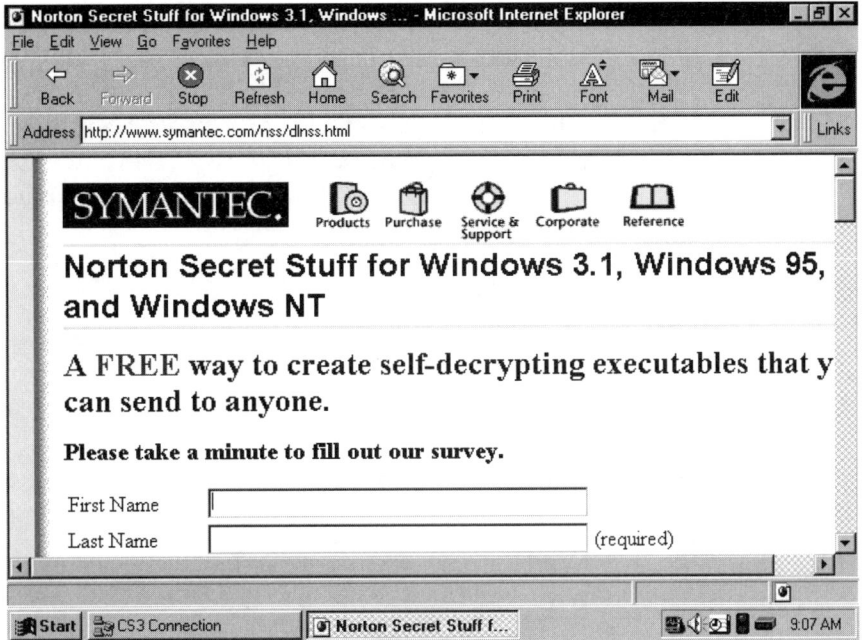

Figure 4–26   Norton Secret Stuff, free (for the moment) on Symantec's Web site.

Turn Your PC Into a High-Powered Workstation

Inside your run-of-the-mill Windows PC sits the throbbing heart of a (nearly) state-of-the-art UNIX workstation. You just need to coax it out. Millions of people worldwide are doing just that—with Linux,

Linux is a free, UNIX-like operating system that runs on standard 386, 486, and Pentium-class PCs. Linux was invented by a real person: Linus Torvalds, a Finnish computer science student. Since then, a team of programmers worldwide has worked to enhance it, adding many features including world-class networking.

183

The result is an extremely powerful, flexible, and reliable 32-bit operating system that supports a surprisingly wide range of hardware (though not as much as Windows 95). An industrial-strength operating system that is—drumroll, please—*free*.

Having said that, you *can* pay for Linux (or at least the disks it comes on)—and you probably should. Several companies have organized the huge collection of Linux files and related software and put them all together on convenient, relatively easy-to-install CD-ROMs. (The alternative is some very large downloads.) The most well known of these "Linux distributions" include

Red Hat 4.1
Red Hat Software
www.redhat.com

Slackware '96
Walnut Creek Software
www.cdrom.com

Plug & Play Linux
Yggdrasil
www.yggdrasil.com

Linux Developer's Resource
InfoMagic
www.infomagic.com

Each of these products is widely available for under $50.

What's it like to live with Linux? This is a full-fledged UNIX-style environment, a very different beast from Windows or the Mac. With Linux, the user faces much more immediate complexity—but once you learn your way around, the reward is much more customization and control than are typically available from DOS, Windows, or Macintosh environments. Many users also report that Linux gives them much better performance than Windows on the same hardware.

Better performance doing *what*? Linux is an excellent option for

- ▲ Hosting Web sites
- ▲ Managing your internal network or intranet
- ▲ Learning C or C++ programming
- ▲ Learning UNIX
- ▲ Doing anything that involves heavy-duty networking
- ▲ Running technical applications (many of which were originally created for Sun's Solaris or other commercial versions of UNIX, but can easily be used with Linux)
- ▲ Setting up a UNIX environment at home to mirror one you may already be using at school or work

Linux is *not* an excellent way to run the market-leading business applications. There's no Microsoft Excel for Linux. (There is, however, a Linux version of Doom!) You can find a list of more than 2,600 Linux applications—many programming oriented—at the Linux Software Map, **www.boutell.com/lsm/**. You'll find a list that includes more business-oriented applications at **www.redhat.com/linux-info/linux-app-list/** (see Figure 4-27).

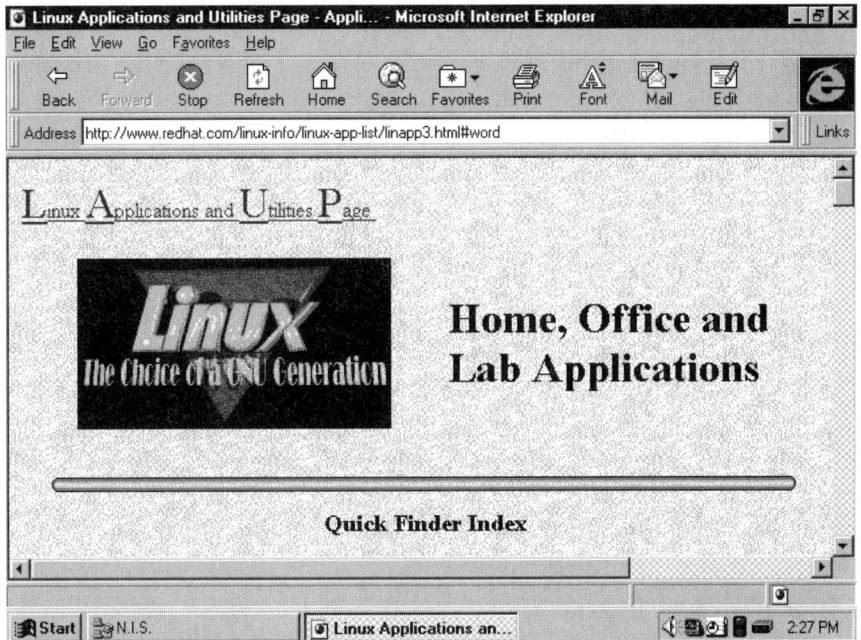

Figure 4–27   The list of Linux-compatible business applications at Red Hat Software's site.

You can usually install Linux in a DOS partition and switch back to DOS or Windows whenever you need to perform those prosaic tasks the real world seems to demand on occasion. And if you want to experiment with Linux without jumping in too heavily, some distributions of Linux can be run straight from the CD-ROM, without a full installation on your PC.

Summary

So there you have it: the complete guide to getting software "on the cheap." Still don't have enough software? See Chapter 12 to see what's on the Cheapskate's CD-ROM. Ready to change the subject? In Chapter 5, we'll cast a Cheapskate's eye on peripherals and hardware upgrades, to help you keep as much money as possible where it belongs: in your pocket.

Printers, CD-ROM drives, sound boards, modems, speakers, processor upgrades…ever feel as if you're on a merry-go-round? Or at least, someone *wants* you to be? In this chapter, we'll take a Cheapskate's look at peripherals and upgrades, to help you decide what's worth it—and what's a waste of your time and limited resources.

> Before you purchase any peripherals or hardware, check the Web to see if there are any FAQs available to help you understand what you're buying. Currently, FAQs exist for sound cards, CD-ROMs, video cards, monitors, modems, and many other items.

The Limits to Upgrading

Short of going the bare-bones route, where you transfer some or all of your computer's organs into a whole new body, how should you think about upgrading? Which upgrades are worth it? When is it time to sell the old computer and purchase something new (or newer)?

Nowadays, the one upgrade that is most likely to be worth the money is adding memory to a system that has very little. Taking a Windows 3.1 system from 2 or 4 Mb to at least 8 Mb will almost always significantly improve its performance. Taking a Windows 95 system from 8 Mb to 16 Mb will do the same—and if you are running high-powered applications such as Microsoft Office 97, upgrading to 24 Mb will help even more.[1]

Be more cautious about other upgrades. You want an upgrade that achieves one or both of the following goals:

1. *Significantly extends the life of your system at a much lower per-year cost than replacing and selling it.* My rule of thumb: A successful upgrade should extend the life of your system by no more than $150 per added year.

   So, if an upgrade extends the life of your system by 12–18 months, it should cost no more than $150–$175. On the other hand, if a motherboard upgrade can reasonably extend the life of your system for *three* years, it may well be worth a few hundred dollars. In these examples, you're paying 30–40 cents per day, or less, for your computer's added usage.

   By this rule of thumb, inexpensive processor upgrades from companies like Evergreen may be worth the money, but expensive Intel Overdrive upgrades that can cost $350–$500 probably aren't. A memory upgrade that takes you from 4 Mb to 12 Mb for around $60 probably *is* worth the money; an expensive new video card inserted in a system that wasn't designed for it probably *isn't*.

2. *Gives you a benefit now—and allows you to keep benefiting even after you purchase your next computer.* If you add a new video card to your system, chances are you'll sell that video card when you sell the system, gaining only a short-term benefit from your purchase. On the other hand, if you purchase a new printer, you can keep using that printer for several years to come. A new hard drive falls somewhere in between. You can always transplant the older, smaller drive back into your computer when you sell it and take the new one with you—if you're prepared to go through the trouble.

   Keep in mind that some upgrades, especially processor upgrades, don't add much to the value of your system when you sell it. They're like adding a swimming pool to your house: They can actually alienate buyers who prefer not to have them.

▲ ▲ ▲ ▲ ▲ ▲ ▲ ▲ ▲ ▲ ▲ ▲ ▲ ▲ ▲ ▲ ▲ ▲ ▲

1. Things get iffier when you start adding memory to a system that already has quite a bit. For example, Microsoft and Kingston recently ran a promotion encouraging owners of 486 systems to add 32 MB to those systems for $199. The per-megabyte price was attractive, but much of that added memory was largely going to waste, according to benchmarks from *PC Week*.

Memory: The Universal Upgrade

Nothing lubricates PC performance like a little more memory (though as I've said elsewhere, there *is* a point of diminishing returns). In this section, we'll discuss memory from the Cheapskate's perspective: Why it's priced the way it is, how to buy it, and where to buy it. Later, in Table 5-1, there's a memory buyer's checklist you can use to compare suppliers.

The Mysterious Memory Market

So what gives with memory? For years, it's consistently $35–40 a megabyte—while virtually every other computer component is plummeting in price. Then, in a matter of months, it's less than $10 a megabyte, and by early 1996, you could get it for $5/Mb or even less. But whisperings are heard on the street: *Memory prices are headed up again*. And what happens? They go *down*. Why so unstable?

Memory chips are built in manufacturing plants that can cost more than $1.5 billion and take two years to build. Building a plant like that is one big decision. You have to guess what memory demand will be like two years in advance, and you have to guess how long demand will remain strong for the products you can build there. Technology changes so quickly that a plant designed to build one generation of memory chip usually won't be able to build the next.

If a few manufacturers misjudge demand, or if critical suppliers do, then supply and demand can get completely out of whack—leading to either very high or very low prices.

Once the plant's finally up and running, its owner has to sell *tons* of chips to pay for it. Those chips are sold in two ways. Most are sold to companies who buy at least 5,000 units through fixed-price contracts which last from three months to a year. The rest are sold to distributors, who resell them to smaller companies.

Companies that buy memory on contract can misjudge demand, too. (Let's say Windows 95 ships late, so customers don't need memory upgrades for several months longer than was expected.) When that happens, they resell memory to brokers who buy and sell it worldwide—much like stockbrokers. As with stock, memory prices can be extremely volatile, changing several times daily. The memory itself can bop around some, too—through the hands of several brokers before it gets to you.

So why am I telling you this? With memory prices at all-time lows, manufacturers all over Asia have reportedly delayed new plant construction. So if you're thinking of buying memory, keep an eagle eye on prices.

The best way to find out what's happening with memory prices *right now* is to visit the Chip Merchant's pricing page (**www.thechipmerchant.com/prices.htm**) every couple of days; they update their memory prices every weekday. For medium- to long-term memory pricing trends, see if there's any news at the usual sources, **www.zdnet.com** and **www.cnet.com**.

If you see prices starting to go up, you might want to pounce. They could go up a *lot*.

What Memory? I Forget

So you've got an old computer but you don't know what kind of memory you need for it?

If you have a brand-name computer, you can usually find this information in your manual, or check with the manufacturer. First, you'll want to know how much memory you already have; you can check that by running the MEM command at a DOS prompt. I'd be hard-pressed to invest in more memory for a very old PC, such as an 8088-, 8086-, or 80286-based system. It gets more interesting when you get to 80386 and 80486 systems. There are millions of 80386 and low-end 80486 systems being forced to run Windows 3.1 on 2 or 4 Mb. Expanded to 8 Mb, they'll run Windows 3.1 a whole lot more efficiently—and they'll be able to handle powerhouse applications like Word 6.

80386 machines generally use 30-pin SIMMs, which are becoming scarcer (and therefore somewhat more expensive). 80486 machines typically use 72-pin SIMMs. A few years ago, as people found they couldn't transplant SIMMs from their 80386s to their newer 80486 machines, companies began selling devices that allowed you to mount two or more 30-pin SIMMs in the same 72-pin SIMM socket. The same kind of device is now also used to connect two 4-Mb 72-pin SIMMs, transforming them into one 8-Mb 72-pin SIMM.

With new memory running about $4-$5/Mb, these devices aren't very cost-effective. Worse, they're not perfectly reliable. Two 4-Mb SIMMs that work perfectly on their own might give you trouble when combined on one of these devices, due to timing or electrical signal problems. I'd like to recommend them; so far, I can't.

In fact, the whole issue of transplanting memory from one system to another is getting dicey. You have to worry not only about memory *sizes*; there are also *speeds*. (Many 80386 systems used 80-ns RAM; many 80486 and some Pentium systems used 70-ns RAM; most faster Pentiums use 60-ns RAM. You can always give a system faster memory than it expects, but slower memory is a recipe for trouble.)[2]

Last but not least, there are changes in memory technology. For a few years, the industry standardized on Fast Page Mode (FPM) memory. Then, it moved on to slightly faster[3] Extended Data Out (EDO) memory. Most computers that accept EDO memory will also take the older FPM memory, but the reverse isn't true: Computers that expect FPM will rarely accept EDO. More recently, yet another type of memory has been introduced: Synchronous Dynamic RAM (SDRAM). This memory uses not 72-pin SIMMs but 168-pin Dual Inline Memory Modules (DIMMs). It's about 20–30 percent more expensive. The advantage? It can work in faster computers, adjusting to their speed as needed, up to and including bus speeds well beyond anything available right now.

Problem solved? Just buy SDRAM (assuming your computer will handle it) and you're covered forever? Close your eyes and imagine Johnny Carson: "Wrong again, dogbreath." By 1999, Intel systems will start using nDRAM, a new high-speed memory technology that will operate several times as fast as SDRAM may ever work. (nDRAM's predecessor can already be found in the Nintendo 64 game machine.) Since Intel owns a piece of the company that invented this technology, and since not all memory manufacturers have agreed to manufacture nDRAMs, these beasts just might cost more.

▲ ▲ ▲ ▲ ▲ ▲ ▲ ▲ ▲ ▲ ▲ ▲ ▲ ▲ ▲ ▲ ▲ ▲ ▲

2.   There's also the prosaic issue of *leads*: most systems these days use tin leads in their memory sockets. Ideally, you want to fill those sockets with memory that also has tin leads, not gold. And vice versa: if the system has gold leads in its sockets, you want gold edges on your SIMMs. This isn't an issue of life or death, but mismatched leads can, over years, lead to corrosion—especially in humid climes.

3.   If your system has level 2 cache, EDO won't make much of a difference. If it *doesn't*, EDO will help significantly.

All this is to say: When it comes to memory, live for today. If you're going to keep your current system for another couple of years and more memory will improve its performance, that's an upgrade worth considering. But don't buy memory thinking you'll be able to transplant it into your next computer, because the odds are stacked against you.

> If you're not sure what kind of memory you need, try downloading KEPLER for Windows from the Kingston Technology Web site. Kingston is a leading memory producer, and this software package is designed to help its customers figure out what kind of memory their computers need. Of course, the parts numbers it gives you are Kingston part numbers. But whether you choose to purchase Kingston or not, KEPLER will tell you how many memory slots you have, what speed memory you need, and other things you really ought to know. Of course, it's free.

Where to Buy Memory

It *is* possible to buy really rotten memory. Manufacturers sell so-called "C-grade" RAM chips for use in devices such as calculators and pagers, but some of those chips find their way into SIMMs you can buy. Unfortunately, it's not easy to tell. Some lower-quality chips are marked with their country of origin. Others have been "remarked"; original information has been sanded or etched away, and new information stenciled on. Chips that appear *unusually* dull or unreflective may have been remarked.

> Simply the best source of detailed information about memory—and memory scams—is the *Memory Buyer's Guide* by Dean R. Kent of Real World Industries, available at **www.realworldtech.com**. (There's also an invaluable companion booklet, the *PC Upgrader's Troubleshooting Guide*, available "next door" at **www.realworldtech.com/tshoot.htm**.)

You could be extra safe and buy only name-brand memory from large retailers or mail-order houses—but you'll pay a lot more that way, often at least 30 percent more. There *are* quality memory resellers who charge less. The best way to find them is to ask other computer users whom they've been satisfied with. Here are a few more pointers:

▲ Ask what kind of warranty you're getting. Even though a lifetime warranty may just be a "bet" on the manufacturer's part that nothing will go wrong with your memory while you still own the computer, it's still a comfort. Settle for no less than five years.[4]

▲ Test your memory as soon as you install it (see Chapter 8 for a discussion of diagnostics software).

▲ Keep an eye out for unexplained system crashes that occur after you install the memory. If they seem to occur more often than they used to, you may have memory that's getting ready to fail.

Used Memory

Yes, you *can* buy used memory. In fact, if you have a 386 or early 486 computer requiring older 30-pin SIMMs, or an even older computer requiring other types of RAM, buying used memory could save you a significant amount of money. If newer 72-pin memory starts increasing in price, I suspect used RAM may begin to offer real cost advantages for newer systems as well.

Some experts claim that used memory is less reliable, because the individual RAM chips may have undergone the physical stress of being heated for removal from one SIMM and then being resoldered for attachment to another. Others say it's *more* reliable than new, because it's been "burned in"—and many memory problems occur the first few days a chip is in use. Realistically, it will depend on the individual SIMM—and the reliability of your source. If your applications aren't "mission-critical," I'd say it's worth a try.

▲ ▲ ▲ ▲ ▲ ▲ ▲ ▲ ▲ ▲ ▲ ▲ ▲ ▲ ▲ ▲ ▲ ▲ ▲

4. At Surplus Direct, one of my favorite sources for many other products, the memory warranty is only 30 days. That's *not* enough.

If you decide to pay for *new* memory, it will be nice to know you're *getting* new memory. There's really no way to know for sure, but here's a clue: Most chip manufacturers place a code somewhere on their chips which indicates the year they were manufactured. On a Hitachi chip, for example, the number 9537 indicates that the chip was manufactured in 1995. (The number 37 is often a week code, but it doesn't necessarily correspond to the thirty-seventh week of the year.) If you see dates that are more than a year old, chances are the memory is used. Similarly, if you see chips from different manufacturers—or dates that are more than a few weeks apart— you may be getting used memory that has been reassembled from separate SIMMs.

Memory Sources

The following sources provide new memory; a few accept memory trade-ins and sell used memory as well.

The Chip Merchant
4870 Viewridge Avenue
San Diego, CA 92123
1-800-426-6375; 1-619-268-4774
www.thechipmerchant.com
My favorite memory reseller on the Web.

Memory 4 Less
1-800-821-3354
www.memory4less.com

MicroMall Direct
16812 Hale Avenue
Irvine, CA 92606
1-800-346-7172; 1-714-833-3222

The Memory Liquidators
531 Main Street, Suite 1174
El Segundo, CA 90245
1-800-718-7755; 310-326-5656

The Memory Place
1-800-306-8901
www.buymemory.com

Intol Computers
22065 US Highway 19 North
Clearwater, FL 34625
1-800-551-1449; 1-813-796-0806
www.intol.com

The Memory Exchange
1-800-501-2770
www.memoryexchange.com

The CPU & Memory Exchange Club
1-408-654-9090

Hard Drives

In this section, I will help you
- ▲ Decide whether you *really* need a new hard drive.
- ▲ Get the best deal on one if you do need it.

Do You Need a New Hard Drive At All?

Your hard drive is full. Naturally you need a new one, right? Hold on a minute. Every once in awhile there really *is* something for nothing, and this *could* just be one of those moments. You *might* be able to turn your cramped hard drive into a bigger hard drive without spending a dime. There are two ways to do it: *data compression*, or *repartitioning*.

Data Compression: Something for Nothing?

With data compression, you run a program that recodes all your data and programs into more compact form by squeezing the redundancy out of your data. Strings of bytes constantly reappear throughout your files; data compression software substitutes shorter codes for these recurring patterns. In DOS and Windows, data compression programs also find more efficient ways to use the physical space on your hard drive—even if it means "tricking" the underlying operating system into thinking everything's the same as it's always been.

Using these and other techniques, data compression software can typically add 75 percent to 125 percent to the apparent size of your hard drive.

Table 5–1 Memory Buyer's Checklist

Your Computer's Memory Specs				
Amount of memory per SIMM (1, 4, 8, 16, 32, 64 Mb, etc.)				
Type of SIMM (FPM, EDO, SDRAM, other)				
Number of pins (30, 72, 168)				
Speed (80 ns, 70 ns, 60 ns, other)				
Leads (tin, gold)				
	Product #1	Product #2	Product #3	Product #4
New/used?				
Free phone support (# days)				
Warranty				
Price				
Shipping				
Tax				
Total Price				

If you have MS-DOS 6.0, MS-DOS 6.20, MS-DOS 6.22[5], Windows 95, or the most recent versions of IBM DOS, Novell DOS and OpenDOS (see Chapter 4), you have data compression software. All you need to do is use it.

> The only *imaginable* reason to purchase Microsoft PLUS! is that it offers a more sophisticated, powerful compression program than off-the-shelf Windows 95. It will compress larger drives and compress them more tightly.

Should you? What are the trade-offs of compression?

It can slow your computer down a little. You now have to compress and decompress every bit of data on their way to and from your hard drive. (On the other hand, you're reading smaller chunks of data, which compensates in part.)

And there's an ever-so-*slight* risk to your data. Data compression has come a long way, and it's quite reliable. However, it still does add complexity to your system. Microsoft's DoubleSpace and DriveSpace store all the data on your compressed drive in a single humongous file, named (for example) DRVSPACE.000. If something bad happens to that file, you could lose your data.

There are plenty of built-in precautions. For example, Windows 95 won't compress a drive without checking the entire physical surface of your hard disk first. However, if you're going to use data compression, make sure you back up your critical files regularly. If you're simply too stubborn, lazy or busy to make backups, then only compress programs you can easily reinstall and keep your data on an uncompressed portion of your drive.

▲ ▲ ▲ ▲ ▲ ▲ ▲ ▲ ▲ ▲ ▲ ▲ ▲ ▲ ▲ ▲ ▲ ▲ ▲ ▲

5.   But not MS-DOS 6.21. Microsoft was then in the process of defending (and losing) a lawsuit by Stac, then the developers of the leading compression software. As a result, Microsoft was forced to pull data compression from MS-DOS for several months, until it could reengineer a version that didn't risk infringing Stac's patents.

Repartitioning: Waste Not, Want Not

If I've spooked you about data compression, you may be able to get some of its benefits without any of its risks by repartitioning your hard drive. You can do this the *hard* way, for free, or the *easy* way, which of course isn't free.

The way DOS (or Windows 95, for that matter) manages your hard drive, every file requires a cluster no matter how small it is, and if a file gets larger than the clusters already assigned to it, the file gets an entirely new cluster, even if it's only needed for 1 byte of information.

The bigger your drive partitions, the bigger the clusters are. Imagine that you purchase a computer with a drive between 1024 Mb (1 Gb) and 2048 Mb (2 Gb)—and you don't bother to divide it up before you start filling Drive C with data. Your cluster size is a whopping 32K.

That means every e-mail message you store takes up at least 32K— even the quickest "hello" from your grandkids. Nowadays, these inefficiencies can easily eat up 15–20 percent of the space on your hard drive.

What you want is cluster sizes that are as small as possible—without creating so many drives that you can't keep track of them all. Table 5-2 shows you the cluster sizes associated with drives of various types. It will help you decide how big your partitions ought to be.

Table 5–2 Hard Drive Cluster Sizes

Hard Drive Size	Cluster Size
16 Mb–127 Mb	2K
128 Mb–255 Mb	4K
256 Mb–512 Mb	8K
512 Mb–1,024 Mb	16K
1,024 Mb–2,048 Mb	32K
2,048 Mb–4,096 Mb	64K

So if, for example, you can use partitions *just below* 512 Mb, you can cut your cluster size to 8K, while still having drives of reasonable size.

Unfortunately, DOS' and Windows 95's FDISK tool for changing partitions *stink*. The bottom line is, when you change partition sizes using FDISK, you destroy all your data on all the partitions involved. That means you have to completely back up all your data first. As a practical matter, it typically means you'll have to reinstall much or all of your software—and you'll lose any customizations you've made to your system along the way.

In short, this is the kind of thing you only do on a long, rainy afternoon when the family's away.

> **tip** Of course you save yourself this hassle by partitioning your drive as soon as you get it.

There is an alternative: a program called Partition Magic, from Quest Corporation, which lets you change partitions "on the fly" without destroying data. Partition Magic 3.0, the current version, costs around $50–$60—a bit steep unless you expect to repartition more than once. But you can get Partition Magic 2.0 from Surplus Direct for well under $30, and *that's* a deal.

> **tip** Microsoft's newest file system, FAT32, makes drives more efficient by reworking the cluster/sector relationship—but it's only available in new systems shipping recently (with a version of Windows 95 called OEM SR2) and in the forthcoming Windows 98. Unfortunately, it won't work with many current disk utilities.

Buying a New Hard Drive

OK, you've done all that (or considered and rejected it), and you still need a new hard drive. First two questions: How *big* and how *much*?

In Chapter 2, you learned how to evaluate your storage needs for a new computer; you can use the same techniques in purchasing a second, or replacement drive. Now, let's take a little closer look at hard drive pricing.

As with computers, there's a "sweet spot" in the hard drive market-place, where you're paying the least amount of money for each *incremental* megabyte.

The sweet spot moves, but it's always *somewhere*. Table 5-3 shows pricing on Western Digital hard drives in February 1997. You can see that as you move from 1280 Mb to 1620 Mb, you're paying less than 6 cents for each extra megabyte, but if you move from 2113 Mb to 2559 Mb you're paying 9 cents per megabyte. The sweet spot on *this* chart is 1620 Mb. It will be much higher by the time you see this book, possibly *twice* as high.

Table 5–3 Western Digital Hard Drive Pricing (February 1997)

Size	Price	Price per Megabyte	Price per Incremental Megabyte
1280 Mb	$189.99	$0.148	N/A
1620 Mb	$209.99	$0.130	$0.059
2113 Mb	$249.99	$0.118	$0.081
2559 Mb	$289.99	$0.113	$0.090

Of course, there really are a couple of other questions. One is, How fast? Most standard IDE drives run at from 9 ms to 12 ms (lower is better). You shouldn't notice a dramatic difference among any of the drives in this range, especially since several factors besides raw seek speed affect drive performance.

> If you do want to squeeze every inch of performance out of your hard drive, though, milliseconds do matter—and so do a few other specs. All things equal,
>
> ▲ PIO Mode 4 is better than PIO Mode 3.
> ▲ Higher rpm (rotation rates) are better than lower ones.
> ▲ More on-drive cache may be slightly better than less: 128K or 256K are better than 64K (though today's software caches are so much bigger that it doesn't matter as much as it once did).

Final question: IDE or SCSI? IDE (nowadays E-IDE or Fast ATA-2) is cheaper and just as reliable. SCSI is more efficient for high-powered network servers, and for applications that require steady, uninterrupted, and fast streams of data, such as video editing. For Cheapskates with unexceptional needs, I vote IDE.

Warning! Many older systems contain BIOSes that won't support hard drives bigger than 540 Mb. Before you purchase a larger drive, make sure your computer will support it. If not, you may be able to purchase a replacement BIOS, or your new drive may come with software such as OnTrack that will provide support. If you go the software route, make sure the software works with the operating systems you intend to run.

Bare Drive or Package?

There are three ways to buy a hard drive:

- ▲ Bare drive
- ▲ Retail packaging
- ▲ A "cross between the two"

When you buy a bare drive, that's *all* you're getting: no cables, no mounting hardware, and often, no manuals. Most companies that sell bare drives purchase them wholesale in "OEM" format—in other words, as if they were planning to install those drives in computers for resale.

On the other hand, when you buy a retail package, you get all the goodies, an attractively printed manual—and you usually pay a premium price for all that.

Insight, the leading hard drive reseller, takes a middle position. They repack "OEM" drives in their own inexpensive (but secure) packaging—along with everything you might need to install the drive:

- ▲ 5-1/4″ mounting frame
- ▲ Bezels
- ▲ Data cable
- ▲ Jumper blocks
- ▲ Manual
- ▲ Rail set
- ▲ Screws

You *might* not need all that stuff. For example, if you are mounting a 3.5″ drive in a 3.5″ drive bay, you won't need the 5-1/4″ mounting frame—and if you're experienced with this, you might get away without a manual. Much of the technical information you need will be imprinted right on the drive, or it will be available on the Web—and most newer computers are equipped to recognize today's drives without much intervention. On the other hand, if you do need this stuff, it's very nice to know it's there. And if you ask a bare drive vendor to add the stuff, you may be surprised at how much they charge. The buying checklist in Table 5-4 will help you choose the right drive and supplier.

> Before buying a hard drive (or CD-ROM drive), check to see that you have an extra power connector available from your power supply, and that it can reach the drive bay where you want to insert the drive. If you don't have a spare power connector, get a Y connector that turns one existing connector into two. If you *have* a power connector but it doesn't reach far enough, you *could* get a power extender—but a better move is to get a Y connector anyway and stick electrical tape over the unused end. Then, when you install your "next" new drive, you'll have a power line ready and waiting.

Table 5–4 Hard Drive Buying Checklist

	Product #1	Product #2	Product #3	Product #4
Size				
Price per megabyte				
Interface (EIDE, Fast-ATA, IDE, SCSI?)				
Speed (ns)				
Complete kit or bare drive?				
Free Phone Support (# days)				
Warranty				
Price				
Shipping				
Tax				
Total Price				

Hard Drive Sources

Insight
6820 South Hart Avenue
Tempe, AZ 85283
1-800-INSIGHT
www.insight.com

These folks sell more hard drives than anyone on Earth. The prices are very good (not quite excellent, but definitely very good). They've been at it for more than a decade. I've bought several drives from them, and I've never had a complaint.

Dirt Cheap Drives
3716 Timber Drive
Dickinson, TX 77539
1-800-473-0960

Comp-U-Plus
20 Robert Pitt Drive
Monsey, NY
1-800-287-2323
www.compuplus.com

I hesitated mentioning Comp-U-Plus. As they claim, they really **do** *have the lowest prices advertised in* Computer Shopper *on bare drives—but they charge premium prices for the little cables and whatnots you may need. If you have a cheap alternative source for that stuff, you might give them a try.*

> When you install your IDE hard drive, remember to
> 1. Assign one hard drive as master and another as slave.
> 2. Consider running Windows and your primary software from the faster drive (typically, the newer one).

CD-ROM Drives

The first dirty little secret about CD-ROM drives is that faster isn't always better. The second secret is that, more than any other computer component except memory, the price of CD-ROMs has fluctuated dramatically over the past two years. Quite simply, CD-ROM drive supply and demand keep slipping out of balance.

In 1995 and early 1996, consumers moved from 4X to 6X and 8X drives, leaving a glut of perfectly useful 2X and 4X drives to be sold dirt cheap. One drive manufacturer, Reveal, sold nearly a quarter-billion dollars in hardware one year—and went bankrupt the following year, when it couldn't manage the product transition.

Some of Reveal's drives are still floating around as close-outs, or showing up in auctions. They're cheap—occasionally available for less than $50. I can't recommend them, however, because there's no longer any tech support (except through a third-party 900 number, at $2 per minute). Moreover, users have had mixed results with the Windows 95 Reveal drivers that are available on the World Wide Web.

This past winter, the vendors started moving to faster drives before customers were ready to accept them. That meant shortages of 8X drives, which suddenly couldn't be found for less than $100—while 10X and 12X drives were easy to find, if you were willing to pay a premium. In spring 1997, 12X and even 16X drives became de rigeur.

Do you need them? Probably not.

A faster CD-ROM drive has two benefits. First, if you install quite a bit of software from CD-ROM, you can get the job done more quickly. You might install an office suite in 5–10 minutes instead of 15 to 30 minutes.

Second, a faster CD-ROM streams data to your processor more quickly. That often means faster transitions between scenes in computer games—but it doesn't necessarily mean that the games themselves will play more quickly. Faster data transfer may also be helpful if you make heavy use of computer databases, such as telephone directories.

If you don't fit into these categories, you probably don't need a high-speed CD-ROM drive. Keep in mind that most software titles are still developed for the broadest installed base: 2X and 4X drives. One major magazine tested 12X drives recently and found they only averaged 20 percent better performance than 6X drives, possibly because of interface bottlenecks.[6]

Unfortunately, "slow" drives are practically impossible to find these days. My suggestions:

- Keep an eye out for 6X drives. These were popular only briefly, and some suppliers may have overstock.
- Look for those all-too-rare bargains on 8X drives. Some may appear in the form of complete multimedia upgrade packages.

---

6.   You can sometimes do better by purchasing the slowest CD-ROM drive you can find and adding a software cache accelerator.

▲ If the price is right, consider 10X drives: 10X is another drive speed that came and went quickly but is perfectly functional.

▲ Make sure to purchase either IDE or SCSI drives—that way you won't have to worry about hard-to-find custom interfaces.

More CD-ROM Buying Tips

Make sure you get everything you need, including the power cable and the interface cable. I was once quoted an exceptionally low price for a bare CD-ROM drive—but then $12 more for the power cable and another $12 for the interface cable.

Often, the biggest issue with older CD-ROM drives is finding the right driver for the operating system you want to use. When Windows 95 was introduced, many CD-ROM drives required new drivers—and not every vendor provided them. One of the best places to find new Windows 95 (and Windows NT 4.0) drivers is the Windows Sources Driver Finder, at **http://finders.zdnet.com**; another useful compendium of CD-ROM drivers is at **http://final.dystopia.fi/~jargon/files/drivers/cdrom_d.html**.

Recently, 4X CD-ROM changers—which can hold three or four disks at a time—have become widespread. My experience with these hasn't been good. These drives have been known to confuse Windows 95, which does not always keep accurate track of disks as you change them. There have also been reports of quality problems with 4X changers manufactured by Sanyo and sold under a variety of names, including Torisan. Check on the Web before buying.

Where to look for inexpensive CD-ROM drives? Here are a couple of potential sources:

NEC LikeNew
1-800-NEC-INFO
Sells refurbished products by NEC, a top-quality Japanese manufacturer.

A2Z Computers
1-800-983-8889
Still sells 4X and 6X internal drives at press time.

Computer Geeks Discount Outlet
5931 Sea Lion Place #108
Carlsbad, CA 92008
1-619-603-9242
www.compgeeks.com
Also still sells 4X and 6X internal drives—even Sound Blaster 2X Multimedia Kits for under $70!

The buying checklist in Table 5-5 will help you compare product features and suppliers.

Table 5–5 CD-ROM Buying Checklist

	Product #1	Product #2	Product #3	Product #4
Speed (#X)				
Windows 95 Drivers?				
Other OS Drivers				
Source for Driver Updates				
Interface (IDE, SCSI, proprietary?)				
***Interesting* Software (exclude software you won't use)**				
Company in business?				
Free Phone Support (# days)				
Warranty				
Price				
Shipping				
Tax				
Total Price				

The Spectre of Multimedia Past

Two multimedia companies that are dead and gone, but whose products linger on in Cheapskate channels, are MediaVision and Reveal. Count on getting no technical support for products from either of these companies. (Well, actually you *can* get technical support for Reveal products at $2.00/minute by calling 1-900-225-3000. But it won't take long for the support to cost you more than the product did.)

If you're stuck with a product from an orphan company that needs a driver, another strategy is to try to identify a chipset inside that product, and see if a driver is available from the chipset manufacturer. For example, many Reveal CD-ROMs used Opti 929 chipsets and will work under Windows 95 with drivers created for those chipsets.

Monitors: What You See, and What You Get

There are two ways to judge a monitor: by specifications, and by the way you feel when you're working at it. Specifications are important; your eyes' subjective opinion is more important. We'll consider the "objective" specs first.

Monitors by the Numbers

For 14", 15", and 17" monitors, look for a dot pitch of 0.28" (0.25" for Trinitron-style monitors). Lower numbers mean crisper images. 0.31 is a judgment call, 0.39 is horrific, 0.42 downright criminal. These days, most new monitors have 0.28 dot pitch. Now and then you'll find an exception, for example, some low-end Orchestra® brand and Packard Bell monitors. With used monitors, you have to check extra carefully.

By the way, a 14" monitor isn't really 14" diagonal. The number you really care about is "viewable area." For example, many 17" monitors have a viewable area of 15.1" or 15.5". Imagine if Campbell's filled their soup cans to 15.1 ounces and called them 17 ounce cans!

No matter *what* size the monitor is, make sure it's noninterlaced. Interlacing is an old shortcut borrowed from television, but it leads to a noticeable flicker that can hurt your eyes and drive you nuts. Again, interlacing is mostly a thing of the past, but make sure.

The last number you want to know is refresh rate. The higher the better. You want 60 Hz minimum. Newer, more expensive monitors can run at 75 Hz or even 85 Hz. Refresh rates vary depending on how high a resolution you intend to use. For example, a monitor might have a refresh rate of 75 Hz at standard 640x480 VGA resolution, but a lower refresh rate at 1024x768 SuperVGA.

> **tip** It is entirely possible that your monitor may cost you more in electricity during its life than it did to purchase. (Monitors use between 60 and 200 watts of power. At a dime per kilowatt hour, that's between $240 and $800 in electricity over five years, if you leave your monitor on all the time.)
>
> Turn your monitor off when you're not going to use it for awhile. Or consider purchasing an "Energy Star" monitor that meets the EPA's energy-saving guidelines.

> *Warning!* In almost all cases, stay away from older "CGA" or "EGA" monitors. They're useless for Windows 95, and while EGA monitors will work with Windows 3.1, you'll pay more for new glasses than you'll save.

A Ten-Step Guide to Evaluating Monitors

Now for the subjective side of testing a monitor. The Internet's video FAQ is an exceptionally good source of information on monitors; much of the following is borrowed from there. [7]

7. This is the FAQ associated with the **comp.sys.ibm.pc.hardware.video** newsgroup. This FAQ was compiled and written by Michael Scott with contributions by Ralph Valentino, Sam Goldwasser, Bill Nott, Andy Laberge and Dylan Rhodes. This FAQ may be found in many locations on the Web, including **www.heartlab. rri.uwo.ca/vidfaq/** ©Michael Scott.

1. Warm up the monitor for at least 10 minutes before you check it.
2. Eliminate extraneous glare.
3. Set the monitor's contrast fairly high.
4. Check the back of the monitor: It should be warm but not exceptionally hot.
5. Check bright text against a black background, first in the center and then at the corners of the screen. Make sure all letters are readable, especially letters that can easily blur, such as lowercase "e."
6. Check white lines against a black background. If they're white, great. If you see distinct bands of colors that shouldn't be there, not so great.
7. Check whether images bend or bulge toward or away from the center of the screen. The easiest way to do that is to place something straight—such as a piece of paper—against the side of the screen image.
8. Display solid reds, greens, and blues—make sure they appear solid in color throughout.
9. Display a white screen; make sure the brightness is consistent and there are no colored blotches.
10. Step back, and just look at the monitor. Is it clear? Bright? Sharp? Flicker-free? Do you *like* it?

Warning! Some systems manufacturers, such as Monorail, have begun offering computer systems that use notebook-PC style passive-matrix LCDs instead of monitors. These LCDs are just *not* good enough for day-in, day-out use—and the LCDs that *are* good enough still cost too much to be included in standard desktop PCs.

The buying checklist in Table 5-6 will help you compare product features and suppliers.

Table 5–6 Monitor Buying Checklist

	Product #1	Product #2	Product #3	Product #4
Size				
Viewable area				
Dot pitch				
Noninterlaced?				
Refresh rate				
Maximum resolution				
Company in business?				
Free Phone Support (# days)				
Warranty				
Price				
Shipping				
Tax				
Total Price				

Good Deals on Refurb Monitors

New monitor prices *are* dropping—but since much of a monitor's value is in old-fashioned stuff like picture tubes, these prices aren't dropping as quickly or as consistently as other computer equipment.

One way to save on a monitor is to buy a refurb or overstock model. Most major computer manufacturers contract out monitor manufacturing to one of a small number of respected manufacturers. The monitors may carry names like AST and Dell, but they're manufactured by companies like Mitsubishi and MAG. As with computers, when sales fall short or customers return monitors, these monitors become available for resale. In some cases, the manufacturers commonly sell them to distributors, or at auction, and smaller companies then offer them to you. In other cases, they're available directly from the computer company.

Currently, 14" monitors average around $200; 15" monitors roughly $250; 17" monitors around $475. These prices are all roughly 20–25 percent below comparable new monitors.

Sources for refurbished and overstock monitors include

NEC LikeNew
1-800-NEC-INFO

Surplus Direct
P.O. Box 2000
Hood River, OR 97031-2000
1-800-753-7877
www.surplusdirect.com

Krex Computers
9320 Waukegan Road
Morton Grove, IL 60053
800-222-KREX, 847-967-0200
www. krex800.com

Second Source Engineering
800-848-8700
www.second-source.com

Synnex Budget Computer Depot
4155 Stevens Creek Blvd.
Santa Clara, CA 95051
1-408-249-7266
www.synnex.com/mspec.html

Computer Discounters Inc.
10543 Ewing Road
Beltsville, MD 20705
301-595-0500
www.computerdiscounters.w1.com

Computer Discounters retail location
8383 Leesburg Pike
Vienna, VA 22180
1-703-556-7782

Silver Reef
1-714-366-6864
www.billboards.com/sreef1.html
Specializes in Sony monitors for Macintosh.

Data Trend Inc.
South Braintree Park
1515 Washington Street
Braintree, MA 02184
1-800-366-7060

Data Trend International also now operates an outlet store for AST
Computer, Inc., AST Outlet Direct, 1-800-540-7060;
www.astoutlet.com.

Electrified Discounters
110 Webb Street
Hamden, CT 06517
1-800-678-8585; 203-787-4246
www.electrified.com
Refurbished IBM monitors.

Computer Service Point
69 Bloomingdale Road
Hicksville, NY 11801
516-937-3800
Refurbished NEC monitors.

Chipheads Unlimited
167 Cove Drive
Coppell, TX 75019
972-393-4216

Also try the ONSALE auction at *www.onsale.com.*

tip

Giant Monitors, Tiny Price

Huge monitors. Sure would be great to have one, but they cost upwards of $1,500. Most of us Cheapskates are hard-pressed to make that kind of financial commitment.

But here's an idea: You can sometimes find 21" monitors from older UNIX workstations for very low cost, occasionally even free. (Ask around at your local university, at any engineering or R&D organization in your neighborhood, or at one of those DRMS military surplus stores we mentioned in Chapter 3.) Not only are the monitors inexpensive; many of them were also manufactured by some of the top names in "monitor-dom," including Sony, Hitachi and Mitsubishi.

The workstations are obsolete, and their owners really have no use for the monitors now. Moreover, these are "fixed-frequency" monitors that weren't designed to work with standard PC video cards. You *can*, however, make them work with your PC—with a little effort and the right cable.

There are two ways to go about it. If you're technical, visit the Fixed Frequency Video FAQ at **www.devo.com/video/** to learn whether you can cobble together a hardware solution that will make your standard VGA card and fixed-frequency monitor work together. For everyone else, the solution is a custom video card designed specifically to work with the fixed-frequency monitor you have. Companies that make these specialized video cards include

PCG
1-800-255-9893; 1-310-260-4747
www.photonweb.com

Software Integrators
1-800-547-2349
www.si87.com

Mirage
1-800-228-3349; 1-310-301-4545
www.mirage-mmc.com

These video cards are more expensive than standard SVGA cards, but they're still a small fraction of the cost of a standard 21" monitor and video card.

> **Mirage offers discounts to customers who mention the Internet's video FAQ.**

Video Cards

The first thing you need to know in buying a video card is: What kind of slot are you going to put it in? Nearly all current PCs come with PCI slots; most 486s came with a VL-Bus slot specially intended for video; in older standard systems,[8] you simply use one of your standard "ISA" slots. Not surprisingly, PCI cards tend to offer better performance than VL-Bus cards, which offer better performance than ISA cards—though performance can vary widely depending on the individual card and operating system you're using.

If you have an older ISA-only system, when would you even consider a video upgrade? Most of the time, you wouldn't. On the other hand,

▲ If you have an ISA video card with only 256K, you might find it worth the $30 or so needed to get a generic 1-Mb VGA card.

▲ If you have upgraded to Windows since you purchased your computer, you might find it worth the money to purchase an inexpensive "Windows accelerator" video card.

---

8.   Excluding most PS/2s.

If you have a 486 system with VL-Bus, chances are your video card already takes advantage of it. But, if for some reason you have a VL-Bus system with an ISA video card, *and* you use high-bandwidth applications like video games, *and* you're planning to keep the computer awhile, you might consider a close-out VL-Bus video card. An example: the Paradise 32-bit card recently available from Surplus Direct for $39.99.

In any case, I wouldn't invest more than $50 in a video card upgrade for a pre-Pentium system.

Sources for inexpensive video cards include

> Computer Geeks Discount Outlet
> 5931 Sea Lion Place #108
> Carlsbad, CA 92008
> 1-619-603-9242
> **www.compgeeks.com**

> XWY Direct
> 313 South Second Street
> Laramie, WY 82070
> 1-307-745-5608

Modems: When to Buy?

Modems appear to follow a roughly consistent pricing curve throughout their product life cycles; you can decide for yourself how long you want to wait.

Stage 1: New modem technology is introduced to consumers at premium prices, $200–$250.

Stage 2: Competition drives prices down well below $200.

Stage 3: Lower-cost technologies are introduced to make it possible to deliver the same speed for around $125; meanwhile, the price of modem chipsets drops, allowing for generic modems that tend to drive prices down further. Leading manufacturers attempt to resist price erosion as long as possible through rebates and added features.

Stage 4: Leading manufacturers prepare to introduce the *next* generation of modems, as prices for the current generation settle around $100, and second-tier manufacturers offer modems for as little as $75.

Of course, this time around, nobody knows what the next generation will be; 56K appears to be the end of the line: The industry is consolidating, and manufacturers like U.S. Robotics are expanding into new products. So we'll see. But you can expect today's 56K modem to cost 30–40 percent less in a year, no matter what.

A Closer Look at 56K Modems

If the Web does nothing else, it sure sells a lot of modems. The latest hot deal is 56-Kbps modems. Should you bite?

Nobody could fault you for wanting faster Web access. If only the Web were fast, it would be just about perfect. But there are some things you should know about buying modems—and 56-Kbps modems in particular.

First of all, when it comes to modems, *standards matter*. The international standards process is slow, cumbersome, and bureaucratic, so it's no surprise that modem vendors sometimes try to beat it to the punch with new, nonstandard modem technologies. Unfortunately, modems that use nonstandard technologies can't communicate at top speed with modems that don't.

Today's "prestandardized" 56-Kbps modems follow two very different sets of standards; U.S. Robotics' x2 and Rockwell's K56 (sometimes called K56Plus or K56flex). It now appears that these two standards will be merged into one—especially if U.S. Robotics completes its planned merger with 3COM. But it hasn't happened yet. So before you purchase a 56-Kbps modem, make sure you know exactly what upgrade commitments the vendor has made, so you'll wind up with a modem that meets the final standard.

Even if the standards get worked out, there are some other things you should know about 56K modems:

1. They're 56K *receive only,* at the user's end: the maximum speed for sending is still 33.6K, even if you're sending to another user with the same 56K modem.

2. There's currently an FCC regulation limiting modems to 53.3K—and modem speed depends heavily on the quality of your phone lines. If you're having trouble getting the full 33.6K or 28.8K your current modem is supposed to provide, you'll have trouble getting anywhere near 56K. Many users may find themselves achieving 40–45K—much better than 28.8, but not what you might be expecting.

3. For the first time, 56K modems require you to have a telephone connection that utilizes digital technology which isn't universal. Before investing, ask your Internet Service Provider (ISP) whether your telephone exchange qualifies.

4. If you're planning to use a 56K modem to access the Internet, you need an Internet Service Provider that supports the modem you're using. Many don't—especially smaller providers who will need to invest several thousands of dollars in new equipment. Even larger providers such as CompuServe and America Online may only support 56K in certain cities.

5. No matter what fast modem you buy, you need to make sure your computer has a fast 16550 UART chip. Most Pentium systems do; most earlier systems don't; there are exceptions to both rules of thumb. The easiest way to solve the problem is to purchase an internal modem that costs less and has a fast UART chip built into it.

The Long-Term Move to Software Modems

Modem hardware doesn't do anything that couldn't be done with software if only your computer were powerful enough. Every year, computers get more powerful, so it becomes possible to move more capabilities from hardware to software—theoretically, at least, allowing for modems that are cheaper and easier to upgrade.

Really *fast* Internet access is the pot of gold at the end of the rainbow—always just tantalizingly out of reach. If you're considering investing hundreds of dollars in a fast modem, you may want to know where your alternatives stand.

Integrated Services Digital Network (ISDN), from the local telephone companies, is finally widespread—and after a solid decade, most phone companies are finally figuring out how to adequately support it. Standard residential ISDN operates at 64K (one "B-channel") or 128K (two "B-channels"); costs tend to be 1 to 3 cents per minute per B-channel. Plus installation, typically at least $100 sometimes more. Plus an ISDN adapter, typically $200-$300. On top of that, many service providers will charge you extra for all the extra data you're getting, especially if you run your Web connection at 128K. It gets expensive quick. If you're seriously considering ISDN, choosing a 56K modem instead might save you a bundle.

Cable modems take advantage of the fact that your cable company's coaxial cables can carry tons of data alongside Nick-at-Nite and the Cartoon Channel. They could *conceivably* deliver the Internet at 10 to 50 times the speed of ISDN. The cable modems themselves have recently dropped in price, to around $300—the target price the cable companies have been shooting for. However, the cable companies' infrastructure is designed to be one-way; much of it has to be reconfigured for two-way data transmission. That takes money. Many cable companies are already carrying enough debt to choke a horse—and satellite companies are skimming away their best customers. So it remains to be seen when cable modems will show up in *your* backyard—and what the service will cost. Best guess: $35-$50 per month.

xDSL technologies (ADSL, SDSL, and a bunch of other initials) are the phone companies' answer to cable modems. Originally designed to squeeze pay-per-view movies through standard telephone lines, xDSL can also deliver several megabits of data per second, and in early tests, it seems to work. But the back-office equipment isn't in place to deliver that much data to millions of customers. It may take until the year 1999 or 2000, according to some insider estimates—and even then, not in all areas. And the phone companies aren't notorious for rushing to sell new technologies that cannibalize older, slower technologies (like ISDN) that they're still paying for.[a]

(continued on next page)

a.   Make a liar out of me! At presstime, Ameritech announced that its ADSL trials were going so well, it would begin deploying ADSL *before* 1998. Maybe you can teach an old dog... .

(continued)

Satellite dish technologies may be the sleeper in all this. Right now, the fastest way for most people to get Internet service is DirecPC, a sibling of DirecTV that delivers 400 Kb of Internet service via a dish similar to the DSS TV dish. DirecPC is *expensive*: $400+ for the dish, $100–$200 for installation, $40/month for the most basic off-peak service plan, plus the cost of an Internet service provider. But it works, and DirecTV is introducing a dish that will receive both TV and the Web—making this potentially more attractive.

The real excitement, however, may be in a new joint venture between DirecTV, Microsoft, and Adaptec to deliver a constant high-speed Internet feed via satellite— as much as 300 Gb per day. You download the sites you want onto your hard disk, where you can browse them whenever you feel like it. Again it remains to be seen how much this will cost—and whether it will make the entire Web available, or just a carefully controlled commercial element of it. IBM and Gateway have promised systems that include this technology, possibly by Christmas 1997. Add-on boards that do the same thing are expected in 1998.

None of this stuff is exactly "priced for Cheapskates," but if you use the Web heavily for business (or entertainment), one of these options may be worth it. You might want to hold out a little longer to see how things shake out in *your* neck of the woods.

The first step in this direction was called Rockwell Protocol Interface, or RPI. So-called RPI modems depended on your computer for data compression and error correction. From the start, RPI modems were often 30 percent less expensive than comparable non-RPI modems. Unfortunately, they needed special communications software which supported RPI. Many standard communications packages didn't, and some still don't—leading to failed or dropped connections, corrupted data, and enormous frustration. For more information on making RPI modems work the way they're supposed to, visit **www.nb.rockwell.com/mcd/bman/rpi_faq.html**

A list of first-generation RPI modems follows in Table 5-7.

Table 5–7 RPI Modems That Require Special Care, Feeding, Data Compression, and Error Correction

Brand	Model
Aspen	14.4
Best Data	1442VF, 1442FTQ, 1442VTQ, 1442FTX
Boca	1440Ae
Cal Com	1442I
Cambridge Telecom	1414HI
Cardinal	MVP144I, MVP144XF, MVP144iv2, MVP144xv2
Delrina	Delrina 4 in 1
Dynalink	1414H
Global Village	Gold II
Logicode Quicktel	14.4LH
Maxtech (GVC)	F(M)-114H
Prometheus	14.4I
Supra	Express 144I (not Express Plus)
U.S Robotics	Sportster SI 14.4
Zoltrix	FM 144 ATI, FM 144 ATE, FM 144 ATF
Zoom	14.4 PC, 14.4 EX, Serial #s: xxxZA1ixxx, xxxZA2ixxx, xxxZF1ixxx, xxxZF4ixxx

Later versions of RPI, called RPI+ and WinRPI, use a special Windows driver that handles data compression and error correction; this should solve many of the problems. U.S. Robotics' WinModem is a very popular example. Still, RPI in any form remains unpopular with some on-line services, especially CompuServe.

Whenever you move processing from specialized hardware to PC software, you load more work onto your system's processor. You probably wouldn't want to run an RPI modem on a system slower than, say, a 486/66.

In the next year, keep an eye out for modems that go far beyond RPI, off-loading both modem control and "data pump" functions onto your processor. These are sometimes called Host Signal Processing (HSP) modems.

HSP modems eat computing power like crazy. Many of them will require *at least* a Pentium 166 with MMX, maybe more, to deliver top-notch performance. They'll also lock you into specific operating systems that run their software. But they offer the potential of driving down modem costs significantly—and simplifying upgrades.[9] And they're the harbinger of a long-term trend toward integrating communications into your computer.

In five years, you may be asking the same question you might have asked five years ago: *What's a modem?*

If You Only Need Fax

Virtually every modem sold for the past several years has send and receive fax capabilities built in—the same fax capabilities built into fax machines costing hundreds of dollars. Assuming you have fax software, about the only thing these modems *won't* do is let you fax documents you've created or marked up by hand. (If you have a scanner, you can do that, too.)

And if you have a laser printer, you can print your incoming faxes there—banishing low-quality, expensive thermal paper from your life forever.

It's common for small businesses (and some individuals) to have computers that will never be used to surf the Web but *will* be used to send faxes. (The productivity reasons are compelling: With PC-based fax, you don't have to print a document, you don't have to walk over to the fax machine, you don't have to wait your turn—you just "print" your document to fax, and the computer takes care of everything else.)

The point is, you don't need a fast new modem to do this—*just a modem that will send and receive faxes at 9600 bps.* Even many modems that transmit data as slowly as 2400 bps will send and receive faxes at 9600 bps. And just about any brand will do, including generic brands.[10]

▲ ▲

9.   To give you an idea, Computer Geeks Discount Outlet currently sells the PC-Tel 33.6-Kbps software modem for $43.00 plus shipping. Minimum—I repeat, *minimum*—system requirements are a 100-Mhz Pentium.

10.   There are a few esoteric brands that Windows 95's built-in fax software has trouble with, including early Gateway Telepaths, some expensive AT&T Paradyne faxmodems, and a number of European brands. But a generic no-name Hayes-compatible fax modem will do just fine.

Fax is mature technology, easy for fax board manufacturers to implement—they just buy a standard chipset, dirt cheap.

> *Warning!* When faxmodems were first introduced, some sent faxes at 9600 bps but received at only 4800 bps. Unless you virtually never receive a fax, avoid these.

All the Modem Answers You Could Ever Want

By the way, if you're having problems getting all the performance out of your modem that you paid for, I'll bet you'll find the answer at the Navas Modem FAQ™ site, by John Navas and the Navas Group. Navas has compiled answers to just about every modem question imaginable, including remarkably detailed guidance on

- ▲ The best ways to share one incoming phone line for voice, fax, and data, and avoid the cost of a second line
- ▲ Oddball problems that seem to afflict market-leading U.S. Robotics modems
- ▲ When to finally invest in a 56K modem
- ▲ How to troubleshoot modems that just plain won't work

It's all at: **http://users.aimnet.com/~jnavas/modem/faq.html** (see Figure 5-1).

Where to Buy

For new modems, the best sources are the major mail-order houses. The easiest way to compare current prices is with Computer Shopper's NetBuyer service, at **www.netbuyer.com**.

Computer Discount Warehouse
1020 E. Lake Cook Road
Buffalo Grove, IL 60089
1-800-608-4239
www.cdw.com

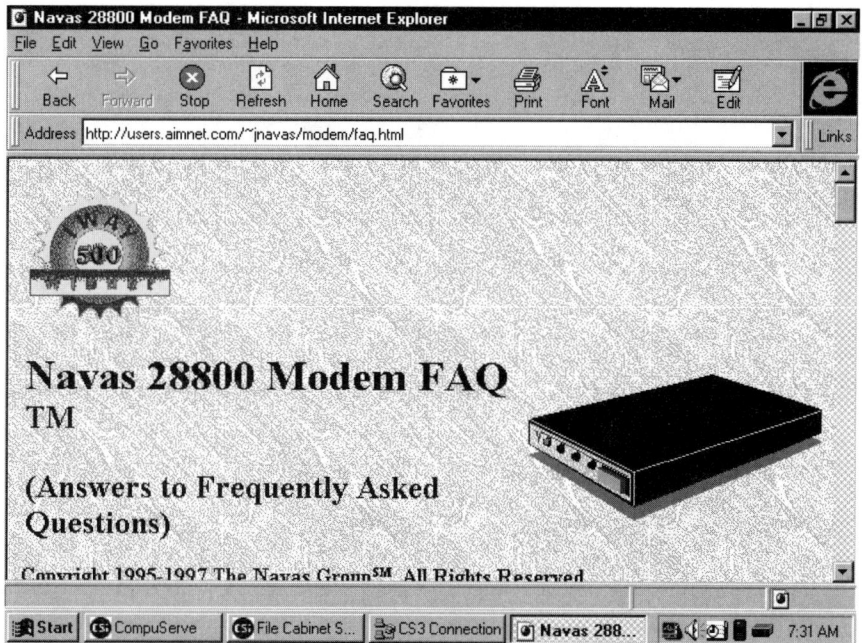

Figure 5–1   Everything you ever wanted to know about why your modem doesn't work as well as advertised.

PC Connection
6 Mill Street
Marlow, NH 03456
1-800-800-5555
www.pcconnection.com

Comp-U-Plus
20 Robert Pitt Drive
Monsey, NY
1-800-287-2323
www.compuplus.com

The Buying Checklist in Table 5-8 will help you compare products and sources.

Table 5–8 Modem Buying Checklist

	Product #1	Product #2	Product #3	Product #4
Speed				
Internal/External?				
Protocol (x2, K56flex, V.42, etc.?)				
Traditional hardware modem (or WinRPI, or HSP)?				
Company in business?				
Free Phone Support (# days)				
Warranty				
Price				
Shipping				
Tax				
Total Price				

Sound Cards

I won't spend a lot of time on sound cards, because I don't have a lot of really good Cheapskate advice. "Frequency modulation" (FM) cards are cheaper than "wavetable" cards and don't sound as good. If you're not heavily into sound, FM cards are fine. 16-bit cards sound better than 8-bit cards. (Many people believe the Sound Blaster AWE32 is a 32-bit sound card, but it isn't—32 refers to the number of "voices" the card can generate at once.)

For some reason, it's proven difficult to clone Sound Blaster audio hardware properly, so many of the cheap "Sound Blaster-compatible" cards out there really aren't 100 percent compatible and can give you trouble under Windows 95. At minimum, you're likely to need custom drivers (if they're available for the operating system you want to use).

If your sound needs are minimal, they might be worth a try. Otherwise, just use the cheapest official Creative Labs Sound Blaster card you'll be comfortable with, from the least expensive source selling it.[11]

If you have better Cheapskate advice than that (or successes to report using clone cards), let me know about it. In the meantime, Table 5-9 lets you compare sound cards and their suppliers.

Printers

If you're considering a new printer, the best source of information is *PC Magazine's* annual printer issue, typically published in late October with an early November cover date. (Missed it? Search for "personal printers" at **www.zdnet.com** to read the individual reviews.) Your second best source of information is *Consumer Reports*.

Printers have changed a lot over the past few years: daisy-wheels are long gone; even dot-matrix printers are pretty much on the way out except for duplicate forms printing. (Of course, that means you can find rock-solid old Epson or Panasonic dot-matrix printers at every second yard sale, often for $20 or less. You might consider picking one up as a backup printer, or if money's tight, as a student's printer—especially if it's a *24-pin* model. The output from 24-pin dot matrix printers can be surprisingly good, if slow.)

The latest change: Inkjet printers have finally become more competitive with laser printers. The new generation of inkjets offers extraordinary color quality and black and white quality that's almost as good as laser printers (though it may still not be good enough if you're using the printer extensively for business, or for desktop publishing). And color inkjets can cost at least $100–$150 less than roughly comparable black-and-white lasers. Not surprisingly, more than five inkjets were sold for every laser last year. There are a lot of us Cheapskates out here.

11.　Sound Blaster licenses its "Vibra" chipset to a few other manufacturers, including computer companies that integrate the card directly on their motherboards. Those boards *are* Sound Blaster-compatible.

Table 5–9 Sound Card Buying Checklist

	Product #1	Product #2	Product #3	Product #4
Bits (16, 8?)				
Wavetable or FM?				
True SoundBlaster chipset?				
Windows 95 Drivers?				
Other OS Drivers?				
Source for Driver Updates?				
IDE interface for CD-ROM?				
Interesting Software (exclude software you won't use)				
Company in business?				
Free Phone Support (# days)				
Warranty				
Price				
Shipping				
Tax				
Total Price				

Black-and-white ink prices have come down somewhat. If you choose the inkjet route, you should look for a printer that does black-and-white pages for no more than 3 cents per page, list price. That's still a penny more than a contemporary laser—which means that all else equal, a $400 laser printer will become cheaper than a $300 inkjet after you print your 10,000th page. Of course all things are never equal: Comparing printer consumables costs is a lot like comparing long distance companies. They don't make it easy.

By the way, those "average" pages have 5 percent coverage. If you print posters, newsletters, pictures, things get more expensive. And if you start actually *using* the color in your color inkjet printer, well, your costs go through the roof. See Chapter 6 for some ideas on reducing the cost of inkjet printing.

These days, pretty much every new inkjet printer is a color inkjet. If you don't need color, that means you can get some terrific deals on older black-and-white inkjets. At the moment, the easiest one to find is the DECwriter 100i, for around $75.

If you're leaning toward laser, of course the market leader is Hewlett-Packard. They make excellent printers and charge you accordingly. They've established a price umbrella: Almost every other printer manufacturer comes in underneath that umbrella. You won't go wrong with a laser printer from Okidata, NEC, or Epson, and you'll probably pay at least $50 less.

As with modems, there's a trend to lower the cost of laser printers by allowing the host computer to handle more of the processing that would have been managed by the printer. This only makes sense if you have a fast computer with plenty of memory, or if your printing needs are relatively light. If you have, for example, a low-end 486 and you send a large print job to one of these printers, you may find that your system slows to a crawl while you're printing. Also, these printers work only in Windows. In fact, they use Windows' built-in Graphics Device Interface (GDI) to send already formatted images to the screen.

The best solution might be a so-called "hybrid" printer, which does some processing on your computer and some in the printer. You still save some money, but you sacrifice much less performance. One such device is the NEC SuperScript 860.

Whether you're considering inkjet or laser, you can Table 5-10 below to make your comparisons:

Table 5–10 Printer Buying Checklist

	Product #1	Product #2	Product #3	Product #4
Resolution (dots per inch)				
Speed (pages per minute)				
Color? (If color, how many ink containers?)				
Windows 95 drivers?				
Other OS drivers				
Sound for driver updates				
Interesting software (exclude software you won't use)				
Require expensive IEEE parallel cable?				
Toner/inkjet cartridge cost				
Consumables cost/page				
Economy mode?				
Free phone support? (# days)				
Warranty				
Price				
Shipping				
Tax				
Total Price				

Refurbished Printers

Laser printers are dependent on mechanical parts, so buying a refurbished laser isn't quite the no-brainer that buying a refurbished PC can be. Still, there are some prominent sources for refurb laser printers. Surprisingly, the popular Hewlett-Packard 5L is available as a refurb. MEI/Micro Center (1-800-634-3478) has been offering it for $299, a full $100 less than new. You can also purchase refurbished Okidata, Epson, and Lexmark printers from Electrified Discounters (see Figure 5-2), 1-800-678-8585.

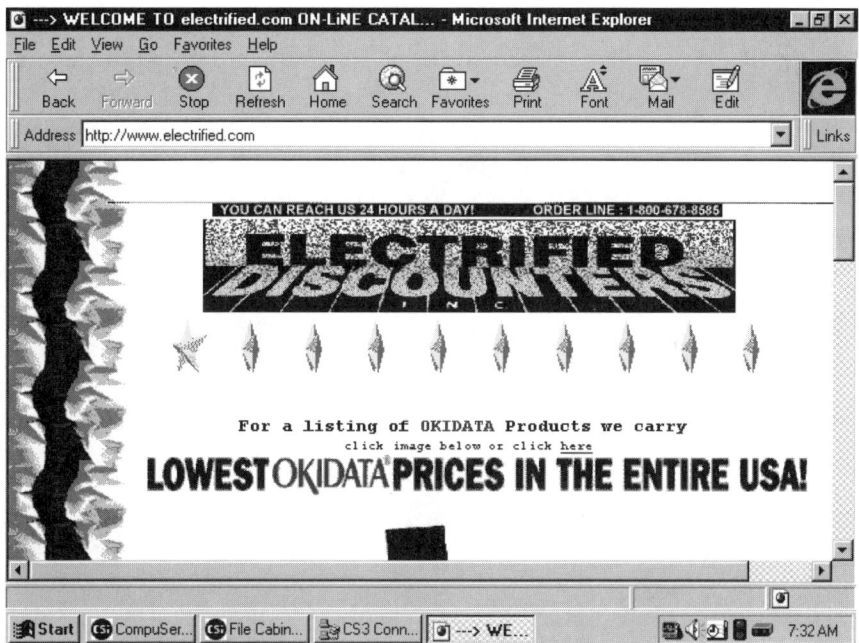

Figure 5–2   Electrified Discounters, the center of the universe for people who want to buy refurb Okidata printers.

> **tip**
> On many inkjet printers, you'll have to replace an expensive printhead several times during the life of your printer. PC Connection (1-800-800-0009) sells remanufactured printheads at a significant discount.

Processor Upgrades

Processor upgrades can be very seductive: Replace one chip, and suddenly your system goes from pokey to state of the art. Of course it's rarely like that, but if you have the right system—and the right expectations—a low-cost processor upgrade could extend its life for another year or two.

And *that* would very likely be worth the money.

Several companies manufacture chip upgrades intended to increase the speed of a 486 system to roughly that of a Pentium 75. That's a fairly low-end Pentium, but still a sizable performance improvement—*if* you're upgrading from a low-end 486 such as a 486/25 or 486/33 system. (If you replace a 486/100 chip with one of these upgrades, you'll hardly see any improvement at all.)

Most of these upgrades use the same processor: the Am5x86-P-75. (This processor has had a number of incarnations; for a long time, it was called a 5x86-133, implying equivalence with a Pentium 133—greatly misleading, to say the least. It's really a 486 on serious steroids.) Most of these upgrades cost as little as $80–$120—not surprising, because the chip itself can be purchased for under $40 these days.

> **tip**
> If you're technically oriented and have some time to kill, you *may* be able to perform a comparable upgrade yourself at significantly less cost by combining a standard AMD Am5x86-P-75 microprocessor, a voltage regulator that allows 5-volt motherboards to use the 3.3-volt Am5x86-P-75 chip and a fan/heat sink. One good source for the voltage regulator you'll need is JDR Microdevices (*www.jdr.com*).

Installation tends to be surprisingly easy, but many of these upgrades require a driver to work—which means you only gain the benefits when you're running operating systems the manufacturer has provided drivers for.

These upgrades work in most 486 systems but by no means all. For one thing, your system board must provide jumpers or switches to set clock speed and bus speed. This doesn't mean you should avoid the upgrades altogether, but it does mean you should

▲ Check the Web sites of the upgrade manufacturers to see if they've certified your system as compatible.

▲ Make sure to purchase your upgrade from a company that will give you a money-back guarantee *with no restocking charges.*

Some newer products use Cyrix 6x86 chips to upgrade low-end Pentium computers to much faster Pentium systems. So far, however, these upgrades are very expensive—and don't include MMX. And speaking of expensive, of course there are Intel's authorized OverDrive upgrades, some of which do include MMX—but typically cost several hundred dollars. That's more than you would pay for a bare-bones system that would upgrade *everything* on your motherboard, not just the processor.

Processor upgrade manufacturers include

Kingston Technology
17600 Newhope St.
Fountain Valley, CA 92708
1-800-337-8410
www.kingston.com
Turbochip 133, Am5x86-P-75 processor, for 486s, roughly Pentium 75 performance, list price $109.

CCT
P.O. Box 3350
West Sedona, AZ 86340-3350
1-800-CCT-MENU
www.cct.com
CCT 486-100-MHz kit, 486/100 processor, roughly Pentium 60 performance, list price $79; CCT 586-133, Am5x86-P-75 processor, for 486s, roughly Pentium 75 performance, list price $109.

VisionTek
1175 Lakeside Drive
Gurnee, IL 60031
1-800-726-9595, 1-847-360-7500
www.visiontek.com
*Extreme CPU 5x P75 (Am5x86-P-75 processor, for 486s, roughly
Pentium 75 performance, $88.28 at CDW)*

TrinityWorks
12201 Technology Blvd.
Suite 145
Austin, TX 78727
1-800-278-4944
www.trinityworks.com
*PowerStacker 6x86; available in a variety of speeds; uses Cyrix
6x86 chips to upgrade Pentiums to much faster Pentiums; prices at
PC Connection $250 to (whoa!) $950.*

Evergreen Technologies
806 NW Buchanan Avenue
Corvallis, OR 97330-6218
1-541-752-9851
www.evertech.com
*Evergreen 586T processor upgrade, Am5x86-P-75 processor, for
486s, roughly Pentium 75 performance, $109.95 at PC Warehouse;
also new, comparatively low-cost 6x86 upgrades for low-end Pentium systems.*

Improve Technologies
TransEra Corporation
345 East 800 South
Orem, UT 84058
1-801-224-0355
www.transera.com

Overclocking: Live Fast, Die Young?

If you drive a little too fast and live a little too dangerously, you can do the exact same thing with your computer. The technical term for this digital James Dean act is *overclocking*: goosing your microprocessor to work faster than it was rated to work.

Many microprocessors have a significant safety factor built in—they can run significantly faster than they're rated to run.[12] Overclocking means narrowing that safety factor, and it's about as risky a topic as I'll mention in this book. With computers, faster usually means *hotter*—and heat, left unchecked, is deadly to computers. Make sure you have a top-notch, working fan before you try this (PC Power & Cooling makes the best, 1-800-722-6555; 1-619-931-5700, **www.pcpowercooling.com**).

The best sources of information about overclocking are The Official Overclocking FAQ (**www.computercraft.com/docs/offover.html**) and the Overclocking Guide (**http://sysdoc.pair.com/overclock.html**). Read these carefully, especially the parts about all the things that can go wrong. And don't tell anyone I told you about this.

Assorted Stuff That Doesn't Fit Anywhere Else

In this section, we'll mention a few discount sources that didn't fit anywhere else in this chapter.

Notebook port replicators. So you have a notebook, and you'd like to add a port replicator—a device that makes it easy to connect or disconnect your notebook from the monitor, keyboard, and peripherals you use when you're at home or at the office. But port replicators from your notebook's manufacturer typically cost an arm and a leg. Check out the basic, low-cost port replicators sold by Xtend Micro Products (**www.xmpi. com/./html/ port_replicators.html**). Xtend currently sells port replicators for the following notebooks:

- ▲ Compaq Armada 1120/T
- ▲ Compaq Contura 400 through 430 Series
- ▲ IBM ThinkPad 365 Series
- ▲ Toshiba Satellites and Satellite Pros

▲ ▲

12.   Some overclocking aficionados swear the safety factor on Intel chips is higher than their competitors.

Xtend also sells batteries and accessories for many discontinued notebooks and laptops, including older IBM ThinkPads and Apple PowerBooks.

Computer batteries. One discount mail-order source for replacement notebook computer batteries is: Batteries Etc., 1-800-697-9900.

Mice and input devices. If you're in Northern California, a good source for quality mice and sound cards is

Logitech Factory Outlet
6505 Kaiser Drive
Fremont, CA 94555
510-795-8500
www.logitech.com

Summary

In this chapter, I've brought a Cheapskate's perspective to the major purchases you might be faced with after you buy a computer. In the next chapter, I'll try to help with those sneaky *little* purchases that add up… and add up… and add up.

Computer stores love the margins on consumables. Even super-stores, which may be earning only 5 percent margins on low-end PCs, can often triple those margins on laser toner, inkjet inks, specialty papers, cables, and the like.

That's a cue to you: Pay close attention to the way you buy accessories and consumables. Here are some overall tips:

- ▲ Plan your purchases and buy in bulk.
- ▲ Consider mail-order sources, except for heavy items such as paper.
- ▲ Pay attention to superstore and office warehouse sales and loss leaders.

This chapter covers specific strategies for saving money on accessories and consumables—and some of the best sources for doing so.

Diskettes

As far as I'm concerned, a disk is a disk is a disk.

Yes, I know there are different grades of diskettes (higher grade diskettes are sometimes called "duplicator-grade" or "OEM grade"). I know that some people claim preformatted diskettes are dirtier than regular diskettes, and that used diskettes are floating around as new.

All that may be true, but I've used thousands of diskettes over the past several years, and I've found no quality differences between expensive and dirt-cheap diskettes in day-to-day use. In fact, the only diskettes I've ever had trouble with were branded by top manufacturers.

> You'll find some anecdotal information on major diskette manufacturers who seem to have experienced occasional quality problems at *http://hugse1.harvard.edu/~wangal/disk.html*. While I can't vouch for the objective accuracy of the list, I *can* say I've had some of the same problems with the same manufacturers, including Sony and Maxell. Your experience may be different, of course. One relatively low-cost, brand-name manufacturer I've had a lot of good experiences with is BASF.

That being the case, where can you get diskettes at the lowest cost?

Superstore Loss Leaders

Was it Samuel Johnson who said that "consistency is the hobgoblin of small minds"? That makes me feel better about breaking two of my own rules: *Don't* shop for consumables in a superstore, and *don't* make purchases that involve rebates.

Every couple of months, Computer City or CompUSA circulars offer packs of 50 to 150 diskettes, with a rebate that brings the price down well under $10. Often after rebate the diskettes are free. (One recent Computer City catalog also offered free CD jewel cases, mice, reams of inkjet paper, CD holders, dust covers, and other accessories—all after rebate, of course.)

It's a loss leader, of course, designed to draw you into the store to purchase higher-profit items. But who says you have to?

If You Can't Wait

If you need diskettes *now*, and you don't want to bother with rebates, buy generic. Some inexpensive diskette sources include

Media Factory, Inc.
1930 Junction Ave.
San Jose, CA 95131
1-800-879-9536
www.mediafactoryinc.com

MEI/Micro Center
1100 Steelwood Road
Columbus, OH 43212
1-800-634-3478

Diskettes Unlimited
6206 Long Drive
Houston, TX 77087
1-800-364-DISK; 1-713-643-9939

Midwestern Diskette
509 West Taylor
Creston, IA 50801
1-800-221-6332
www.mddc.com/mdi/mdi.html

Best Computer Supplies
P.O. Box 2042
Sparks, NV 89432-2042
1-800-544-3472

Exxus Direct, Inc.
200 San Mateo Avenue
Los Gatos, CA 95030
1-800-557-1000; 1-408-399-7655
www.disksdirect.com

Often, generic disk manufacturers sell disk labels separately. But you don't have to use "official" disk labels: You can use any sticky label you want, including mailing labels, which are much less expensive than disk labels.

> *Warning!* You used to hear about these two alleged money savers more than you do nowadays, but just in case:
>
> 1. No, you *don't* want to buy a hole puncher that turns 720K 3.5" diskettes into diskettes that 1.44-megabyte floppy drives recognize as one of their own. Those diskettes are 720K for a *reason*, and they won't be reliable at the higher density. Worse, you might leave crud behind in your diskette that can damage the drive itself.
>
> 2. No, you *don't* want to use 360K and 1.2M 5.25" diskettes interchangeably—nor do you want to format low-density 360K diskettes on high-density 1.2M disk drives. It's not worth the space to explain why: Just *don't*.

Use 5.25" Diskettes if Possible

As 3.5" 1.44-Mb diskettes have become the widely accepted standard, demand has plummeted for 5.25" 1.2-Mb diskettes, and so has the price. If your system has both a 1.2-Mb and 1.44-Mb drive, consider using 1.2-Mb diskettes for "scratch" use whenever possible. They cost significantly less.

The Late, Lamented AOL Diskette Airlift

For years, it's been possible to count on an endless supply of free America Online diskettes. To build its membership past the 8,000,000 level, AOL has been carpet-bombing the country with junk mail and free diskettes—just reformat them, relabel them, and use them.

Unfortunately, the disk airlift appears to be slowing down. AOL's serious service problems have forced them to reduce the floppy flights—and they're increasingly sending out CD-ROMs, as well. So if AOL can get past those nagging busy signals and keep the attorneys general of all 50 states off their backs, you may have to settle for an endless supply of free coasters and miniature frisbees from now on.

Laser Labels

If you've ever printed labels on your laser printer, you know how expensive they are. Here are a couple of tips for holding the cost down.

▲ Use plain paper to print test pages until you're 100 percent certain that your labels will print the way you intended.

▲ Look for generic labels, or failing that, use MACO brand labels. They're significantly cheaper than Avery, the leading brand.

Laser Printer Paper

Laser printer paper weighs a ton, so mail order is not usually a realistic option here. My strategy for saving over 40 percent on laser printer paper is simple: Go to your nearest office supply warehouse (or membership warehouse if you're already a member) and buy a ream of the cheapest paper they sell. Most personal laser printers will do just fine with the cheap stuff, though high-speed office lasers tend to be a bit more finicky.

At Staples and OfficeMax, there's a generic brand beneath the house brand. Buy *that*, if it's available by the ream. Then run your laser printer on it. If you don't experience paper jams, go out and buy a case of the same stuff. If you aren't likely to use a whole case of paper (that's 5,000 sheets) in the next year, find someone to share it with.

> One mail-order source that does occasionally offer excellent pricing on generic paper—and ships virtually all orders over $25 free of charge, no matter what they weigh—is Viking Office Products, 1-800-421-1222.

Laser Toner

The time to buy laser printer toner is *before* you run out. Otherwise, you're likely to pay through the nose—even if you visit an office supply warehouse like Staples or OfficeMax. You'll often save from 10–25 percent if you order laser toner from one of these sources:

MEI/Micro Center
1100 Steelwood Road
Columbus, OH 43212-9972
1-800-634-3478

American Ribbon & Toner Company
2895 West Prospect Road
Fort Lauderdale, FL 33309
1-800-327-1013
www.icanet.net/arctoner

Laser Cartridges: Remanufactured vs. Refilled

It seems an awful waste to throw out those toner cartridges once you're done with them, especially since you can recycle them for much lower-cost *remanufactured* toner cartridges.

Time was that most toner cartridge recyclers simply drilled a hole in your cartridge, refilled or "recharged" it, and shipped it back to you. Since the cartridge wasn't opened, none of the parts inside it were checked for wear. Customer results with recharged cartridges were uneven, to say the least.

Some toner cartridge recyclers still simply recharge cartridges, but it's now more common to find *remanufacturers* who actually open cartridges, check components, and then refill and reassemble them. Remanufactured cartridges are generally quite reliable, and occasionally even superior to originals (though not as often as remanufacturers claim).

Among the many mail-order and on-line sources for remanufactured cartridges are:

A-ARVIN Toner Store (see Figure 6-1)
8200 E. Pacific Place #103
Denver, CO 80231-3220
1-800-555-3150; 1-303-338-1763
www.tonerstore.com
Six-month warranty.

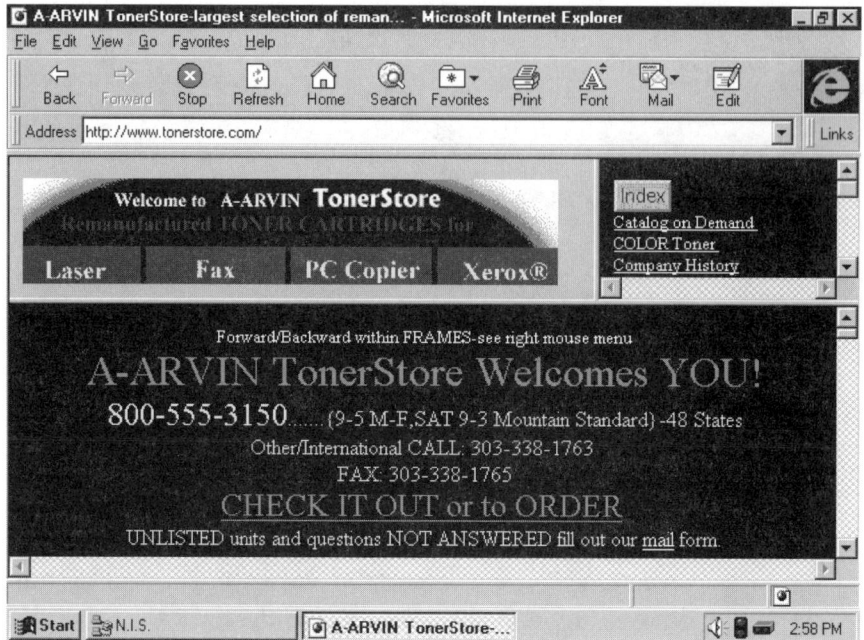

Figure 6–1 A-ARVIN TonerStore, one of the leading on-line sources of remanufactured toner cartridges.

Environmental Laser
www.toners.com

Pendl Company
1825B Dolphin Drive
Waukesha, WI 53186
1-800-869-7973; 1-414-896-8888
www.pendl.com

Nu'life Cartridge Corporation
662 BeBout Road
Venetia, PA
412-331-7553

Tonerworks
5844 Kirby Road
Clinton, MD 20735
1-301-297-4340

Laserlux
P.O. Box 814
Mercedes, TX 78570-0814
1-800-366-4053
210-565-9596
www.laserlux.com

Quality Laser Alternatives
133 North 8th Street
Reading, PA 19601
610-373-0788
www.qla.com

Laser Technology Systems, Inc.
527 Industrial Way West
Eatontown, NJ 07724
1-888-389-3704

Enviro-Charge Corp.
#2 Whittier Hill
Purdys, NY 10578
1-800-487-0447; 1-914-232-9582

Toner Charge, Inc.
Fairfax, VA
1-800-301-9298; 1-703-560-7800

Marlborough Supplies
1-800-777-2949
Also a source of Okidata and Panasonic remanufactured drums.

Atsumi
Brooklyn, NY
1-800-889-9722

Ultimate Image, Inc.
3498 N. San Marcos Place, Suite 10
Chandler, AZ 85224
1-800-459-9876; 1-602-966-8973
www.ultimateimage.com

"Economode" Printing

Many laser printers, such as the Hewlett-Packard LaserJet 5L, have an "Economode" that reduces toner usage by as much as 50 percent. While not appropriate for final documents, you may want to experiment with this low-toner mode for drafts and other "transient" documents.

If your printer has an Economode or similar setting, you can typically control it through your Windows (or Macintosh) printer driver. If you're running Windows 95, choose File, Print in any application; then click Properties to change the printer driver's settings, as shown in Figure 6-2.

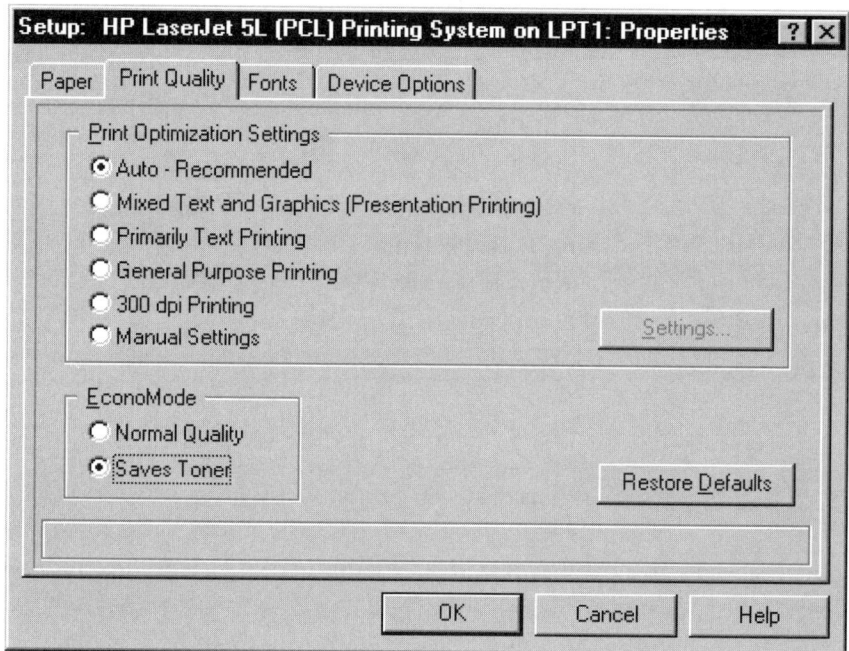

Figure 6–2   Setting a Hewlett-Packard LaserJet 5L to Economode.

Inkjets: Initial Cost vs. Consumables Cost

Inkjets are the cheapest kind of printer you can buy. But they're not the cheapest kind of printer you can use. New inkjet cartridges can really put a dent in your wallet. And the price of printing can vary dramatically from one printer to another. Table 6-1 compares several printers that cost around $350 or less, each from leading manufacturers. The cost information is provided by the manufacturers themselves.

Table 6–1 Evaluating the Cost of Inkjet Printers

	Canon BJC-4200	Epson Stylus Color 500	HP DeskJet 693C	Lexmark 2050 Color Jetprinter
Purchase Price	$279	$279	$355	$252
Ink Cost per Page (color)	14 cents	8 cents	11 cents	15 cents
Ink Cost per Page (black and white)	4 cents	4 cents	4 cents	3 cents

For some inkjet printers, it is possible to purchase third-party inkjet cartridges that are significantly cheaper than the original manufacturer's cartridges. As with diskettes and laser toner, one good source for third-party cartridges is MEI/Micro Center (1-800-634-3478).

Inkjet Refills

Inkjet printing will never be cheap, but it can be much cheaper—if you refill your inkjet cartridges. All-in-one refiller kits can cut the cost of inkjet printing by 50–75 percent.

As with all the do-it-yourself ideas in this book, the key words are *be careful.* You may want to wait until your printer is out of warranty, since many manufacturers will void your warranty if they discover you've been refilling. That's 75 percent self-interest on their part: They want to sell you expensive new cartridges. But it's also at least 25 percent honest concern: Careless refills, substandard ink, or the wrong ink *can* damage printers. Believe it or not, there are more than 40 types of inkjet ink, with many more on the way.

Having said that, if you *are* careful, I vote wholeheartedly for refilling. Now, how to do it successfully?

Once you've decided to refill, don't cheap out on the ink. More expensive inks have better viscosity, so they'll flow through print heads more smoothly and produce a more consistent image.

Second, make sure you don't let your inkjet cartridges run completely dry before you refill them. Most inkjet cartridges contain a foam sponge which can quickly dry out if the cartridge is allowed to become completely empty. Once this happens, the cartridge is susceptible to many problems, especially inconsistent light and dark printing, and fewer pages per refill. You may want to "top off" your cartridge every 250 pages to prevent this problem.

It's not just the sponge in an inkjet cartridge that can dry out; so can the print head. Water in the print head's microjets can evaporate quickly, leaving a residue of dried ink that causes blockages which can't be fixed. The solution: Leave your cartridge in the printer until you're ready to refill it. (Of course this means you may be better off refilling the cartridge yourself than sending it to a refilling service.)

Make sure you keep your print head clean. For some inkjet printers, normal cleaning cycles aren't enough; you can gently clean the print head with a soft cotton cloth dipped in water.

Most inkjet printers also have a purge cycle, which heats and cleans a cartridge's microjets from the inside out. Consider running the purging cycle every few weeks.

When is a cartridge beyond salvaging? As we've mentioned, if you've let the cartridge's foam sponge or print head microjets dry out and you're getting poor quality print from it, nothing you can do will help. Also, cartridges do eventually simply wear out. One symptom: slanted or wavy print, which means that the cartridge's built-in resistors are wearing out.

A couple more obvious pointers: Read the instructions, and never insert a wet or leaking cartridge into your printer.

Where can you get inkjet refills? A bit surprisingly, they're often available at office supply warehouses such as Staples. BJ's Warehouse Club stocks Repeat-O-Type brand refills; you can see which model you need, or find your local BJ's Wholesale Club at **www.repeatotype.com/refills.html.**

You can also purchase refills by mail. Here are some sources:

Micro Center
SoftCentre Inc.
30 Petersburg Road
Hackettstown, NJ 07840
800-366-3311

Computer Friends
14250 NW Science Park Drive
Portland, OR 97229
1-503-626-2291
www.sourcedata.com/500/000183.htm

Nu-Jet
9918 Spruce Ridge Drive
Converse, TX 78109
1-800-216-7850; 1-210-599-7045
www.nujet.com

Cables

Unfortunately, when you need a cable, you tend to need it *now*. But if you can wait a day, or a few days, you can often get a significantly better price from one of these mail-order sources:

Computer Gate International
2960 Gordon Avenue
Santa Clara, CA 95051
1-408-730-0673
www.computergate.com

Cables America
1-800-348-8724

Dalco Electronics
P.O. Box 550
275 Pioneer Boulevard
Springboro, OH 45066
1-800-445-5342
www.dalco.com

CableNet
1-800-788-8488
Specializes in networking cables.

Books

You may already know the best sources for discount books in your neck of the woods. But what if you need a book for an older software version? National sources of remaindered, close-out, overstock, and discount computer books include:

Paradise Books
Wholesale Discount Outlet
www.paradisebooks.com/menu_computer.shtml
Publishers' close-outs, overstocks, and discounts; refund or exchange within 30 days from shipment date.

Readme.Doc
1-800-678-1473
readmedotdoc.com
Twenty-five percent off many titles.

All Publishers' Outlet
1-888-255-7826
www.tucson.com/allpub/all-pub-outlet.html

The Book Bargainbot Search Agent

If you're buying books on the Web, you probably already know about **www.amazon.com**, but it's far from the only Web source for books. With Bargainbot, you can price several sources at once to find the best on-line deal.

Bargainbot is a "threaded, multi-connection, autonomous agent prototype." Got that? In English: You tell Bargainbot the name and author of the book you're interested in, and it checks several top on-line bookstores to find which ones stock the book, and what they charge.

See a price you like, click, and bang: You're at the bookstore. You'll find Bargainbot at **www.ece.curtin.edu.au/~saoundb/cgi/nph-bargainbot** (see Figure 6-3).

Yo! This is how Web commerce is *supposed* to work!

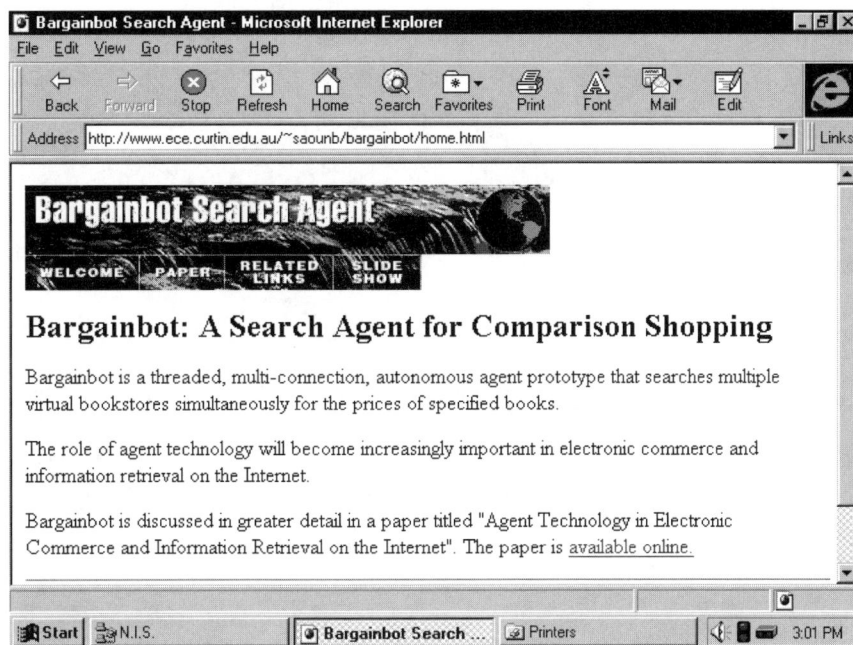

Figure 6–3   Bargainbot at work.

Free Books On-line

Ventana Press (**www.vmedia.com**) offers free on-line access to several of their Internet-related titles, including the Official Netscape Navigator 3.0 Book, and the Internet Business 500, a list of 500 of the most useful, valuable on-line business resources.

One source for tons of books in the same place is the *PC Library, Volume 2* CD-ROM (see Figure 6-4). Originally available from Allegro New Media for as much as $99.95, it's now published by Essex Interactive for $9.95 (see page 158). *PC Library* contains the full text of 46 computer reference books covering a wide range of topics, from PC troubleshooting and repair to using Microsoft Word, Excel, and many other applications. At this point, the books are a few years old, but if you're using old systems or software, there's a wealth of information here.

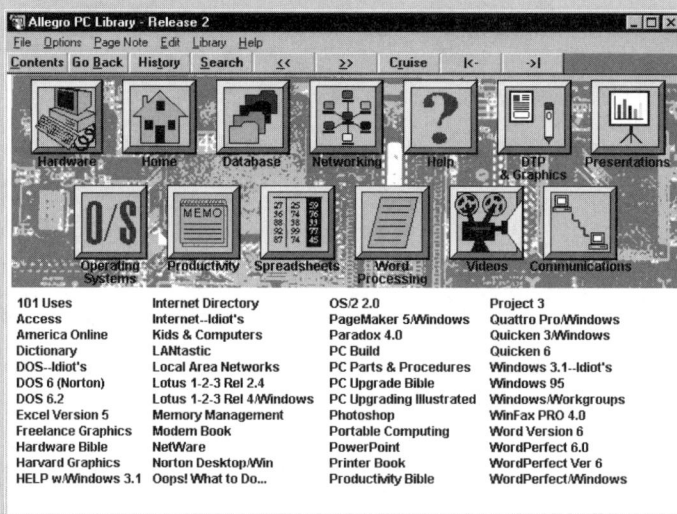

101 Uses	Internet Directory	OS/2 2.0	Project 3
Access	Internet--Idiot's	PageMaker 5/Windows	Quattro Pro/Windows
America Online	Kids & Computers	Paradox 4.0	Quicken 3/Windows
Dictionary	LANtastic	PC Build	Quicken 6
DOS--Idiot's	Local Area Networks	PC Parts & Procedures	Windows 3.1--Idiot's
DOS 6 (Norton)	Lotus 1-2-3 Rel 2.4	PC Upgrade Bible	Windows 95
DOS 6.2	Lotus 1-2-3 Rel 4/Windows	PC Upgrading Illustrated	Windows/Workgroups
Excel Version 5	Memory Management	Photoshop	WinFax PRO 4.0
Freelance Graphics	Modem Book	Portable Computing	Word Version 6
Hardware Bible	NetWare	PowerPoint	WordPerfect 6.0
Harvard Graphics	Norton Desktop/Win	Printer Book	WordPerfect Ver 6
HELP w/Windows 3.1	Oops! What to Do...	Productivity Bible	WordPerfect/Windows

Figure 6–4   PC Library, Volume 2: Forty-six slightly older computer books on one CD-ROM.

Summary

Accessories and consumables have a way of adding up. Let's look at the costs of a typical year for an average computer user with a laser printer in Table 6-2.

Table 6–2 Consumables Costs per Year, Typical User

	Buying Careless		Buying Cheap	
100 Diskettes	10 individual boxes @ $6.00	$ 60.00	100 diskettes purchased at superstore (including rebate postage)	$ 1.00
5,000 Sheets Laser Paper	10 reams purchased individually @ $5.00	$ 50.00	1 case generic paper from office warehouse	$ 22.00
2 Toner Cartridges	Purchased at retail	$140.00	Purchased mail order	$120.00
1 Cable	Purchased at retail	$ 11.00	Purchased mail order	$ 7.00
3 Books	Purchased full price	$100.00	Purchased 25 percent off	$ 75.00
	Total	**$361.00**	**Total**	**$225.00**

That's nearly 40 percent savings for doing nothing more than paying attention. Not bad.

In the next chapter, we'll leave the mundane world of toner cartridges and reams of paper for the heights of cyberspace and show how to apply Cheapskate principles to the virtual world, too.

7

Cheapskates On-Line!
Inexpensive and Free
On-Line Resources

255

As everyone knows, the world now officially revolves around the Internet. For Cheapskates, that presents new challenges, and a world of new opportunities. You may *want* information to be free, but that doesn't mean it *is*.

In this chapter, I'll help you sort through your options for getting on the Net inexpensively—and introduce you to resources that can save you a bundle once you're there.

Choosing an Internet Service Provider: A Cheapskate's Guide

There are many routes onto the Internet, and they can vary dramatically in both cost and quality. In this section, I'll help you discover whether you may be eligible for free or highly discounted Internet access. Later in the chapter, I'll show you how to compare commercial providers and strike the best deal possible.

Internet Access through Colleges

If you have a relationship with a college or university, as a student, faculty member, staff person, or possibly as a participant in a university organization, or an alumnus(a), you may be eligible for a free or inexpensive

Internet services account through your educational institution, or at least for Internet access at public workstations on campus.

Internet Access at Your Public Library

It's increasingly likely that your library has an Internet connection of some kind. A comprehensive survey of libraries[1] in 1996 showed that 44.6 percent have some Internet connectivity, and for libraries that serve areas with more than 100,000 residents, the percentage soars to 82 percent. These numbers are nearly twice what they were in 1994. Of those libraries that were not connected to the Internet, well over half planned to become connected by March 1997.

Admittedly, some of those connections are staff only, and some provide only limited Internet services, not always full-fledged Web access. Still, if you're planning to use the Internet only occasionally, you might check whether your library has a Web connection before you spend $20+ per month to get your own.

Occasionally, you may hit the jackpot. For example, the Baltimore County Public Library system not only offers Internet access on site, it also provides full Internet accounts for $75 per year to Baltimore residents, $100 to others. For information, call 410-887-3297.

Be in the Right Place at the Right Time

As with college scholarships, you can sometimes find free or very low cost Internet accounts if you look for them.

For example, K–12 teachers in Maryland have access to free accounts through the University of Maryland. You can find out more at (hold your breath, now): **www.inform.umd.edu:8080/EdRes/Topic/Education/K-12/mdk-12/resource/access/contents.**

Some large companies, such as Bell Atlantic, offer significant employee discounts for the Internet access services they already provide to customers.

▲ ▲

1.   The *1996 National Survey of Public Libraries and the Internet: Progress and Issues Final Report*, 1996, National Commission on Libraries and Information Science (NCLIS), 1110 Vermont Avenue, NW, Suite 820, Washington, DC 20005-3522, **www.nclis.gov**.

Free Introductory Internet Access Offers

Several national and regional Internet service providers offer no-strings attached, 30-day unlimited free trial offers for dial-up Internet service. Among the service providers currently making this offer are

▲ Sprint
▲ Bell Atlantic.Net (Northeast U.S.)
▲ BellSouth.Net (Southeast U.S.)
▲ America Online
▲ The Microsoft Network

If you're not sure whether you intend to keep your Internet service provider after your free service ends, consider using a service such as Hotmail (which we'll cover on page 292). Hotmail will give you a free e-mail address you can keep using even if you change service providers.

Hourly Rates for Light Internet Users

So you're a light Internet user and you don't even want to pay $19.95 per month? Unlimited plans get all the publicity, but many Internet service providers offer lower-priced plans for people who intend to use relatively fewer hours. For example,

▲ *MindSpring* charges $6.95 per month for 5 hours; $2 per hour afterwards; or $14.95 per month for 20 hours, $1 per hour afterwards
▲ *Sprint* offers Internet access for $1.50 per hour
▲ *AT&T WorldNet* offers five hours for $4.95 to AT&T long-distance customers; others get 3 hours for $4.95. (Sorry: The five free monthly hours of Internet access offer that made AT&T WorldNet famous is no more.)

Free, Advertiser-Supported Internet Service

If virtually everything on the Web can be free and advertiser supported, how about Internet service itself? That's the theory behind a growing number of companies that plan to convince advertisers to pay the freight.

It remains to be seen whether this business model will fly: the revenues required to deliver quality Internet service appear to be higher than the revenues available from advertising, at least until now. Having said that, Internet advertising revenue has recently started to increase significantly, so who knows? Maybe one of the following companies will actually pull it off.

• *A "FreeRide" on the Internet*

FreeRide Media, is offering free Internet access in selected markets throughout the United States. The catch: You have to earn enough FreeRide points each month to qualify. How do you get those points? By

▲ Purchasing merchandise from companies advertising with FreeRide
▲ Subscribing to magazines advertising on FreeRide, currently including *Newsweek, Rolling Stone, US Magazine* and *Men's Journal*
▲ Visiting sites of FreeRide sponsors

You also have to use a service provider that has affiliated with FreeRide (see Figure 7-1). As of January 1997, the company has established partnerships with two national and 70 local Internet service providers.

You might want to wait and see on this deal. According to FreeRide, most users will need about 1,000 points to get a free month's access. But magazine subscriptions only earn you roughly 160 points, and Web site visits only earn you 10 points. So far, it looks like you'll be spending an awful lot of time and money to get that free Web access.

Having said that, *someone's* buying in: As of January 1997, FreeRide claimed 100,000 subscribers.

• *"One-Time Fee" Internet Service*

Along similar something-for-nothing lines, one company has begun offering lifetime, unlimited, advertising-supported Internet service for a one-time fee and little or no additional ongoing charges. The company, Bigger.Net, is currently operating only in the San Francisco area, though it plans to roll out its service to seven more cities by the end of 1997.

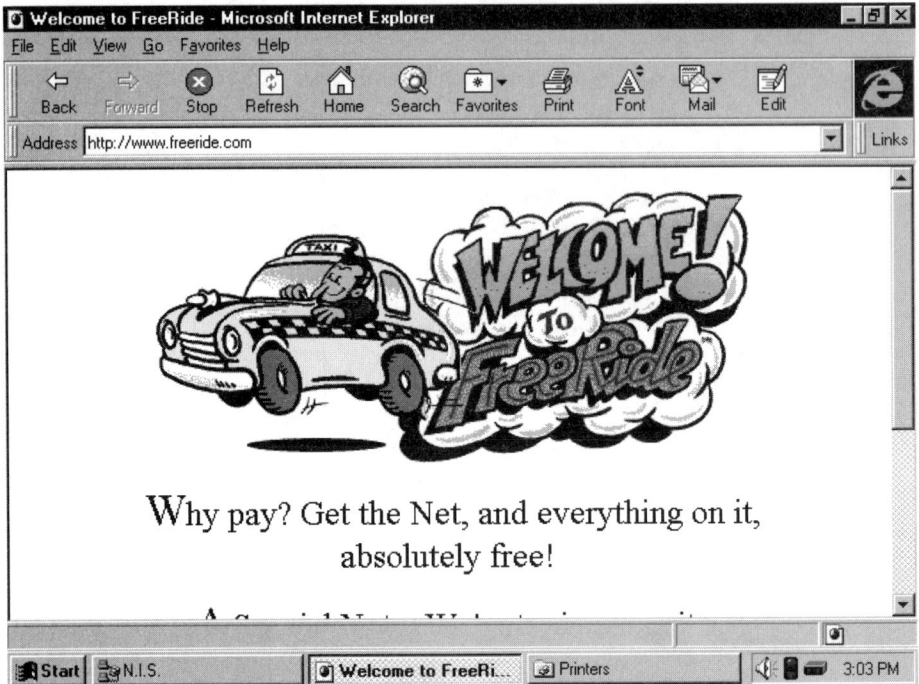

Figure 7–1   If you're seriously into couponing, you might just go for FreeRide.

Bigger.Net asks $59.95 as a setup charge, then $10 a year to maintain an e-mail account.

Before signing on with any free Internet service, visit its Web site, get a sense of how disruptive its advertising will be—and also how quickly the site responds. That may be an omen of how fast and reliable its service will be.

> Bigger.Net
> 1-800-228-1992; 1-408-283-3703
> **www.bigger.net**

Pay-in-Advance Discounts

Some Internet Service Providers (ISPs) are trying desperately to maintain price competitiveness by offering lower prices if you pay three months, six months, or a year in advance. The prices can be *significantly* lower. In the most extreme example I've seen, in the New York metropolitan area, Erol's advertises in *The New York Times* that it will provide two years of Internet service for $9.50 a month paid in advance; $12.00 a month if you buy in for one year. (Incidentally, that's a better deal than they offer on their own Web site, **www.erols.com**, which advertises $156.00 for a full year's service.)

At least two major phone companies, Ameritech and BellSouth, also offer discount plans for annual payments. In the Midwest, for example, Ameritech.net's (**www.ameritech.net**) plan currently costs $189/year, prepaid in full once a year. That's $15.75 per month.[2]

> *Warning!* If an ISP is familiar to you, and if you're comfortable that they will provide reliable service, deals like these can be very attractive. But I'd want to be very careful investing more than a few month's charges with a company I wasn't sure about. It's very tough to make a profit as an Internet service provider nowadays, even at $19.95 a month. Some providers are using the pay-in-advance technique for a fast cash infusion, while hoping long term that their businesses will improve. What guarantee do you have that they'll be around?

Account Sharing

The rules and costs vary widely, but some Internet service providers allow you to add separate user IDs under a master account at low (or no) cost. You may be able to use these IDs to share inexpensive Internet access with family members at other locations.

---

2.   Be aware that for regulatory reasons, regional phone companies like BellSouth and Ameritech that offer Internet service may currently add on a separate charge for a global service provider, the equivalent of a "long-distance" Internet carrier. This is a charge you won't run across if you deal with other ISPs.

Pseudo-SLIP Shell Accounts

If you have a lowly UNIX shell account, you may be able to transform it into something approaching a swan, using a freeware program called SLiRP, which emulates a full-fledged SLIP/PPP connection. With SliRP running on the host system, you can use Web browsers like Netscape and Internet Explorer on both Windows and Macintosh computers.

Of course, your service provider needs to be running a UNIX server (most are); needs to offer shell accounts and offer them at low cost (shell accounts are in relatively low demand these days), and needs to consent to the presence of SLiRP on their system. That's the tough part, since service providers realize SLiRP is a way for you to avoid purchasing a full-featured SLIP/PPP account, while still taxing the server with graphics that wouldn't normally be sent to UNIX shell account users. Again, however, it doesn't hurt to ask.

The real hotbed of SLiRP usage is universities, which have provided UNIX shell accounts for years and are often more tolerant of workarounds like SLiRP.

> Configuring SLiRP can be tricky. You can get more information about SLiRP at *http://blitzen.canberra.edu.au/~danjo/* or from the newsgroup **alt.dcom.slip-emulators**.

A commercial product, The Internet Adapter from Cyberspace Development, Inc., did much the same thing as SLiRP, but the manufacturer withdrew it in July 1996.

Community Networks and Freenets

Lest you think that everything on the Net is commercial, or that everything that's free is advertiser supported ...

There are more than 200 community networks, sometimes called freenets, throughout the United States. These are nonprofit organizations dedicated to providing on-line resources to people who would most likely never get access to them in any other way. The organizations are very diverse. Some provide Internet or Web access; others don't. Many are just getting off the ground; others are well-entrenched institutions in their communities.

Virtually all of them have a few things in common, however. They see information technology as a means of rebuilding local communities and empowering individuals within those communities. In the words of Frank Odasz, director of Big Sky Telegraph, a community network for rural Montana, "community networking is people coming together electronically to make good things happen. Community networking is fundamentally about people, not technologies."

Most freenets provide their services at extremely low cost, or at no cost, often focusing on public access through schools, libraries, and other community institutions. Not surprisingly, few of them are rolling in money—so it can be a struggle for them to provide reliable, high-speed access at peak hours.

Nevertheless, the community networking movement reminds us that the Internet can be something more than just a great new advertising medium: It can be a profound new way for human beings to communicate with each other. If you would like to participate in building your community through a freenet, and at the same time get on-line at low or no cost, check the list on the next few pages for a freenet in your own backyard.

Since freenet contacts can change quickly, the best way to find out how to get in touch with your local freenet—or whether one exists—is to contact the Organization for Community Networking (OCN). Visit **www.ofcn.org**, or write

Organization for Community Networks
P.O. Box 32175
Euclid, OH 44132

- *Freenet Listings*

  Alabama
  Mobile Area Free-Net
  West Alabama Free-Net (Alabama)

  Alaska
  AnchorNet (Anchorage)
  FairNet (Fairbanks)

  Arizona
  AzTeC (Tempe)
  City of Phoenix
  City of Tucson

  California
  Belmont-Access for the Community (BAC)
  City of Palo Alto
  City of San Carlos
  City of San Diego
  Davis Community Network
  Los Angeles Free-Net
  Mendocino Community Network
  NapaNet Community Network (Napa Valley)
  Net at Two Rivers (Sacramento)
  Northern California Regional Computing Network (Chico)
  Orange Country Free Net (Orange County)
  Redwood Free-Net
  San Diego Community Free-Net
  Santa Barbara RAIN
  Silicon Valley Public Access Link (SV-PAL)

  Colorado
  Boulder Community Net
  Denver Free-Net
  FortNet: Fort Collins Community Network
  Littleton Community Network
  Southwest Colorado Access Network (Durango)

Connecticut
Danbury Community Network

Florida
Alachua Free-Net (Alachua County)
Naples Free-Net
SEFLIN Free-Net (Broward County)
SEFLIN Free-Net (Dade County)
SEFLIN Free-Net (Palm Beach County)
Suncoast Free-Net (Tampa Bay)
Tallahassee Free-Net

Georgia
Blakely/Early County Free-Net (Blakely)
Southwest Georgia Telecommunications Alliance (Americus)
Worth County-Sylvester Free-Net (Sylvester)

Hawaii
Hawai'i Home Page (Honolulu)

Illinois
Aurora Online Community Network
Heartland Regional Network
LincolnNet ("Grand Prairie" Region of Chicago Metropolis)
NorthEast Chicago Community Network
NorthStarNet Community Information Network (northern
Cook County, Lake County, parts of Kane and McHenry Counties)
Prairienet (Champaign-Urbana)
Shawnee Free-Net (Carbondale)

Indiana
Access Evansville
Access LaPorte County
Boone County Community Network (BCCN)
CarrollNet
CommuniNet (Wabash County)

East Central Indiana Community Network
Falls Cities Community Net (Clark and Floyd Counties)
Fort Wayne Area InfoNet
HoosierNet (Monroe County)
Huntington CommNet (Huntington County)
Indianapolis OnLine
Johnson County Community Network
LakeNET (Lake County)
Michiana Free-Net Society (Granger and South Bend)
Noble Community Access Network (NobleCAN) (Noble County)
SCICAN (South Central Indiana)
Sheridan Community Network (Indiana)
SouthLake Net (Lake County, Indiana)
WCIC Net (West Central Indiana Community Network)

Iowa
CedarNet (Cedar Falls)
Iowa Knowledge Exchange
Thomas County Free-Net (Colby)

Kentucky
Owensboro Free-Net (Owensboro)
Pennyrile Area Free-Net (Hopkinsville)

Louisiana
Acadiana Free-Net (Lafayette)
Greater New Orleans Free-Net

Maine
Aroostook Free-Net (Caribou)

Maryland
Chesapeake Free-Net (Easton)
Garrett Communiversity Central (McHenry)

Massachusetts
Cambridge Civic Network (Cambridge)

Michigan
Allegan County Free-Net (Allegan)
Almont Expression (Almont)
Capitol City Free-Net (Lansing)
Genesee Free-Net (Flint)
Grand Rapids Free-Net
Great Lakes Free-Net (Battle Creek)
Greater Detroit FreeNet
Huron Valley Community Network (Ann Arbor)
Macatawa Area Free-Net (Holland)
Manistee Universal Free-Net (Manistee)
MSTC Free-Net (Big Rapids)
Seaway Community Free-Net (Port Huron)
St. Johns Free-Net (St. Johns)
Traverse Community Network (Traverse City)

Minnesota
Northfield Free-Net (Northfield)
State of Minnesota
Twin Cities Free-Net (Minneapolis/St. Paul)

Mississippi
Magnolia Free-Net (Jackson)

Missouri
Columbia Online Information Network (COIN)
KC Free-Net (Kansas City)
Ozarks Regional Information Online Network (ORION)
(Springfield)
Show-Me Free-Net (Cape Girardeau)
Westplex Information Network (WIN) (St. Charles County)

Montana
Big Sky Telegraph (Dillon)
Yellowstone Valley Free-Net (Sidney)

Nebraska
Omaha Free-Net
Ordon Rushville Information Network (Rushville)
Kearney Free-Net (Kearney)

Nevada
Free-Net Nevada (Las Vegas)
Northern Nevada Free-Net (Wells)

New Jersey
North Jersey Public Information Exchange (Summit)
Garden State Free-Net (Mount Laurel)

New Mexico
La Plaza de Taos
Santa Fe Free-Net

New York
Buffalo Free-Net
Capital Region Information Service (CRISNY) (Albany)
CNYNet (Central New York State)
IthacaNet (Central New York)
New York Free-Net (Manhattan)
Rochester Free-Net (Rochester, New York)

North Carolina
Charlotte's Web (Charlotte)
Forsythe County Free-Net Project
Mountain Area Information Network (Asheville)
RTPnet (Raleigh/Durham/Chapel Hill)

North Dakota
SENDIT (Fargo)

Ohio
Blanchard Valley Area Network (Findlay)
Cleveland Free-Net (Cleveland)

Dayton Free-Net (Dayton)
Greater Columbus Free-Net
Greater Portsmouth Area Free-Net (Portsmouth)
HeartLAN Community Free-Net (Kenton)
Lakeland Free-Net (Kirtland)
Lorain County Free-Net (Elyria)
Medina County Free-Net (Medina)
Oak Web Internet Access (Washington Court House)
Richland Free-Net (Mansfield)
SEORF (Athens)
Toledo Free-Net (Toledo)
Tristate Online (Cincinnati)
Tuscarawas Valley Free-Net (New Philadelphia)
Washington County Free-Net (Marietta)
WCNet: The Wood County Free-Net (Bowling Green)
WORC-Net (Lima)
Youngstown Free-Net (Youngstown)

Oklahoma
Pioneer Free-Net (Ponca City)

Oregon
Eugene Free-Net
GroveNet (Banks, Cornelius, Forest Grove, Gaston, Washington County)

Pennsylvania
Bloomsburg Area Free-Net (Bloomsburg)
Chester County InterLink (West Chester)
Libertynet (Philadelphia)
MERLINK: Mercer County Free-Net (Sharon)
Niagara Free-Net (Erie)
Three Rivers Free-Net (Pittsburgh area)

Rhode Island
Ocean State Free-Net (Providence)

South Carolina
MidNet (Columbia & the Midlands)
GRINet (Greenwood)

South Dakota
State of South Dakota

Tennessee
Jackson Area Free-Net (Jackson)
KORRnet (Knoxville-Oak Ridge)

Texas
Austin Free-Net (Austin)
Fayette Free-Net Information Service (La Grange)
Rio Grande Free-Net (El Paso)
San Antonio Free-Net (San Antonio)

Vermont
NorthNet (Morrisville)

Virginia
ALEX, Electronic Alexandria Community (Alexandria)
Blacksburg Electronic Village (Blacksburg)
Central Virginia's Free-Net (Richmond)
City of Staunton (Staunton)
SEVAnet (Newport News)
VaPEN (Richmond)

Washington
LinkNet (Bremerton)
OPEN (Port Angeles)
Seattle Community Network (Seattle)
TINCAN (Spokane)
Tri-Cities Free-Net (Tri-Cities)
Yakima Valley Free-Net Foundation (Yakima)

Washington, DC
CapAccess: National Capital Area Public Access Network

Wisconsin
Chippewa Valley Free-Net (Wisconsin)
DANEnet
Kenosha Public Free-Net (Kenosha)
Marquette County Coalition Free-Net (Montello)
NorthCoast Free-Net (Ashland)
Wisconsin River Free-Net (Mosinee)

Internet Access: They're Not Making It Any Cheaper

If, like most home Internet users, you choose a commercial route to the Internet, I have some bad news. Commercial Internet access charges are headed up.

First of all, the local phone companies that connect you to your Internet service provider are squawking louder and louder. Where local calls are free, and Internet service is flat-rated, people just keep their Net connections open all day long, stressing the phone network. We should be paying for the trouble we're causing.[3]

Of course, these same local phone companies have rationed out bandwidth with a teaspoon for over a century now, they're accustomed to strictly regulated environments that encourage them to keep working that way—and aren't particularly enamored of business models that offer unlimited *anything*. Why, people might use those Internet connections to *make phone calls*.

How much the Internet is really impacting phone service is hotly contested. But you can expect to hear a lot more about this—if for no other reason, because the local phone company lobbyists are about as heavy-duty as they come.

▲ ▲ ▲ ▲ ▲ ▲ ▲ ▲ ▲ ▲ ▲ ▲ ▲ ▲ ▲ ▲ ▲ ▲ ▲

3. Of course, the argument is typically put in a more genteel way: "Flat-rate pricing is a disincentive that prevents the marketplace from moving toward higher-speed Internet access, such as ISDN, which would allow us to fulfill the promise of the information superhighway."

> To stay up to date on this issue, which could *dramatically* impact your Internet access costs, visit the Internet Access Coalition, at *http://internetaccess.org/action.htm.*

In any event, nobody's making a dime on those $19.95 per month unlimited service deals. Large Internet service providers like Netcom have already eliminated them, and others like UUNet have repositioned themselves as value-added business Internet providers. Meanwhile, America Online is fending off outraged customers and stockholder lawsuits over their $19.95 per month offer, and IDT is repositioning itself as a phone company.

I haven't made many rash predictions, but here's one: The $19.95 unlimited service offers that will survive the longest will be AT&T's and Microsoft's. Those are the two companies with the deepest pockets—and the most to gain from added Internet market share. AT&T can tie its WorldNet Internet service to its long-distance service, providing one-stop shopping that makes long-distance customers less likely to switch. And Microsoft, which has said it will accept billions of dollars of losses to gain a foothold in the Internet marketplace, can tie its MSN Internet service to its strategy for continued dominance of the desktop.

Choosing the *Right* Internet Service Provider

Unfortunately for us Cheapskates, Internet service isn't quite a commodity item yet. There are dramatic differences in the quality offered by different suppliers. It's no wonder that nearly half of all Internet users reported dissatisfaction with their current provider in a recent survey. Internet service is no bargain if you can't get connected—or you can't get help when you need it.

In this section, I'll show you what questions to ask—and what independent research you can do—to minimize your chances of choosing a lemon.

Finding ISPs

You can now find ISPs in the phone book, but if you're already on the Web, you can get a quick list of service providers in your neck of the woods by checking **www.thelist.com**. The site includes direct links to most service providers listed—something your phone book can't do quite yet.

Basic Questions to Ask Any Service Provider

✍ *What are your nearest phone numbers? (If you want to impress them, ask: **What's your nearest point of presence?**) You obviously want a phone number that you can call free, assuming that your local phone company provides free local calls. In many cases that won't be available. Some service providers offer 800 number access as an alternative. It's not cheap: On average, it costs 8 to 15 cents per minute—which is dramatically more than the Internet service itself.*

> *Assuming that you can't find a service provider with a local point-of-presence, ask your phone company how the service provider's 800 charges compare with the cost of simply making toll calls. Many toll calls cost as little as 3 to 5 cents per minute—which makes 800 numbers a bad bargain. In addition, some phone companies offer a flat-rate monthly service that allows you to specify an exchange outside your immediate area and treat calls to **that** exchange as local calls.*

✍ *How many users do you have per modem (or comparable device)? The generally accepted standard is roughly nine to ten users per modem. At the height of its troubles last spring, America Online had a ratio of 40 to 1. Now do you know why you kept getting busy signals?*

✍ *How fast are your connections? By now they should all run at 28.8 Kbps. If you have a 33.6-Kbps modem, you'll want 33.6-Kbps access—but keep in mind that successful 33.6-Kbps connections depend on external factors such as the quality of your phone lines, and in the real world, they're fairly unusual. 33.6-Kbps modems do often connect at 31.2 Kbps, and they're much more likely to successfully connect at 28.8 Kbps than older 28.8-Kbps modems are.*

You want a service provider that doesn't make its connections via standard analog modems, but via digital/PRI circuit modems—special access products provided by companies like Ascend, Cisco, and U.S. Robotics.

✎ **How will you support 56 Kbps?** *The right answer to this depends on your modem—or your plans to buy one. U.S. Robotics, the market leader, already offers 56-Kbps modems which use its own proprietary X2 technology. The rest of the world trails several months behind U.S. Robotics but will ultimately use Rockwell or Lucent chipsets that support a competing standard.*

Service providers need to buy special equipment to support either standard. (Some who already own U.S. Robotics equipment may have an easier upgrade path, via lower-cost firmware upgrades.)

You'll want to know which 56K-compatible equipment they've already purchased, or are planning to purchase. Are they taking one side, or both? If they already have 56-Kbps access, what kind of speeds are typical customers actually achieving? (Early tests show some 56K modems falling far short of expectations.) And one important related question: **Oh, by the way, you won't charge me more for 56-Kbps access, will you?**

✎ **Do you make any service guarantees? How good is your connectivity to the rest of the Internet?** *Busy signals are the bane of every Internet user. And sometimes you establish a connection but can't reach your destination. It's brutally difficult for an Internet service provider to maintain high-quality service while supporting more customers and fending off price-cutting competitors. Some aren't up to the challenge.*

Ask how many separate connections to the Internet the ISP

has. "One" is **not** the answer you want to hear. "Two" is a little better—and it's all that many small ISPs can reasonably be expected to provide. But if you really depend on the Internet, you'll sleep better at night if there are at least three.[4]

All else equal (and it rarely is), the faster the service provider's connections the better. 56-Kbps connections are clearly inadequate. T-1 connections are good; multiple T-1s are better. T-3—a 45-Megabit per second connection—is the best, but far out of the reach of most local service providers. Of course, even the largest connections can be overwhelmed by a fast-growing customer base—or undermined by technical staff that doesn't know how to configure them properly.

If you're really curious, a few Internet providers will even give you a look at their network map!

If you are an Internet insomniac, ask how the ISP handles outages overnight. Is the network monitored 24 hours a day? Is someone available to fix problems 24 hours a day?

✍ **What kind of customer support will you offer me?** Will you talk me through getting connected? Do you have any printed materials that will help? Are you familiar with the type of computer I'm using—Windows 3.1, Windows 95, or Macintosh? (Many service providers know little or nothing about Macs.) Whom can I call if I'm having problems? (E-mail addresses will do you little good if your e-mail isn't working!) Is the call free? How long are your customers waiting on hold these days? What is your ratio of customers to Customer Service Representatives (CSRs)? There's no perfect answer to this question, but some local providers are able to maintain ratios of 1 to 200 or 1 to 500, while some national providers only have one CSR per 5,000 or more customers.

✍ **How long have you been in business?** Very few ISPs have been in business for more than a few years, but it would be nice to

▲ ▲

4.   Conversely, you might not sleep at all, if you're among the millions of Internet insomniacs out there.

*know your provider has lasted even **that** long. **Are you growing?** That's wonderful news. How are you handling that growth? Have you hired more customer service people?*

✍ ***Can you provide references from customers like me?*** *In an earlier chapter, we suggested asking a computer reseller for references with business customers. If you're looking for home Internet service, however, you won't find business references all that useful. Many service providers are repositioning themselves to focus on businesses instead of consumers. Accordingly, they may have excellent business references, but when **you** come to them for help, you may have to stand in line behind those bigger customers.*

✍ ***Do I get a free Web page along with monthly access?*** *Short answer: You should—and you should expect at least 5 Mb of storage space. That's plenty for most personal needs. Related question: Will you be there to answer questions while I'm getting my page up and running? Will you upload my pages for me? (Or conversely, if you prefer: **Will you let me do it myself?**)*

✍ ***What will this cost me?*** *Are there extra fees I need to be aware of? Which alternative plans do you offer? What do you charge for additional e-mail addresses if I need them? How unlimited is your "unlimited" plan? (Many service providers are quietly slipping limits into these plans.) Is there a startup charge? That's money gone forever if you decide you don't like an ISP. A few ISPs will waive or reduce startup fees for customers switching from another provider. It doesn't hurt to ask.*

✍ ***Do you provide all the software I'll need?*** *This is less of a problem than it used to be (especially for you, since this book's CD-ROM contains complete versions of Microsoft's Internet Explorer Web browser for Windows 95, Windows 3.1, and the Macintosh). But some service providers do offer free copies of Netscape Navigator, e-mail clients like Eudora, and other useful software. Related question: **Can I use any software I want?** A* *few service providers still limit you to customized browsers they provide. These browsers are typically updated more slowly, so you may have to wait for access to the most exciting new Web features.*

✍ **What if I travel?** *If you want to access your Web connection from another location, you'll want at least the option of an 800 number or a local number in the location you're visiting. Of course national and large regional service providers are more likely to be able to provide that.*

With that, Table 7-1 provides a checklist you can use to pick the ISP of your dreams:

Table 7–1 Internet Service Provider Buying Checklist

	Provider #1	Provider #2	Provider #3	Provider #4
Monthly charge				
Setup and other one-time charges				
Hourly charges, if any				
Telephone company per-minute charges (free local call, toll call, or 800 number?)				
Total anticipated monthly cost (monthly charge + monthly additional costs, including toll or 800 charges, based on _____ hours/month on-line)				
Current connection speed?				
Plans to support 56K (U.S. Robotics, Rockwell/Lucent or both?)				
Modem-to-user ratio (should be 10–1 or better)				
Service guarantees?				

Table 7–1 Internet Service Provider Buying Checklist *(continued)*

	Provider #1	Provider #2	Provider #3	Provider #4
ISP connectivity to the rest of the Internet (56K, T1, T3?)				
Toll-free customer support?				
Customer support hours?				
Free software?				
Local references?				
Independent reviews?				

• *Independent Reviews of Service Providers*

Measuring service provider performance is very difficult, since there are few objective yardsticks, and network performance can vary dramatically from moment to moment, due to factors that are sometimes beyond the control of any service provider.

However, measuring *customer satisfaction* is possible, and C|Net, the online computer news service, has done just that. C|Net runs an ongoing customer satisfaction survey that now ranks more than 600 national, regional, and local providers. While the survey samples for local providers are sometimes too small to be meaningful, the information about regional and national providers can be quite telling—and quite surprising.

You can view lists of the top 10 and bottom 10 national ISPs, or search for ratings of providers who do business in your state. The survey can be found at **www.cnet.com/content/reviews/compare/isp/**.

> **tip**
>
> For another detailed look at 12 top national service providers, see the February 1997 issue of *PC World*, or visit *www.pcworld.com/software/ internet_www/articles/feb97/1502p125.html*.

Spend Less Time, Spend Less Money

So you're already paying for Net access by the minute. Or you see the writing on the wall: You're about to be dragged there kicking and screaming. Here are three ways to minimize the damages.

1. Turn off images, Java, and ActiveX programs—you know, all the multimedia stuff that makes the Net fun. (Well, OK, just turn them off when you don't need them.)

2. Make smarter searches. Refine your searches using the advanced search techniques available at most search engines. If you're expecting to use several search engines, consider using software like Symantec Internet FastFind, which automates searching of multiple sites at once.

> **tip** Or try the shareware Search Stream for Windows 95, included on the CD-ROM, which does much the same thing as Internet Fast Find. Your first 25 searches are free; then Search Stream is $29.95, roughly $15 less than Symantec Internet FastFind.

3. Do more of your work off-line. Make sure to prepare your e-mail off-line; consider a free e-mail service like Juno which doesn't require Net access. And if you plan to spend a significant amount of time on a specific site, consider downloading some or all of that site using a program like WebWhacker.

Taking the Wait out of the Web

Whether your Internet service is metered or not, why not make your time on-line as efficient as possible? Two inexpensive products can help you do just that: PeakNetJet and WebWhacker.

- *Peak Net.Jet*

In normal browsing, according to Peak, modems are idle 90 percent of the time. Peak Net.Jet from Peak Technologies (see Figure 7-2) keeps them chugging right along, constantly. While you're on-line, browsing a Web page, Net.Jet scans that page—identifying linked pages, connecting to those pages in the background, retrieving information from them. It also keeps track of the sites you visit most often, making sure they're up to date in case you get a notion to visit them again. The result: Almost any page you choose to click next will display its information almost immediately, because it will already have been retrieved.

Peak NetJet is somewhat controversial, because it adds Web traffic to an already crowded Internet, but in its defense, it *does* retrieve only small text files, not large, bandwidth-intensive graphics. And it works: Users report that Peak Net.Jet dramatically improves the perceived speed of the Web, without modem upgrades or expensive ISDN lines. (Of course, the more graphics on the sites you're visiting, the less improvement you'll see.)

It works with both Netscape Navigator and Microsoft Explorer 3.0. If you decide to buy the product, it's widely available for around $29.95.

Early versions of Peak Net.Jet were prone to inadvertently displaying older versions of pages and other technical problems. For example, Net.Jet takes over for your proxy server, using your "real" proxy server as a point of reference. When people changed proxy servers, early versions of Net.Jet didn't always recognize this properly—leaving browsers unable to find what they were looking for.

If you're considering Peak Net.Jet, first download a trial version from their Web site, *www.peak-media.com.* You can always de-install it if you decide you don't like it. If you like Peak Net.Jet and decide to purchase it, buy direct from Peak's Web site to make sure you get the latest version. Web-related software evolves fast, and it's common for retailers to stock older versions.

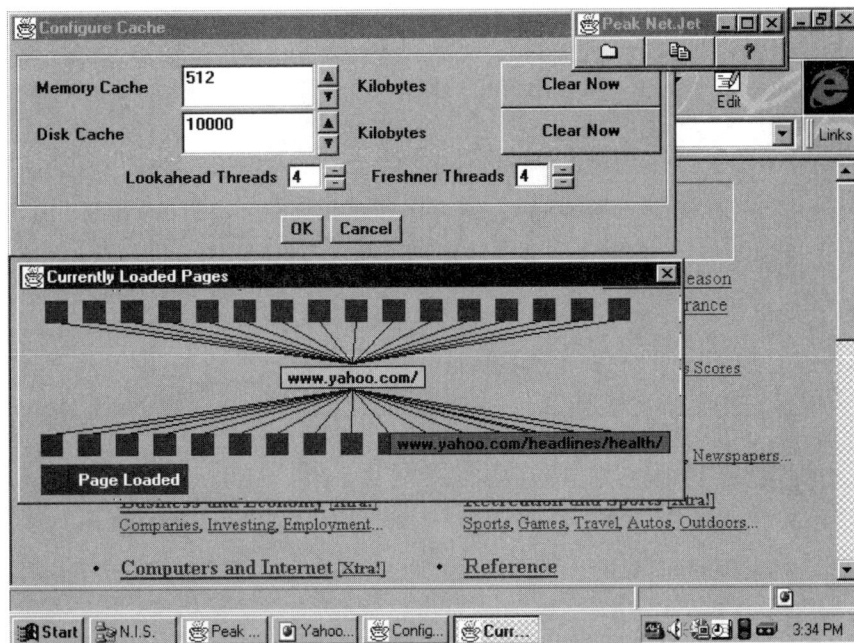

Figure 7–2   Peak Net.Jet keeps your modem hopping to anticipate your every click.

• *WebWhacker*

WebWhacker from ForeFront Group (see Figure 7-3) is another product that lets you be there now, even when you're elsewhere. Billed as "the ultimate off-line browsing and content delivery application," WebWhacker allows you to download specific pages or entire Web sites, including text, images and links—then view them quickly, because they're already stored on your computer. It also allows you to automatically monitor sites, only retrieving new pages and information.

You can get a free 30-day demo of WebWhacker at ForeFront Group's Web site, **www.ffg.com/whacker/**—or you can purchase the product for $49.95 on-line, or at many retailers and mail-order houses.

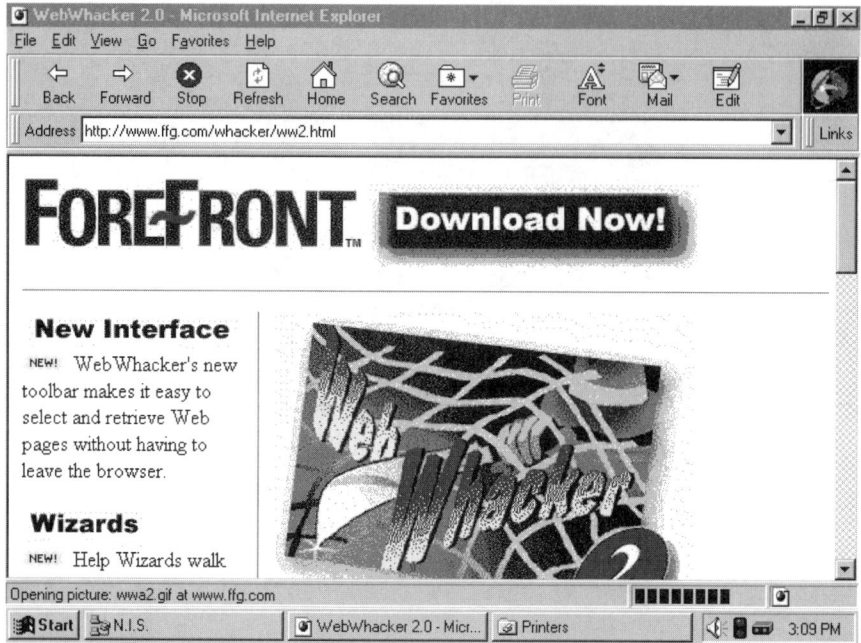

Figure 7–3   WebWhacker: Download whole sites in a single click.

Free and Evaluation Web Browsers

The accompanying CD-ROM contains versions of the leading free Internet Web browser: Microsoft Internet Explorer for Windows 95, Windows 3.1, and the Macintosh. Internet Explorer is currently the world's number 2 Web browser, trailing only Netscape Navigator.

You can expect both Explorer and Navigator to be upgraded in the near future. To download free upgrades of Internet Explorer, visit Microsoft's Web site at **www.microsoft.com/ie/download**.

Evaluation copies of Netscape Navigator, and the Netscape Communicator Internet communications suite that is replacing it, are will be available at **www.netscape.com**. Netscape Communicator includes e-mail, groupware, conferencing, and additional features not previously available on Netscape browsers.

If you are a student, faculty member, or staff member of an educational institution (K–12, junior college, college, or library), or an employee of a charitable nonprofit, nongovermental organization, Netscape currently grants you a license to use Navigator at no charge; others may evaluate the software for 90 days before purchasing a license.

Surfing the Web from DOS

So you have one of those $99 DOS machines we talked about in Chapter 1; you can get on the Web, too. It's a miracle that proves the infinite nature of human ingenuity.

The first programmer to achieve this Everest-like goal was Garrett Arch Blythe, author of DosLynx. At this writing, DosLynx' latest release is 0.8. It's still an alpha release (read: *buggy*). But it has been designed to run on computers as old as 8086s with as little as 512K free memory, as long as they use versions of DOS after 3.0. For information on downloading and configuring DosLynx, visit **ftp://ftp2.cc.ukans.edu/pub/DosLynx/ readme.htm**.

Now there's a second DOS browsing program, too, and one that's getting very good reviews: NetTamer. It's also capable of running on systems as old as XTs, and even more remarkably, there's even a version for older Hewlett-Packard palmtop systems, such as the HP200LX.

NetTamer is shareware by David Colston with a $35 lifetime registration fee, and you'll find it at the following Web site: **http://people.delphi.com/davidcolston/**.

Free Web Pages for Businesses

We've already mentioned that most good service providers will now give you free space for your own Web page. If you have a business or professional practice, you can also get a free Web page through Inc. Online, the Web Site of *Inc. Magazine*. You fill out a simple on-line form, and *Inc.* builds the Web page—nothing fancy, but this may be the fastest and easiest way for many businesses to get on the Web. To find out more, visit **www.inc.com/createsite/**.

For the Courageous Cheapskate: Free Web Servers

So you want to actually *host* a site yourself, on your premises? May the force be with you. You'll have access to tons of free resources. And lots of companies, big and small, will want to be your friend—in exchange for the early market share they view as critical to their long-term success.

Don't forget to carefully factor in the hardware, communications lines, and the *time* you're going to need. Normally, the Cheapskate solution is to outsource this kind of thing, but hey, even Cheapskates like a challenge.

• *Apache*

Apache is now the world's #1 Web server, running on more than 40 percent of all Web sites worldwide, according to a recent survey.[5] It's the direct descendant of the Web server that dates back to the very beginnings of the Web, in those halcyon days at the National Center for Supercomputing Applications, before everyone (well, it *seems* like everyone) went public and got rich. In fact, the name Apache derives from the fact that the first version of Apache was *a patchy* version of NCSA's Web server software.

Apache runs on a variety of UNIX platforms, including Linux, the free UNIX-like operating system discussed in Chapter 2. You can download the current version of Apache at **www.apache.org** (see Figure 7-4). You might, however, find it faster and more efficient to purchase the inexpensive Red Hat distribution of Linux (4.0 or higher), which comes with Apache and gives you the opportunity of automatically installing it during the Linux setup process.

Apache is both powerful and fast. Even with Red Hat helping you out, though, if you're unfamiliar with both UNIX and the mechanics of running a Web server, your learning curve will be steep, and it will be a while before you'll feel comfortable. Many of the Linux and Apache resources available on the Web and elsewhere assume you know quite a bit about either UNIX or the Web.

▲ ▲

5.   A survey of more than 1 million Web sites worldwide, May 1997, NetCraft Inc., Bath, England reports 44 percent are running Apache.

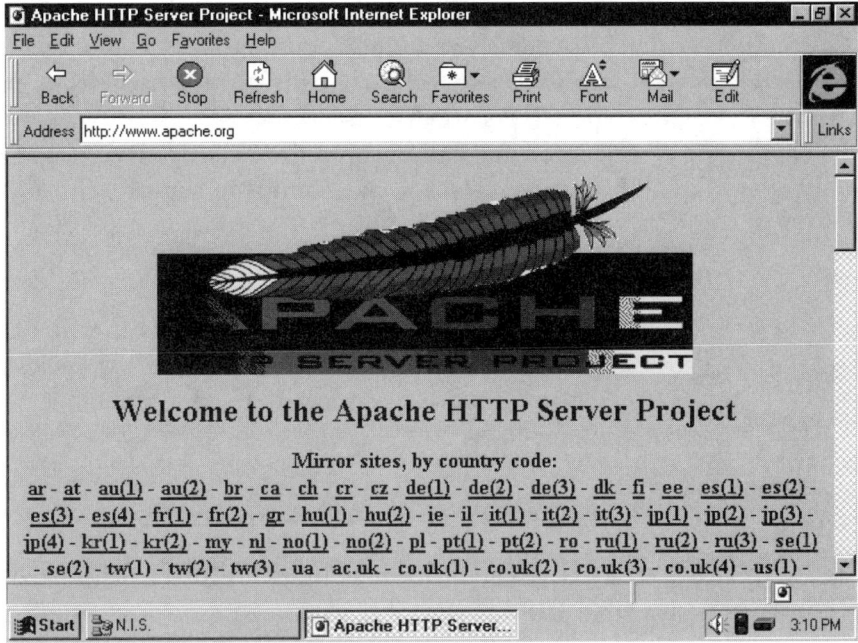

Figure 7–4 **www.apache.org**, home of the world's most popular free Web server.

> You can keep track of what's new with Apache at *www.apacheweek.com.*
>
> tip

• *Free Netscape Servers for Nonprofits*

If you are an educational institution, charitable nonprofit organization, or public library, you almost certainly qualify for the Netscape Free Server Software Program, which allows you to download and use any of the server products available on Netscape's Web site, free of charge. Some of these advanced servers are sold to the corporate market for thousands of dollars. Most run on UNIX and Windows NT platforms; Netscape's Fast Track server also runs on Windows 95.

Support and printed documentation aren't included with this free offer, but extensive on-line documentation exists for most of these products, and you may also be able to get help from newsgroups where Netscape servers are discussed.

For more information about the Netscape Free Server Software Program, visit **http://live.netscape.com/comprod/server_central/edu_ drive.html**.

• *Free Web Servers for OS/2 Warp*

If you use OS/2 Warp, IBM has made its Internet Connection Server for OS/2 available for free download at **www.ics.raleigh.ibm.com**. There's also an OS/2 version of Apache, downloadable at **www.slink. com/apacheOS2/**.

• *Microsoft Internet Information Server*

The extremely powerful Microsoft Internet Information Server is also available free for download from Microsoft at **www.microsoft.com**. Of course, there's a catch: You have to run it on Windows NT Server 4.0 or higher, which typically costs over $700. Oh, well.

If it's any consolation, Microsoft is currently happy to send you a free four-month trial CD-ROM containing both NT Server 4.0 *and* Internet Information Server. Visit them at **www.microsoft.com/iis/promo/ download3/** for the details.

• *Microsoft FrontPage and Microsoft Office 97*

If you've purchased either Microsoft Office 97 or the Microsoft FrontPage Web authoring tool, you already own Microsoft's Personal Web Server (see Figure 7-5). While Personal Web Server is typically used to test Web pages you create with Office or FrontPage, you can actually use it to run a small corporate intranet with either Windows 95 or Windows NT.

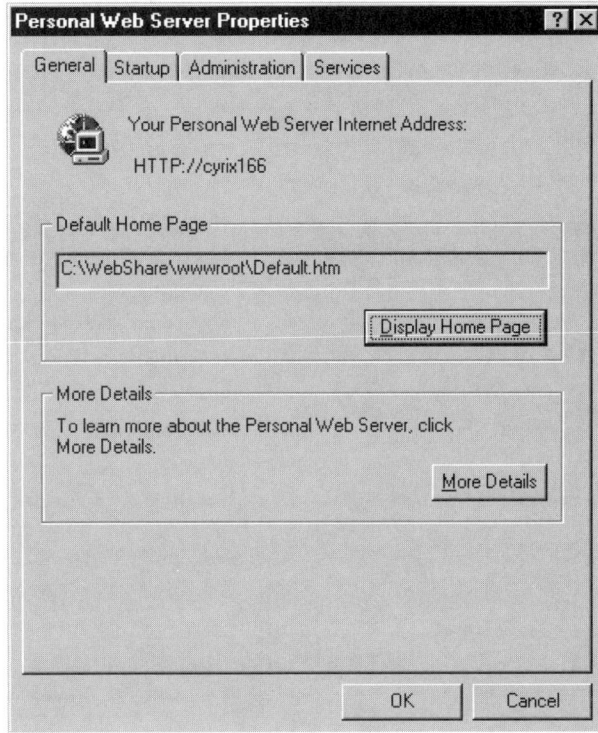

Figure 7–5 Microsoft's Personal Web Server *might* be just enough for a small company intranet, and if you own Office 97 or FrontPage 97, you already own it.

Now That You're on the Web

Now that you're on the Web, you'll find you've arrived in Cheapskates' paradise. The sheer quantity of free stuff to be found is extraordinary. Free news, free software, free e-mail, free products … you name it. (And the freebies aren't all computer related: Check out the *Next to Nothing* site, **www.winternet.com/~julie/ntn1.html**, for an up-to-the-minute compilation of free offers at both Web sites and 800 numbers.)

Of course, this is the information superhighway we're talking about. So much of what's free is information. You can see a sampling of what's free in Table 7-2.

Net Freebies

Table 7-2 Some Net Freebies

You *Could* Pay for It …	Or You Could Access It *FREE* on the Web at…
The *CIA World Factbook 1995*	http://www.odci.gov/cia/publications/95fact/index.html
White Pages Directory Assistance	http://www.databaseamerica.com http://www.whowhere.com
Encyclopedia Britannica	http://www.eb.com (7-day free trial only)
Dictionary listings	http://www.onelook.com (searches multiple dictionaries at once)
Stock quotes	PointCast (http://www.pointcast.com) Yahoo (http://www.yahoo.com) After Dark Online (http://www.afterdark.com) NASDAQ (http://www.nasdaq.com)
The New York Times	http://www.nytimes.com
Official company information from SEC filings	http://www.sec.gov http://www.edgar.whowhere.com
Business news	http://www.individual.com
Long-distance and international telephone calls	http://www.vocaltec.com (Vocaltec Internet Phone trial software) http://www.intel.com (Intel Internet Phone) http://www.microsoft.com (Microsoft NetMeeting) and other locations to download and use Internet telephony software
E-mail service	http://www.hotmail.com http://www.juno.com
Nationwide classified ads	http://www.yahoo.com
Current TV and cable listings	http://www.tottv.com

Free Directory Assistance

In Chapter 4, we told you that previous-year PhoneDisc nationwide residential and business telephone directories are available for $30 or less through sources like Surplus Direct and MEI Micro Center. But you can get directory assistance listings on the Internet, without spending a dime. PhoneDisc's publisher offers a free lookup service on its Web site, at **www.phonedisc.com/411.htm** (see Figure 7-6).

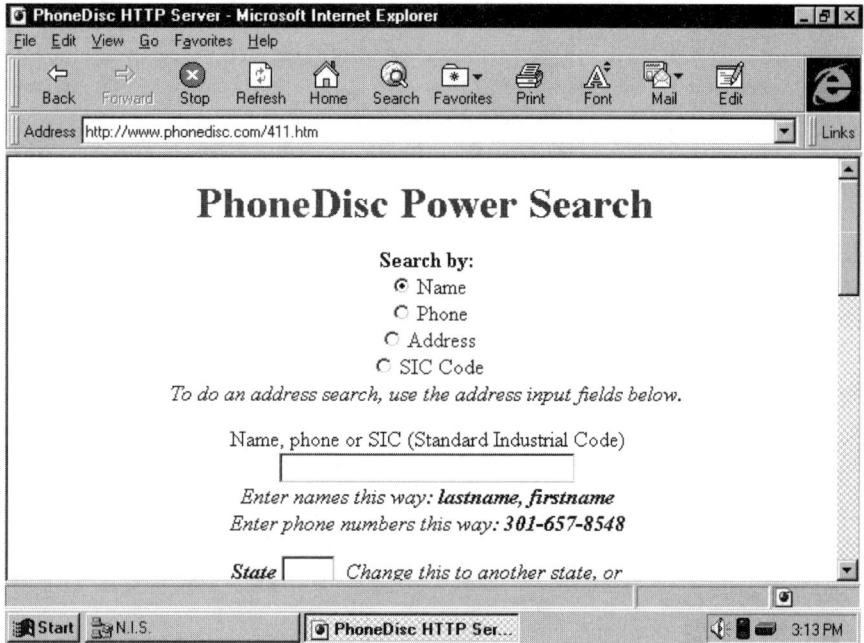

Figure 7–6 Free phone listings on the Web from the folks who bring you PhoneDisc.

If it's an e-mail address you're looking for, try the Four11 service (**www.four11.com,** see Figure 7-7). It's free, and while it's not comprehensive *yet*, with more than 10 million current listings, it's sure headed in the right direction.

Four11 gets its listings from three sources: more than 2,000,000 voluntary individual registrations; public sources, such as postings to Usenet newsgroups; and automatic registration, in which Internet service providers register all their users at once.

Four11 has recently supplemented its e-mail directory with national telephone listings, links to directories of Internet phone users who use any of six different Net phone products; and e-mail directories of government officials and celebrities—all equally free.

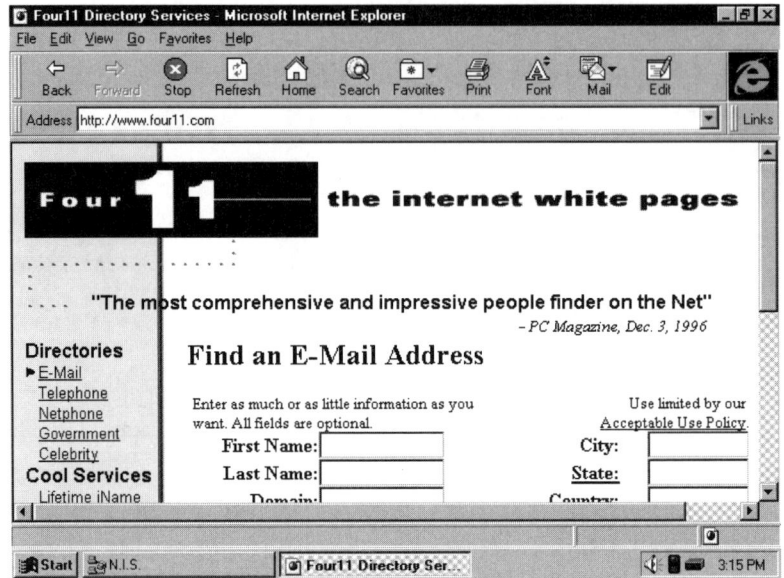

Figure 7–7   Lonely tonight? Here's where to find your high school sweetheart's E-mail address—even if her name is Madonna (Madonna@wbr.com).

Free E-Mail

If you already have Internet access at home or at work, you probably already have an e-mail address. But, what if:

- ▲ You don't have an Internet connection at home or at work?
- ▲ You want to check your e-mail from a computer or a location where you can't reach your service provider?
- ▲ You want a private account that isn't shared by your family, or owned by your employer?
- ▲ You want an account you can keep using even if you find a better deal, and change your service provider?

As it happens, several companies, led by Juno and Hotmail, are vying to give you free, advertiser-supported e-mail that will follow you wherever you may go. Each works somewhat differently, but one of them may well be for you. These services may also be just the ticket for community nonprofits who want to provide e-mail to their members.

Juno

Without questioning anyone else's intentions, Juno appears to be in it for the long haul. Its lead investor, David Shaw, is the principal in a $700 million investment bank, and perhaps the world's most well respected expert on using technology to beat the markets.

You don't need an Internet connection to use Juno e-mail, but you do need a Windows 95 or Windows 3.1 PC. Widely publicized as one of the best-financed Internet startups, Juno claims that it can provide local access to more than 95 percent of the U.S. population, so chances are you won't have to make a toll call to access your e-mail.

To get a free copy of the Juno software, you can e-mail a request to **signup@juno.com**—or since you may not have an e-mail address, call 1-800-654-5866. Juno is rolling out its service very deliberately, to make sure it can handle the load—so you may have to wait a little while.

Judge for yourself whether you can handle the advertising (see Figure 7-8).

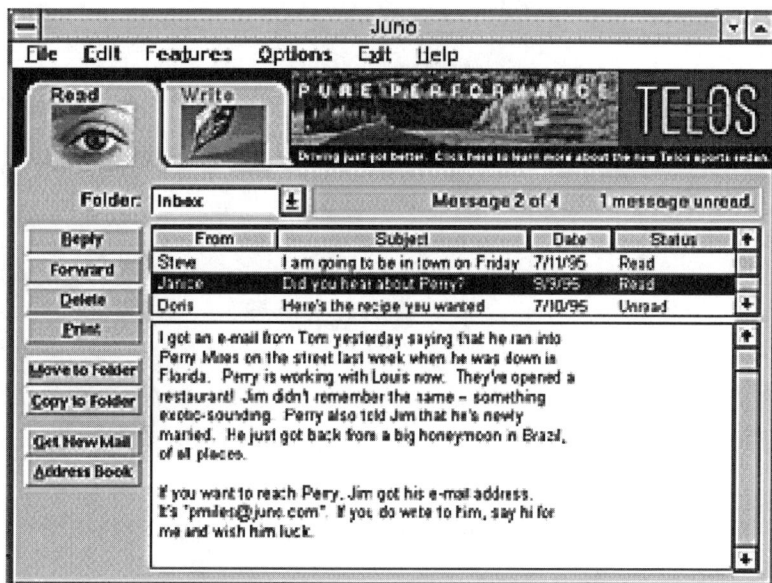

Figure 7–8 Juno's E-mail software runs on virtually any Windows PC.

Hotmail

In March 1997, Hotmail (see Figure 7-9) claimed 2,000,000 subscribers—twice as many as just a few months before. No wonder Hotmail has been busily upgrading and rearchitecting its own computer network.

Unlike Juno, Hotmail requires no special software, but it does require a Web connection and a standard Web browser. Any Web connection will do: You can connect at work, or at a library, Internet café, or other public Internet connection. If there are ever Internet terminals in airports and rail terminals, as has been widely promised, those will do the job swimmingly.

To register, you fill out a brief questionnaire which allows Hotmail to target advertising to your specific interests. Once registered, to check your e-mail, you enter a password at the Hotmail Web site (**www.hotmail.com**). You can then retrieve any messages that have been left for you.

Hotmail allows you to set up folders for filing your mail, maintain a personal address book, read mail, even e-mail files to yourself for pickup at another destination.

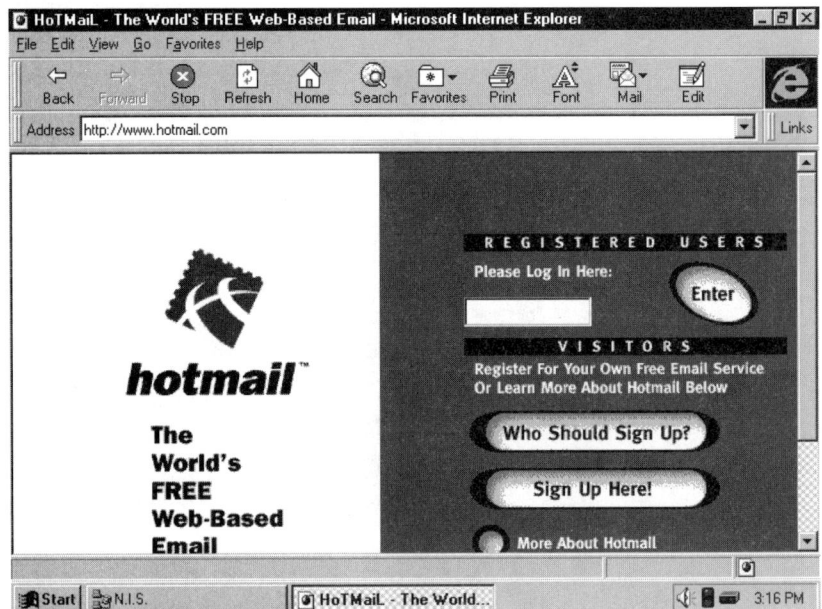

Figure 7–9   If you can get on the Web, you can get your e-mail at Hotmail.

More Free E-Mail Sites

A third entry, NetAddress (**www.netaddress.com**), borrows capabilities from a variety of sources. As with Hotmail, you can pick up your mail at the NetAddress Web site. Or, you can use your own Internet mail reader—any program that supports standard Internet protocols. You can also use NetAddress' MailRover feature to collect your e-mail from other mailboxes, as often as every 15 minutes. And if you simply hate advertising, they'll gladly remove the e-mail advertising tags from your incoming mail—for the low, low price of $24.95.

> There's also TravelTales *(www.traveltales.com)*, targeted specifically to travelers who aren't carrying computers but may stop at cybercafés or other public Internet access sites to pick up their e-mail. In fact, the site contains a list—scanty, but growing—of free internet access points and cybercafés worldwide.

The Same E-Mail Address, Forever

With Internet access prices on the way up, and many Internet Service Providers (ISPs) on the way down, you may be wondering whether it's time to make a change. There's one reason many Internet users stay with providers they aren't satisfied with: It's too much of a hassle changing business cards and letting all your contacts know about a new address.

Bigfoot (see Figure 7-10) offers a potential solution. Once you register with Bigfoot—it's free, of course—you get a forwarding address through which *all* your e-mail comes. That's the address you give your contacts: *you@bigfoot.com*.

Next, you let Bigfoot know which ISP you're currently using, and where you want your E-mail forwarded. If you're on AOL, for example, Bigfoot can forward your mail to *you@aol.com*. If you move to AT&T WorldNet service, inform Bigfoot and they'll start forwarding your mail to you@*att.worldnet.net*.

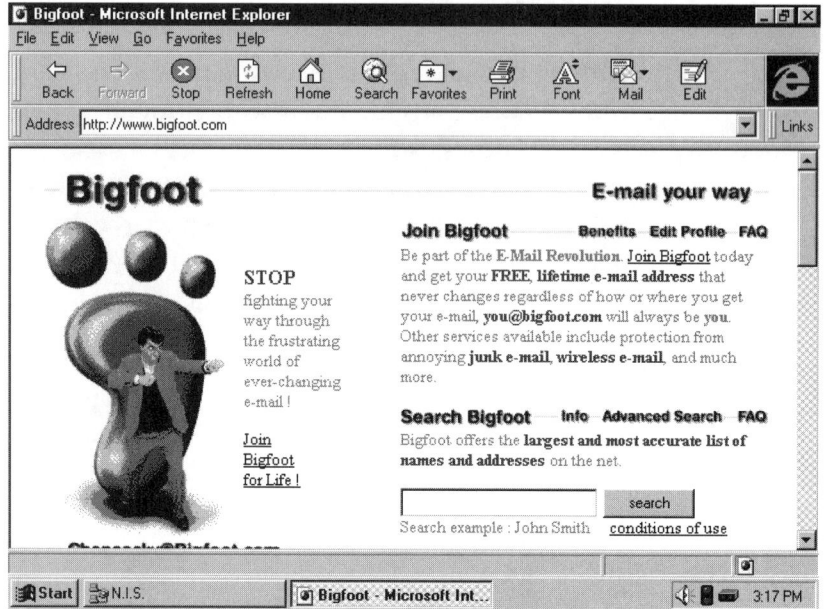

Figure 7–10   Getting a permanent e-mail address at Bigfoot.

If you're feeling especially cheap, you *could* hop back and forth between ISP special offers (assuming there are still any)—using Bigfoot to forward your mail while you keep your Internet access inexpensive or free for the next several months.

Of course, all this only works if *Bigfoot* stays in business a while—but so far, there's no sign they're going anywhere.

Free Long-Distance Phone Calls

If you have an Internet connection, there's a bonus you should be aware of: free (or extremely inexpensive) long-distance telephone calls. Instead of using your telephone and the phone company's network, if you have a sound card and microphone you can establish a voice connection through your computer and the Internet.

Why isn't everyone doing this? Until very recently, both parties had to connect to the same Internet location at the same time. There was no way to call someone who hadn't prearranged to be at the right place at the right time. Nor could you call a regular phone from your "Internet" phone. You and the person at the other end also had to use the same software. (Imagine if your phone only connected to other people with the same model!)

Worst of all, to be blunt, the sound quality of Internet phone calls has been poor. (Depending on the software you use, it may be *moderately* poor or *unbelievably* poor, but unless you have an expensive dedicated high-speed connection to the Internet, it has definitely been *some* kind of poor.)

Things are slowly improving. If you are fortunate enough to have a fast modem and an Internet service provider that supports it, you might find voice quality that's nearly competitive with cellular calls—especially if you can make your calls at off-hours when the Internet is less crowded.

Meanwhile, Internet voice companies are beginning to provide gateways that allow you to call people at their telephones, not their Internet connections. Internet directories are improving, and standards are slowly evolving to help ensure that Internet phone software from different vendors can work together (see Figure 7-11).

VocalTec is the market leader in Internet telephony: They were there first, have the largest installed base, and are generally considered to offer the best voice quality—in an industry that hovers somewhere between CB and walkie-talkie quality at best. VocalTec offers limited-time free downloads of its products. That limited time is currently *quite* limited: just one to two weeks, in many cases. This makes it difficult to fully evaluate the products, unless you've carefully planned in advance to have someone ready at the other end.

On the other hand, when you *do* buy VocalTec Internet Phone or a related product, you get two licenses. That means you can share a copy of the software with whomever you talk to most often, without worrying about compatibility problems.

Plenty of people are using Internet telephony (and even cruder Internet video) to meet, umm, interesting strangers on the Web. If that's not your bag, the best applications for Internet telephony are

▲ International calls that would otherwise be inordinately expensive
▲ Planned calls between two people who already talk regularly via long distance

295

Why not at least try the Internet alternative, and see what results you get? You have nothing to lose. There's a copy of Microsoft's NetMeeting on the accompanying CD-ROM; you install it as part of the Internet Explorer installation process. (NetMeeting provides both telephony and document sharing.) You can also download free (or evaluation) Internet telephony software at the sites listed in Table 7-3.

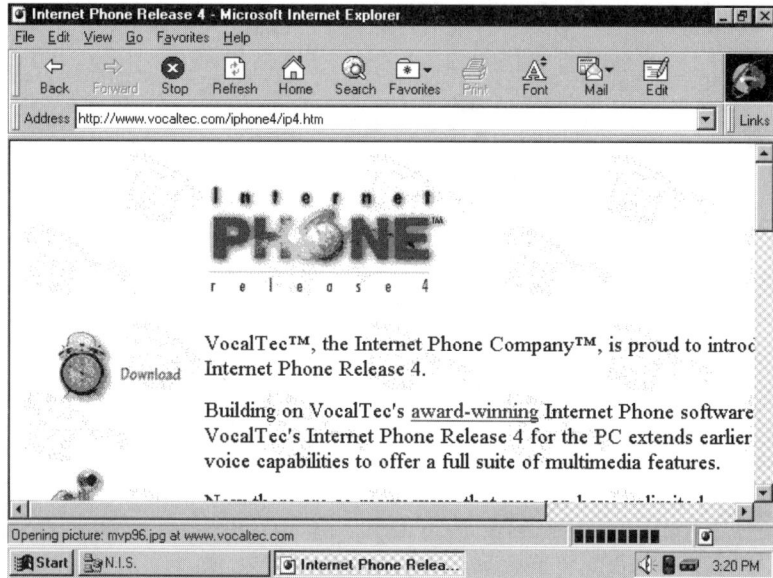

Figure 7–11   Downloading a trial version of VocalTec's Internet Phone, the market leader in Internet telephony.

The long-term outlook for Internet telephony is that quality will improve, but costs will go up, too. Infrastructure improvements such as gateways and new protocols that allow voice packets to take priority are going to cost money. Companies are likely to provide telephone service that resembles traditional telephony but carries calls over the Internet instead of traditional voice networks; those companies will charge less than conventional phone companies, but quite a bit more than typical Internet access companies. Finally, the same technologies and software that allow for voice transmission will increasingly support document sharing and low-quality video as well. That's already happening with products like Microsoft's Net-Meeting and Vocaltec's Internet Conference Professional.

Table 7–3 Sites to Download Free or Trial Internet Telephony Software

Product	Web site
Vocaltec Internet Phone	**http://www.vocaltec.com**
Microsoft NetMeeting (upgrades to newer versions as they are introduced; see Figure 7-12)	**http://www.microsoft.com/ie/conf**
Intel Internet Video Phone (also supports video if you have a video input device such as a Connectix QuickCam)	**http://connectedpc.com/iaweb/cpc/iivphone/**
Netscape Cooltalk (an extension to Netscape Navigator)	**http://www.netscape.com**

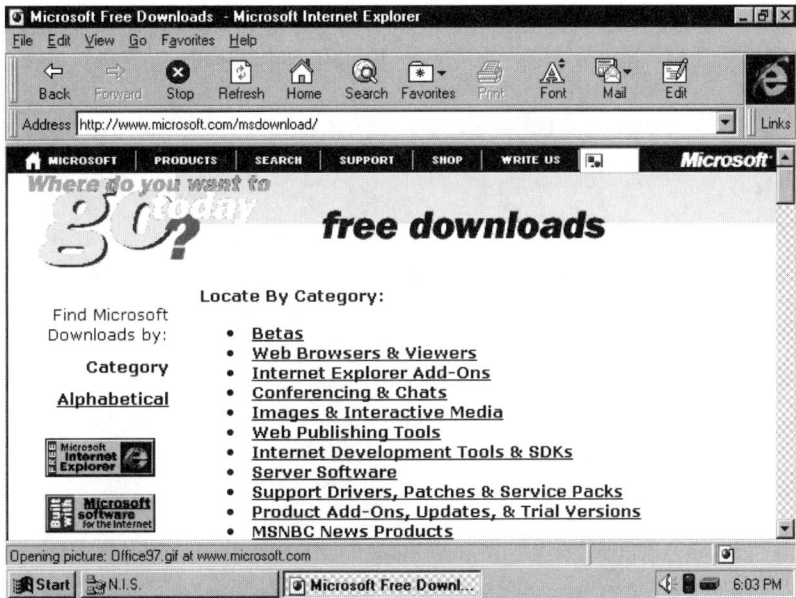

Figure 7–12   Downloading Microsoft NetMeeting to hold free meetings on the Web.

> You can get up-to-date information on the entire field of Internet telephony at *http://rpcp.mit.edu/~asears/voice-faq.html*, and also at www.pulver.com, a site operated by Jeff Pulver, one of the Internet telephony industry's leading experts.

Discount Videoconferencing

If you've gotten tired of waiting for AT&T to deliver the PicturePhone® of your dreams, you can now set up your own videoconferencing system for well under $300, using the Web and your regular phone lines.

Well, perhaps that doesn't quite qualify as cheap, but it's very cheap compared to all the traditional alternatives.

The most popular on-the-cheap videoconferencing system starts with Connectix' QuickCam black-and-white desktop camera, available for roughly $99 (and less if you can find a refurb; they've sold for as little as $59 at Surplus Direct). The software is White Pine Software's Enhanced CU-SeeMe, which began life as shareware at Cornell University and is now a full-featured commercial product for $99. You can get a 30-day demo at **www.wpine.com/cudownload.htm**, or you can satisfy yourself with the older shareware version.

A less expensive software alternative is Vfone 2.0 from SummerSoft (**www.summersoft.com**), currently priced at $49.95 + $3.95 shipping and handling, at 1-800-879-4141. Vsoft offers a full-featured, free trial version with only one limitation: Calls made with the trial version cannot exceed five minutes.

Free News

Earlier in this chapter, I listed some sources of information that used to cost an arm and a leg but are now free on the Net. Now, let's take a closer look at a couple of ways you can get a free customized newspaper that just might be good enough to replace the one you may be paying hundreds of dollars a year for.

PointCast

If you're on the Web, you ought to be on PointCast (see Figure 7-13).

The first and still the best at delivering free information to you across the Internet, PointCast lets you choose among more than 15 channels of world-class, regularly updated news and information. Then, on any schedule you want, it retrieves the new information and displays it on an elegant screen-saver that runs whenever you're not typing. If you want more information, click on the screensaver, and PointCast appears, showing you everything it has downloaded.

Figure 7–13   PointCast: The first and still the best on-line news broadcaster.

What do you pay for all this up-to-date information? Nothing, if you download the PointCast software on-line at **www.pointcast.com** (though if you're determined to pay, you *can* purchase a shrinkwrapped copy of PointCast in your local computer store for around $19.99). Animated ads run in about one-fourth of the PointCast screen, but they're fun and easy to ignore if you so choose.

PointCast currently delivers news from the following sources:

- ▲ Reuters News (International, U.S., Business, and Sports)
- ▲ News by industry (primarily but not entirely press releases)
- ▲ Weather (including detailed radar maps, and even allergy forecasts)
- ▲ CNN and CNNfn (CNN Financial Network)
- ▲ *The New York Times*
- ▲ The *Chicago Tribune*

- The *Boston Globe*
- The *Miami Herald*
- Philadelphia On-line
- Mercury Center (The *San Jose Mercury News*, one of the best sources of Silicon Valley news)
- *Wired* magazine
- *Health News*
- *Lifestyle News*
- Time/Warner Pathfinder

After I browse PointCast in the morning, and then visit *The Dilbert Zone* (**www.unitedmedia.com/comics/dilbert/**) for a Dilbert comic strip (one week delayed from its appearance in print), I rarely feel the need to buy a newspaper. And that's a print *fanatic* talking, someone who writes books and was once a reporter.

Individual NewsPage

Among the many other companies that are currently battling for the right to give you free, targeted news, one of the best is Individual, Inc.'s NewsPage.

NewsPage excerpts current news from more than 700 sources, including magazines, newsletters, newspapers, and newswires. You choose from among 2,500 distinct topics of interest; having done so, whenever you visit NewsPage you will get new headlines and news briefs about those topics. Individual also claims its technology is superior to traditional search engines, using content-based analysis to "eliminate garbage and duplicate stories."

If you want to know more about a story, for about 40 percent of the headlines—typically the ones that came from press releases and other low-cost sources—you can simply click and get the entire article.

For $3.95/month you get free access to a tier of premium articles, as well as the right to access pay-per-view articles that cost more. For $6.95/month, they'll e-mail the news to you every morning instead of waiting for you to visit their Web site.

Mercury Mail

If you don't want to bother installing or visiting anything, Mercury Mail will e-mail you the latest news, sports, and weather up to three times a day, based on a personalized profile you fill out at **www.merc.com** (see Figure 7-14). One nice touch: You can tell Mercury Mail about any birthdays or anniversaries you'd like to be reminded about, and it will send you free e-mail reminders one week and one day before the big day.

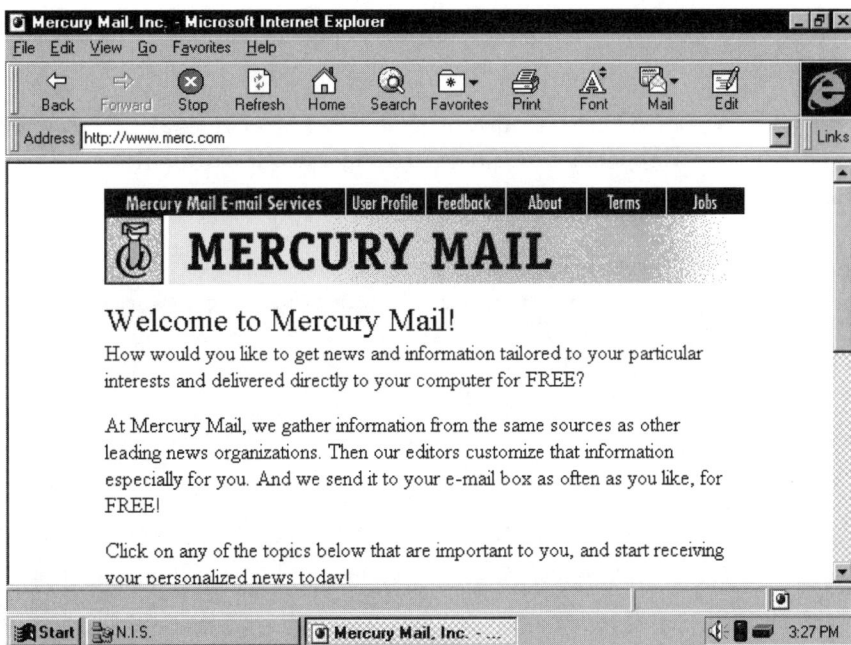

Figure 7–14   Mercury Mail, another contender in the drive to give you free e-mail.

Trade Magazines on the Web: Insider's Secret

For the regular Joe or Jane Cheapskate PC user, trade magazines are among the world's coolest secrets. These magazines provide up-to-date insider coverage of computers, multimedia, Web stuff—just about any technology you're into. Best of all, they've always been free.

There used to be a catch: You used to have to fill out a subscription form claiming that you were involved in buying decisions for some huge number of computers, or that you managed some huge number of employees. Well, for some of you that was no problem: It's the truth, Boy Scout's honor. But for others, the only way to get the magazines for free was to lie. And we can't have that.

Now, however, there's the Web. Many of these magazines have posted all their content, available to everyone, for free. And (at the moment, anyway), few of these sites ask you to be a subscriber, or to validate yourself in any other way.

With that in mind, Table 7-4 is a Cheapskate's guide to trade magazine Web sites with up-to-date technology information.

Table 7–4 Free Access to Computer and Network Trade Magazines

What's New with...	Print Publication	Web Site
PCs	*PC Week*	**http://www.pcweek.com**
	InfoWorld	**http://www.infoworld.com**
		(requires registration to access some information)
Macintoshes	*MacWeek*	**http://www.macweek.com**
The Web	*Web Week*	
	Interactive Week	**http://www.webweek.com**
Multimedia	*New Media (monthly)*	**http://www.hyperstand.com**
Networking	*Communications Week*	**http://www.techweb.cmp.com/cw/cwi**
What the *phone companies* are up to (e.g., when they're going to finally give us fast Web access and cheap cellular)	*Tele.com*	**http://www.teledotcom.com**
What the *cable companies* are up to (e.g., when they're finally going to give us fast Web access. We know they'll never give us cheap cable!)	*Multichannel News*	**http://www.multichannel.com**

Summary

So there you have it: the Cheapskate's guide to getting on-line as cost-effectively as possible and grabbing all the goodies you can once you're there. Now that we've had our fun, in the next chapter we'll face the inevitable: What to do when your computer starts misbehaving.

8

The Cheapskate's Guide to Troubleshooting, Repairs, and Preventive Maintenance

The worst has happened. You turn on your PC and—*nothing*. Or, suddenly your computer isn't recognizing Drive C, where all your valuable data are. Or that CD-ROM drive worked yesterday, but today—*nothing*.

Now what? Finding a Cheapskate computer repairman isn't much easier than finding, say, a Cheapskate dishwasher repairman. Should you bring it in? Is it worth fixing? Is it really broken? Could you fix it yourself? And if you can't, how do you know the repairman's worth his or her salt?

In this chapter, we'll take a look at these questions and others. But first, because we're the true Cheapskates we are, let's see how we can reduce our risks of having problems in the first place—and minimize their severity when and if they occur.

Your Computer's Physical Environment

By simply treating your computer well, I'm convinced you can avoid one-third to one-half of all computer repairs. What does your computer need? Surprisingly, it's pretty much the same stuff *you* need: a clean environment that's not too hot or cold, no cigarette smoke, a minimum of dust to inhale, and as few shocks to the nervous system as possible.

Smoke Gets in Your Drives

Let's take care of the quickies first. If at all possible, don't smoke near your computer. (Shucks, now even the *hardware* is objecting to your habit.)

Computers dislike all types of smoke and dust, and you'll be amazed how much can find its way into your computer, even though the case is closed.

One statistic may be enough to convince you: In today's hard drives, the drive head that reads and writes data must consistently operate at *one to two millionths* of an inch above the drive platter where information is stored—all while the platters are spinning at several thousand rotations per minute. A typical speck of dust is *four to eight millionths* of an inch high: If one finds its way inside your drive, it's more than enough to cause serious data damage. Obviously, the more dust you have, the more likely one will.

Vacuum out your computer every now and then. The preferred way to do this is with canned air.[1] Cheapskates may object in principle to paying for air, but these products are a lot better than your DustBuster™ for safely blowing dust and dirt away from motherboards, circuit boards, and system fans—and equipment with clean innards lives longer.

Static Kills

Computers also hate static electricity. If you routinely give off sparks when you walk across your carpet in the wintertime, you may have an electric personality, but *please* touch a key to your metal file cabinet before you go anywhere near your computer. One more thing: Magnets destroy data. Don't stick refrigerator magnets on your PC; don't put telephones (which contain magnets) on top of your floppy disks.

Feel the Power: You Won't Like It

Computers like a steady diet of clean power, and unfortunately, that's not as common as we'd like to think. Part of that is the utilities' fault: Summer brownouts are just the most prominent examples of power problems that can shorten the life of PCs. Part of it is *us*, though.

Try not to put your PC on the same line as devices that draw large amounts of energy. That includes the obvious stuff, like air conditioners,

▲ ▲ ▲ ▲ ▲ ▲ ▲ ▲ ▲ ▲ ▲ ▲ ▲ ▲ ▲ ▲ ▲ ▲ ▲

1.   Well, actually, a variety of chemicals are used, not precisely "air." One inexpensive source for canned air is Best Computer Supplies (1-800-544-3472), which currently offers Dust-Off Jr. Canned Air for $3.97 per 3.58-oz. can.

refrigerators, or space heaters. But unfortunately it also includes the not-so-obvious staples of the modern home office: coffeemakers, laser printers, copiers, and the like.

Unfortunately, most surge protectors are *a long way* from foolproof.[2] One good zap, and typical surge protectors are worthless. Some of the *slightly* better ones have lights that will go out when a large surge attacks them. Problem is, several small zaps will also kill the surge protector—but they won't kill the light. You'll think you're protected, until one day, *you're* the one who's zapped.

Just as unfortunately, the devices that *do* help—power conditioners and Uninterruptible Power Supplies (UPSs)—cost an arm and a leg. As a Cheapskate I'm hard pressed to follow the standard advice and recommend a $300–400 UPS, especially if you're protecting only $600–$1000 worth of equipment. That is, *unless* you're storing especially valuable data on it. In that case, you need a UPS—*and* daily backups, as we'll cover shortly.

> **tip** If you want a UPS, MEI/Micro Center (1-800-634-3478) sells the Deltec brand for substantially less than most name-brand units. Brand name UPSes are beginning to drop in price, though the low-end 200-300V models are sufficient to protect recent-vintage systems.

OK, then what? If you're in an area with few obvious power problems, such as regular brownouts or large thunderstorms, you may choose to live dangerously, and try to get away with

----

2. Actually there are some excellent surge protectors, called "series" surge protectors. But they cost quite a bit more. For the record, two companies that manufacture series surge protectors are

ZeroSurge
944 State Route 12
Frenchtown, NJ 08825
1-800-996-6696

Brick Wall Division
Price Wheeler Corporation
P.O. Box 9150
Trenton, NJ 08650-1150
908-996-3100
www.brtinc.com/brickwall/home.htm

1. Purchasing quality surge protectors *and replacing them every six months to a year* (or whenever the light goes out, indicating failure). You can use the failed surge protectors as standard outlet strips. Your toaster won't care.
2. Turning off the computer during brownouts or potential brownouts.
3. Disconnecting the computer (and disconnecting any phone jacks connected to your modem) during thunderstorms, or when you go away on vacation.

This strategy is merely a form of self-insurance. You could get burned (or fried). But you've made a conscious decision to retain *part* of the risk rather than paying a substantially higher upfront cost to eliminate it.

There's one more big thing you can do to reduce your risk of electrical-related damage: Minimize the number of times you turn your PC on and off. That's when the components and power supply are stressed most. (Many computer experts recommend leaving a system on 24 hours a day, though I'm hesitant to recommend that to Cheapskates. But think about it: When do your light bulbs fail? Typically, it's when you turn them on and off. Same deal here.)

Whenever possible, reboot by pressing the Reset button instead of the on/off switch. Leave the computer on if you leave the room for a while (though if you're lucky enough to have a laptop or desktop system with reliable power management, it's OK to use that).

> **tip** If you're not comfortable with wasting energy, leave the computer on but turn the monitor off. (See Chapter 6 for a discussion of monitor energy costs.) Another solution is a PowerMiser-type device, which sits between your monitor and your computer and turns off the monitor when it sees you haven't been using it for awhile. Surplus Direct has been offering IBM's version for just $5.00 as a close-out.

The Heat Is On (and *On*, and *On*)

Heat inside your PC is yet another killer. And while devices like hard drives run a lot cooler than they once did, microprocessors run hotter than ever. You could actually boil water on some of them, if left unprotected.

A typical computer will have from one to three fans: one attached to the power supply; conceivably one mounted somewhere in the case, and in nearly all newer systems, a third fan mounted directly on the microprocessor. Usually, they're poorly made, and it's not uncommon for at least one of them to fail, sometimes within months.

That's a problem—a big one.

You can do something to help keep your fans going. Regularly vacuum out every air vent on your computer's case, especially the circular fan vent on the back of the power supply, usually located on the back of the case.

The power supply fan is the only one you can check without opening the box. With the machine on, place your hand at the back of the computer, near the on/off switch: You should feel a breeze. If you ever *don't* feel a breeze there, save your data and shut the system down *immediately*...then replace the fan *immediately*.

Whenever you open your computer's case, vacuum the vents leading into the power supply (the big silver box with all the relatively heavy colored wires running in and out). Turn the machine off and disconnect the power before doing this, of course.

If you have an 80486DX/66 or faster CPU, any Pentium or any Pentium Pro, you may also find a fan on the CPU. Especially in older systems, there may be additional fans scattered around the machine, either against the inside of the box side or on plug-in "fan cards" stuck in expansion slots. Before you replace the cover on your case, find any additional fans that may be present. Then, plug in the machine, turn it on, and see if they run.

If one of your fans fails, everyone in the business makes the same recommendation: Use fans from PC Power and Cooling. They cost more, but they're extraordinarily reliable and effective. Of course, that's an investment you may want to make only if you're planning to keep your computer around for awhile. If you're getting ready to sell or retire it, you could probably get away with less.

PC Power and Cooling, Inc.
5995 Avenida Encinas
Carlsbad, CA 92008
1-800-722-6555; 1-619-931-5700
www.pcpowercooling.com

By the way, fearing heat, some people simply run their computers with the top off. If you discover that one or both of your fans have failed, that's a *temporary* solution—but it's not a long-term solution. You get more dust that way, and as we've discussed, dust also damages systems. Second, in well-designed systems, someone has carefully considered air flow. An open computer case changes the dynamics and can occasionally lead to air pockets that are hotter than they would have been with the case closed.

One last point about heat: Thermal shocks associated with rapid changes of temperature can also damage your computer. If you've moved a PC or laptop during extreme temperatures, wait for it to cool off or heat up before you turn it on.

Protecting Your Software and Data

Now that we've done all we can to keep your chips happy, let's see what we can do about preventing damage to your software and data. Of course, job number 1 is to make sure you keep copies of *all* your important data. *Hard drives do die.* For some reason, everyone seems to have to learn this the hard way. I know I did. So let's talk a bit about backup from the Cheapskate's perspective.

If it seems as if I'm belaboring this, remember that it can cost hundreds, or even thousands of dollars to retrieve or re-create the data on your hard drive. Imagine your drive being disassembled in a special clean room with air filtered to 100 times normal cleanliness, by men and women dressed from head to toe in sterile bunny suits. That's how it's done.

Backups: The Topic Everyone Hates

This is like flossing. Everyone hates it, but it's necessary. How often should you back up your files? As befits a Cheapskate, do your own cost-benefit analysis:

▲ How much time are you willing to invest in backups, against the likelihood that one day you'll lose data?

▲ How much data can you afford to lose?

▲ If you lose data, how much could you reconstruct, and how long would it take?

▲ How important are the data you would lose?

Many computer users—especially people who primarily use the computer to write short documents and don't use a lot of formatting—can get away with once-a-week floppy backups. If you've got accounting information on your computer, you'd better back up every day!

MS-DOS, Windows 3.1 and Windows 95 *all* come with basic backup software designed to work with floppy drives; the Windows 95 program works with some tape drives as well. You can see each of these programs in Figures 8-1, 8-2 and 8-3. The DOS and Windows 3.1 programs are downsized versions of Symantec's backup software, while the Windows 95 program is an adaptation of software created by Hewlett-Packard's Colorado division, which sells its own tape drives.

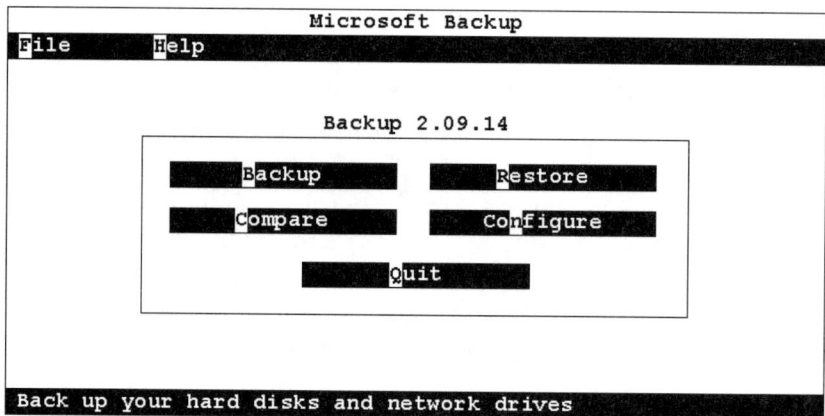

```
                        Microsoft Backup
 File          Help


                        Backup 2.09.14


            Backup                   Restore

            Compare                  Configure

                        Quit



 Back up your hard disks and network drives
```

Figure 8–1   MS-DOS 6.22's built-in floppy backup software.

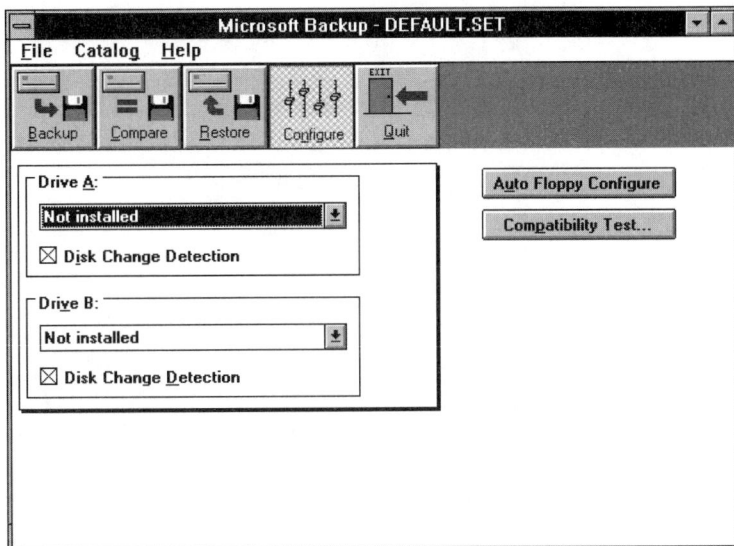

Figure 8–2   Windows 3.1's built-in floppy backup software.

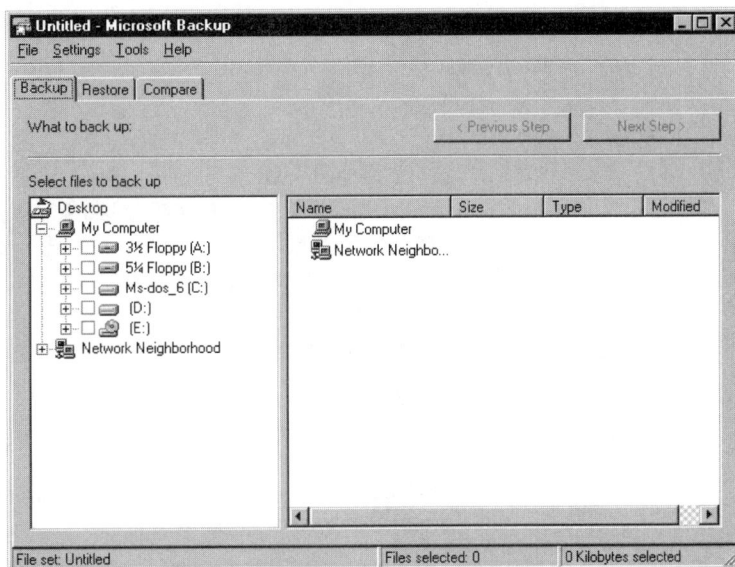

Figure 8–3   Windows 95's built-in floppy and tape backup software.

> For very low-end backups, you might not even need formal backup software. Data compression programs like PKZIP and WinZip (both on the accompanying CD-ROM) can come in very handy in helping you squeeze your most important files onto just a few floppy diskettes.

A few notes about Windows 95's backup software: It won't work with tape drives that predate 1992, nor will it work with QIC Wide, QIC 3020, SCSI, or Travan tape drives—most of what's currently popular, in other words. If you're buying a tape drive for use with Windows 95, make sure it comes with Windows 95 compatible backup software. Don't use the old DOS or Windows 3.1 software—it can't keep track of Windows 95's long file names!

Making Sure Your Tape Backups Really Back Up

When the worst happens, there's only one thing worse than not having a backup: It's having a backup which doesn't work or isn't available. If you're using a tape backup system, there are a few things you can do to improve your odds:

- ▲ Test your backups regularly by attempting to restore a few files from different parts of your tape. (It's remarkable how many people never check to make sure their backup tapes work!)
- ▲ Keep your tapes away from anything magnetic, including telephones and speakers.
- ▲ When you make backups, use your software's Compare or Verify feature, which checks your tape drive's work and fixes any errors. It will take longer, but you'll be glad you did.
- ▲ Occasionally retension (stretch) your tapes and clean your tape drive heads, as your tape drive manual recommends.
- ▲ Keep a recent backup off-site. That way, if your computer falls victim to flood or theft, the backups won't also be lost.

Make a System Startup Disk

If you run into problems with DOS or Windows, you'll be a lot happier if you have a startup "bootable" floppy that you can use to start your computer, access your files, and perhaps use to do some troubleshooting. In later versions of MS-DOS, the first setup disk is bootable. But you may not have the first setup disk any more. You can create a bootable floppy by formatting a floppy diskette with the DOS command:[3]

```
FORMAT A: /S
```

This diskette will now contain the most basic files DOS needs to load.[4]

In Windows 95, you're given the opportunity to make a startup disk when you install. Anytime thereafter, you can make a startup disk as follows:

1. Click Start, Settings, Control Panel.
2. Double-click the Add/Remove Programs icon.
3. Click the Startup Disk Tab.
4. Click Create Disk.
5. Label a disk "Windows 95 Startup Disk," insert it into Drive A, and click OK.
6. When Windows 95 finishes copying the diskette, click Close and remove the disk.

▲ ▲

3.   All the DOS commands in this chapter assume that your DOS utilities are stored in a directory that is listed in the "path" where your computer looks for programs. If this isn't the case, use the CD command to change to your DOS directory before entering the command.

4.   If the drive your computer boots from is a SCSI or compressed drive, things get more complicated. Neither using **FORMAT A: /S** nor using the first setup disk are sufficient. Briefly, run the command **setup /f** to copy a minimal installation of DOS to a floppy diskette. Remove the floppy and reboot. Put the floppy back in, and copy the drivers you need onto the diskette. The most common driver file names you may need are **ASPI4DOS.SYS** for SCSI drives or either **DRVSPACE.SYS** or **DBLSPACE.SYS** for drives compressed with Microsoft's DriveSpace or DoubleSpace utility. Once you have all those files on your floppy, also copy **AUTOEXEC.BAT** and **CONFIG.SYS** to it – these are the files that DOS runs to actually load the drivers you copied. Take a breath; you're almost there. Now you have to tell **CONFIG.SYS** to look on the floppy instead of the hard drive for your drivers. Open CONFIG.SYS with a text editor such as DOS' Edit, or Windows' Notepad. For each driver you've copied, edit the corresponding statement (something like **DEVICE=C:\DOS\ DBLSPACE.SYS**) to point to your floppy drive. If that's drive A, the equivalent command would be: **DEVICE=A:\DBLSPACE.SYS**. Having done all that, you qualify as a true Master of Disaster. And relax: You only have to do this once!

Windows 95 Registry Problems: Be Prepared

Windows 95 depends heavily on two files that together make up something called the Registry: SYSTEM.DAT and USER.DAT. These Registry files store detailed information about your computer and the software running on it. Windows 95 is constantly making changes to these files; for example, new information is written to them when you install new software or change the settings on software that is already installed.

If these files are ever missing or damaged, you're likely to have *major* system problems. Therefore, Windows 95 makes copies of these files every time you successfully start your computer; the copies are named SYSTEM.DA0 and USER.DA0. If Windows 95 runs into problems the next time it starts, you can restart *again* and Windows 95 will use the data in SYSTEM.DA0 and USER.DA0, which are presumably good.

Sounds good, so far. But what if a problem appears in one of these files, and you don't realize it until the problem has been copied into both stored versions? You may start to get "registry errors" that are annoying at best, or worse, completely prevent you from working.

That's why I recommend creating a separate weekly backup of SYSTEM.DAT and USER.DAT elsewhere on your hard drive (or on a floppy, if they'll fit). Then, if you start having problems, you can run Windows from a startup disk and copy the two files back into your system manually.

Know When to Leave Well Enough Alone

Occasionally you'll see a letter in a computer magazine: "I was trying to clean up my hard drive so I deleted file such-and-such, and now my computer won't work." *Know what you're deleting.*

Some files are more important than others. We've already mentioned two: SYSTEM.DAT and USER.DAT. Depending on your operating system, others you might come across include COMMAND.COM, AUTOEXEC.BAT, CONFIG.SYS, IO.SYS, MSDOS.SYS, DRVSPACE.BIN, DBLSPACE.BIN, SYSTEM.INI, WIN.INI, IBMBIO.COM, and IBMDOS.COM. Some of these files will normally (but not always) be invisible—and therefore be a little harder to erase. Others are the type of files you could easily erase through carelessness. *Don't.*

See That Button? Don't Press It

If you're running Windows 95, Windows 3.1, OS/2, or a Macintosh, *never* switch off your computer without following the normal system shutdown procedure (unless the system locks up and you have no choice). That's a good way to confuse the living daylights out of your system, causing all sorts of disk problems and lost data.

Run the Latest Antivirus Software

There seem to be two common reactions to computer viruses: panic and denial. Neither is appropriate. Many computer users will never encounter a virus. Some will. Better be safe than sorry. Use protection. The commercial antivirus packages—Symantec, IBM, McAfee—are all good, though none is perfect. There's also a good shareware alternative: F-Prot, available on the Web at **www.datafellows.com.** (And for Cheapskate Mac users, there's the freeware Disinfectant.) Make sure you get a package that can be updated easily to handle new viruses.

There is one new class of virus you should know about: the macro virus. Macros are scripts or programs that run within a program and allow it to perform tasks it wasn't originally designed for. So far, most macro viruses have been designed to make life miserable for users of Microsoft Word and Microsoft Office, though they could in principle be written for Corel WordPerfect or Lotus SmartSuite as well.

Macros give sophisticated users awesome power. Unfortunately, a few of those users have gone over to the dark side and written viruses that can damage your data. Macro viruses seem especially hard to get rid of, and until recently, antivirus software didn't recognize them. If you use Microsoft Word or Microsoft Office, be especially careful to keep your antivirus software up to date.[5]

▲ ▲ ▲ ▲ ▲ ▲ ▲ ▲ ▲ ▲ ▲ ▲ ▲ ▲ ▲ ▲ ▲ ▲ ▲

5.   In the meantime, Word 97 has a feature that notifies you about the presence of macros in any document as you open it—not whether those macros are good or evil, just their presence. That way, if you're *not* expecting macros in your document, you can close it before any damage is done. To turn on this feature, choose Tools, Options, click the General tab, and check the Macro Virus Protection box.

A Little Routine Drive Maintenance

MS-DOS 6.0, MS-DOS 6.2[6] and Windows 95 each come with two important hard drive maintenance utilities. You don't need to be obsessive about using them, but you should get to know them and use them once in a while.

The first and most important is ScanDisk, which checks your hard drive for both logical and physical errors that can cause data to be lost. In many cases it can actually fix the errors. In other cases, it can only salvage data in a form that's unlikely to be useful.

Use ScanDisk as part of your routine system maintenance. Also use it when files or directories are missing when they shouldn't be; when you have trouble accessing a disk; when your disk starts behaving erratically; or when applications that ought to load properly don't.

To run ScanDisk from Windows 95 (see Figure 8-4),

1. Choose Start, Programs, Accessories, System Tools, Scandisk.
2. Select the drive or drives you want to scan (ScanDisk works on both floppies and hard drives).
3. Check Standard only if you want to check for logical errors; Thorough if you also want to check the disk's physical surface.
4. Click Start to begin scanning.

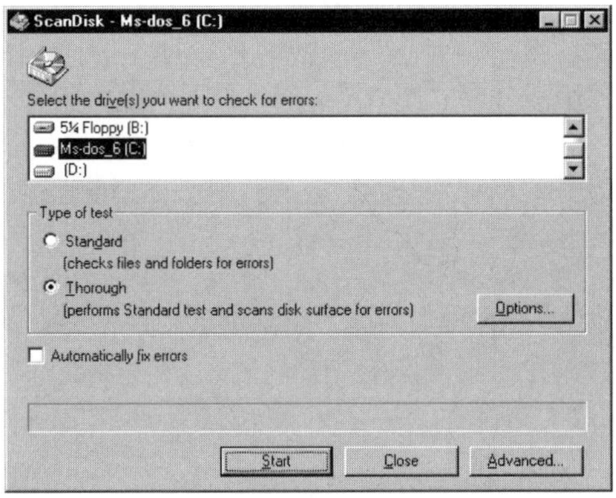

Figure 8–4   ScanDisk for Windows 95.

6.   These are the disk utilities to use whether you're running only DOS 6.x or you are also running Windows 3.x on top of it.

To run ScanDisk from DOS 6.x (see Figure 8-5),

1. Exit Windows if you're running it. (Don't just open a DOS session from within Windows.)
2. From a DOS prompt, enter the ScanDisk command and the name of the drive you want to scan; for example,

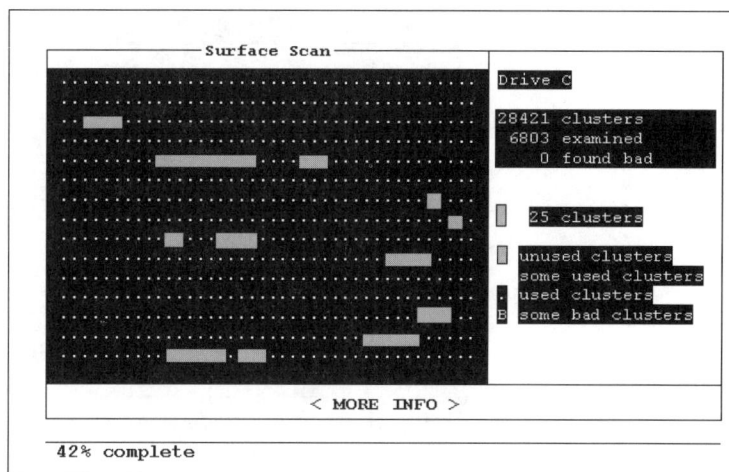

   ```
   SCANDISK D:
   ```

```
┌─────────────── Surface Scan ───────────────┐
│ ................................  ┌──────────────┐
│ ......▓▓▓▓.....................   │ Drive C      │
│ ................................  │              │
│ ..............▓▓▓..............   │28421 clusters│
│ ................................  │ 6803 examined│
│ ...............................▓  │    0 found bad│
│ ......▓▓▓....▓▓▓...............   │ ▓ 25 clusters│
│ .........................▓▓▓...   │              │
│ ...............................▓  │ ▓ unused clusters│
│ .....................▓▓▓▓......   │   some used clusters│
│ ...............▓▓▓.............   │   used clusters│
│ ................................  │ B some bad clusters│
│                 < MORE INFO >     │
│ ──────────────────────────────────────────│
│ 42% complete                               │
└────────────────────────────────────────────┘
```

Figure 8–5 ScanDisk for DOS 6.x/Windows 3.x.

In addition to backup and ScanDisk, both DOS 6 and Windows 95 come with disk defragmentation utilities. No, this doesn't mean your disk drive is currently scattered in hundreds of fragments inside your computer's case. But your *data* are. DOS and Windows plunk chunks of data wherever it's convenient to put them. Then, when it's time to retrieve your data, they're scattered hither and yon—and it takes longer to retrieve. Put simply, defragmenters get everything organized, so your hard drive works faster.

This isn't something that needs to be done every day, or even every week. But if you never defrag, your drive may eventually slow down enough that you'll notice the difference. If you're constantly adding and deleting files and software, consider defragging your drive at least every month or two.

To run Windows 95's Disk Defragmenter (see Figure 8-6),

1. Choose Start, Programs, Accessories, System Tools, Disk Defragmenter.
2. Select the drive or drives you want to scan.
3. Click Start.

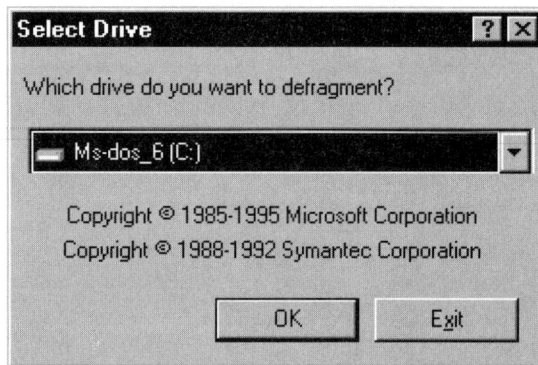

Figure 8–6   Disk Defragmenter for Windows 95.

To run Defrag from DOS 6.x,

1. Exit Windows if you're running it. (Don't just open a DOS session from within Windows.)
2. From a DOS prompt, enter the DEFRAG command and the name of the drive you want to scan; for example,
   ```
   DEFRAG D:
   ```

Inventory Your System

In just a few minutes, you can print an excruciatingly detailed report about what's inside your computer—a report that will be invaluable if you ever run into trouble.

If you're running MS-DOS and/or Windows 3.x, exit Windows. Then enter the command MSD. The Microsoft Diagnostics program opens. Choose Print Report from the File menu.

If you're running Windows 95, you can print an even more detailed report from Device Manager, as follows:

1. Click Start, Settings, Control Panel.
2. Double-click the System icon.
3. Click the Device Manager tab.
4. Click Print.
5. Choose All devices and System Summary.
6. Click OK.

> **tip** These reports can also help you sell your system when the time comes: They'll impress the daylights out of your potential buyer.

While you're printing out your system report, take a few minutes to gather up all your system manuals and make sure they're in one accessible location. Take note of any manuals that are missing, so you can start looking for them or possibly contact the manufacturer for a replacement.

Drivers, He Said

Sound boards, CD-ROMs, SCSI drives and most other devices come with driver software that allows them to operate under Windows 3.1 or Windows 95. But it's possible for driver files to become damaged, preventing the hardware from operating properly. So make sure your driver diskettes and CD-ROMs are all somewhere you can find them.

> If you're trying to upgrade old hardware to Windows 95 or Windows NT, but you can't find the drivers you need, try the Ziff-Davis Driver Finder, at *http://finders.zdnet.com.*

See What's in CMOS

Get out your notebook; we're going to take some notes. Shut down and turn off your computer; now turn it back on, and before your operating system loads, enter your Setup program. These are the critical settings your computer needs in order to start up properly. If your computer's battery ever fails, they'll disappear.

Write down all the settings, especially any settings related to your hard drive. (Unfortunately, you can't print them from here.) Then exit your Setup program *without saving any changes*. Keep the information with your manuals and diagnostics software; you may need it one day.

Get Yourself a Diagnostics Program

If you purchased a name-brand computer, chances are it came with a diagnostics program designed to help test all the things that can go wrong with hardware. Since you never use it, it's easy to lose. Go find it and make sure it's somewhere safe.

If you don't have a diagnostics program, you need one.

There are dozens of diagnostics programs at widely varying prices, many designed specifically for professionals. As a Cheapskate, you'll want something that does the job without too much fuss and won't cost you a fortune.

I have a suggestion. Windsor Technologies offers a downsized version of its professional PC-Technician professional diagnostics software. The "amateur" version, TuffTEST, costs $9.95, and works with any system using an 80386 or higher. It's available only via download, at **www.tufftest.com.**

TuffTEST isn't quite as systematic as professional diagnostics software. But it is easy enough for real people to use and thorough enough to be of real value. (For $29.95, you can download TuffTEST Pro, which is virtually identical to the PC-Technician product Windsor Technologies has been charging $199 for.)

If you're not ready to spend even $9.95, at least download AMIDiag Limited Edition at **www.megatrends.com/utilities/amidiag50.html**. It's free for evaluation, but it doesn't contain all of the features built into the complete AMIDiag product. It's missing some important tests; for example, it will test your base 640K memory but not your extended memory. But it's significantly better than nothing.

The Worst Happens. Now What?

If you do everything in the previous sections, I believe you'll head off many all the serious problems you're likely to encounter—and you'll make many of the remaining problems significantly easier to fix.

But that still leaves plenty of room for trouble.

In the next few pages, I'll help you determine whether a problem is one you're likely to be able to solve on your own—and show you a few techniques that could save you an expensive repair visit. I'll talk a little about navigating technical support lines. I'll help you decide whether an older computer is worth repairing. Last but not least, I'll help you choose the right repair person and communicate effectively with them.

Some Overall Troubleshooting Guidelines

First rule for troubleshooting your computer: Do what you feel comfortable doing. If you are truly afraid to pull off a connector, that's the point where you need a pro.

Second rule: It will almost never happen, but if you ever hear sparks, smell smoke, see smoke, or see flames, stop everything, pull all the plugs, and get the (nonwater-based) fire extinguisher.

Third rule: Always take your time and think things through. Be methodical: Never assume you did something right. I recently went nuts installing a backup tape drive that worked at first and then insisted every tape was no good. It turned out I'd installed it without screws. The first time I pulled out a tape, I partially pulled off the data connector and didn't think to recheck it before I was ready to declare it "bad," because the error message said "bad tape" not "bad connection." Shoving the connector back on properly (and screwing the unit into place so it can never happen again) solved the problem.

Fourth rule: As Hippocrates said, *Do no harm.* Make sure you're not zapping your computer with static. (Follow the instructions on page 307, or better yet, *wear an antistatic strap*: You can get one at Radio Shack.) Hold boards by their corners; *never* get your grubby fingers on edge connectors or chips. Don't force things that just won't go: Step back and make sure you're really doing it right.

Fifth rule: Write things down. Take notes. Draw diagrams. Like Hansel and Gretel, you need a way to retrace your steps. And if you happen to cause any more mischief along the way, your service technician will want to know exactly what you did in there.

Sixth rule: Your computer contains hundreds of millions of transistors, countless other electronic components, dozens of cables and connectors, assorted small motors, and software of virtually infinite complexity. No repair guide can tell you all you need to solve every problem. The best solution is to know your machine: Learn all you can about it. You don't need to become an engineer; far from it. But knowledge is power—in this case, the power to save money on repair bills.

One day when you've got nothing else to do (yeah, *right!*) spend a few minutes looking around inside your computer. See where the tight crevasses are. Find the hard disk(s), floppy disk(s), CD-ROM, memory SIMMs, empty memory slots (if any), and empty slots for boards. See which components look as if they would be easy to replace or upgrade—and which would require you to take practically the whole computer apart. That will help you decide in advance which upgrades or repairs you're comfortable handling yourself, and which you'll want to delegate to professionals.

Seventh Rule: Gather all your manuals and documentation. You'll probably need them.

Eighth Rule: Set aside enough time to do what you'll need to do. If you don't have the time, admit it and hire someone.

Forgive Me for Asking a Stupid Question, But

OK, the computer's completely dead. Before you panic, forgive me, but please answer these dumb questions:

- ✍ *Is everything plugged in?*

- ✍ *Is your outlet strip plugged into the wall, **and switched on?***

- ✍ *Is your **outlet** working?*

- ✍ *Is your monitor connected to your PC?*

- ✍ *Are your keyboard and mouse connected to your PC?*

- ✍ *Is the system turned on? Is the monitor turned on?*

- ✍ *Did someone misadjust your monitor to appear dark?*

- ✍ *Did you inadvertently leave a floppy disk in your computer when you turned it on, preventing the operating system from starting properly?*

You won't be the first smart person to assume the worst, when all that's happened is someone kicked out the power plug.

"I Turned the Computer On And *Nothing* Happened"

One of the most common PC problems is a power failure. If you've checked the checklist above and your computer still isn't working, the next step is to make your best guess as to whether the problem is with the motherboard, the power supply, the connection between them, or over-heating.[7]

Overheating problems are usually easy to identify. Turn off the machine and let it cool down for several hours—or open it up and blow a

▲ ▲

7.   If you smell something burning, shut off the computer fast, and don't turn it on again until you find out why. Computer fires are *extremely* rare, but if it concerns you, get an extinguisher. Halon extinguishers were the best, but are no longer made because Halon damages the ozone layer. If you see a used one that's still charged, buy it: the Halon will eventually leak out whether you use it or not. A distant second: CO_2. Third-best: your common, cheap dry-chemical fire extinguisher. It will put out the fire, destroy your computer, but leave your house standing. Never, ever use a water-based fire extinguisher on anything electrical, unless you like spreading the fire and risking electrocution.

fan or air conditioner into the case. If these methods revive the computer, you need either a fan on your CPU chip, a new cooling fan in your power supply, or a supplemental cooling fan or fan card, available from many computer parts suppliers. For the time being, as we mentioned earlier in this chapter, you might try running the system with the case removed.

This symptom could also be a sign of a chip getting "weak." With added cooling, the weak chip may last another week—or another 100 years—before dying for good.

> **tip** Another sign of an overheating problem: Your system works fine all morning, then in the afternoon it locks up. You reset it; in a few minutes it locks up again—and so on. This can sometimes happen after you add internal boards to a computer, changing its internal airflow patterns.

• *Power Supply Problems*

If this doesn't solve the problem, and nothing's working at all—not even the fan or the lights on your front panel—it's likely that your power supply has failed. Power supplies have the hardest job (electronically) in your computer system—turning 120 volts of AC house current into the highly-regulated low voltage DC—and the highest death rate. One of the major reasons power supplies die is that their cooling fans die and bake them to death.

Replacement power supplies on generic clones can cost as little as $25–$30, though custom power supplies for brand-name computers such as Compaqs can cost much more. If you're planning to keep your computer for a long time, you *might* consider investing in a premium power supply from—you guessed it—PC Power and Cooling, the same people who make those great fans we discussed earlier.

If you have your power supply replaced by a professional, you're also looking at an hour's labor. In my neck of the woods, that's $60–$75—and of course they'll mark up the parts as well. The experts say you can easily replace a power supply yourself. For example, according to Winn L. Rosch in *Your Old PC:* "Changing a power supply is among the easiest things you can do to your PC. The entire operation usually can be completed in 10 minutes."[8]

It may well be simple. But you'll have to (1) make sure you get the *right* power supply for your computer; (2) be comfortable working in tight spaces; (3) be careful enough to keep track of everything you disconnect and reconnect it the exact same way; (4) be prepared to disconnect and reconnect some completely unrelated devices, just to get them out of your way; (5) be mature enough to not even *think* about opening the power supply itself—which could easily kill you. If you're OK about all that, absolutely, go for it.

One last point, which may be obvious. If it turns out that your power supply or motherboard has blown and there's no obvious cause, it's time to double-check the steps you're taking to make sure your computer is receiving clean, consistent power.

• *One Possible Cheapskate Fix*

Before you replace your power supply, it's conceivable that there's simply a problem with the connections between your power supply and the motherboard. Possibly a connector has come loose, or another loose wire from your power supply is creating an electrical short somewhere inside your computer. And *those* are problems that most people can fix by themselves.

Before you start working, make sure you're not carrying a static charge. Then, disconnect everything that's connected to the outside of your computer—monitor, keyboard, mouse, speakers, printer, phone jack, *and especially, power!*

Now open your computer. If you still have the manual, follow the instructions printed there. Otherwise, look for four to six screws on the back of the box, unscrew them, and gently lift up and slide out the back cover.

Place your computer down gently, so you can look straight down at the motherboard. Look for the power supply: It's the big silver box with a large fan that sticks out the back of your computer. Not sure? The power supply is the part of the computer you plug your power cord into.

You'll see a bunch of colored wires snaking out of your power supply to locations all over the inside of your computer. These are the wires that send power to your drives, the lights on the front panel ... and your motherboard.

▲ ▲ ▲ ▲ ▲ ▲ ▲ ▲ ▲ ▲ ▲ ▲ ▲ ▲ ▲ ▲ ▲ ▲ ▲ ▲

8.   *Your Old PC: The Complete Upgrading and Renovating Guide,* Winn L. Rosch, Brady, September 1993, ISBN: 156681047, out of print

For now, we're only concerned with the connectors on the motherboard. Most standard PC motherboards have two large white connectors where the power cables are connected. The power cables are named P8 and P9; sometimes the names are printed on them, but not always. You'll generally find them at the top left or top middle of the motherboard.

The P8 cable contains six wires from left to right, as follows: *orange, red, yellow, blue, black, black*. Sometimes the red wire is absent. The P9 cable contains another six wires from left to right: *black, black, yellow, red, red, red*. I'm telling you this because I'd like you to disconnect and reconnect these—and you'll have to reconnect them properly, or you'll finish off whatever's left of your motherboard. You may have to jiggle them to disconnect them (assuming there's room).

As I mentioned, it's also possible there's a temporary electrical short somewhere inside your computer. That's especially possible if you've been mucking around in there, or if you recently moved the computer. See if any power supply wires have fallen onto the motherboard; if so, bundle them up and gently tie them out of the way. While you're at it, see if any wires are very tightly kinked; try to move them so they hang a little more easily (without letting them drop onto the motherboard or other boards in the system).

Blame the "Cable" Company (So, What Else Is New?)

Now for the deep dark secret of the computer repair fraternity: Cables and connectors may be the most frequent causes of computer failure, and they fail for apparently no reason. Why? Many are made to the standards of those old Eastern European cars you can trade for a pair of Levis. Also, wherever metal touches metal, you get corrosion and a place for dirt to build up.

Let's say your sound card has suddenly stopped working properly. Gently pull it away from your motherboard. Apply a liquid conductor if you have it. (See the following section on Tweek.) Plug it back in. If there's a cable involved, do the same.

Turn on the system and see if the symptoms disappear. If not, and there's a cable involved, beg, borrow or steal a "known good" cable, plug it in, and, again, and see if things improve. You'd be surprised how often they will.

• *Making Sure You Plug Things Back In Right*

Your biggest fear: Putting the cable back in the wrong way. You can fix it so that will never happen. Before removing or adjusting any cable in your computer,

1. Go through your documentation to see if you have a diagram showing the cables and connections you're adjusting.
2. Get a superpermanent magic marker, preferably an extra-fine-point marker. For black connectors, you may need a white marker.
3. On your diagram, note how any cables with "key wires" face. These are cables with multicolored wires or a single colored stripe. Record the order of the colors, or where the colored stripe on the cable goes.
4. Here's the crucial step—the one you can do even if you don't have any documentation. Using the marker, draw a single mark across the cable and socket, in such a way that both marks will match up *only* when the connector is on properly.

• *Tweek: The Magic Compound*

If you can, go to a high-priced stereo shop and buy a bottle of Tweek, a liquid conductor which only adheres to metal. This is magic stuff *if you can find it.*[9] You wipe it on the pins of cables and memory SIMMs and chips before you insert them. "Impossible" erratic problems vanish in seconds. A small bottle runs about $15, but even if you were constantly swapping boards and building systems, a bottle could last you a year.

▲ ▲ ▲ ▲ ▲ ▲ ▲ ▲ ▲ ▲ ▲ ▲ ▲ ▲ ▲ ▲ ▲ ▲ ▲ ▲

9. Legal disputes have kept Tweek off the market for roughly a year, but its manufacturer expects them to be resolved soon. In the meantime, an alternative is Stabilant-22 from D.W. Electrochemicals Ltd., Richmond Hill, Ontario (call 416-889-1522 for a local dealer). This product is a little more expensive and concentrated, but it does the job.

Beep! Checking POST Codes

If your power supply is working, but your computer isn't, the problem may be somewhere among the millions of circuits on your motherboard. A repair person would find out for sure by connecting a Power-On Self Test diagnostic card that reports whether power is reaching the motherboard, and if so, which circuit on the motherboard may have failed. Chances are, you don't have a POST card in your attic.[10] But there's a second-best solution.

Look and listen carefully when you turn on the machine. Your computer's BIOS will try to report out major errors with POST messages, either by flashing them on the screen or sending out a series of beeps. The manual which, with any luck, came with your computer, should list the meaning of each of the beep codes.

If you don't have the manual, call the manufacturer and ask the company to send you a manual or at least a POST code list. If you're fortunate enough to have access to a second computer, you can also try the manufacturer's Web page.

Often, you won't be able to solve the problem the beep codes are telling you about—but knowing the code in advance could help you reduce your repair costs, because you'll have more information for your service technician. It can also help you evaluate the estimates you're being given.

And occasionally, knowing the POST code *will* help you fix the problem—possibly by reseating a component, such as a memory chip; tightening or replacing a connector; or replacing an easy-to-swap part such as a keyboard.

"It Can't Find My Hard Drive!"

You turn on the computer and it comes on, but—it can't find your hard drive! Panic. Regrets that you never made a backup. Promises that *if only your data are still there, you'll never skip a backup ever again.*

First—as usual—check your cables. Turn the computer off, and tighten the cables that connect your drive to the motherboard or interface card, as well as the power cable connected to the power supply. If this

---

10.   Even though Surplus Direct has been selling one lately for only $25.

doesn't work, disconnect the connections completely, and reconnect them from scratch. Get out the bottle of Tweek again.

Second, check your computer's setup program. Many computers store information about hard drives in a special CMOS memory chip that is kept alive by battery. When the battery fails, the information can disappear. The temporary solution is to run the setup program again; see if your drive's information is present, and if not, reenter it. Nowadays this information is usually printed right on the drive, but if it isn't there or you can't find it, you can call the company that manufactured the drive. Or if you have a computer still working, try their Web site. If you don't have the correct information, *don't guess.*

If you enter accurate setup information and that brings your drive back to life, get a replacement battery immediately. We'll talk about replacement batteries in the next section.

Would your disk happen to be a SCSI disk, or a removable cartridge? Then it needs a driver—and it's possible that something's happened to either the driver file or the CONFIG.SYS file which tells your computer where to look for the driver. Open the CONFIG.SYS file in a text editor and look to make sure you have a line that says something like

```
DEVICE=ASPIDISK.SYS
```

There may also be references to files like ASPI2DOS, ASPI4DOS, ASPI7DOS, or ASPI8DOS. Check your drive manual or README file to see exactly what it should say.

Have you added any other SCSI devices lately? Remove them and then try the drive. If it's a removable, try another disk.

If none of this works—or if you hear scraping, clicking, grinding, or other noises that just shouldn't be there—you now have the satisfaction of knowing you have a real, *big* problem.

"It Just *Hangs*—Even More Than It Used To"

Computers crash and hang. It's a fact of life. But if yours is suddenly crashing and hanging more than it used to, spend a little time troubleshooting the software before you assume there's a hardware problem.

Have you just installed any new software? Try uninstalling the software and see if things improve. If you're running a screen saver, get rid of it.

Run a disk-checking utility like ScanDisk to see if you have any lost disk clusters mucking up the works. Run your antivirus program, just in case.

Have you just upgraded to a new operating system, such as Windows 95? Newer operating systems give your memory more of a workout than older ones did. Remove your system's SIMM chips, apply Tweek again, reinstall memory, and see if that clears up the problem.

• *If You Suspect a Memory Problem*

In Chapter 5, you learned that cheap memory can cause your system to have intermittent problems, or fail altogether. In many cases, the memory test that runs when you start your computer won't catch these problems. Now's the time to run the diagnostics program we told you to get earlier in this chapter.

Battery Problems

Starting with 80286 models, first IBM, then all the clone makers decided to add flexibility to their systems with the inclusion of a small CMOS memory chip to store crucial system setup data.

CMOS means "complementary metal oxide semiconductor." And what it means to you is "batteries." Because all the data in a CMOS chip vanish when you turn the power off, all machines after the original IBM AT were given small batteries, sometimes hidden, to preserve the CMOS setup information. And one day, your battery is going to die.

You'll know it's dead if your computer starts forgetting the date and time, or worse, fails to find (or messes up) crucial setup information. Since you've copied all that information down (as we told you to on page 322), you can reenter the information in CMOS and keep working. But don't turn off the machine until you've purchased a new battery, or you'll have to do it over again.

Several generations of PCs use several types of backup batteries—and the first hassle can be finding the thing.

The first ATs and many of their clones, and some machines to this day used relatively large (2" x 3" or so) lithium battery packages which were attached to the side of the inside of the case, usually with velcro, and attached to the motherboard via a black and red twisted wire with a flat plug on the end. (If you have one of these, see our advice on marking cables before you unplug it.)

Advantage: These will last a good long time, often a decade or more. *Disadvantage*: Well, first of all, it's most likely already *been* a decade or more since they were installed. These batteries are relatively expensive and difficult to find. You'll have to go to a computer store or fair, an electronics store, or a mail-order source to find a replacement. These are sometimes known as "Tadiran" batteries after the Israeli company which made the first ones. *To replace*: Turn off the machine, unplug the battery pack, plug in a new one, and go.

Here's a mail-order source for these and other hard-to-find PC batteries:

Powerline

4268 Los Angeles Avenue

Simi Valley, CA 93063

1-800-234-2444

www.powerline-battery.com

Some clones substituted a battery holder with four AA-size batteries for the Tadiran package. *Advantage*: You can find AA batteries anywhere. *Disadvantage*: AA batteries die far sooner, and far more often, than their lithium equivalents. *To replace*: Turn off the machine, unplug the pack, change the batteries, and replace with good alkaline cells (good choices are Energizers or Duracells depending on whose ads you like better). Plug the battery pack back in and go.

If there is any corrosion on the battery holder due to a leaky battery, clean it off with a damp cloth, dry thoroughly, and coat with Tweek (there's that Tweek again!) to prevent further damage.[11]

Both types of batteries were replaced by some clone makers with nickel-cadmium rechargeable batteries. The idea is that whenever the computer is

▲ ▲

11.   If the corrosion is *really* bad, with enough ambition and creativity you can replace the holder yourself. Go to Radio Shack; buy a plain four-AA battery holder with unattached wires, cut the connector and wire off the old pack, and attach the red to the red, black to black by stripping the plastic off the wires, twisting the exposed wires hard, soldering them or using proper electrical solderless splices if you know how, then taping over the exposed joint with good electrical tape. Of course, stay away from your PC with that soldering gun <g>. If you are doing the AA pack replacement and the old pack is glued down and you don't want to break it off, just cut off the connector, leave the old pack behind (without the leaking batteries) and use double-sided white foam tape to stick the new pack on top of or next to the old one. (We're getting close to the kind of advice you get in *The Tightwad Gazette*: Arguably a bit goofy and obsessive, but hey, it *works*.)

turned on, the battery, which looks like a small caterpillar soldered directly to the motherboard, is recharging. *Advantage:* If your system has been off a long time and the CMOS "forgets" everything, plugging it in and leaving it turned on for a day may recharge and revive it. Try this before going for the repair job. *Disadvantage:* Ni-Cads eventually go bad. If you spot crud on the side of the Ni-Cad, even if everything's OK, power everything down, carefully wipe the crud with a wet cloth, and, yup, cover with Tweek. That may hold you for a while. When the Ni-Cad dies, if you don't happen to solder, you'll need a service technician who *does*.

Newer motherboards may have either of two additional types of batteries, or something even better. The first is the lithium "coin cell," the smaller cousin of the "Tadiran" pack. It sits on the motherboard and looks like a three-quarter inch silver coin held to the motherboard by a tab. This is *good news*: When these die, you power down the system, reach in, and pop the battery right out from under that tab. There's usually a cutout or thumb notch to make this easier. Camera stores carry the most popular varieties.

If you can't find a battery at all, look for a black box marked "Dallas Semiconductor" that's bigger and thicker than your average chip. It will usually say that it's a battery-backed-up clock. The battery is under the black cover, and on many, but not all models, you can pop off the cover and replace the lithium coin cell as described above.

Some manufacturers seal the covers with a nylon strap. Unless your system is still under warranty, which is unlikely, feel free to cut through the strap over the Dallas clock package with a pair of diagonal-cutting pliers or sharp-tipped scissors to get at the batteries.

An unusual technology that replaces the battery on some motherboards is the "supercap" or supercapacitor. This device stores energy when the machine is running and is not likely to ever die before something far more critical goes. If you cannot find a battery, look for a relatively small cylinder mounted circle-side down that says it's a supercapacitor. Otherwise, just assume it's there. Either way, if you've got one of these, leave it alone.

A Few "Easier Said Than Done" Ideas

The following ideas may fall into the category of, "yeah, if I had the time and resources to do *that*, I wouldn't *need* you."

If a given peripheral or card is giving you trouble, try borrowing an identical good one from someone (make sure identical means *identical*—with jumpers and switches all set the same) to see what happens.

Try rebuilding your computer into a "minimal" system: In stages, until you find the hot spot, disconnect first the printer, then modem (remove internal modem cards), sound cards, backup tape drives, even hard drives and controllers (use your emergency boot disk to boot from your floppy drive), and any extra memory you may have added. (You may have to adjust your CONFIG.SYS or AUTOEXEC.BAT files to make sure the system doesn't spend time looking for devices that aren't there.) Then add things back, one at a time until the system dies. Vary the order until you find the problem.

Resurrecting PS/2s from the Dead

Ahh! You have an IBM PS/2. You have a rock-solid, highly reliable, premium machine, a real IBM, not just some clone. Of course, you also need different memory, different motherboards, in most cases different add-ons, and different information.

Since there are literally millions of PS/2s out there, we'll take a little detour to focus on some PS/2-specific troubleshooting and upgrade issues.

Back in the 1960s and 1970s, every second closet contained some kid's old baseball card collection. Now it sometimes seems that every second closet contains an old IBM PS/2 that has stopped working for lack of a battery, an IBM reference disk, or a password.

For a motivated Cheapskate, these are easy problems to fix. Invest an hour or less, and you'll wind up with an IBM system that will probably last you for years.

Symptom: You turn on the computer and you're told the system settings aren't present. Or you get a 162 or 163 error code.

Solution: Chances are your CMOS battery has died. We've already talked about batteries at length. Call Powerline at 1-800-234-2444 to get a new one.

Then, you'll need to reinstall the settings. For that, you'll need the PS/2's original *reference diskette.* I'll bet you don't have it; nobody does. If you have a working, Web-connected PC, you can get a copy on-line at IBM's Web site. Search for the right files, using your model number, at **www. pc.ibm.com/searchfiles.html**. (You may need to retrieve both the reference disk file and the program **ldf.com** which allows you to extract it.)

If you need more detailed information on getting a reference disk from IBM, and what you can do with it once you've got it, point your browser to **www.computercraft.com/docs/ ps21.html**.)

> If you have no way to download a reference disk, Computer Reset (214-276-8072) sells some of them for $19 apiece.

> If you run the programs on your reference diskette and you're still having problems, your PS/2 may contain a Micro Channel card but *not* have the information it needs to work with that card. If you know who manufactured the board, you can get the correct .ADF file from them. Failing that, remove the card. The most common Micro Channel architecture cards are "token-ring" network cards. I'll wager you're not going to use that PS/2 on a token-ring network. If so, just remove the card.

To get the reference disk, you'll need to know exactly what kind of PS/2 you have. If you're not sure—or if you want to know more about your PS/2 so you can decide how much time to invest in it—Table 8-1 will help you. In many cases, we've even listed the file you'll need to download.

Symptom: You turn on the computer and you're asked for a password you don't have.

Solution: Open the box, locate the CMOS battery, remove it, leave it out overnight, then reinstall it. (Obviously you'll also need to restore your settings. Make sure you have your reference disk.)

Symptom: You have a PS/2 and your hard disk won't start up properly.

Solution: PS/2 Model 70s are prone to hard disk startup problems, due to poor contacts on the motherboard. The official solution is to take everything apart, clean out any dust, apply Tweek or some other contact cleaning spray to edge connectors and sockets, and then reassemble the computer.

But here's an alternate approach, straight from Harvard via the Usenet newsgroups:

We have a computer room with 20 PS/2 70's which exhibited that problem all the time. I have found that a light blow (about as hard as you would hit the desktop when frustrated) to the right hand side of the case, near the back, will fix the problem.

It made for good comedy. Student comes to me complaining that a machine is broken. I'd go over, yell "You are healed," while striking the machine (you know, like TV evangelists do). I proceeded to turn it on, and it would work. I had them convinced I had supernatural powers.

Lawrence Khoo, Micro Systems Manager, Harvard University

Voila! Working computer.

It's *Alive.* Now What?

Now that you've resurrected your PS/2, what next?

What you can do with it depends largely on processor and memory, as with any other PC. Machines with processors older than 386SX/16s won't run Windows—nor will PS/2s that were designed as network workstations and don't have hard drives.

Of course, you *may* have a PS/2 preloaded with IBM's OS/2 operating system. If it's OS/2 version 2.0 or higher, it should run Windows 3.1 programs pretty well. While OS/2 is a cultivated taste, it has its charms. But if you happen to have a version *older* than OS/2 2.0, just format your hard disk and start over with DOS.

The next question is: Do you have a Micro Channel Architecture system or an ISA machine? As we discussed in Chapter 3, ISA means your machine uses the same add-on boards as everyone else's. Micro Channel Architecture was IBM's unpopular proprietary standard.

If you're buying a PS/2, pay less for a Micro Channel system. It's a great negotiating point. (Watch them blanch: They'll think you didn't know!) You can still add external devices like modems with no problem, and PS/2s have video built in, so *that's* not a problem. Just don't expect to use that cheapo sound card you've been looking at.

Table 8–1 PS/2 Models: A History

PS/2 Model #	Processor	Bus	Slots (Typ. Avail.)	Memory Expandable[a] to	Introduced	Reference Disk File(s)	Notes
25	8086/8	ISA	2	640K	1987	25START.TG0 TGSFX.COM	Typically no hard disk. CGA graphics.
25LS	8086/8	ISA	1	640K	1988		Typically no hard disk. CGA graphics.
30	8086/8	ISA	3	640K	1989	30START.EXE	Most have 30-Mb hard disk. CGA graphics.
25 286	286/10	ISA	0–2	4M	1990	RS25286A.TG0 TGSFX.COM	Most have 30-Mb hard disk.
25SX	386SX/16	ISA	2	16M	1992		Typically no hard disk.
30 286	286/10	ISA	3	4M	1987–1991	MOD30286.EXE	Hard disks 20–45 Mb.
35SX	386SX/20	ISA	3	16M	1991	3540ST.EXE	Most have 40-Mb hard disk.
35LS	386SX/20	ISA	2	16M	1991		Typically no hard disk.
40SX	386SX/20	ISA	5	16M	1991	3540ST.EXE	40-Mb or 80-Mb hard disk.
L40SX	386SX/20	ISA	0	16M	1991		60-Mb hard disk.
50	286/10	M[b]	3	2M–16M	1987	RF5060A.EXE	20-Mb hard disk.
50Z	286/10	M	3	8M–16M	1988	RF5060A.EXE	30–60-Mb hard disk.
55SX	386SX/16	M	3	8M–16M	1989–1991	RF5565A.EXE	30–80-Mb hard disk.
55LS	386SX/16	M	2	8M–16M	1990		Typically no hard disk.

Table 8–1 PS/2 Models: A History *(continued)*

PS/2 Model #	Processor	Bus	Slots (Typ. Avail.)	Memory Expandable[a] to	Introduced	Reference Disk File(s)	Notes
56SX	386SX/20	M	3	16M	1992	RF85567.EXE or RF95567.EXE	40–80-Mb hard disk.
56SLC	386SLC/20	M	3	16M	1992		80–160-Mb hard disk.
56LS	386SX/20	M	2	16M	1992		Typically no hard disk.
56SLC LS	386SLC/20	M	2	16M	1992		Typically no hard disk.
57SX	386SX/20	M	5	16M	1991		80–160-Mb hard disk
57SLC	386SLC/20	M	5	16M	1992		80–160-Mb hard disk.
M57SLC	386SLC/20	M	3	16M	1991–1992		80–160-Mb hard disk. XGA graphics.
60	286/10	M	7	1M–16M	1987	RF5060A.EXE	44–70-Mb hard disk.
65SX	386SX/16	M	7	8M–16M	1990	RF5565A.EXE	60, 120 or 320 Mb hard disk.
70 386 (8570-E61)	386DX/16	M	3	6M–16M	1988	RF7080A.EXE	60-Mb hard disk.
70 386 (8570-061, 081, 121, 161)	386DX/20	M	3	6M–16M	1989–1991	RF7080A.EXE	60, 80, 120 or 160-Mb hard disk.
70 386 (8570-A61, A81, A21, A16)	386DX/25	M	3	8M–16M	1989–1991	RF7080A.EXE	60, 80, 120 or 160-Mb hard disk.
70 486	486DX/25	M	3	8M–16M	1989	RF7080A.EXE	60–120-Mb hard disk.

Table 8–1 PS/2 Models: A History (continued)

PS/2 Model #	Processor	Bus	Slots (Typ. Avail.)	Memory Expandable[a] to	Introduced	Reference Disk File(s)	Notes
P70 386 (8573-031)	386DX/16	M	2	8M–16M	1990	RF7080A.EXE	30M hard disk.
P70 386 (8573-061, 121)	386DX/20	M	2	8M–16M	1989–1990	RF7080A.EXE	60–120-Mb hard disk.
P75 486	486DX/33	M	4	16M	1990	RF7080A.EXE	160–400-Mb hard disk. XGA graphics.
80 386 (8580-041, 071)	386DX/16	M	7	4M–16M	1987	RF7080A.EXE	44–70-Mb hard disk.
80 386 (8580-081, 111, 121, 161, 311, 321)	386DX/20	M	7	4M–16M	1987–1990	RF7080A.EXE	80-, 115-, 120-, 160-, 314-Mb hard disk.
80 386 (8580-A21, A16, A31)	386DX/25	M	7	8M	1990	RF7080A.EXE	120-, 160-, 320-Mb hard disk.
90 XP 486 (8590-0G5, 0G9)	486SX/20	M	3	64M	1991		80–160-Mb hard disk; XGA graphics.
90 XP 486 (8590-0H5, 0H9)	486SX/25	M	3	64M	1991		80–160-Mb hard disk; XGA graphics.
90 XP 486 (8590-0J5, 0J9)	486DX/25	M	3	64M	1990		80–160-Mb hard disk; XGA graphics.
90 XP 486 (8590-0K9, 0KD, 0KF)	486DX/33	M	3	64M	1990–1991		320–400-Mb hard disk; XGA graphics.
95 XP 486 (8595-0G9, 0GF)	486SX/20	M	6	64M	1991		160–400-Mb hard disk; XGA graphics.

Table 8–1 PS/2 Models: A History *(continued)*

PS/2 Model #	Processor	Bus	Slots (Typ. Avail.)	Memory Expandable[a] to	Introduced	Reference Disk File(s)	Notes
95 XP 486 (8595-0H9, 0HF)	486SX/25	M	6	64M	1991		160–400-Mb hard disk; XGA graphics.
95 XP 486 (8595-0J9, 0JD, 0JF)	486DX/25	M	6	64M	1990		160-, 320-, 400- Mb hard disk; XGA graphics.
95 XP 486 (8595-0KD, 0KF)	486DX/33	M	6	64M	1990–1991		320-, 400-Mb hard disk; XGA graphics.

a. Where two numbers are specified for maximum memory, the second number indicates additional memory requiring an add-on board.

b. M stands for MicroChannel Architecture

Here are some terrific sources for finding out more about your PS/2:

ComputerCraft PS/2 Resource Center

ComputerCraft

14 Center Street

Jersey City, NJ 07302

201-946-1178; 201-795-0909

www.computercraft.com

General Technics

38 Raynor Avenue

Ronkonkoma, NY 11779-6618

1-800-GT-SALE-8

www.gtweb.net

Another excellent source is the **comp.sys.ibm.ps2.hardware** Internet newsgroup (see Figure 8-7).

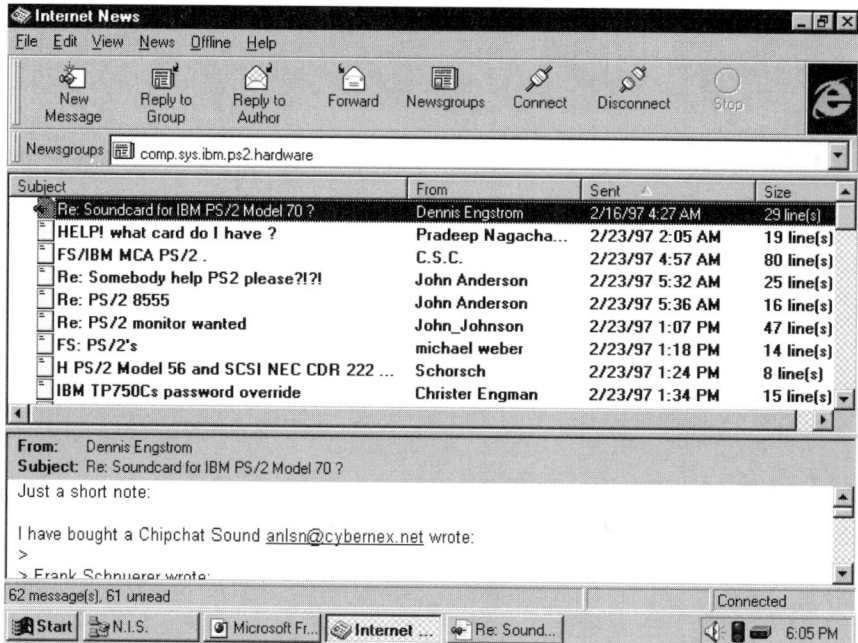

Figure 8–7   Browsing messages in the **comp.sys.ibm.ps2.hardware** newsgroup.

Not as good but still useful is IBM's own Web site at **www.pc.ibm.com**. The problem isn't the information, which is authoritative, as you would expect. The site is just plain slow to access and tough to navigate— though you can tell, as usual, that the folks at IBM have the best of intentions. Then there's also IBM Tech Support at 1-800-772-2227.

You can also get automated help via fax from IBM, at 1-800-IBM-3395. It will help to know which documents are available, and you can get a list on-line from our aforementioned friends at **www.computer-craft.com**.

Now for a few sources for IBM PS/2 upgrades and add-on equipment:

Netstream International Inc.
1002 N. Central Expressway Suite 311
Richardson, TX 75080
972-664-0383
www.wwtrading.com/ps2.htm
These folks have remarkably inexpensive PS/2 Micro Channel cards, notably Ethernet cards for as little as $25.

Evergreen Technologies
915 NW 8th Street
Corvallis, OR 97330
1-800-733-0934; 1-503-757-0934
www.evertech.com
Evergreen sells processor upgrades that replace your PS/2's microprocessor and make your computer go significantly faster. How much faster depends on your system and the available upgrade.

Kingston Technology Corporation
17600 Newhope Street
Fountain Valley, CA 92709
1-800-835-6575; 1-714-435-2600
www.kingston.com
Reliable PS/2 memory and processor upgrades.

General Technics
38 Raynor Avenue
Ronkonkoma, NY 11779-6618
1-800-GT-SALE-8
www.gtweb.net

In addition to maintaining a great PS/2 information site on the Web, these folks sell hard drives, memory, CD-ROMs, modems, processor upgrades, Micro Channel Architecture-compatible cards, and all sorts of other stuff to extend the life of your PS/2. In particular, they've been selling some really interesting upgrades for PS/2 Model 70s.

Page Computers
1-800-886-0055

PS/2 new and used systems and parts, including used motherboards.

Advanced Microcomputer Systems, Inc.
1460 SW 3rd Street, Suite B-8
Pompano Beach, FL 33069
1-800-972-3733; 1-305-784-0900

Micro Channel cards, including modems.

Index Computer Remarketing, Inc.
3601 West Commercial Blvd. #38
Fort Lauderdale, FL 33309
1-954-730-0900

PS/2 system board upgrades; ThinkPad parts.

Solutronix
1-800-875-2580

Last but not least, if you can't get your PS/2 running, these folks specialize in PS/2 repair.

Repairs and Upgrades in Order of Difficulty

In this section, we'll take a quick look at the repairs and upgrades you're most likely to confront and help you decide whether to take a shot at them yourself.

✍ *Category 1: Repairs and upgrades most careful computer users shouldn't be afraid to do:*

- ▲ Add or replace memory
- ▲ Add or replace an internal board
- ▲ Replace a floppy drive
- ▲ Add an internal tape drive

✍ *Category 2: Things that are significantly tougher, but still doable by many amateurs:*

- ▲ Replace a hard drive
- ▲ Add multimedia
- ▲ Add components to a bare-bones system
- ▲ Depending on the system, swap a power supply

✍ *Category 3: Things that will require you to do an awful lot of things right:*

- ▲ Replace a motherboard
- ▲ Build a system from scratch

Cheapskate or Computer Nerd?

There's a fine line between Cheapskate and computer nerd. You begin to get perilously close when you start stockpiling cables in case you'll need a spare. Having said that, there are a few items you may want to keep around in the event you run into trouble, because in the long run they'll probably save you more money than they cost you.

We've mentioned two of them already: *Tweek*, the magic potion for getting rid of intermittent connection-related problems, and an *antistatic strap*.

Next, beyond a set of small screwdrivers, if you'll be poking around inside computers, hemostats will make your job a lot easier. You've seen these on every medical show where they show surgery close-ups when the doc yells "clamp!" They're locking pliers that resemble scissors and come in a dozen different sizes with straight and curved jaws.

Hemostats are perfect for reaching into a crowded box to grab a dropped screw. Sometimes the only alternative is turning the whole computer upside down and shaking it. Either way, you'll have to get that loose screw out; it could cause an electrical short on your motherboard if you don't.

If you bought hemostats meeting American Medical Association standards, they'd cost you a bundle. However, at many computer shows you'll find people selling Asian tools that may not be quite up to human standards but are just fine for computers.

Then, there are three books I recommend.

The first is by an old college friend of mine—so you know about my conflict of interest right upfront. It's Mark Minasi's *Complete PC Upgrade and Maintenance Guide*.[12] This is your book if you want to feel as if there's an expert looking over your shoulder, making sure you don't stick the plugs together the wrong way. The book also has wonderful coverage of preventive maintenance, far more coverage than we've got room for here. Mark travels the world teaching this stuff, and the most recent edition of his book comes with a CD-ROM full of video clips from his seminars.

The second is *Troubleshooting Your PC* by Jim Aspinwall and Mike Todd, which includes a nifty Problem Index that follows logically from symptoms to possible causes and recommended solutions. The recently published third-edition includes new coverage of Windows 95, Windows NT, Plug and Play, and the Internet.

The third book, respected by just about everyone for its detail and authoritativeness is *Upgrading and Repairing PCs*, by Scott Mueller, now in its sixth edition. This is one of the world's best sources for the detailed charts, tables, graphs, and specifications often needed for serious repairs.

▲ ▲ ▲ ▲ ▲ ▲ ▲ ▲ ▲ ▲ ▲ ▲ ▲ ▲ ▲ ▲ ▲ ▲

12.　　*The Complete PC Upgrade and Maintenance Guide,* 7th Ed., Mark Minasi, Sybex, October 1996, ISBN: 0782119565, $54.99.

Troubleshooting Your PC co-author Jim Aspinwall, who is also the Windows advisor columnist for *Computer Currents* Magazine, will attempt to answer any technical support questions you e-mail to him at *wb9gvf@raisin.com.*

One last resource: the *PC Upgrader's Troubleshooting Quick Reference* by Dean R. Kent. It's short—just six pages. It's pithy. It's practical. And it's free: You can download it at **www.realworldtech.com**.

Cutting the Cost of Technical Support

So you've followed all this good advice and your system still isn't working. Or you've been trying to get some contraption working in your computer without success and regretting that you didn't buy a Macintosh.

You're one step away from calling one of the technical support phone numbers in Table 8-2. Nowadays, the first thing to know about technical support is *What's it going to cost me?* The second question is *How long will it take for me to speak with a real human being?* All too often, you won't like the answers. So, before you start the meter running on a paid technical service call, have you

▲ Read the README.TXT file on your software or driver diskettes?
▲ Left questions at the appropriate CompuServe or AOL forum? (You can also try Usenet newsgroups, though the results can be more inconsistent.)
▲ Tried the fax-back support line, if one exists (see Table 8.2)?
▲ Visited the Web site and searched for a "Knowledge Base" or similar technical support library?

Table 8–2 Manufacturer's Support Resource Guide

Company	Technical Support	Fax-Back	Web Page
Acer America	800-845-2237	800-554-2494	http://www.acer.com
Apple Computer	800-766-2333	800-510-2834	http://www.apple.com
AST Research	800-876-4278	800-926-1278	http://www.ast.com
Canon	800-423-2366		http://www.ccsi.canon.com/ computers/
Compaq	800-345-1518	800-345-1518	http://www.compaq.com
Dell	800-613-3355	800-950-1329	http://www.dell.com
Digital (DEC)	800-344-4825	800-344-4825	http://www.pc.digital.com
Epson	800-922-8911		http://www.epson.com
Fujitsu	888-466-8434	800-936-5209	http://www.fujitsu-pc.com
Hewlett- Packard	800-752-0900		
Hitachi	800-555-6820	800-565-9621	http://www.hitachipc.com
IBM PC Co.	800-426-2968	800-426-4329	http://www.pc.ibm.com
Micron	800-209-9686	800-270-1232	
NEC	800-632-8377	800-366-0476	http://www.nec.com
Olivetti	888-465-4838		http://www.olivettipc.com
Packard Bell			http://www.packardbell.com
Panasonic	800-662-3537		http://www.panasonic.com/ pcsc/
Samsung	800-656-9826		http://www.samsung.co.kr/ product/computer/
Sharp	800-237-4277		http://www.sharp-usa.com/products/
Texas Instruments	800-848-3927	800-848-3927	http://www.ti.com/
Toshiba	800-334-3445	800-999-4273	http://www.toshiba.com/tais /csd/
Zenith (ZDS)	800-227-3360	800-582-8194	http://www.zds.com/

Still no luck? Here's a checklist of information you can provide that can shorten your call and often save you money:

✍ *Clear and detailed explanation of the problem, and exactly when it occurs.*

✍ *Information about any system changes you made shortly before the problem occurred.*

✍ *Your product serial number (helps technical support determine when the product was manufactured, and which firmware or software is being used).*

✍ *Basic information about your system (operating system, memory, hard drive, etc.).*

✍ *Detailed information about your system (output from MS-DOS MSD program or Windows 95 Device Manager, as discussed on page 320-21).*

Finding the Right Service Technician

All else has failed, you're no longer under warranty, and you need a service technician. It's the same as finding an electrician: The best way to find a reliable computer repair service is to ask for references.

Then, talk to the company that got the best recommendation, ideally to one of the service technicians. Here are a few questions to ask:

▲ How would you expect to troubleshoot this problem?

▲ Have you seen this problem before? What did it turn out to be then?

▲ What do you charge for an estimate? Is the estimate cost applied against the total cost of the repair? Will you call me in advance if the repair turns out to be more expensive than anticipated?

▲ How will you test the system to make sure it's been fixed properly?

▲ What is your warranty? On parts? On labor?

▲ What is your turnaround time?

Repair or Replace?

Before getting a repair estimate, think about how much you'll be willing to pay to repair your system: What's the threshhold at which you'll consider replacing it?

If it turns out that your motherboard needs to be replaced, find out whether you will also need to replace the memory, microprocessor, or other boards in the system.

If a repair comes in over $300 on an older system (motherboard repairs on systems with custom parts, such as Compaqs, easily could), it's worth asking what the repair company would charge to transplant all the good parts into a new bare-bones system that you can provide. (See the discussion of bare-bones upgrades on page 71.)

Because we are Cheapskates, let's take a more systematic, step-by-step look at the repair vs. replace question. Here's a worksheet you can use to quantify this.

Repair versus Replace Worksheet

1. How long were you planning to keep your existing system?		_____ years
2. What is the cost of the repair?		$_____
3. What is the value of the parts you can salvage from your existing system?	Monitor?	$_____
	Keyboard?	$_____
	Mouse?	$_____
	Modem?	$_____
	Sound card?	$_____
	CD-ROM?	$_____
	Video card?	$_____
	Memory?	$_____
	Other?	$_____
	Total	$_____
4. What is the cost of a *replacement* system?	System:	$_____
5. How long would a new system last you?		_____ years
6. What is the *per year* cost of making the repair? (#2 divided by #1)		$_____
7. What is the *per year* cost of *not* making the repair, and purchasing a replacement system instead? (#4 divided by #5)		$_____
8. How much more (or less) per year would it cost to purchase a replacement system? (#7 minus #6)		$_____

Let's walk through a typical scenario, using this worksheet.

Step 1: How long were you planning to keep your existing system? *"Let's see. It's a 486SX/25; it's a little slow, but I was counting on getting roughly two more years out of it."*

Step 2: What is the cost of the repair? *"They quoted me $300."*

Step 3: What is the value of the parts you can salvage if you don't repair your system? *"My monitor's working perfectly. So is my keyboard. The repair technician says my sound card and CD-ROM are OK, too. I'll probably have to replace the memory if I get a new computer, though. That's roughly $300 worth of stuff I can salvage, near as I can guess."*

Step 4: What is the cost of a replacement system—including transplants? *"I'm sure I could be very happy with one of those refurbished IBM Pentium 90s with 16-Mb RAM that IBM Credit is selling for $800. And I think I can transplant the CD-ROM and sound card myself, so that won't add any cost."*

Step 5: How long will a new system last you? *"If I do buy a new system, I'd really like it to last at least four years."*

Step 6: What is the per-year cost of making the repair? *"Well, at $300 for two years, that would be $150 per year."*

Step 7: What is the per year cost of *not* making the repair? *"At $800 for four years, that would be $200 per year."*

Step 8: Compare the costs. All else equal, if the two figures are close, *replace* the system; if they aren't close, *repair* it.

Summary

In this chapter, I've done all I can to help you avoid repairs, minimize their costs, and think rationally about when to throw in the towel. I've shown how preventive maintenance can dramatically reduce the likelihood of expensive system problems; helped you organize yourself and your data to make system problems as painless as possible; shown you how to perform a wide variety of troubleshooting tasks; and helped you decide when it's time to throw in the towel.

Now, for all you PC Cheapskates, something completely different. Come along on a visit to planet Mac.

The Cheapskate Mac

So you love Macs. Always have. Always will. And you're grumbling to yourself: Awful lot of stuff about Windoze in the last few chapters. What about me?

Or you're a new computer user, and you've been told, over and over again: Macs are easier. You want one. Or your child's school is filled with Macs, and you want your child to have the same kind of computer at home.

OK, Mac Cheapskates, this is your chapter.

I'll show you where to get cheap Macs, how to buy used Macs, and what to know about Mac clones. We'll take a stroll down Mac memory lane, showing you what to expect from each old model of Mac. I'll show you some pitfalls (and models) to watch out for. And I'll point you to some cool sources for Mac software, peripherals, and accessories.

But first, a word about the Mac—and its future.

Macs in the Late 90s: The Big Change

What an elegant piece of machinery; one that, as you're probably well aware, is going through a profound transition. Former wunderkind Steve Jobs, who led the project that delivered the first Mac way back in 1984, is back with Apple, if only as a part-time consultant. Every week, there's new news about what to expect. Most especially, new news about what owners of current Macs can expect.

354

The current deal is this. For a while at least, there are going to be two Mac operating systems. The first, code-named Rhapsody, will combine the Mac interface with Steve's industrial-strength NextStep operating system. Rhapsody will have the superior multitasking and memory management capabilities the Mac has sorely lacked. If all goes well, it should work more smoothly, and crash much less, than Macs have lately. It should be an operating system your brokerage firm could depend upon—just as NextStep is now.

Rhapsody will run existing Mac software. But it will do so by "emulating" the current Mac OS operating system. If you've ever pretended to be someone you weren't, you know how much energy that can take. Expect Rhapsody to run current Mac OS software more slowly than it runs the new stuff. (Apple says "existing Mac OS software is expected to work within Rhapsody at PowerPC speeds," which means it isn't promising all that much yet.)

Apple did a spectacular job of maintaining compatibility and performance through its last major Macintosh transition, but they've got their work cut out for them this time.

Apple has promised that Macs sold today *will* run Rhapsody—but hasn't made any promises about older Macs. Today's best guess is that the cutoff line will be somewhere within the last three years—most likely within the last two years. It remains to be seen whether older Macs will have the power to run Rhapsody even if they *are* compatible. It also remains to be seen how quickly real Rhapsody software will appear. It may be a few years before all the major programs Mac users depend on have "gone native."

Apple says it will also continue to upgrade the current Macintosh operating system, Mac OS, starting with System 8.0 in summer 1997, and one new release per year afterwards. So current Apple users shouldn't be completely left behind—at least not until all the exciting new Mac programs appear only on Rhapsody.

If You're Buying Now

What does this mean to you, the Mac Cheapskate? Fall 1997 will be a challenging time to make a Mac buying decision. It will be hard to predict exactly when Rhapsody will be released, exactly what it will do for you,

355

when compelling software will appear, and how much hardware you'll really need to run it well. New operating systems tend to need more power than anyone expects—or advertises. Ask Windows 95 users about that.

If you buy now, you could find yourself having to upgrade a nearly new computer when Rhapsody arrives. And you'll certainly have to pay for the Rhapsody upgrade itself. Yet if you wait for Rhapsody, you could be waiting another full year.

If you're buying your first Mac, and you're buying it for the home—not for professional applications like graphic design—my suggestion is to ignore Rhapsody entirely and focus on buying a system that does the job for you *now*. That gives you the freedom to buy a low-end system, a clone, a refurb, or a used Mac. The alternative is to spend thousands more on a high-end system with no real sense of why you need it, what it will do for you, or even whether it'll turn out to be adequate.

Macs are like other PCs in two respects. First, the real profits are at the high end, where manufacturers can squeeze the people who need the power and can afford it. Second, as soon as you drive your Mac away from the dealer, it loses a significant portion of its value. Cheapskate Mac aficionados take note.

Eric Yang, who maintains the Macintosh Evolution Web site at **www.primenet.com/~ericy/MacEvolution.html**, has carefully tracked the extraordinary recent improvements in recent Mac price/performance. His conclusion:

> *…it usually takes about 8 months for processors used in Apple's high-end systems to get passed to mid-range systems and another 4 months to make their way into low-end systems.*

There's more to performance than just the processor, but that's still a very telling fact: *A high-end Macintosh system today is a low-end system in one year.*

There's nothing worse than buying a system and, a few days later, discovering that the price has dropped. If only you'd waited![a]

Wouldn't it be great if someone would tell you who's *about* to lower their Mac OS prices? Believe it or not, someone *will*. For up-to-the-minute information on which Apple and clone systems are being closed out, who's just announced lower prices—and who's *about* to—visit the Buying a Mac Web site at *www.digiserve.com/buying-a-mac/* (see Figure 9-1). They'll even tell you who's got the best PowerBook prices.

a. Of course, if your mail-order firm or reseller offered price protection, you might actually be able to get a refund!

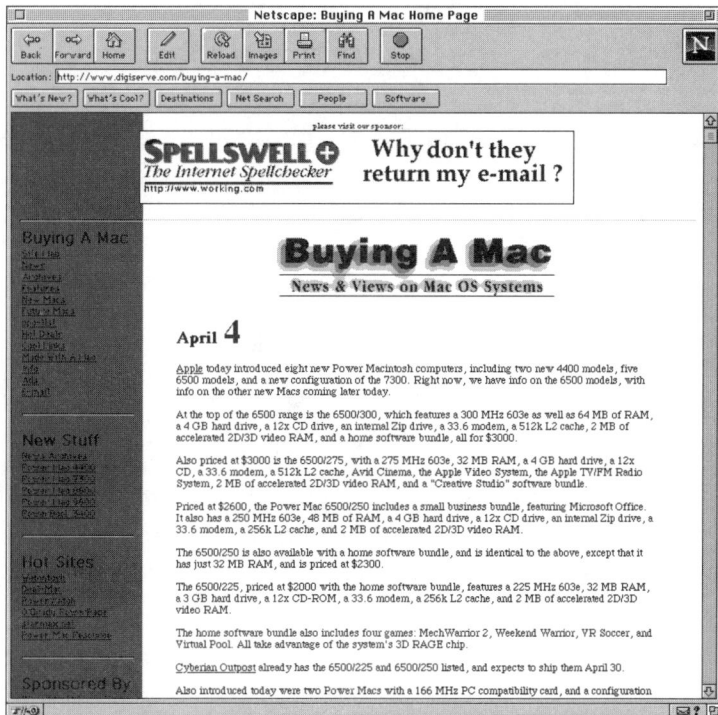

Figure 9–1   The Buying a Mac site.

What to Ask When Rhapsody Arrives

If, in two years, Rhapsody looks so great that you simply must have it, sell your current Mac and buy a new one designed for Rhapsody from the ground up—a system that already comes with Rhapsody. Meanwhile, when Rhapsody arrives, stay close to the Mac market. See what the experts are saying. And, as we've said throughout this book, stay focused on *your* needs:

▲ What will Rhapsody (and new Rhapsody software) let me do that I can't do now? Is this new capability worth what it costs?

▲ Will Rhapsody help me perform my current tasks better? Better enough to be worth the investment?

▲ How important is improved stability and multitasking in the work I do? Am I having trouble with my current Mac? Is Rhapsody actually delivering the reliability it promised?

A Guide to Apple's Macs—and the Clones

Once, if you wanted a Macintosh, you had to buy from Apple.

Not any more. At this writing, a sizable and growing minority of new Mac-compatible systems come from clone vendors. And while Mac clone vendors can easily be numbered on the fingers of two hands as I write this, for the first time there's a new Mac at *most* of the same price points you can get a new PC for.[1]

There's one big exception. On the PC side, there are generic companies selling stripped down or bare-bones systems for as little as a few hundred dollars. It's a market fueled by the presence of hundreds of small motherboard makers, each of whom can easily license the technology they need to make PC compatibles. On the Mac side, where only a few large companies are licensed to manufacture Mac-compatible logic boards, that doesn't exist yet—though a higher-priced barebones market is beginning to take shape.

▲ ▲

1. Apple itself has a lot to do with determining how price competitive the cloners will be. Right now, Apple charges roughly $50 to license the Mac OS and anywhere between $10 and $100 for the hardware license. These fees are now being renegotiated, and if they increase, it will be more difficult for cloners to maintain their price differential.

In this section, we'll take a quick look at today's leading Mac OS vendors—and tell you where to find out more about each company. We'll also give you a few tips about buying clones—tips you might not have needed when Apple presided over the marketplace as a relatively benign monopoly.

Getting Buying Information on the Web

Cheapskates ought to be, first and foremost, *informed* buyers. Whether you buy a new Mac, a clone, or a used Mac, there's an enormous amount of useful, *free* buying information on the Web. With radical changes on the horizon for the Mac, these sources are even more important to Mac users—and to anyone interested in the future of the Mac platform.

Make the rounds of *these* Web sites listed in Table 9-1 before you plunk down one hard-earned nickel.

Table 9–1 Great Web Sites for Cheapskate (and Other) Mac Users

Site	Description
www.macsurfer.com	A compilation of the latest headlines from every Mac medium.
www.macintouch.com	*MacWeek* columnist Ric Ford's extensive resource for anyone concerned with Mac hardware and software issues (see Figure 9-2).
www.macweek.com	Up-to-the-minute news on the Mac marketplace *(see Figure 9–3).*
www.shareware.com	Comprehensive source of Mac shareware.
http://ng.netgate.net/~engstrom/cc.html	Detailed Macintosh and clone specifications and performance benchmarks
www.velodrome.com/umac.html	The ultimate Macintosh site: A comprehensive collection of Mac news and links to other Mac sites on the Web.
www.macfixit.com	Detailed information on Macintosh hardware problems and repair solutions.
www.uce.com	United Computer Exchange.

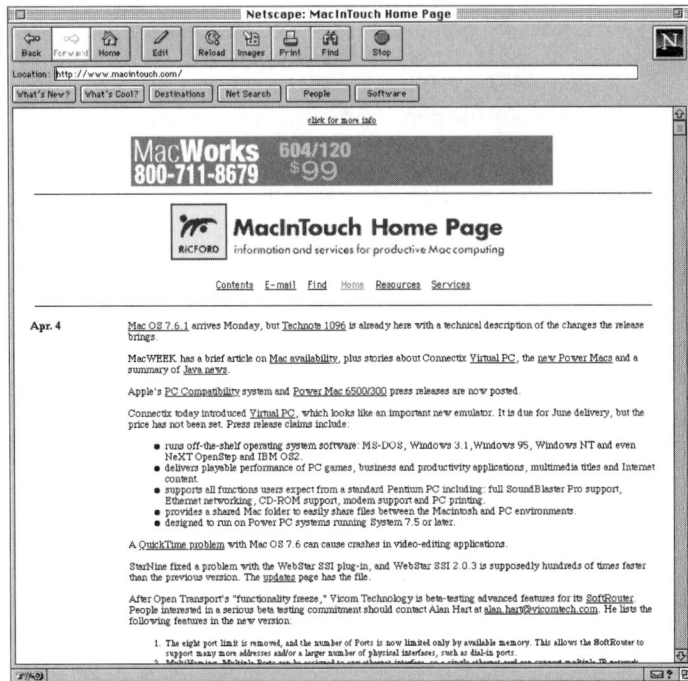

Figure 9–2   Ric Ford's MacInTouch site: Up-to-the-minute information on Mac hardware and OS issues.

Apple

Of course, there's Apple itself. Relatively poor price/performance relative to most of its competitors (though much better than it used to be). Apple's hardware and quality control used to be rock solid, but it's slipped a few notches. (Later in this chapter, we'll show you a few Apple products to be wary of.) Compensating in part for any falloff in Apple quality, however, the company has consistently offered world-class customer service and technical support (though Apple's well-respected 800-SOS-APPL phone number has recently become a paying phone number).

Later in this chapter, Table 9-2 details basic specs for all Macintosh models. You can get even more detailed information and spec sheets about any Apple Macintosh system—including discontinued models—at Apple Facts Online, **http://product.info.apple.com/productinfo/ datasheets/**.

PC users have *Computer Shopper*; Mac users have *MacWeek*.

MacWeek's display classifieds include some of the world's best deals on Mac stuff (along with the occasional scam artist—get references or call the Better Business Bureau). If you're involved with Mac buying decisions at the office, you may be able to qualify for a free subscription to *MacWeek*. Fill out your application at *www.zdnet.com/zdsubs/*.

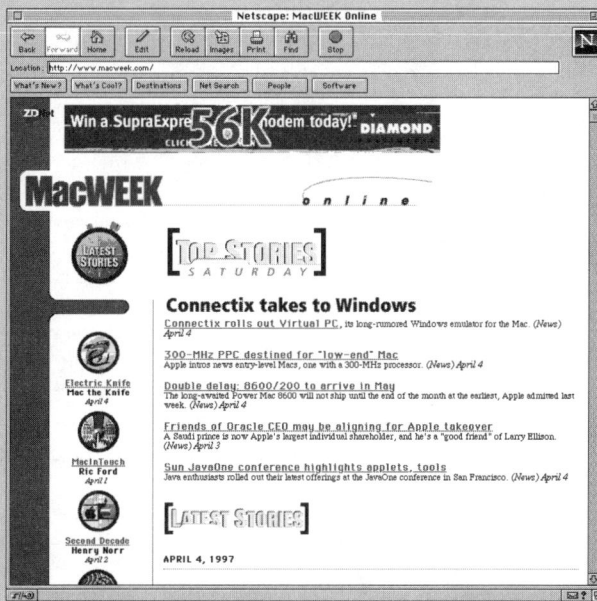

Figure 9–3   What happened *today* in the world of Macintosh? See **www.macweek.com** for the answer.

Discount Sources for Apple Macintoshes

Other World Computing
224 West Judd Street
Woodstock, IL 60098
1-800-275-4576

tip If you want to get performance data on a whole bunch of Macintoshes and clones at once, the fastest, most efficient way is to visit *http://ng.netgate.net/ ~engstrom/cc.html*, the Macintosh Performance Guide. If you're paying for Web access by the minute, download the Macintosh Catalog database from ZDNet (*www5.zdnet.com/mac/catalog.html*).

If you don't have FileMaker Pro, make sure to get the catalog version that includes the Mac Catalog Runtime—the catalog will then work as a stand-alone application. Then you can do all the comparisons you want off-line.

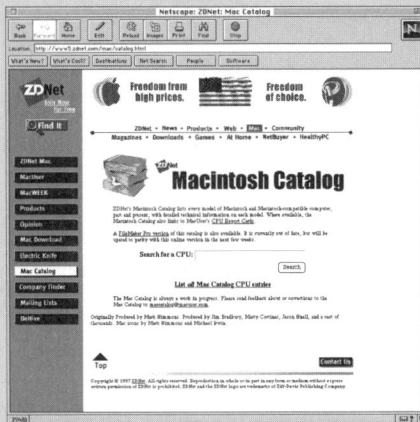

Figure 9–5   Downloading ZDNet's Macintosh Catalog.

CompuAmerica
1-800-533-9005
www.compu-america.com

ComputerTown
52 Congress Street
Boston, MA 02109
1-800-613-0622 (24-hour order line)
www.computertown.com

Power On Computer Services
4323 Anthony Ct., Unit #1
Rocklin, CA 95677
1-800-673-6227; 1-916-652-1880
www.poweron-line.com

SoftClub Computer Systems, Inc.
68 Bellingham Street
Chelsea, MA 02150
1-888-MACS-NOW
www.softclub.com
The good news: Great prices, BBB member. The bad news: Credit card surcharge.

Power Computing

Then there's Power Computing. Awesome price/performance—probably the best of any Mac clone vendor. Wonderful intentions. These are people who love the Mac and show it in every way they can, from their hiring to their advertising.

However, they've offered uneven quality, poor support, and only fair customer service at best. The biggest complaint: They haven't come anywhere near meeting their promised ship dates. So if you need your computer on a certain date, you may not want to take the chance on Power Computing.

Power Computing
255 North Interstate 35
Round Rock, TX 78664
1-800-999-7279; 1-512-388-6868
www.powercc.com

There are some early signs that, just maybe, Power Computing is getting past its growing pains. For example, there seems to be less grousing on Power's CompuServe forum of late. It would be nice if you could routinely depend on these folks by the time you read this. There's one quick way to find out: PowerWatch at **www.lostworld.pair.com/powerwatch/** (see Figure 9-6). This site keeps a close, independent eye on doings at the company, including the real scoop on what's shipped and what hasn't.

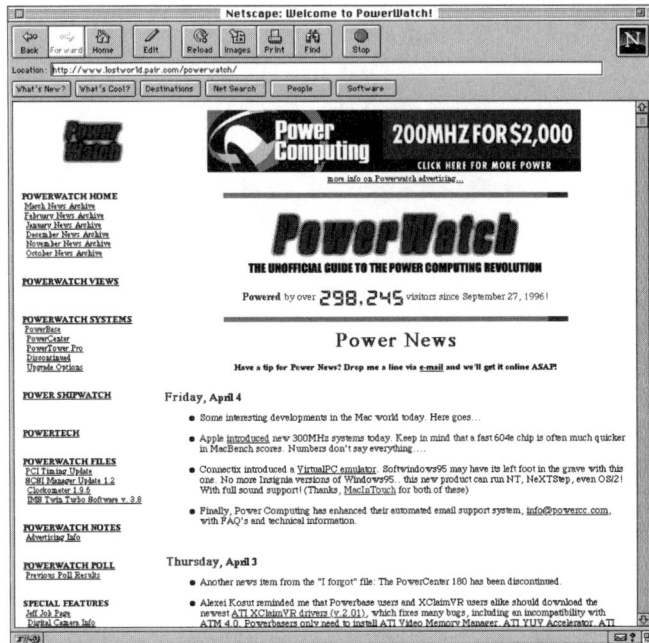

Figure 9–6   PowerWatch

UMAX

Next, there's Umax. This Taiwan-based company—well known for scanners—purchased the rights to Radius' Mac clone technology and now markets systems under the SuperMac brand. These are solid systems, from the top of the line down to entry level. UMAX' current "value" offerings include the 603e-based C500 and C600 systems, which can be upgraded to faster 603e processors later.

UMAX Technologies
3353 Gateway Boulevard
Fremont, CA 94538
1-510-651-9488
www.supermac.com/products/

364

Motorola StarMax

One of the best current Mac clone options is Motorola's recently introduced line of StarMax systems. These systems have three major advantages. First, Motorola's reputation for quality and strong technology.
Motorola is also the company that designs the PowerPC chips at the heart
of all current Macintoshes—which gives it a headstart in designing new
systems based on those chips. Then, there's Motorola's five-year warranty.[2] That's unheard of in the PC business—and the best part is, you
can be fairly sure Motorola will actually exist in five years. Third, Motorola's first systems have been introduced at surprisingly low prices.

Motorola Computer Group
2900 S. Diablo Way
Tempe, AZ 8582
1-800-359-1107; 1-512-434-1526
**www.mot.com/GSS/MCG/products/systems/ds/star-
max/SMfamily.html**

> **For the independent scoop, including a host of minor
> StarMax problems and solutions—and an URL that's
> a whole lot easier to type—visit www.starmax.net
> (see Figure 9-6). I can't say enough good things about
> this site.**

Starmax.net includes a wonderful pricing page, *www.starmax.net/
ref/pricing.html,* that tracks the prices of StarMax systems at 12 different
suppliers. Among the lowest-price StarMax providers tracked by star-
max.net in April 1997 were

MicroComputer Systems
2615-184th Street., SW #105
Lynnwood, WA 98037
1-800-422-5182; 1-206-778-7337
www.micro-computer.com/

▲ ▲ ▲ ▲ ▲ ▲ ▲ ▲ ▲ ▲ ▲ ▲ ▲ ▲ ▲ ▲ ▲ ▲ ▲

2.   Though the last two years of the warranty only guarantee that you'll be reimbursed the residual value of your
        system— which after five years won't be all that much.

Figure 9–7 The unofficial Web site starmax.net, covering Motorola StarMax computers.

Small Dog Electronics
RR#1 Box 171-1
Prickly Mountain Road
Warren, VT 05674
1-802-496-7171
www.smalldoggy.com

SoftClub Computer Systems, Inc.
68 Bellingham Street
Chelsea, MA 02150
1-888-MACS-NOW
www.softclub.com
Enter this site at www.softclub.com/welcome2.html, *and you may be eligible for bonus software with your StarMax purchase. Tell them: "Ben sent me."*

Back at starmax.net again, check out the page *www.starmax.net/comm/test/ resellers.html*, which compiles unedited user experiences with many leading StarMax resellers. Even if you're planning to purchase another system, it's awfully instructive.

APS Technologies

New to the Mac clone market—but not to Mac hardware—is APS. For more than a decade, APS has been a leading third-party supplier of hard drives for Macintosh systems, and they've built a significant business in Macintosh hard drives and other peripherals. They have a strong reputation in the Mac community.

Now they're selling the M*Power series of Mac OS compatibles. In some respects, these are relabeled Motorola systems with a twist: You can mix and match the exact configuration you want from a wide range of options for hard drive, memory, video card, and CD-ROM. If you want an M*Power system, you call APS: They sell direct, not through dealers.

> APS Technologies
> 6131 Deramus
> Kansas City, MO 64120
> 1-800-235-8935
> **www.apstech.com**

PowerTools: Build Your Own Bare-bones Mac

PowerTools (see Figure 9-7), a company that previously specialized in Mac upgrades, has introduced the first truly "bare-bones" build-your-own Mac clones. PowerTools' Infiniti series starts at $899 for a stripped down 180-MHz 603e system that includes Mac OS System 7.6, but no hard drive, monitor, memory—or even mouse.

The Infiniti takes standard SCSI drives—and lower-cost IDE drives designed for PCs. It uses standard EDO DIMM memory, standard VGA monitors, and standard keyboards and mice—either traditional Mac, or cheaper PC-style. PowerTools will walk you through purchasing each component from them—or you can buy the stripped down Mac and do it yourself.

PowerTools Corp.
P.O. Box 3000-343
Austin, TX 78764
1-800-891-4307; 1-512-891-0646
www.pwrtools.com

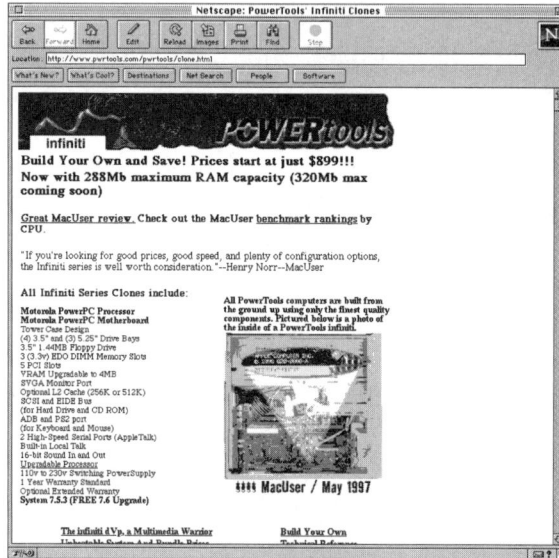

Figure 9–8   Bare-bones Macs! What a concept.

> **tip**
>
> The guts of a clone Mac is its logic board (motherboard), and many Motorola, APS, and PowerTools computers all use the same "Tanzania" boards. Long term, these are expected to be replaced by lower-cost boards that meet a new standard called PowerPC Platform (PPCP). If and when this ever happens (and it's far behind schedule), it will become significantly easier to clone the Mac, and the business *could* get a lot more price competitive.

Clone Buying Tips

It's not as easy to buy a Mac as it used to be when only Apple made them. Now you have to ask more questions.

- ▲ Call the service and support line—see how long it takes to reach someone. That will give you an idea of what to expect when *you* need help.
- ▲ Read your warranty carefully.
- ▲ Make sure you know exactly what your clone comes with—and what it doesn't come with. A simple example: You can't always count on getting a mouse any more!
- ▲ Shop around on the Web. There are substantial variations in price and availability, especially for Umax and Motorola systems—and the lowest prices will often come from smaller companies that have chosen to focus their businesses on Mac clones. (See the Web and mail order buying tips in Chapter 2.)
- ▲ Take into account the Mac OS version that will ship with your computer. For example, if you want Mac OS 8.0 and your system ships only with System 7.6, will you have to pay extra to upgrade? Will your system be compatible?
- ▲ There are now a wide variety of technical specs that affect performance and vary among vendors: cache, upgradability, hard drive performance, to name a few. Check the Macintosh Performance Guide we mentioned earlier for objective MacBench performance ratings; then calculate benchmark ratings against price for a rough estimate of system price/performance. You'll be surprised how much it can vary.

Buying a Used Mac

Used Macs wear well, especially if you don't have to use the latest software. In this section, I'll take a look at each generation of Mac—and give you some buying tips. In Chapter 1, you took a brief look at the different generations of Mac. Now we'll take a closer look. Use Table 9-2 as your quick reference to any used Mac you might come across.

Table 9–2 Macintosh Systems, 1984–1997

Macintosh Model #	Processor	Memory Expandable to	Expansion Slots	Introduced	Notes
68x00 series					
128K	68000 8 MHz	128K	0	1984	First Macintosh released; built-in monitor
512K	68000 8 MHz	512K	0	1984	Built-in monitor
512Ke	68000 8 MHz	512K	0	1986	Built-in monitor
Centris 610/ Quadra 610	68LC040 20 MHz	68M	1 PDS	1993	
Centris 650	68040 25 MHz	4–136M	3 Nubus, 1 PDS	1993	
Classic	68000 8 MHz	1–4M	0	1990	Built-in monitor
Classic II	68030 16 MHz	2–10M	0	1991	Built-in monitor
Color Classic	68030 16 MHz	4–10M	0	1991	Built-in color monitor
Color Classic II	68030 33 MHz	4–10M	0	1991	Built-in color monitor
II	68020 16 MHz	1–20M	6 (Nubus)	1987	Up to 68 Mb with SuperDrive upgrade
IIci	68030 25 MHz	1–128M	3 Nubus, 1 cache	1989	
IIcx	68030 16 MHz	1–128M	3 Nubus	1989	
IIfx	68030 40 MHz	4–128M	6 Nubus, 1 PDS	1990	
IIsi	68030 20 MHz	1–17M	1 Nubus or PDS	1990	
IIvi	68030 16 MHz	4–68M	3 Nubus, 1 PDS	1992	
IIvx	68030 32 MHz	4–68M	3 Nubus, 1 PDS	1992	
IIx	68030 16 MHz	1–32M	6 (Nubus)	1988	
LC	68020 16 MHz	2–10M	1 (LC)	1990	

Table 9–2 Macintosh Systems, 1984–1997 *(continued)*

Macintosh Model #	Processor	Memory Expandable to	Expansion Slots	Introduced	Notes
LC 475	68LC040 25 MHz	4–36M	1 (LC)	1993	
LC 520	68030 25 MHz	4–36M	1 (LC)	1993	
LC 550	68030 33 MHz	4–36M	1 (LC)	1994	
LC 575	68LC040 33 MHz	4–36M	1 (LC)	1994	
LC 580	68LC040 33 MHz	8–52M	1 (LC)	1994	
LC 630	68LC040 33 MHz	4–36M	1 (LC)	1994	DOS-compatible version includes 486DX2/66 DOS card
LC II	68030 16 MHz	4–10M	1 (LC)	1992	
LC III	68030 25 MHz	4–36M	1 (LC III PDS)	1993	
LC III+	68030 33 MHz	4–36M	1 (LC III PDS)	1993	
Performa 200	68030 16 MHz	2–10M	0	1992	Built in 9" B&W monitor
Performa 400	68030 16 MHz	4–10M	1 (LC)	1992	
Performa 405	68030 16 MHz	4–10M	1 (LC)	1993	
Performa 410	68030 16 MHz	4–10M	1 (LC)	1993	
Performa 430	68030 16 MHz	4–10M	1 (LC)	1993	
Performa 450	68030 25 MHz	4–36M	1 (LC)	1993	
Performa 460	68030 33 MHz	4–36M	1 (LC III PDS)	1993	
Performa 466	68030 33 MHz	4–36M	1 (LC III PDS)	1993	
Performa 467	68030 33 MHz	4–36M	1 (LC III PDS)	1993	
Performa 475	68LC040 25 MHz	4–36M	1 (LC)	1993	
Performa 476	68LC040 25 MHz	4–36M	1 (LC)	1993	
Performa 550	68030 33 MHz	4–36M	1 (LC)	1993	14" Sony monitor
Performa 560	68030 33 MHz	4–36M	1 (LC)	1994	14" Sony monitor
Performa 575	68LC040 33 MHz	4–36M	1 (LC)	1994	14" Sony Monitor

Table 9–2 Macintosh Systems, 1984–1997 *(continued)*

Macintosh Model #	Processor	Memory Expandable to	Expansion Slots	Introduced	Notes
Performa 577	68LC040 33 MHz	4–36M	1 (LC)	1994	14" Sony monitor
Performa 578	68LC040 33 MHz	8–36M	1 (LC)	1994	14" Sony monitor
Performa 580CD	68LC040 33 MHz	5–52M	1 (LC)	1994	14" Sony monitor
Performa 600	68030 32 MHz	4–68M	3 Nubus, 1 PDS	1992	
Performa 630	68LC040 33 MHz	4–36M	1 (LC)	1994	Performa Plus display 630 CD model includes CD-ROM and 8 Mb standard
Performa 631CD	68LC040 33 MHz	4–36M	1 (LC)	1994	
Performa 635CD	68LC040 33 MHz	4–36M	1 (LC)	1994	
Performa 636CD	68LC040 33 MHz	4–36M	1 (LC)	1994	
Performa 637CD	68LC040 33 MHz	8–36M	1 (LC)	1994	
Performa 638CD	68LC040 33 MHz	8–36M	1 (LC)	1994	
Performa 640CD DOS Compatible	68LC040 33 MHz	4–52M	0	1994	Includes 486DX/2-66 processor and Windows 3.1
Plus	68000 8 MHz	1–4M	0	1986	Built-in monitor
Portable	16 MHz 68HC000	4–9M	1	1989	Transportable
Quadra 605	68LC040 25 MHz	4–36M	1 LCIII PDS	1993	
Quadra 610	68040 25 MHz	XXX	XXX	1994	DOS compatible version includes 486SX-25 DOS card

Table 9–2 Macintosh Systems, 1984–1997 *(continued)*

Macintosh Model #	Processor	Memory Expandable to	Expansion Slots	Introduced	Notes
Quadra 630	68040 33 MHz	4–36M	1 (LC)	1994	
Quadra 650	68040 33 MHz	4–132M	3 Nubus, 1 PDS	1993	
Quadra 660AV	68040 25 MHz	XXX	XXX	XXX	
Quadra 700	68040 25 MHz	4–20M	2 Nubus, 1 PDS	1991	
Quadra 800	68040 33 MHz	8–136M	3 Nubus, 1 PDS	1993	
Quadra 840AV	68040 40 MHz	4–128M	3 Nubus	1993	
Quadra 900	68040 25 MHz	4–256M	5 Nubus, 1 PDS	1991	
Quadra 950	68040 33 MHz	4–256M	5 Nubus, 1 PDS	1992	
SE	68000 8 MHz	1–4M	1 (SE PDS)	1987	Built-in monitor (FDHD version introduced 1.4-Mb SuperDrive)
SE/30	68030 16 MHz	1–32M	1	1989	Built-in monitor
TV	68030 32 MHz	4–8M	0	1993	TV monitor built in
XL	68000 5 MHz	0.5–2M	0	1985	Adapted from pre-Macintosh "Lisa" computer
PowerPC Series					
4400/200	603e 200 MHz	16–160M	2 (PCI)	1997	
5200/75 LC	603 75 MHz	16–64M	1 (LC)	1996	Sold in the U.S. to K–12 market only. May have logic board problems eligible for free repair.
5260/100	603e 100 MHz	16–64M	1 (LC)	1996	

373

Table 9–2 Macintosh Systems, 1984–1997 *(continued)*

Macintosh Model #	Processor	Memory Expandable to	Expansion Slots	Introduced	Notes
5300/100 LC	603e 100 MHz	16–64M	1 (LC)	1995	Sold in the U.S. to K–12 market only. May have logic board problems eligible for free repair.
5400/120	603e 120 MHz	16–136M	1 (PCI)	1996	Built-in 15" monitor
5400/180	603e 180 MHz	16–136M	1 (PCI)	1996	Built-in 15" monitor
5400/200	603e 200 MHz	24–136M	1 (PCI)	1996	Built-in 15" monitor
5400/225	603e 225 MHz	32–136M	1 (PCI)	1996	Built-in 15" monitor
6100/60	601 60 MHz	8–72M	1 (Nubus)	1994	
6100/66	601 66 MHz	8–72M	1 (Nubus)	1994	
6100/66AV	601 66 MHz	8–72M	0	1994	
6200/75	603 75 MHz	8–64M	1 (LC)	1995	May have logic board problems eligible for free repair.
6400/180	603e 180 MHz	16–136M	2 (PCI)	1996	
6400/200	603e 200 MHz	16–136M	2 (PCI)	1996	
6500/225	603e 225 MHz	32–768M	2 (PCI)	1997	
6500/250	603e 250 MHz	32–768M	2 (PCI)	1997	
7100/66	601 66 MHz	8–136M	3 (Nubus)	1994	"AV" version includes CD-ROM and two S-video to composite video adapters
7100/80	601 80 MHz	8–136M	3 (Nubus)	1994	"AV" version includes CD-ROM and two S-video to composite video adapters
7200/75	601 75 MHz	8–256M	3 (PCI)	1995	

Table 9–2 Macintosh Systems, 1984–1997 *(continued)*

Macintosh Model #	Processor	Memory Expandable to	Expansion Slots	Introduced	Notes
7200/90	601 90 MHz	8–256M	3 (PCI)	1995	
7200/120	601 120 MHz	16–256M	3 (PCI)	1995	
7300/180	604e 180 MHz	16–512M	3 (PCI)	1997	
7300/200	604e 200 MHz	32–512M	3 (PCI)	1997	
7500/100	601 100 MHz	8–512M	3 (PCI)	1995	
7600/120	604 120 MHz	16–512M	3 (PCI)	1996	
7600/132	604 132 MHz	16–512M	3 (PCI)	1996	
8100/100	601 100 MHz	8–264M	3 (Nubus)	1994	"AV" version includes CD-ROM and two S-video to composite video adapters
8100/110	601 110 MHz	16–264M	3 (Nubus)	1994	
8100/80	601 80 MHz	16–264M	3 (Nubus)	1994	
8500/120	604 120 MHz	16–512M	3 (PCI)	1995	
8500/132	604 132 MHz	16–512M	3 (PCI)	1995	
8500/150	604 150 MHz	16–512M	3 (PCI)	1995	
8500/180	604 180 MHz	16–512M	3 (PCI)	1995	
8600/200	604e 200 MHz	32–512M	3 (PCI)	1996	
9500/120	604 120 MHz	16–768M	6 (PCI)	1995	
9500/132	604 132 MHz	32–768M	6 (PCI)	1995	
9500/150	604 150 MHz	16–768M	6 (PCI)	1995	
9500/180MP	Dual 604e 180 MHz	16–768M	6 (PCI)	1996	
9500/200	604e 200 MHz	32–768M	6 (PCI)	1996	
9600/200	604e 200 MHz	32–768M	6 (PCI)	1996	
9600/200MP	Dual 604e 200 MHz	32–768M	6 (PCI)	1996	
9600/233	604e 233 MHz	32–768M	6 (PCI)	1997	
Performa 5200	603 75 MHz	8–64M	1 (LC)	1995	May have logic board problems eligible for free repair.

Table 9–2 Macintosh Systems, 1984–1997 *(continued)*

Macintosh Model #	Processor	Memory Expandable to	Expansion Slots	Introduced	Notes
Performa 5215CD	603 75 MHz	8–64M	1 (LC)	1995	May have logic board problems eligible for free repair.
Performa 5260	603e 120 MHz	16–64M	1 (LC)	1995	
Performa 5400, 5420	603e 120 MHz	16–136M	1 (PCI)	1996	Comes with 15" monitor
Performa 6110	601 60 MHz	8–64M	1 (Nubus)	1994	
Performa 6200 series (6205, 6214, 6216, 6218, 6220, 6230)	603 75 MHz	8–64M	1 (LC)	1995	May have logic board problems eligible for free repair. Some models come with monitor.
Performa 6290	603e 100 MHz	8–64M	1 (LC)	1996	
Performa 6300CD	603e 100 MHz	16–64M	1 (LC)	1995	
Performa 6320	603e 120 MHz	16–64M	1 (LC)	1995	
Performa 6360/120	603e 120 MHz	16–64M	1 (LC)	1995	
Performa 6360/160	603e 160 MHz	16–64M	1 (LC)	1995	
Performa 6400/180	603e 180 MHz	16–136M	2 (PCI)	1996	
Performa 6400/200	603e 200 MHz	16–136M	2 (PCI)	1996	

Start by taking a quick look at the PC buyer's tips in Chapters 2 and 3—many of them apply here, too. For example, when evaluating a used Mac, remember that Macs don't like dust, smoke and animal hair any more than PCs do.

Then, there are some Mac-specific tips you should be aware of.

The first relates to pricing. As a Mac cheapskate, you have one terrific resource your PC brethren don't: the United Computer Exchange. This organization tracks "bid" and "offered" prices for virtually every Mac, updating them every week at **www.uce.com**. See what the market is like before you start searching.

The second tip seems obvious, but doesn't always seem to be. Know what you want to use your Mac for before you go searching for one. If all you need is a simple word processing system—and you're writing short documents, not a book—you might be able to get away with an older compact Mac—possibly for $200 or less. We'll talk more about compact Macs later.

If you plan to use your Mac to keep track of your business finances, check the requirements of the software package you plan to use. For example, if you're planning to run QuickBooks 4.0 for the Macintosh, the current version,[3] the manufacturer recommends at least a 68030-25 processor, with at least 8-Mb RAM and at least 15–20-Mb disk space. That eliminates the compact Macs, but you can still consider a computer like the Macintosh IIci or Performa 450—and you can build a complete system around these computers for under $500. (MacResQ offers the Mac IIci with Apple 13" Trinitron monitor and keyboard for $399, but you'll have to add about $50 worth of memory.)

On the other hand (this will sound hauntingly familiar if you've read the rest of this book), if you're running heavy-duty business applications based on the current version of Microsoft Office for the Macintosh, you realistically need a PowerMac—and probably at least 16 Mb minimum. A first-generation PowerMac, such as a 7100/80, can now be purchased used for well under $700. Add a monitor and you're still under $1,000—but not by much.

If your needs go *beyond* this, you may want to consider a new Mac or clone.

One last pointer: It's become tougher than ever to judge the speed of a Mac by its chip speed. A Mac with a 603 microprocessor will actually be slower than a Mac with an older 601 microprocessor running at the same speed. (That's why a newer Performa 6200 with a 75-MHz 603 doesn't run any faster than an older Power Macintosh 6100/66 with a 66-MHz 601.) But, a *603e* chip will run about as fast as a 601 at the same clock speed. And the newer *604e* will run a whopping 50–60 percent faster than the 603e at the same clock speed.

OK, where can you get used Macs? Here are some of the best sources.

▲ ▲ ▲ ▲ ▲ ▲ ▲ ▲ ▲ ▲ ▲ ▲ ▲ ▲ ▲ ▲ ▲ ▲ ▲ ▲

3.   And apparently the *final* version—Intuit has announced that it doesn't plan to upgrade QuickBooks for the Mac.

Sources for Used Macs

MacResQ

179 Mason Circle

Concord, CA 94520

1-888-44-RESCUE; 1-510-689-9488

www.macresq.com

MacResQ (see Figure 9-9) sells to both dealers and the public and offers a wide selection of used, refurbished, and demo Macintosh equipment. MacResQ also provides service and repair, and takes trade-ins.

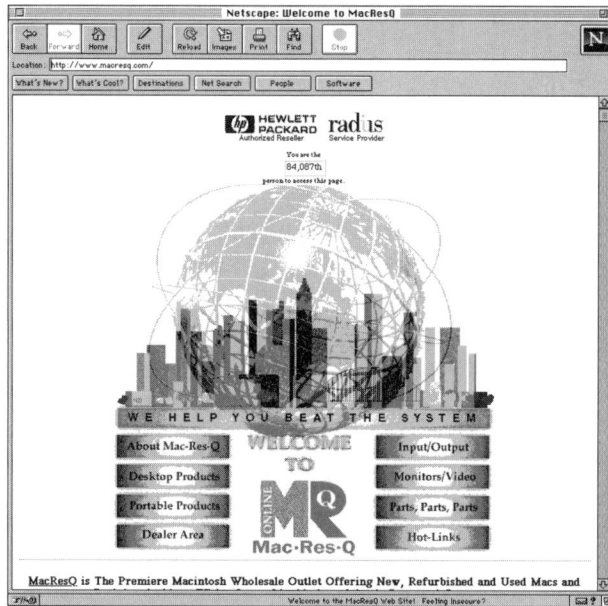

Figure 9–9 MacResQ: Home of used Macs.

Que Computers

2323 E. Hennepin Ave.

Minneapolis, MN 55413

612-623-0903

www.quecomp.com

Recent deals: Mac IIsi 5/80, $175; Mac IIci 5/80; $195; packaged with 13" monitor, keyboard, and mouse, $399.

Que Computers satellite store:
Village East Center
2112 Hoffman Road
Mankato, MN 56001

Mac Sale International
1150 W. Alameda Drive, Suites 1 & 2
Tempe, AZ 85282
1-800-729-7031; 1-602-858-0900
www.macsaleint.com
Recent deal: Apple refurbished Macintosh 5200/75 8/500/CD, 15"
monitor, $999 (reflecting cash discount).

Rentex Computer Rentals
337 Summer Street
Boston, MA 02210
1-800-545-2313
www.rentex.com

CRA Systems
300 South 13th Street
Waco, TX 76701
1-800-375-9000
www.cra-sys.com

Pre-Owned Electronics
125 Middlesex Turnpike
Bedford, MA 01730
1-800-274-5353

Mac Solutions
1416 Wilshire Blvd.
Santa Monica, CA 90403
1-800-80-WE-BUY
www.macsolutions.com

Mac Rentals
Sales 800-756-6227
Used Macs.

User Group Connection
1-800-350-4842
www.ugstore.com
Used Macs for user group members.

DataTech Remarketing
471 Myatt Drive
Madison, TN 37115
1-800-281-3661
www.datatech-rmkt.com
Offers a six-month warranty on used equipment. Current deals:
Macintosh Classic 4/40, $179.00; Centris 610 8/230, $399.

The ARC (An Apple Resource Center)
1014 Central Avenue
Tracy, CA 95376
800-753-0114; 209-832-4300
www.thearc.com
Also offers Apple II products if you're interested. A little more
expensive than some of the others.

RE-PC
206-623-9151
www.repc.com

Macstuff
5420 E. Broadway #230
Tucson, AZ 85711
1-520-747-7625
www.macstuff.com
Offers occasional hot deals on special purchases, customer returns,
or factory refurbs—both hardware and software.

Two more companies are worth mentioning. They're both significantly more expensive but have excellent reputations for reliability:

Sun Remarketing
P.O. Box 4059
Logan, UT 84323-4059
1-800-821-3221; 1-801-755-3360
www.sunrem.com

> You might also ask around at your local ad agency, graphic design firm or newspaper. These companies are constantly upgrading their Macs to the newest and fastest systems and may be willing to sell their older Macs for less than the going rate if you're ready with the cash. You'll be saving them the trouble of tracking down a buyer.

GE Capital
1-800-431-7713
E-mail: **tms.crsinfo@capital.ge.com**

A Word about Compact Macs

Once upon a time, before today's speedy PowerMacs were a glimmer in anyone's eye, there were compact Macs: those cute little all-in-one boxes that included a petite 9" black-and-white monitor.

Some of them are a little too old, slow—and above all, *odd*—to be productive with today. For example, the original 128K and 512K Macs use hard-to-find keyboards and can't be expanded one iota. I'd also cross the Macintosh Plus off my list.

But once you get past those, things get more interesting. The Mac SE, first introduced in 1987, is still quite usable. (You're better off with the FDHD version that comes with the same 1.4-Mb floppy drive as today's Macs.) The faster SE/30, introduced in 1989, is even better. The Classic and Classic II, circa 1990–1991, are newer versions of these machines. There's even a color version, the Color Classic (and the faster, niftier, harder-to-find Color Classic II.)

If you're buying privately, make sure software's thrown into the deal. Programs that will run well on these machines include Microsoft Word 4.0 or 5.x, the Excel 3 spreadsheet program and the FileMaker 2 (or still older FileMaker Plus) database program.

OK, these Macs are slow. But that's not so terrible. They're tricky to expand. Once you find the custom Torx screwdriver you need to open the case, you then have to maneuver in fairly tight spaces—avoiding the high-voltage monitor stuff that always seems to be in your way. But many folks never open the case, so for them, that's not an issue.

There's really only one other thing that keeps these Macs from being perfect. They're susceptible to video failure. The screen starts to jitter... you may hear high-pitched noises that don't belong...maybe even get a faint sniff of burnt ozone... and then zap: *cut to black.*[4]

If you see even the slightest hint of a screen jitter in a compact Mac someone's selling you, walk away from the deal. If you're purchasing from a commercial source, ask whether they've replaced or fixed any of the video circuitry—especially the "flyback transformer" and the "analog board."

And if you own a compact Mac, this is yet another good reason to keep your files backed up. (Chances are, you're creating files that are plenty small enough to fit on floppies, so backup shouldn't be any colossal deal.) If one day your compact Mac's screen starts to jitter, back up your files ASAP, turn it off, and get it fixed—ideally by a Mac specialist who knows how to make a "component-level" repair, without replacing costly parts that are still working.

This video problem is why I like the Classics and Color Classics better than the SEs and SE/30s: they're three to five years newer, and likely to last significantly longer.

> **You can find much more information about keeping your compact Mac going at Classic Macs Digest, *www.zws.com/classicmacs/*, and at the Low-End User Catalog, stored at *http://tkb. colorado.edu/ OLM/LEU/LEU.html.* Some issues of the Low-End User Catalog are published in eDoc format; at the same site, you can download the eDoc freeware you need to read it.**

▲ ▲ ▲ ▲ ▲ ▲ ▲ ▲ ▲ ▲ ▲ ▲ ▲ ▲ ▲ ▲ ▲ ▲ ▲

4. This and much more terrific information may be found in the Macintosh Hardware FAQ, posted in multiple locations around the Internet.

Free Repairs: Apple Repair Extension Programs

Apple, long known for world-class quality, has hit a few bumps in the road lately. Once Apple acknowledged the problems, it's been forthright about offering free repairs.

You should know about these problems whether you already own this equipment, or are considering purchasing a refurbished or used system. Ask whether the problems have already been resolved. If not, factor in the time and cost of having them resolved yourself. (As we've said, the repair will be free, but you'll be without your system for some time.)

Power Macintosh and Performa 5200, 5300, 6200 and 6300 Series

You may be eligible for a free repair if you have a Performa 5200, 5215, 5300, 6200, 6205, 6214, 6216, 6218, 6220, 6230, 6290, 6300, or a Power Macintosh 5200/75 LC or 5300/100 LC,[5] and

▲ Your monitor suddenly or intermittently changes color hue for no apparent reason
▲ Your computer exhibits frequent system freezes, where the cursor doesn't move and the clock doesn't advance

Note that Macs crash for many reasons, some of them related to software, not logic board defects. Apple won't repair software problems. On the other hand, these machines have had a wide variety of defects reported beyond the ones Apple's formal quality program covers. In fact, there's an entire Web site devoted to *nothing but* problems with these machines: *Performa: the problems & the solutions*, at **www.yetan-other.com/performa/** (see Figure 9-10). If you qualify for a repair under this program, chances are you'll solve many of these problems at the same time.

You can get a free testing utility that can help you determine if your Mac will qualify, at **ftp://ftp.info.apple.com/Apple.Support.Area/ Apple_SW_Updates/US/Macintosh/Utilities/5xxx6xxx_Tester_1.0.sea. hqx**. Call 1-800-SOS-APPL to find out more about this repair program.

▲ ▲ ▲ ▲ ▲ ▲ ▲ ▲ ▲ ▲ ▲ ▲ ▲ ▲ ▲ ▲ ▲ ▲ ▲ ▲

5.   Power Macintosh 5260s and 6320s aren't included. Apple says they aren't affected by these problems.

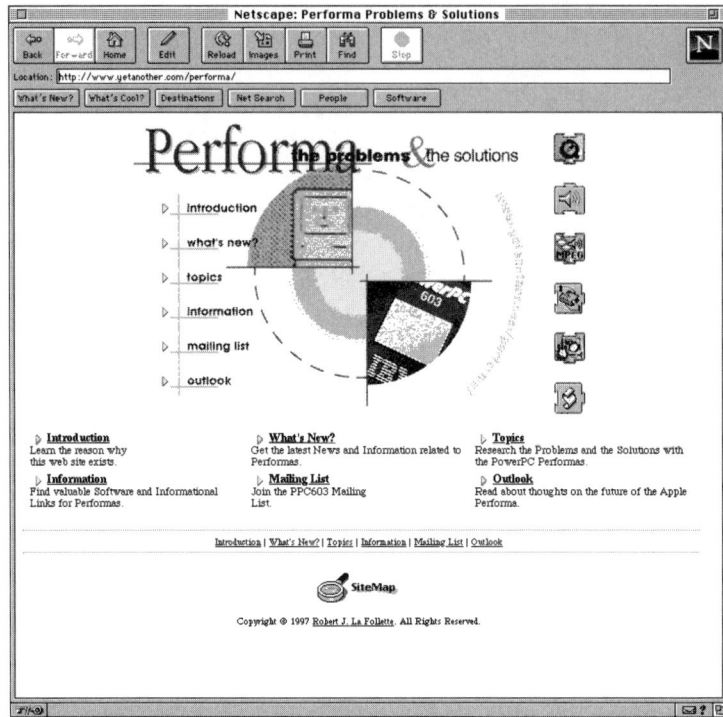

Figure 9–10   Performa: the problems & the solutions

PowerBook Models 5300, 5300c, 5300ce, and 5300cs; 190 and 190cs

The PowerBook 5300s were notorious for poor quality. These are the machines that were reported to burst spontaneously into flames when first introduced. Fortunately, that problem was corrected quickly, and Apple is doing something about the more prosaic problems you might encounter with these machines.

PowerBook 5300 and PowerBook 190 computers

You may be eligible for a free repair if

▲ The plastic housing holding your video display is starting to separate at the seams, especially in the lower-left or lower-right corner.

▲ The AC power connector has come loose or broken.

▲ Your system "hangs" while you're using PC cards (the cursor moves, but clicking the mouse button doesn't do anything).

PowerBook 5300 computers only

You may also be eligible for a free repair if

▲ Your computer takes almost twice as long to boot when plugged into a wall outlet than it does when running off the battery alone.
▲ Your PowerBook drops off of a LocalTalk network for no reason.

Apple says you *shouldn't* be having any of these problems if the third, fourth, and fifth characters of your system's serial number are *above* xx622xxxxx. If your system has a lower serial number, however, Apple encourages you to let them inspect and update your system at no cost. Call them at 1-800-801-6024.

Apple says these free repair programs will stay in effect for seven years after Apple stopped manufacturing these systems. Since most of this equipment is one to three years old, that means you have four to six years to get the work done. I strongly suggest getting it done sooner. There's no telling what could happen to Apple (or *any* technology company) in six years. And if you're planning to sell your equipment, these problems could affect its resale value.

AppleVision 1710 and 1710AV Monitors

When these monitors were first introduced, Apple admits that up to 25 percent of these monitors failed in use. Some outside experts believe the failure rate was even higher. Apple has announced that it will extend the one-year warranty to two years on all AppleVision 1710 and 1710AV monitors with serial numbers beginning with SG522xxxxxx and less than or equal to SG628xxxxxx. If you purchased an extended warranty, Apple should have sent you a refund by now. If you paid for a repair before this warranty program was announced, call Apple Customer Relations at 1-800-776-2333.

You can find out more about Apple repair programs—including any new ones that have been announced since this book went to press at **http://support.info.apple.com/tso/tso-macos.html#late**.

Forgetful Old Macs

Old Macs, like old PCs, sometimes get a little confused in their dotage. They're suddenly convinced it's 1904, or 1956. They get finicky about booting from the startup button on the keyboard. Sometimes they suddenly start displaying in black and white instead of color. (They *really* think it's 1956.)

It's not the logic board. (Usually.)

It's the battery. (Often.)

That's a $10–$20 repair (typically.)

Most (but not all) older Mac batteries are standard 3.6-volt lithium batteries, equivalent to Radio Shack part #23-026. Quadra/Performa 630s use Rayovac 840 4.5V alkalines.

If for some reason, you can't find the battery you need, try

Resource 800
P.O. Box 867328
Plano, TX 75086-7328
1-800-430-7030
www.iitexas.com/gpages/resource.htm

You can find out everything, and I mean *everything* you ever wanted to know about replacing Mac batteries, at **www.academ.com/info/macintosh**.

Cheapskate Software Performance Upgrades

Pretty much everyone agrees the Mac user interface is a sweet piece of work, but most realistic users acknowledge that the underlying Mac OS operating system is held together with baling wire and chewing gum. That's why Rhapsody's happening in the first place.

The Mac OS' creaky underpinnings mean you're almost certainly not getting all the hardware performance you've paid for. There are some inexpensive (and free) software upgrades that just might help.

> Sometimes you can add by subtracting. If you've been using your Mac for a while, it's time to revisit your extensions folder and see what you can live without. Removing unneeded extensions always gives you more free memory, sometimes makes your system run faster, and often improves your Mac's stability and reliability. The best way to find out what might be dispensable on your Mac is to visit the Mac Pruning Pages, *www.ambrosiasw.com/DEF/*.

Connectix RAM Doubler 2.0

In many (but not all) respects, RAM Doubler 2.0 makes your Mac behave as if it has twice—or even three times—as much memory as it actually has. That means you can load more programs.[6]

RAM Doubler does this by

▲ Intelligently reallocating memory your applications aren't using

▲ Compressing the "least recently used" information that's stored in your system memory

▲ When absolutely necessary, swapping data to disk

Unlike the "RAM doubling" products available for Windows, this actually *works*. If you're planning to keep using the Mac OS for a long time to come, it's a great investment.

> *Warning!* On the other hand, if you're planning to upgrade to Rhapsody immediately, think twice about purchasing RAM Doubler (or Speed Doubler). It almost certainly won't work with Rhapsody.

▲ ▲ ▲ ▲ ▲ ▲ ▲ ▲ ▲ ▲ ▲ ▲ ▲ ▲ ▲ ▲ ▲ ▲ ▲

6. It doesn't mean you can give an individual program access to more memory than your Mac has, though. If you try that, RAM Doubler will use disk space to supplement your RAM, slowing down your Mac—just as Apple's built-in virtual memory feature does.

Connectix Speed Doubler 2.0

Connectix employs many of the world's smartest Macintosh system programmers. A while back, those programmers identified several of the
Mac OS' most serious bottlenecks and wrote Speed Doubler (see Figure
9-11) to help clear them. When you look at Speed Doubler, you can't help
thinking that Connectix' programmers are doing the work that Apple's
programmers *should* have done but never bothered to.

Speed Doubler replaces Apple's built-in 680x0 emulator with a new
version that runs nearly twice as fast. That helps most when you're running software that wasn't written specifically for the Power Macintosh,
but it also helps with those parts of the Mac OS operating system that
haven't been rewritten for the PowerMac yet.

Normally, every time a PowerMac encounters an older 680x0 instruction, it must translate that instruction for use on the PowerPC processor.
Speed Doubler translates all the instructions once—and then keeps the
translated instructions available for immediate use.

Speed Doubler also enhances disk performance and copies files faster
than the off-the-shelf Mac OS.

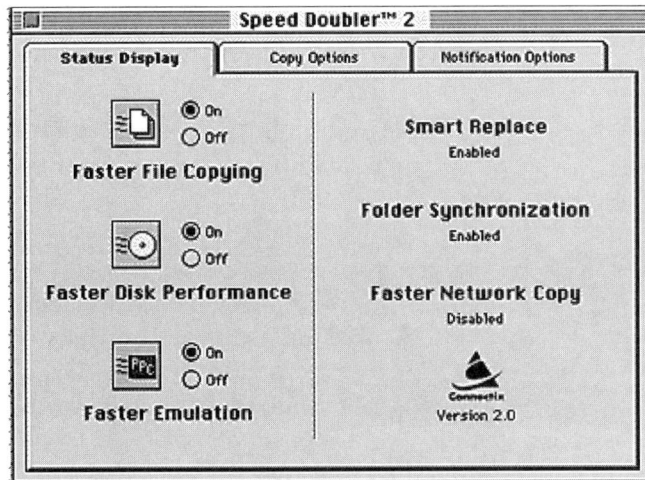

Figure 9–11   Connectix Speed Doubler 2.0.

> I've found both RAM Doubler and Speed Doubler to be quite reliable, but many professional Mac troubleshooters remove them immediately when called upon to track down hard-to-explain system crashes. If these products give you any trouble, visit Connectix' Web site at *www.connectix.com.* The company is usually quite responsive about providing fixes quickly when conflicts are discovered.

Motorola's Free Math Libraries: LIBMOTO

Depending on what applications you're running, there might or might not be a lot of math going on under the hood. For example, CAD and drawing programs tend to depend heavily on math functions; word processors don't.

If you're running a Power Macintosh, Motorola—the developers of your computer's microprocessor—has written a library of math routines that complement the ones Apple provides. Plunk them in your system and you *could* see sizable performance improvements whenever you're using those math functions. They're free. You can read more about them—and *download* them at **www.mot.com/SPS/PowerPC/library/ fact_sheet/ libmoto.html.** Give them a try.

Cheapskate Hardware Performance Upgrades

The same rule applies to Macintosh upgrades that we've used elsewhere in this book: If you can reasonably expect to get another 18–24 months of use out of your system for an upgrade that costs no more than a couple hundred dollars, you have an upgrade worth seriously considering.

A number of companies offer products for upgrading recent Power-Macs to state-of-the-art performance. These products are expensive— though less expensive than buying a new state-of-the-art Mac. They're worth considering if you're a graphics professional, or anyone else whose productivity is dramatically affected by the speed of your computer. Companies providing these top-of-the-line upgrades include

Newer Technology, Inc.
4848 Irving Street
Wichita, KS 67209
1-800-678-3726; 1-316-943-0222
www.newertech.com
Products include MAXpowr single and dual 604e PowerPC upgrade cards for PCI desktop Mac and clone computers, and NUpowr PowerPC 603e upgrade cards for PowerBook 500 and 1400.

PowerTools
P.O. Box 3000-343
Austin, TX 78764
1-800-891-4307
www.pwrtools.com
Products include PowerSource 604/150 and 604e/200 PDS Processor Cards for Power Macintosh 7500, 7600, 8500, and 9500 Power-Macs and some Power Computing, UMAX, and Radius clones.

As a Cheapskate, however, you may be more interested in companies that can help you wring some more life out of your vintage Mac. In this market, there are two leaders:

MicroMac Technology
27121 Aliso Creek Road, Suite 125
Aliso Viejo, CA 92656-3364
1-800-600-6227; 1-714-362-1000
www.micromac.com

Sonnet Technologies
18004 Sky Park Circle
Irvine, California 92614
800-786-6260
www.sonnettech.com

Tables 9-3 and 9-4 describe the products currently available from each company:

Table 9–3 Macintosh Upgrades from MicroMac Technology

System	Product	Price
Macintosh Plus, SE, and Classic	Performer accelerates to 16-MHz 68030 and can optionally add an FPU	$49 $99 w/FPU
Macintosh Plus, SE, and Classic	Performer Pro accelerates to 32-MHz 68030, adding 65K cache and (optionally) an FPU	$99 $149 w/FPU
Macintosh II, IIci, IIvx, IIvi, IIsi, IIcx, IIx, SE/30, LC III, Performa 600	DiiMO 030 accelerates to 50 MHz 68030 with 64K cache and (optionally) an FPU	$199 $249 w/FPU
Macintosh IIci, IIsi, IIcx, IIx	Carrera 040 accelerates to 33 MHz or 40-MHz 68040, with optional 128K cache card	$299 (33 MHz) $349 (40 MHz) $49 cache card
Macintosh LC, LC II, Performa 400, 405, 410, 430	Thunder Accelerator adds 32-MHz 68030 processor and 16-MHz FPU	$99
Macintosh LC, LC II, Performa 400, 405, 410, 430	ThunderCache Accelerator Adds 32-MHz 68030 processor and 32K cache, (optional) FPU	$99 $149 w/FPU
Macintosh LC, LC II, Performa 400, 405, 410, 430, Color Classic	ThunderCache Pro Accelerator adds 32-MHz or 50-MHz 68030 processor and 32K cache, (optional) FPU, and four SIMM slots to allow these computers to go beyond 10 Mb	32 MHz: $249 $299 w/FPU 50 MHz: $299 $349 w/FPU
Power Macintosh 7500, 7600, 8500 or 9500	PowerMaster adds 150-MHz 604, or either a 200- or 225-MHz 604e processor, integrated FPU, and cache	$399 150 MHz 604 $799 200 MHz 604e $999 225 MHz 604e

Table 9–4 Macintosh Upgrades from Sonnet Technologies

Systems	Product	Price
Macintosh SE	Sonnet Allegro SE accelerates to fast 68030, adds an FPU and 4 SIMM slots	$199
Macintosh II, IIx	Sonnet Allegro II accelerates to a fast 68030	$99
Allegro LC	Sonnet Allegro LC accelerates to fast 68030, adds an FPU and 16K level 2 cache	$149
Mac LC, LCII, Color Classic, IIci, IIsi, IIvx, Performa 600	Sonnet Presto LC 040 50/25 accelerates to slow 68040	$199 $249 with FPU
Mac LC, LCII, Color Classic, IIci, IIsi, IIvx, Performa 600	Sonnet Presto LC 040 80/40 accelerates to relatively fast 68040	$299 $399 with FPU and 128K level 2 cache
Quadra/Centris 650, 660AV, 700, 900	Sonnet Quad Doubler 100/50 accelerates to very fast 68040	$399
Centris 610	Sonnet Quad Doubler 80/40 accelerates to relatively fast 68040	$199 $299 with FPU
PowerMac 7500	150-MHz PowerPC 604 for 7500 accelerates to fast 604	$399 with trade-in of existing 601 card

There *are* some limitations on these upgrade products; for example, the Mac IIsi requires an extra-cost adapter to use Sonnet's Presto LC, and some configurations won't run with the popular RAM Doubler utility.

When you consider an upgrade, always compare it against the cost of a (somewhat) newer Mac. For example, if a $350 upgrade will make your Mac IIci as fast as a quick Quadra, but won't do anything about its other limitations, you might be better served by purchasing a used Power Macintosh 6100/600 for $500–$550 and selling the IIci for $200.

Like Cache in the Bank

If you happen to have a Mac IIci without a cache card, you can significantly improve its performance by adding one. They're dirt cheap, if you can find them. Recently, at the **www.onsale.com** on-line auction, $10 was enough to win one of these cards.

If you have a first- or second-generation Power Macintosh, you can substantially improve *its* performance by adding a cache card, too. These aren't *quite* as inexpensive: 256K cache cards are typically around $49; 512K cards $99–$119 depending on your specific model. Sources include

Components Direct
Newport Beach, CA 92660
1-888-4-COMPONENTS
www.componentsdirect.com

Warning! **Cache is a wonderful thing: It makes virtually every Mac go faster. But there's an apparent problem with cache in *some* Power Macintosh 7500s—a problem Apple hasn't officially acknowledged. The issue is too subtle and confusing to cover here, but you can get the details** *at www.cs. miami.edu/~stevent/macresource/exclusives/l2cache.html.*

Clock Chipping

One way to squeeze more performance out of your Mac is to cheat a little.

In Chapter 5, you read about overclocking: running your processor faster than it was intended. On the Mac side, this is called *clock chipping*, because it often involves replacing the crystal "clock chip" that controls a Mac's timing. You can sometimes squeeze 20 percent or more speed from your Mac this way.

Before we go any further: Clock-chipping adds heat and stress to your processor.[7] It's not risk free. And it will void your Apple warranty—if your Mac is still under warranty, that is.

Some Macs are notoriously amenable to clock chipping. It's been widely rumored that Apple's marketing team told the engineers to throttle down the Mac IIsi to avoid cannibalizing sales of the pricier Mac IIci—

▲ ▲ ▲ ▲ ▲ ▲ ▲ ▲ ▲ ▲ ▲ ▲ ▲ ▲ ▲ ▲ ▲ ▲ ▲ ▲

7.   That's why virtually all clock-chipping kits come with a fan to help cool your processor.

so the IIsi is relatively easy to speed up. Many people have also had good luck goosing Power Macintosh 6100/60s to 80 MHz.

On the other hand, many Macs can't be clock chipped at all—and those include models as diverse as the Macintosh SE and the Performa 6200/75.

To share the collective wisdom of the Mac clock-chipping community about your Mac, visit the Clock Chipping Home Page, **http://violet.berkeley.edu/~schrier/mhz.html**. You'll also find the detailed technical information you need to do your own clock chipping: what wires to cut, what to solder—that sort of stuff.

If you're not up for that, you might be more interested in a kit that can simply be clipped onto your processor. You want a "variable-speed" kit that lets you adjust how quickly you're running in the event that your system crashes or overheats at top speed. They're relatively inexpensive and lots of people swear by them. Sources for these products include

PowerLogix
8760A Research Blvd. #240
Austin, TX 78758
1-888-769-9020
www.powerlogix.com
PowerBoost Mach Series of CPU Accelerators for most Macs since the Quadra, excluding Quadra 630, and 5200/6200 series Power-Macs and Performas.

Griffin Technologies
820 Fesslers Pkwy., Suite 315
Nashville, TN 37210
1-615-255-0990
www.nashville.net/~griffin
Mac-celerator line of variable-speed accelerators for many Centris and Quadra computers, for $55.00 plus shipping.

Free Macintosh Technical Support

Believe it or not, you can get *free* answers to your personal Mac technical problem. Unheard of!

Visit the MacAssist Web site (see Figure 9-12): **www.mac4hire.com/ biz/macassist/**. Fill out their on-line form, and within 24-48 hours you should have an answer from MacAssist's volunteer team of Mac experts.

To be fair to these noble folks, *please* check the voluminous Mac troubleshooting resources they've compiled and linked to before you ask them a personal question!

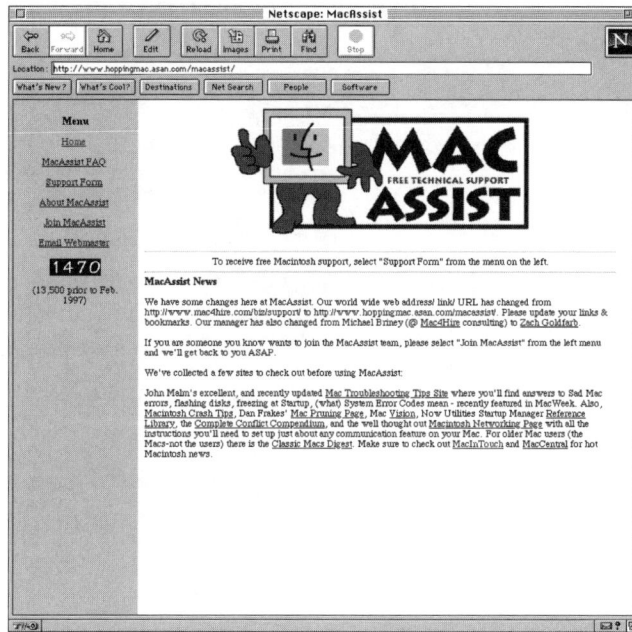

Figure 9–12   The MacAssist site for free Macintosh technical support. (Don't abuse it!)

Get Your Old Monitor to Work With Your New Mac (or Vice Versa)

Mac monitors tend to cost a few dollars more—and there aren't as many of them lying around waiting for you to pick up cheap. What's more, even older Mac monitors won't work with newer Macs. What you need is a video adapter from Griffin Technologies. These folks know everything there is to know about monitor specifications and whether (or how) to make specific monitors work with specific Macintoshes. Their adapters cost between $20 and $50 depending on your Mac and monitor.

Visit Griffin's Web site (see Figure 9-13) to see which adapter your monitor needs. It's a whole lot cheaper than buying a new monitor!

Griffin Technologies
820 Fesslers Pkwy., Suite 315
Nashville, TN 37210
1-615-255-0990
http://www.nashville.net/ ~griffin

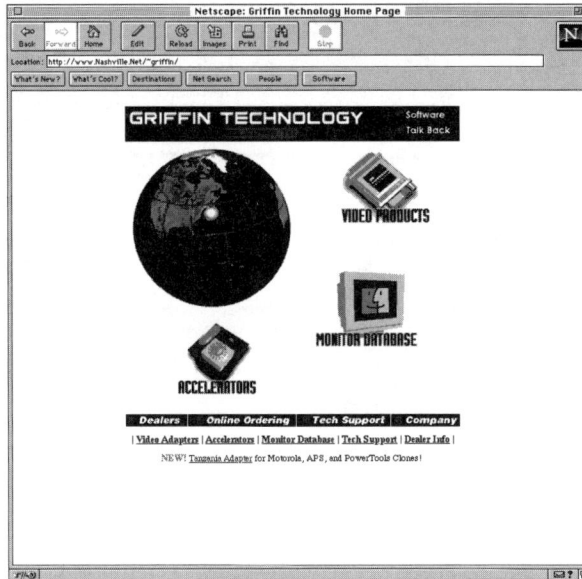

Figure 9–13   Griffin Technologies' monitor database: The world's #1 source for Macintosh monitor compatibility information.

Cheapskate Mac Software Sources

With the exception of Performas, you're pretty much on your own when it comes to getting application software. Apple has chosen not to provide applets comparable to the ones Microsoft delivers with Windows 95. We do have a few Cheapskate suggestions though.

> **tip**
>
> **Speaking of old monitors, here are two great sources for old Mac monitors:**
>
> **Power On Computer Services**
> **4323 Anthony Ct., Unit #1**
> **Rocklin, CA 95677**
> **1-800-673-6227; 1-916-652-1880**
> *www.poweron-line.com*
> *Used Apple, Sony and Hewlett-Packard monitors, even old 21" monochrome monitors for $149.*
>
> **Silver Reef**
> **1-714-366-6864**
> *www.billboards.com/sreef1.html*
> *Specializes in Sony monitors for Macintosh.*

1. See Chapter 4 to see if you or anyone in your family qualifies for academic software. You could save 50–70 percent on the most expensive business and graphics packages you may need!

2. Before investing in Microsoft Office, see if ClarisWorks will do the job. The software will cost you much less. So will the hardware you need to run it!

3. If you need high-end graphics software (e.g., Photoshop), try to buy privately from someone who received a software package they didn't need when they purchased a scanner. Sources for these packages include classified advertisements on America Online and CompuServe, and the newsgroup **misc.for-sale.computers.mac-specific.software** .

4. For home, edutainment, and low-end business software, try Software Clearance Outlet (1-800-230-SOFT, **www.software-outlet.com**).

5. Also try UsoX (**www.midwinter.com/usox/**), the Internet used software exchange discussed at length in Chapter 4.

Cheapskate Mac Buying Tips That Didn't Fit Anywhere Else

Tip 1: If you're lucky enough to have more than one Mac, why not network them? System 7.x has built-in networking software. All you need is standard phone wire—and PhoneNet (or compatible) devices that connect your phone wire to your Macs. Professional Mac users have long since moved on to faster Ethernet networking—which means there are tons of PhoneNet connector devices hanging around going unused. Ask at any office or university that uses Macs. You may be able to get a few of these at no cost.

Tip 2: Mac keyboards are notoriously expensive. Buy your next Mac keyboard from someone other than Apple. At Mac Warehouse (1-800-255-6227), the basic Apple Design keyboard costs $89.95. The PowerUser 105 keyboard costs $49.95. Depending on your tastes in keyboards, you might well like the cheaper one better.

Tip 3: If you're interested in fooling around with UNIX on your Mac, you don't have to pay several hundred dollars for the software. There's now a version of Linux for Power Macintosh (starting with systems based on the PowerPC 601 chip, with others to follow). You can download it, but it's huge. Probably you're better off investing $20 in a CD-ROM, or $50 for the CD-ROM plus a detailed manual.

Tip 4: Until recently, most Macs had woefully small hard drives. And you pay a lot more per megabyte to add a new drive than PC users do, because nearly all Macs use SCSI drives instead of cheaper IDE drives.[8] From a performance standpoint, SCSI is clearly superior. From a Cheapskate standpoint, it's another reason you need to find the best hard drive deals you can. Start your search with

Mac Warehouse
1-800-397-8508
(Power User drives)
www.warehouse.com

APS Technologies
1-800-235-8935
www.apstech.com

▲ ▲ ▲ ▲ ▲ ▲ ▲ ▲ ▲ ▲ ▲ ▲ ▲ ▲ ▲ ▲ ▲ ▲ ▲ ▲

8.   Except for Quadra/Performa 630s, 640s, 6200s and 6300s.

398

While I personally vote for new hard drives only, you might be interested to know that APS also offers "factory recertified" drives for even lower prices at **www.apstech.com/aps-co_products.html**.

Summary

You *can* be a Cheapskate and a Mac owner—and in this chapter, I've shown you how. You've learned about inexpensive sources for new Macs, Mac clones, and used Macs; discovered opportunities for free repairs and free technical support, and more. Now, go forth into a Cheapskate Mac future that's bright—if not positively *rhapsodic.*

Networking

10

- Printer Sharing
- Low-End Data Sharing
- Your Own Private Ethernet Network
- Making Your Network Work
- Summary

No computer is an island—especially if you happen to own more than one. They seem to have a natural urge to mate. So, do you need a network?

If you very rarely share printers or information between computers, or if your computers are separated by several rooms or floors and you don't want to run cable between them, then your best Cheapskate bet may be to keep using "SneakerNet."

If you do need to physically connect your computers, you'll usually get the best price/performance by simply biting the bullet and building yourself a mini Local Area Network. You'll be surprised how little it can cost, often, well under $100 for the whole shebang.

However, if you have reservations about networking, I'll also show you some even less expensive alternatives that *might* be enough to do the job.

Printer Sharing

If you only share printers, then you *may* be able to get away with a simple printer sharing device, sometimes called an A/B switch. You simply run parallel cables to the printer sharing device, and it manages the connections for you.

Unless you're using very old printers, stay away from the mechanical A/B switches, even though they're less than $10. The problem: When you twist the manual switch, it's all too easy to cause voltage and current disturbances that could damage your printer's interface.

Newer, electronic printer sharing switches manage the switching for you automatically, reducing the risk. A basic electronic printer sharing device, such as the ASP Intelligent Autoswitch, can cost less than $25, plus cables.

There are a few things to know, however, that could drive your costs up. Many newer printers use bidirectional communication (i.e., they not only listen, but also *talk back* to your computer). Some use newer IEEE 1284 or ECP parallel ports. If your printer has these requirements, you'll need a printer switch that supports them—and now you're talking $60–$80. Worse, you now need *three* expensive IEEE 1284 cables instead of one: You need one cable from each computer, plus one from the switch box to the printer.

At that point, you should seriously consider a network.

When does a printer switch make sense?

▲ When you can't face the thought of opening your computers and inserting network cards.

▲ When you don't have an operating system that provides built-in networking support, for example, if you're running Windows 3.1 rather than Windows for Workgroups.

▲ When your printers don't require IEEE 1284 parallel ports.

▲ When you don't expect to share anything except a printer.

When *doesn't* a printer switch make sense?

▲ When your computers and printers are too far apart to be connected by parallel cables.

▲ When your printers utilize IEEE 1284 parallel ports and cables.

▲ When you need to share other resources and information, not just printers.

▲ When you already have networking software, such as Windows 95 or Windows for Workgroups, and all you need to add are inexpensive network cards and cables.

Before you buy a switch box, double-check the back of your printer. Some printers, like the HP LaserJet 4 family, may have two parallel ports built in—eliminating the need for printer sharing.

Low-End Data Sharing

It's not well known, but if you only *occasionally* need to move information between computers, Windows 95 and MS-DOS 6.x both come with software to do the job. These are the old-fashioned tramp freighters of networking: the world's cheapest way to move your data cargo, if you're in no hurry and you don't care about amenities.[1]

To use either program, all you need to buy is a $10–$15 "Laplink™"-style cable[2] to connect both PCs' parallel ports, *or* their serial ports.[3] The parallel version is faster (or more accurately, it's less painfully slow). On the other hand, it may require you to disconnect your printer. The serial version is much slower, but you're more likely to have free serial ports on both computers.

MS-DOS 6.x Interlnk

MS-DOS' Interlnk is the program to use if you're running DOS 6.x, whether or not you also have Windows 3.x. It works as follows. You set up one computer up as a "client," which controls the interaction between both computers. The other computer is called the "server," because it serves the information to the client.

The Interlnk *client* program must be run when your computer starts, so you have to include a line such as the following in your CONFIG.SYS file:[4]

```
DEVICE = C:\DOS\INTERLNK.EXE
```

▲ ▲

1. How slow? Well, standard Ethernet theoretically connects at 10 megabits (the reality is somewhat lower); serial cable connections max out at around 1/10 of a megabit, parallel connections just a few times faster.

2. Laplink is a trademark of Traveling Software for software designed to connect and transfer files between two PCs. Since then, other companies (including Microsoft) have adopted compatible cables for the same purpose.

3. Since you're connecting the computers with a parallel or serial cable, they'll need to be relatively near each other.

4. If you only plan to use Interlnk occasionally, and you don't want it taking up a valuable 8–9K of your valuable 640K base memory when you aren't using it, use the command

   DEVICE = C:\DOS\INTERLNK.EXE /AUTO

   With this command, when DOS starts up, it looks for a connected computer running the Interlnk server program. If it doesn't find one, it won't load the client program. (For this to work, you have to run INTERSVR on the server computer before you turn your client computer on.)

Once it's running, you enter the DOS command

```
INTERSVR
```

on the server machine. The two computers look for each other, embrace (well, actually *handshake*—these aren't Macintoshes we're talking about), and establish a connection. Interlnk then "maps" the drive names on the server computer so they appear as extra drives on the client computer. Interlnk can also map parallel ports, giving you remote access to printers from DOS. You'll see this mapping on the server computer.

While the two computers are connected, you can't use the server computer for anything else. You can, however, run most DOS commands (e.g., COPY, XCOPY, etc.) from your client computer.

What if your server computer is running an older version of DOS that doesn't come with Interlnk? You can clone a copy from the client to the server and then run the software on both machines. The commands are a little arcane; type HELP INTERLNK at a DOS prompt to learn more.

All this sounds like a royal pain. When does it really make sense to use Interlnk?

- ▲ When you only need to connect two computers occasionally.
- ▲ When one of your computers is a laptop or notebook PC that doesn't contain a network card.
- ▲ In emergencies, such as when one of your computer's floppy drives isn't working.
- ▲ To install software that comes on CD-ROM on a computer that doesn't have a CD-ROM drive. (You can copy the installation files to the client, and then install from the client's hard drive.)
- ▲ As a slow but workable solution for backing up files when you don't have a tape drive. (You can run an XCOPY command and walk away, rather than sticking around to swap floppies all day.)
- ▲ To print from DOS on a printer that's connected to a different computer.

Windows 95 Direct Cable Connection

As you might expect, Windows 95's Direct Cable Connection is still slow, but it looks a lot better. Unlike Interlnk, it actually emulates a network, so it's easy to access files, printers, and other shared resources across computers. And unlike Interlnk, both computers are available to do other things while Direct Cable Connection is running.

If you've installed Direct Cable Connection, you can run it by clicking Start, Programs, Accessories, Direct Cable Connection. (If it doesn't appear in the list, chances are you haven't installed it. Direct Cable Connection isn't part of the Windows 95 default installation. You can add it through Windows setup: click Settings, Control Panel, Add/Remove Programs, Windows Setup to get there.)[5]

Connect the two computers via a Laplink-type cable. Next, run Direct Cable Connection on both computers; then tell the software which computer will be "Host" and which will be "Guest," as shown in Figure 10-1.

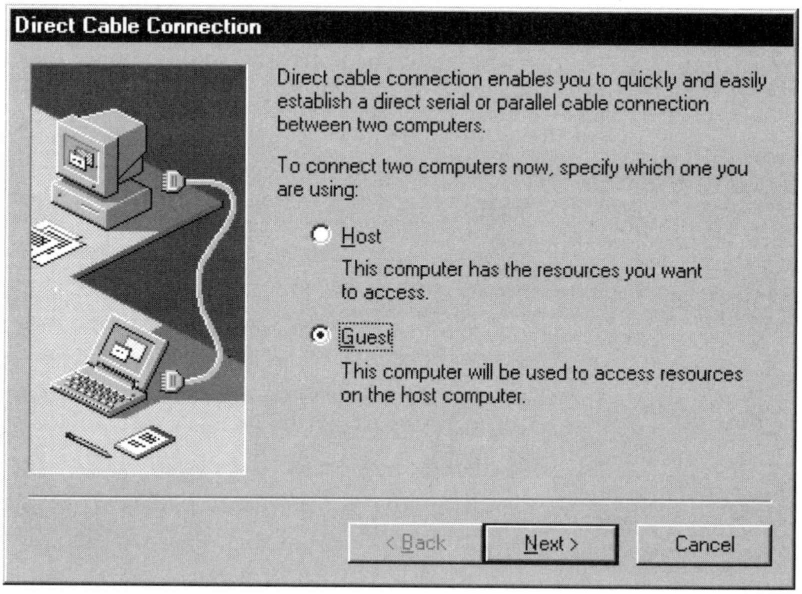

Figure 10-1   Running Windows 95's Direct Cable Connection.

5.   You also need to make sure that file and print sharing is turned on for the drives you want to share.

Host is equivalent to Interlnk's "server," while Guest is equivalent to "client." Then, choose the port you want to use to connect with; you must use the same type of port on both computers. Click Finish. The software will attempt to establish a connection; if it does, you'll be told.

Like Interlnk, Direct Cable Connection is a solution for occasional file backups between computers (unlike Interlnk, it supports long file names). You can use it to install CD-ROM-based software on a computer without a CD-ROM (and unlike Interlnk, you don't have to copy all the files onto the Guest computer first—you can install directly from the Host.)

The disadvantage: It runs like molasses.

Your Own Private Ethernet Network

Now that you've heard the alternatives, here's the Big Kahuna: Build your own Ethernet network.

If you have Windows 3.1x for Workgroups or Windows 95,[6] you already have all the software you need. If you have standard Windows 3.x, you'll need to upgrade to Windows for Workgroups, which costs $49 per machine. If you're in this position, you'll find it tempting to upgrade all the way to Windows 95 for only about another $30. See page 15 for a discussion of the pros, cons, and hidden costs.

If you're running one DOS machine and one Windows for Workgroups or Windows 95 machine, consider downloading Microsoft Network Client v.3.0 for MS-DOS from Microsoft's Web site. It's free, and it adds some (but not all) network capabilities to your DOS system. If you're running two DOS-only machines, you might consider upgrading to Caldera's OpenDOS (see page 136), which has Novell's Personal NetWare networking built in and is absolutely free.

That takes care of software. What about hardware?

Let's dispose of the easy stuff. For 99 percent of all homes and home offices, there's only one kind of network to consider: plain vanilla Ethernet. Not Arcnet, not token-ring, not Moses-Net, or anything else. Ethernet's been around for 15 years, it works, and it's dirt cheap.

▲ ▲ ▲ ▲ ▲ ▲ ▲ ▲ ▲ ▲ ▲ ▲ ▲ ▲ ▲ ▲ ▲ ▲ ▲

6.   Or a Macintosh. See Chapter 9 for the details.

There are newer, faster networking schemes than Ethernet. The most popular is called Fast Ethernet; theoretically it runs ten times as fast as Ethernet, though reality never quite matches theory in networking. Right now it's more than three times expensive as Ethernet, though it's getting cheaper fast. (Right behind it, there's Gigabit Ethernet, allegedly ten times faster still.) There are also pricey, top-of-the-line schemes like FDDI and ATM. If you and your spouse are engineering the next-generation Boeing airliner in your home office, you need one of these. Otherwise, forget it.[7]

There are two ways to build a two-computer Ethernet network. You can purchase an Ethernet hub and two Ethernet cards, and then connect them with 10-BaseT "twisted pair" cable—basically, telephone wire. That's the way most business LANs are built; it's easier to run 10-BaseT cable than coax, and the hub architecture makes network problems easier to troubleshoot. What's more, small hubs have gotten significantly cheaper: you can now get a four-port or five-port hub for $50–$75.

On the other hand, you can skip the hub completely and simply connect your computers using "thin coaxial" cable, which is comparable to what you use to get cable TV. That's what I've always done in my home office. At times I've had as many as four computers hooked up via coax, without a hint of trouble. (The extra "T-connectors" and terminators that coax cables need still cost much less than even the cheapest hub.)

So the choice is yours.

> **tip** If you think you might want to move from coax to 10-BaseT later (let's say you're starting a business that you expect to grow quickly), you can buy cards with both coax and 10-BaseT connectors. These are sometimes called *combo* cards and only cost a few dollars more.

▲ ▲ ▲ ▲ ▲ ▲ ▲ ▲ ▲ ▲ ▲ ▲ ▲ ▲ ▲ ▲ ▲ ▲ ▲

7.   Not satisfied with such a breezy answer? Oh, all right. Let's get slightly more systematic about it. If you are sharing moderately sized data files and programs and e-mail on a small-business network, Ethernet is plenty. If everyone will be accessing the network constantly, an Ethernet network may begin to slow down, though there are a variety of fixes for this, not all of which involve upgrading to Fast Ethernet. If you are planning to share multimedia applications extensively—say, you're planning for desktop videoconferencing—then Fast Ethernet or maybe even something more expensive may make sense. If you're a graphics designer sharing large image files, or an engineer sharing sophisticated design drawings, you probably also want something faster than Ethernet. But if you're one of those folks, you probably already knew that.

Now let's go buy some hardware. Time was when Ethernet cards cost well over $100 apiece. Now, you can purchase a standard ISA Ethernet card made in an ISO 9000 quality-certified factory for under $30. Even if you want a PCI card that will use "Plug and Play" to configure itself, you're still under $50.

Why so cheap? Because the guts of an Ethernet card are found in chipsets that are now manufactured in the millions by chip manufacturers like Lucent Technologies and AMD. Those chip sets are mature technology that can be manufactured for very little cost. And the engineering involved in building a card based on those chips has become so easy that dozens of companies can sell commodity Ethernet cards with little or no R&D cost of their own.

This is why Ethernet usually makes more sense than printer sharing and other solutions.

Look for a card that contains both 10-BaseT and coax connectors, so you can move from coax to twisted-pair later if you want. If you're buying more than one card, buy them both from the same manufacturer. That way, if you've successfully configured one card, you'll know most of what you need to configure the rest. Also look for a card that's "NE2000 compatible." Windows 95 and Windows for Workgroups have built-in, reliable NE2000 drivers. It's just one less thing to worry about.[8]

Who manufactures reliable, cheap Ethernet cards? Here are a few companies to look for:

Allied Telesyn International
950 Kifer Road
Sunnyvale, CA 94086
1-408-730-0950
www.alliedtelesyn.com
ISO 9000 certified.

Linksys
714-261-1288
www.linksys.com
Also offers "Network in a Box"—two Plug and Play cards, a coax

▲ ▲ ▲ ▲ ▲ ▲ ▲ ▲ ▲ ▲ ▲ ▲ ▲ ▲ ▲ ▲ ▲ ▲ ▲ ▲

8.   Unless you're running Linux: in that case, see **www.wp.cc.nc.us/cdrom/bible-src/HOWTO-src/ETHERNET-HOWTO-1.html** for some technical issues concerning NE2000 clone cards before you choose an Ethernet card.

cable, a networked game, and free technical support. A variant, "Network Starter Kit," adds 10-BaseT cabling and a hub.

Netgear
www.netgear.com
Now a division of the high-end networking company Bay Networks.

Addtron
4425 Cushing Parkway
Fremont, CA 94538
1-800-998-4638; 1-510-668-5186
www.addtron.com

And who *sells* them? *Not* some of the mail-order houses you might expect, like CDW, that focus on high-end brands like Intel and 3Com.[9] Try:

PC Connection
1-800-800-5555
Addtron, Boca Research, and MDS House Brand. Recent pricing, Addtron 10-BaseT only ISA card, $21.95; 10-BaseT/coax Plug and Play, $28.95, and up.

Surplus Direct
1-800-753-7877
www.surplusdirect.com
Currently sells Relia brands. Recent pricing: $24.99 ISA Plug and Play; $34.99 PCI Plug and Play, and up.

MEI/Micro Center
1-800-634-3478
Currently sells Addtron and Linksys brands. Recent pricing: $24.97 ISA, $35.97, PCI, and up.

PC Mall
1-800-555-6255
Currently sells Axel brand. Recent pricing: ISA 10-BaseT/coax card, $19.99.

▲ ▲ ▲ ▲ ▲ ▲ ▲ ▲ ▲ ▲ ▲ ▲ ▲ ▲ ▲ ▲ ▲ ▲ ▲

9. If you want the well-known name, you can buy used cards removed from computers owned by large corporations when they upgraded to Fast Ethernet. Sources include GE Capital Information Technology Solutions, 1-800-555-8393, and Federal Computer Exchange, 201-612-0800.

Making Your Network Work

If you're having trouble hooking up two Windows 95 computers, one good source of information is free: Microsoft's Windows 95 Support Assistant includes a troubleshooting "wizard" to help solve networking problems. Windows 95 Support Assistant is free on Microsoft's web site.

In the meantime, here are a few tips.

Make sure the network cards in your computers have no conflicts with other devices in your system, and that they are working properly (check Start, Settings, System, Device Manager).

Make sure the cables are plugged in properly, and terminators are used at both ends of the network.

If you are using Windows' built-in networking, make sure you have installed Client for Microsoft Networks on both computers, and made Client for Microsoft Networks your primary network logon. (check Start, Settings, Network, Configuration).

Next, make sure you've turned on file sharing for your computer. Choose Start, Control Panel, Network, and click the File and Print Sharing button on the Configuration tab; then check the box that says *I want to be able to give others access to my files.*

Then, make sure you've turned on file sharing for the drives you want to share [right-click on a drive in My Computer, and choose Sharing; make sure to provide Full Access to your hard drives (assuming that's what you want to do)].

Make sure you've added both computers to the same workgroup (the default is WORKGROUP, quite reasonably).

Make sure you don't include extra spaces in the names you give your computers.

If you're still stuck, and you think you may have a hardware problem, you might try the Ethernet LAN FAQ (**comp.dcom.lans.ethernet newsgroup FAQ**), available from several locations on the Web, including **www.cis.ohio-state.edu/hypertext/faq/usenet/LANs/ethernet-faq/faq. html**. Another excellent source is Prentice Hall PTR's *Ethernet Tips and Techniques*, by Byron Spinney.[10]

▲ ▲ ▲ ▲ ▲ ▲ ▲ ▲ ▲ ▲ ▲ ▲ ▲ ▲ ▲ ▲ ▲ ▲ ▲ ▲

10.   *Ethernet Tips and Techniques,* Byron Spinney, Prentice Hall, PTR, September 1997, ISBN: 0-13-755950-X, $32.00

Summary

So there you have it. To connect two computers via

▲ Printer sharing will cost $40 to $100 with cables.
▲ Direct cable connections will cost $10 but it's deadly slow.
▲ Ethernet network can cost as little as $60, if you're running a networkable operating system and you skip the hub.

Well, you have to admit that qualifies as *reasonably* cheap.

With that, we've completed our Cheapskate's computer buying tour. In the next chapter, I'll pull together the best print and on-line resources for computing Cheapskates, including our exclusive Top 50 Cheapskates' Web sites. And then, it will be on to the Cheapskates' Software Library: dozens of the best shareware and freeware software resources for Windows, DOS, and Macintosh.

11

Where to Find Out More

- Print and CD-ROM
- The Cheapskate's Top 50+ Web Site List
- Books
- Summary

413

There are a few indispensable print sources for computing Cheapskates—and hundreds of indispensable Web sites. We're living in a golden age of free and cheap stuff. It's hard to imagine that all the folks who are delivering low-cost and free information and software to us on the Internet aren't going to one day wake up and start asking for money. But while it's here, we'll help you take advantage of it. In this chapter, you'll find a list of the best Web sites for computing Cheapskates.

Print and CD-ROM

Two magazines are essential reading for dyed-in-the-wool computing Cheapskates: *Computer Shopper* and *The Processor*. A third, *PC World*, is almost as essential—and if you're going to be making significant purchases, the *PC Magazine* CD-ROM may save you a lot more money than it costs. Here's a brief discussion of each.

Computer Shopper

Certainly one of the *heaviest* magazines in America, *Computer Shopper* is the recognized source for discount computer advertising and information. Typically 750–950 tabloid-sized pages every month, *Computer Shop-per* includes ads from virtually every major direct computer vendor; manufacturers' outlets such as Compaq, Dell, and NEC; dozens of smaller manufacturers of both systems and barebones; and sources for every type of peripheral and accessory. You'll also find indexes listing sources for every category and product—and a source directory containing essential information about vendors' shipping, warranty policies, and technical support.

A "Trends & Technology" section previews what's around the corner, so you can decide whether it makes sense to postpone your purchase another few months. It includes columns by luminaries such as Michael Slater, the industry's most prominent microprocessor analyst.

Better yet, *Computer Shopper* has recently significantly improved its coverage of consumer issues. The new "Smart Shopper" section includes buying tips, current rebates, and a "Shopper's One-Stop Solver" section that puts Computer Shopper's "weight" behind solving the direct-channel problems of individual customers.

If you have the sheer physical stamina, you can pick up *Computer Shopper* at most newsstands for $4.99. Or you can have your mailperson deliver it for a year, for $39.50.

> *Computer Shopper*
> Ziff-Davis Publishing Company
> One Park Avenue
> New York, NY 10016
> **www.cshopper.com**

Processor

Processor is the advertising home for all those small new and used hardware resellers, liquidators, and parts companies that can't afford to advertise in *Computer Shopper*. It's where you'll find the latest offerings from many of the companies listed in this book, including Image Microsystems, Krex Computers, Delaware Computer Center, Electrified Discounters and several others.

Nothing but ads, *Processor* appears weekly, but free subscribers can choose to receive it as often as they wish: weekly, biweekly, monthly, quarterly, semiannually, or annually. Since it appears weekly with an advertising closing date just eight days before the issue date, it contains pricing that's more up-to-date than monthly publications can include.

To fill out a form that may qualify you for a free subscription, visit **www.processor.com/profree1.htm**, or call 1-800-334-7443. While you're on the Processor Web site, check out the Processor Product Exchange at **www.processor.com/prolist/prodex.shtml.** This is a classified ad section that supplements the newspaper.

The Processor
Sandhills Publishing
P.O. Box 82545
Lincoln, NE 68501-2545
1-800-334-7443; 1-402-479-2115
www.processor.com

PC World

PC Magazine "takes the cake" for the most detailed reviews and buying information available. *Computer Shopper* "takes the cake" for most ads— a veritable heaven for comparison shoppers. *But no computer magazine comes close to* PC World *when it comes to watching out for you and your money.* Think of *PC World* as what *Consumer Reports* would be if they really knew computers.

PC World is where you'll find coverage of on-line scams, emerging service problems. It's where you'll find information on companies that have just folded—so you can avoid their merchandise when you see it on the shelves at your local superstore. And it's one of the few commercial magazines that actually publishes articles on inexpensive sources for computer equipment.

They'll welcome your subscription, of course—but at the moment, just about everything in *PC World* is posted free on their Web site, **www.pcworld.com**. The Web site even has some bonuses you won't find in the magazine, including:

▲ PC World Direct Desktop Delivery: Regular E-mailings containing tips and news
▲ Dummies Daily, a free daily computer tip on the topic of your choice, E-mailed from the people who sell the Dummies books
▲ PC World Daily Newsradio: daily broadcasts, and more

PC Magazine CD

Finally, there's *PC Magazine*'s quarterly CD-ROM (see Figure 11-1). The best thing about this CD-ROM isn't the video clips of nerdy looking editors talking up the latest technology, or even the demos of expensive new software packages. It's the 12-month, fully searchable database of excellent *PC Magazine* articles. To save money, I buy the CD-ROM just once a year. That way, I keep a complete collection of *PC Magazine* without overlaps. Off the Web, it's the easiest, cheapest off-line way I know to get the buying information you need.

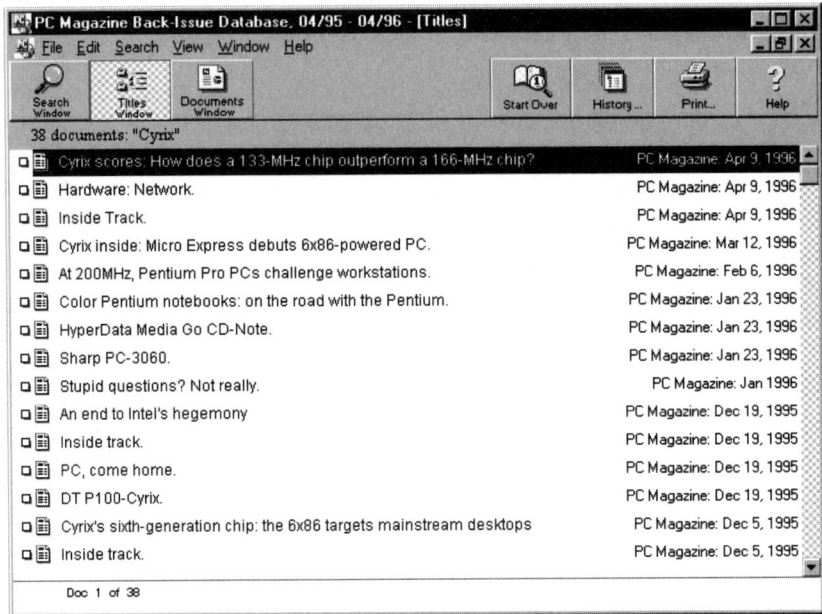

Figure 11–1   Searching the *PC Magazine* CD-ROM.

The Cheapskate's Top 50+ Web Site List

The Net is an extraordinary source of free reviews, free background information, free cantankerous opinions of various quality, free manufacturers quotes, free and discount software, low-cost hardware, peripherals and accessories—you name it. With that, here's our Cheapskate's List of Web sites. (It was going to be a top 50 list, but it "just growed.")

If you want to surf these sites more systematically, the Cheapskate's CD-ROM contains a page that includes all these links. Just click to visit the site you want.

Information

www.pcworld.com
PC World Online: Buying tips for Cheapskates and everyone else.

www.netbuyer.com
Easy comparsion shopping for everything from PCs to toner cartridges.

www.cnet.com
On-line computing and Internet news—and regular buying guides. A recent example: a Cheapskate's guide to building a world-class Web site for under $500.

www.zdnet.com
The central source for searching every Ziff-Davis computing publication for PCs and Macs—along with one of the world's most extensive shareware libraries.

www.techweb.com
The central source for searching every CMP publication, including many of the world's leading computing and networking trade magazines, plus *Windows* magazine.

www.iworld.com
The central source for searching all of Mecklermedia's publications, including *Internet World* and *WebWeek*. A bit disorganized, but still the best free, up-to-date source for news about the Web.

www.crn.com
Computer Retail News: Where to find out what the people who sell you computers are thinking—and doing.

www.cis.ohio-state.edu/hypertext/faq/usenet/FAQ-List.html#P
One of several comprehensive sources for Usenet FAQs about many computer (and noncomputer) related topics.

www.ct.net/~zoo/zoo/
An informal but very telling customer satisfaction poll covering those companies that fly under the big media's radar.

www.altavista.com
Still the most complete and useful search engine on the Web.

www.ionet.net/~rbdavis/
A little on the technical side, but everything you want to know about Cyrix' low-cost alternatives to Intel.

Computers

www.uce.com
United Computer Exchange: The world-renowned clearinghouse and market maker for used Macs.

http://mer.shop.ibm.com/shopping/ibmcredit
Where to get discount IBM PCs off-lease.

www.dell.com/store/index.htm
Dell's price configurator: One of the best ways to buy a computer on the Web.

www.usaweb.com/auction.html
Up-to-date information on live computer auctions.

http://www.drms.dla.mil
Where to find your local military surplus computer store.

www.ustreas.gov/treasury/bureaus/customs/
Information on U.S. Customs computer auctions.

www.onsale.com
ONSALE, the leading Internet on-line auction.

www.usedcomputer.com
Clearinghouse of used computer dealers nationwide, organized by brand name.

www.internetclearinghouse.com
Bonded computer broker that improves the security of transactions between private sellers on the Internet.

www.yahoo.com
Free, nationwide computer classified listings.

www.microweb.com/pepsite/Recycle/ recycle_index.html
National directory of nonprofit computer recycling programs.

Software

www.zdnet.com
One of the Web's leading compilations of shareware and freeware.

www.shareware.com
Another of the Web's leading compilations of shareware and freeware.

www.hyperion/com/usox/
The Web's number 1 clearinghouse for private buyers and sellers of used and older-version software.

www.softwareoutlet.com
Software Clearance Outlet, now the Web's number 1 source of older-version software at discount prices.

www.linux.org
The central Web location for information on Linux, the world's number 1 free operating system.

www.caldera.com
Caldera Corporation, home of OpenDOS, the free DOS-compatible operating system.

www.microsoft.com/msdownload/
Where Microsoft lists all the software it's currently making available for free download.

www.caboodles.com/clipart/
Caboodles of clip art, one of the world's best sources for free and shareware clip art.

www.iaswww.com/source.html
The Software Source, one of the leading suppliers of academic software at discounts from 50–75 percent.

www.syllabus.com/ed.discount.html
Syllabus Magazine's guide to academic discount educational software

www.simtel.net/simtel.net/
Simtel Collection: The world's best source of DOS shareware and
freeware.

www.gamesdomain.com/tigger/sw-kids.html
One of the best sources of children's educational shareware and
games.

Peripherals

www.surplusdirect.com
Surplus Direct specializes in closeout and overstock hardware—
and occasionally even gives some away free.

http://users.aimnet.com/~jnavas/modem/faq.html
In-depth info from one of the world's leading modem authorities.

Accessories and Consumables

www.ece.curtin.edu.au/~saoundb/cgi/nph-bargainbot
The Bargainbot automatically compares computer (and other)
book prices at several top Web bookstores.

www.icanet.net/arctoner
One of the leading Web sources of discount toner cartridges.

Internet Resources

www.ofcn.org
Information about freenet community computer networks
nationwide.

www.thelist.com
The most complete list of Internet service providers anywhere.

www.cnet.com/content/reviews/compare/isp/
Up-to-the-minute customer satisfaction poll results on Internet
service providers nationwide.

www.peak-media.com
Download a free trial version of Peak.Net.Jet, software that
makes the Web seem a whole lot faster.

www.netscape.com
Where you can download the latest Netscape Navigator/Communicator for evaluation (or for *keeps*, if you qualify.)

www.inc.com/createsite/
Your small business can get a free mini-Web site: Just fill out the form here.

www.apache.org
Download the world's number 1 free Web server—for UNIX, Linux, and similar environments.

www.four11.com
Find anyone's e-mail address, free.

www.hotmail.com
Get Web-based e-mail, free.

www.pulver.com
Get the latest scoop on free Internet telephony.

www.pointcast.com
Home of the Internet's number 1 free news service—downloaded free, to your desktop.

www.unitedmedia.com/comics/dilbert/
Free daily Dilbert—what more could you ask?

Troubleshooting

www.datafellows.com
Shareware virus protection.

www.tufftest.com
Downloadable complete system diagnostics, for as little as $9.95.

www.computercraft.com
One of the world's best sources of IBM PS/2-related information.

www.realworldtech.com
Concise but breathtakingly helpful guides to upgrade troubleshooting and memory purchasing.

http://final.dystopia.fi/~jargon/files/drivers/cdrom_d.html
A library of those hard-to-find CD-ROM drivers.

http://finders.zdnet.com
Windows 95 drivers of every stripe.

Mac Stuff

www.macweek.com
The latest news from the Macintosh universe.

www.macintouch.com
Everything you need to know to make Macintosh technology
work the way it's supposed to.

www.uce.com
Up-to-the-minute *used* Mac pricing information.

www.digiserve.com/buying-a-mac/
Up-to-the-minute *new* Mac pricing information.

http://ng.netgate.net/~engstrom/cc.html
Comprehensive Mac and Mac clone performance data.

www.compu-america.com
Discount Macs.

www.softclub.com
Discount Macs.

www.macresq.com
One of the Web's best sources for used Macs.

www.powerwatch.com
Find out whether Power Computing has straightened up its act.

www.macconnect.com/~zubin/StarMax/
The independent scoop on Motorola's powerful Mac clones.

www.zdnet.com/macuser/cpu/
Real benchmarks to judge Macintosh and Mac-clone performance.

http://cdrom.amug.org/
One of the world's best sources for Mac shareware.

www.zws.com/classicmacs/
Detailed information on very old Macs.

www.yetanother.com/performa/
Important information on Performa 5xxx/6xxx technical problems.

http://violet.berkeley.edu/~schrier/mhz.html
Help to decide if you should goose your Mac's processor via clock chipping.

Books

www.amazon.com
Even if they're not always the *cheapest* bookstore on Earth, or even the fastest to deliver, they're the easiest place on Earth to *find out* about the books you're looking for.

www.ece.curtin.edu.au/~saoundb/cgi/nph-bargainbot
And once again, there's Bargainbot—which *will* find you the best deal.

Summary

There you have it: The Cheapskate's best sources. I'd like to hear about any new Cheapskates sites or resources *you* discover. E-mail me at **bcamarda@nisnet.**

Now, on to the software.

•CHAPTER•

12

The Cheapskate's Software Library

- If You're Craving More

- How this CD-ROM is Organized

- Windows 95 Shareware Library

- Windows 3.1 Shareware Library

- MS-DOS Software Library

- Macintosh Shareware Library

- Summary

The Cheapskate's Software Library brings together the best low-cost and free software for Windows 95, Windows 3.1, DOS, and the Macintosh.

This disk contains two kinds of software: *shareware* and *freeware*. In general, freeware is yours to use any way you want, as long as you don't change it. You'll see a few restrictions here or there; for example, one freeware author asks that you send a postcard telling him how you like his software. (He calls his software *postcardware*.) Freeware authors almost always keep the rights to their software, including copyrights. But in general, you won't have to spend a dime.

Then, there's shareware. Shareware is written by people who are trying to make a living, just like the rest of us. With commercial software, you generally have to make a purchase decision before you've tried out the product. Shareware authors distribute their work freely, on the honor system. You can try out their software for a period of time, typically a month.

If it doesn't serve your needs, delete it. No harm, no foul.

If it *does* meet your needs, pay for it. It will almost always cost you less than commercial software. And paying for shareware is the *right* thing to do. (Hey, we Cheapskates are cheap, but we're not thieves!)

If You're Craving Even More

The shareware community is a vibrant one. New shareware is posted every day, especially for Windows 95 and Macintosh systems. Even if

> Most of the programs on this CD-ROM included with this book are published by members of the Association of Shareware Professionals (ASP). It's unlikely you'll ever have a shareware problem that you can't resolve by contacting an ASP member directly, but if you do, the ASP Ombudsman may be able to help. (ASP can't provide technical support for individual products, of course.) Send E-mail to the ASP Ombudsman at 70007.3536@compuserve.com, or write to
>
> ASP Ombudsman
> 545 Grover Road
> Muskegon, MI 49442

you're satisfied with the software on the CD-ROM included with this book, it's worth checking some of the major shareware sites to see if there are updates to the programs you're already using.

Here are several of the best Web sites for locating up-to-date shareware and freeware.

C|Net (**www.shareware.com,** see Figure 12-1)

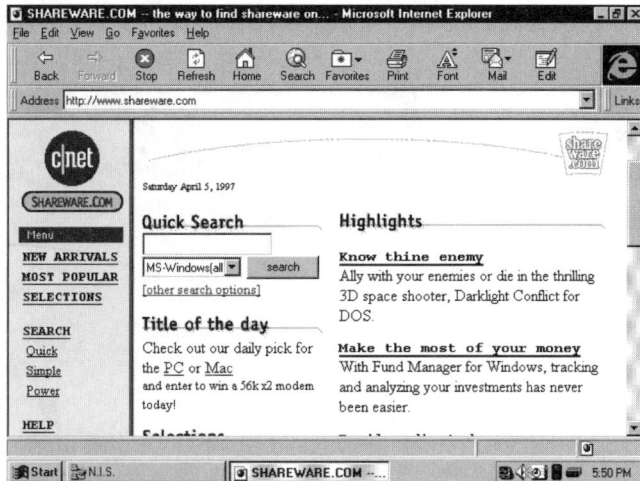

Figure 12–1   C|Net's shareware library.

ZDNet's Software Library (**www.hotfiles.com,** see Figure 12-2)

Figure 12–2   ZDNet's shareware library.

The Shareware Zone (**www.galttech.com,** see Figure 12-3)

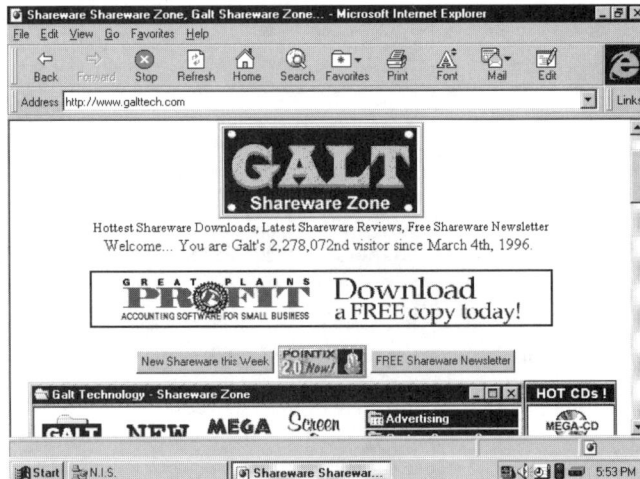

Figure 12–3   The Shareware Zone.

Windows 95 Shareware (**www.windows95.com,** see Figure 12-4)

Figure 12–4   Windows 95 Shareware site.

Tucows (**www.tucows.com,** see Figure 12-5)

Keep an eye out for possible changes to this site. Gateway 2000, which also uses a "cow" visual theme, has been after Tucows to change its name.

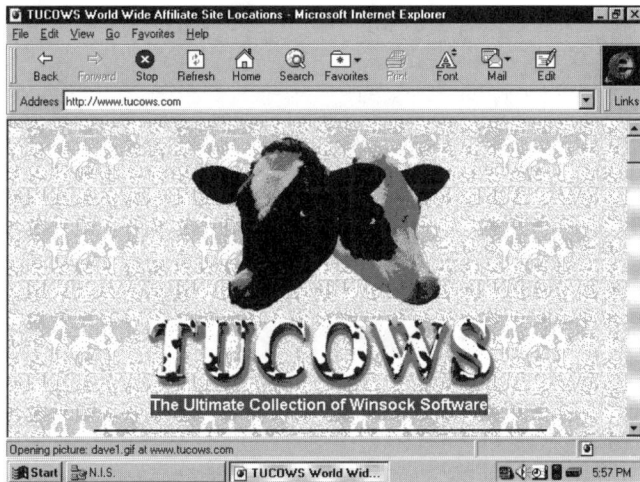

Figure 12–5   Tucows.

431

Walnut Creek (**www.cdrom.com/archive/index.html**)

Walnut Creek CD-ROM site (see Figure 12-6) includes extensive Windows, DOS, and Mac software downloads via ftp, as well as an unmatched catalog of shareware CD-ROMs. You can get information on Walnut Creek's CD-ROMs by sending e-mail to orders@cdrom.com, or writing to

Walnut Creek CD-ROM
4041 Pike Lane, Suite E
Concord, CA 94520

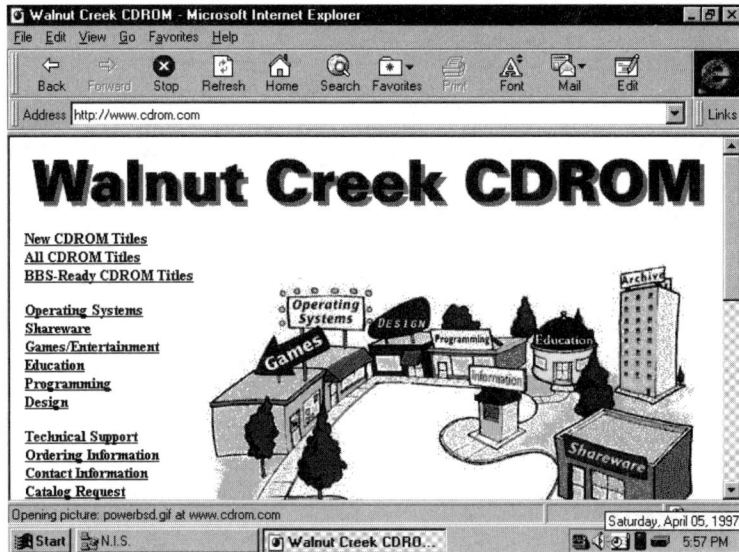

Figure 12–6   Walnut Creek Software.

Windows 95 Shareware Library

The following programs were designed to run under Windows 95 (and in most cases, Windows NT). If you are running Windows 3.1, see the Windows 3.x Shareware Library section of this chapter. In many cases, 16-bit versions of the same programs are included there.

Word Processing

- *WordExpress 2.0 (Trial version)*

WordExpress 2.0 (see Figure 12.7) is a full-fledged word processor with few compromises which requires barely 3 Mb for a complete installation. It includes all the basics: What You See is What You Get editing, sophisticated formatting, graphics, borders, and bullets. It also includes word processing features rarely included in shareware: tables, indexes, tables of contents, fields, mail merge, footnotes, styles, and more.

File Name:	Please run Setup.exe in the Win95\MVD32 folder.
Type of Software:	Shareware
Registration Fee:	$49.95
Requirements:	Windows 95, 4-Mb RAM, 3-Mb hard disk space, VGA
Published by:	MicroVision Development, Inc. P.O. Box 3010 Carlsbad, CA 92009 1-800-998-4555 **www.mvd.com**

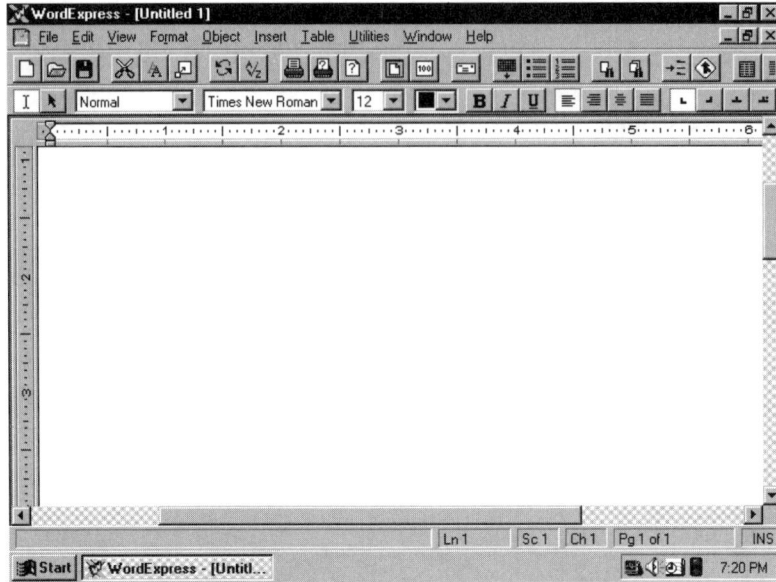

Figure 12–7   WordExpress 2.0

Painting

- *PaintShop Pro 4.12 (Shareware version)*

In many respects, PaintShop Pro (see Figure 12-8) gives Adobe PhotoShop a run for its money—for about one-eighth of the price. It combines extensive image painting and editing tools with image processing—including special effects like drop-shadow, chisel and "hot-wax coating." And it can use PhotoShop-compatible third-party filters. (Combine PaintShop Pro with a close-out copy of Kai's Power Tools 1.0 and you have a remarkably powerful image editing suite for under $100!) It supports nearly all the file formats you're likely to need, including JPG and GIF for Web work. (One significant exception: It will read EPS files but won't save as EPS.) All in all, an excellent value.

File Name:	**psp412.zip (2974K)**
Type of Software:	Shareware
Registration Fee:	$69.95
Requirements:	Windows 95
Published by:	Jasc, Inc.
	P.O. Box 44997
	Eden Prairie, MN 55344
	612-930-9171
	www.jasc.com

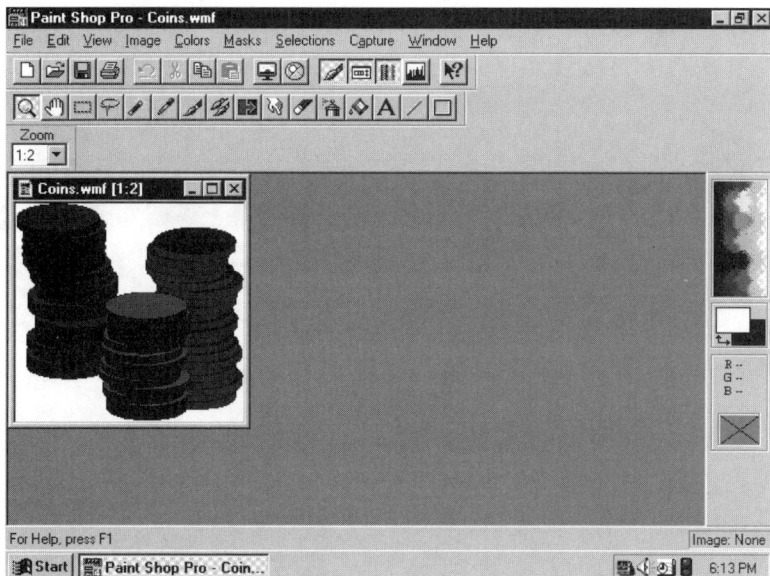

Figure 12–8   PaintShop Pro 4.12.

File Converter

● *Jasc Image Robot (Shareware version)*

If you've ever had to convert a lot of files at once—say from WMF to JPG for use on the Web—Jasc Image Robot (see Figure 12-9) is for you. It

435

will also adjust images, all following the same script—so you can automate the processing of, say, adding a motion blur, or creating to grey scale—and do it consistently for dozens of images at once. This is a very cool new tool from the folks who brought you PaintShop Pro.

File Name:	jir10.zip (1800K)
Type of Software:	Shareware
Registration Fee:	$49.95
Requirements:	Windows 95, minimum: 486 8 Mb, 256 colors; recommended: Pentium, 16M, 24-bit color
Published by:	Jasc, Inc. P.O. Box 44997 Eden Prairie, MN 55344 612-930-9171 **www.jasc.com**

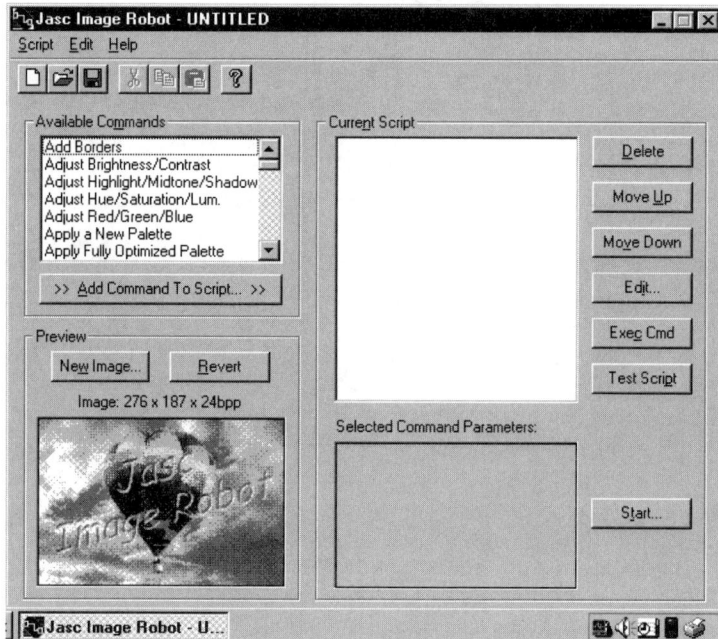

Figure 12–9   Jasc Image Robot.

Compression

- *WinZip 6.2 (Shareware Evaluation Version)*

WinZip (see Figure 12-10) seems to be just about everyone's favorite shareware program. This program manages the on-the-fly compression and decompression of files, so they can be transmitted across the Internet (or other on-line services) more efficiently, and so they'll take up less space on hard disks and floppy disks. It's reliable, elegant, and convenient. For example, you can right-click on one or more file names in Windows Explorer, choose Add to Zip, and WinZip will open to compress them. Once WinZip is open, you can use it much like Windows Explorer: Double-clicking on a file opens it in the appropriate application, or runs the program it contains. WinZip has become a lot more than a zipper and unzipper in the past few years. It now supports a wide variety of common Internet file formats, including TAR, gzip, UNIX compress, UUencode, XXencode, BinHex, and MIME. Share files with people who haven't a clue about zipping and unzipping? Use the WinZip Self-Extractor, Personal Edition. All they need to do is double-click on the file and it unzips itself. Just about anyone can manage that.

Each licensed copy of WinZip 6.2 includes both the 16-bit (for Windows 3.1) and 32-bit (for Windows NT and Windows 95) versions. A user of a licensed copy of WinZip can use either version at any time, as long as the two versions are not used concurrently.

File Name:	Please run the Setup program in the Win95\WinZip\Win32 folder.
Type of Software:	Shareware
Registration Fee:	$29.00
Requirements:	Windows 95
Published by:	Nico Mak Computing P.O. Box 919 Bristol, CT 06011 www.winzip.com

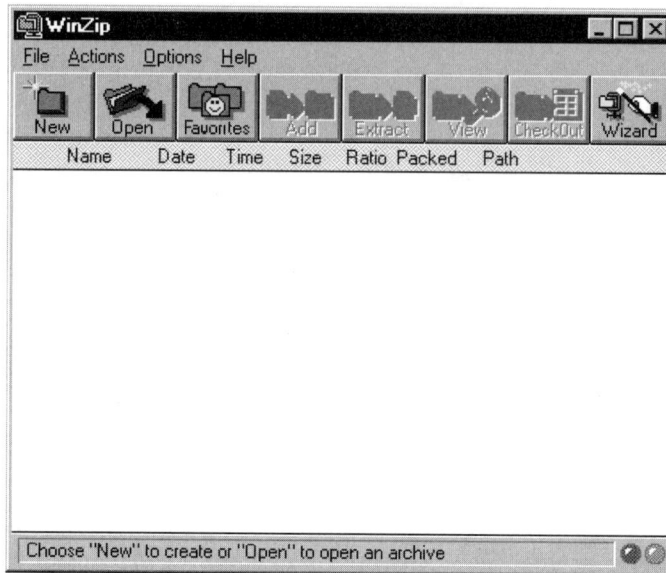

Figure 12–10   WinZip 6.2.

Web Browser

• *Microsoft Internet Explorer 3.02*

Microsoft Internet Explorer (see Figure 12-11) is the world's #2 Web browser, trailing only Netscape Navigator. This full-featured edition is much more than an extremely convenient Web browser with full support for Java, JavaScript, frames, and other popular Web technologies. It also comes with a complete Internet news and mail reader and NetMeeting software for document conferencing over the Internet. And this isn't shareware: it's free. This updated version fixes a number of security problems. Visit **www.microsoft.com/ie** to see if there's an even newer version.

File Name:	msie302m95.zip (10.3 MB)
Type of Software:	Freeware
Registration Fee:	None
Requirements:	Windows 95
Published by:	Microsoft
	www.microsoft.com

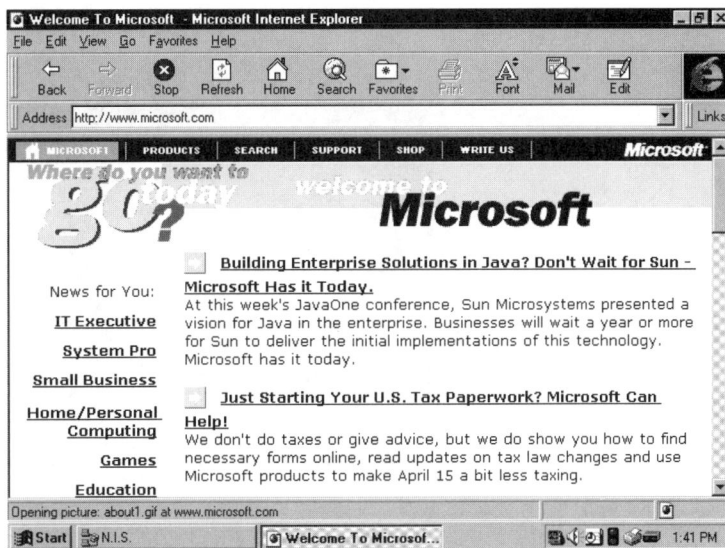

Figure 12–11   Microsoft Internet Explorer 3.02.

Web Authoring

- *Anansi*

Anansi (see Figure 12-12) is an HTML editor that also helps you track every element of your Web site project, including style settings, FTP settings, default directories and other important project elements. Since it keeps track of all that stuff for you, you'll be surprised how much it can automate that has to be done manually in many other editors.

File Name:	an32b3f2.zip
Type of Software:	Freeware
Registration Fee:	None
Requirements:	Windows 95
Published by:	Harry Bosma
	www.xs4all.nl/~hbosma/anansi/
	E-mail: hbosma@xs4all.nl

Figure 12–12 Anansi (16-bit version).

Web Utility

• *Free Agent 1.11 (32-bit)*

One of the world's best Internet newsreaders and newsgroup managers – and it's free!

Copyright© 1995, 1996, 1997 Forte Advanced Management Software, Inc. All Rights Reserved.

File Name:	fa-32-111.exe
Type of Software:	Freeware
Registration Fee:	None
Requirements:	Windows 3.1
Published by:	Forte, Inc.
	2114 Palomar Airport Road, Suite 100
	Carlsbad, CA 92009
	619-431-6400
	www.forteinc.com

• *Search Stream*

You run a Web search at Yahoo! You don't find what you're looking for. You go to Alta Vista and try it again. What if you could search five of the best engines at once? You can, with Search Stream (see Figure 12-13).

File Name:	stream15.zip (1700K)
Type of Software:	Shareware
Registration Fee:	$29.00
Requirements:	Windows 95
Published by:	Robsoft
	2510 Cranston Drive
	Escondido, CA 92025
	fax: 619-695-9356
	www.robsoft.net

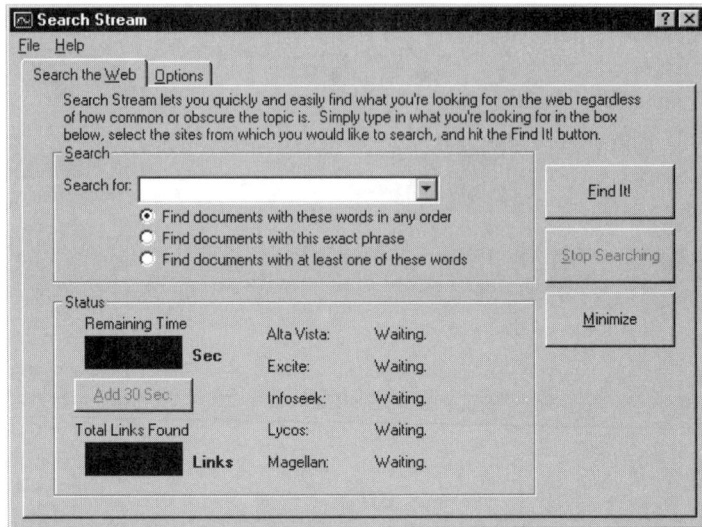

Figure 12–13   Search Stream.

Project Management

- *Firm Plan 32 Version 2.0*

One of the most complete scheduler/calendar systems around, Firm Plan 32 (see Figure 12-14) also offers a handy phone book, the ability to track income, expenses, and projects for everyone in the office, and much more.

File Name:	frmpnt20.zip (1079K)
Type of Software:	Shareware
Registration Fee:	$50.00
Requirements:	Windows 95
Published by:	R.A. Kelly
	Integra Computing
	910 Cobb Place Manor Drive
	Marietta, GA 30066
	770-426-5735
	integracmp@aol.com

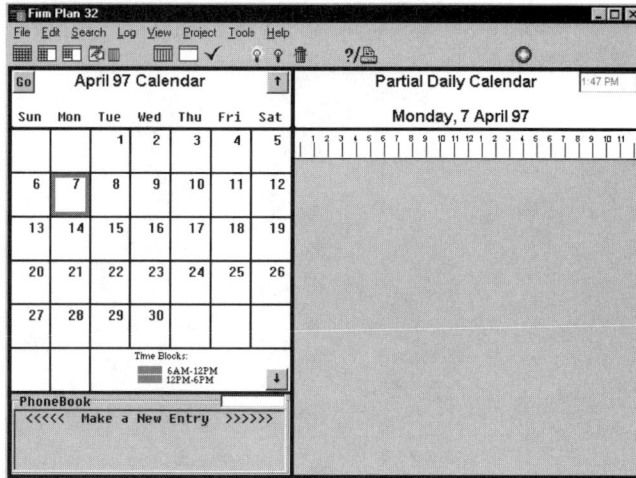

Figure 12–14   Firm Plan 32 Version 1.6.

Children's Educational

• *Roxie's Reading Fish 2.0 for Windows 95*

Roxie's Reading Fish (see Figure 12-15) is a game based on "Go Fish," designed to help young children learn to read. The version on this CD-ROM includes prefirst grade words. If you register the software, you'll get four more levels of words, through the end of second grade—words chosen by educational specialists as the ones your child is most likely to encounter.

File Name:	**rreafb.zip**
Type of Software:	Shareware
Registration Fee:	$9.95
Requirements:	Windows 95
	33 MHz processor, 4-Mb hard drive space, VGA, mouse, sound card
Published by:	Lattice Work Software P.O. Box 362 Lafayette Hill, PA 19444 E-mail: **http://members.aol.com/latticewrk/lattice.htm**

Figure 12–15   Roxie's Reading Fish 2.0 for Windows 95.

• *Dino Spell 4.0*

If your child is beyond Roxie's Reading Fish, he or she may like Dino Spell (see Figure 12.16). The idea: Help Derik the Dinosaur find the strawberries that Rex the Tyrannosaurus has hidden—by spelling words correctly.

File Name:	dspell40.zip (939K)
Type of Software:	Shareware
Registration Fee:	$20.00
Requirements:	Windows 95 or Windows 3.1, 4 Mb, 6-Mb free hard drive space, mouse, VGA; sound card recommended
Published by:	Dyno Tech Software 1105 Home Avenue Waynesville, MO 65583-2231 1-800-396-6832 E-mail: Dtgames@aol.com

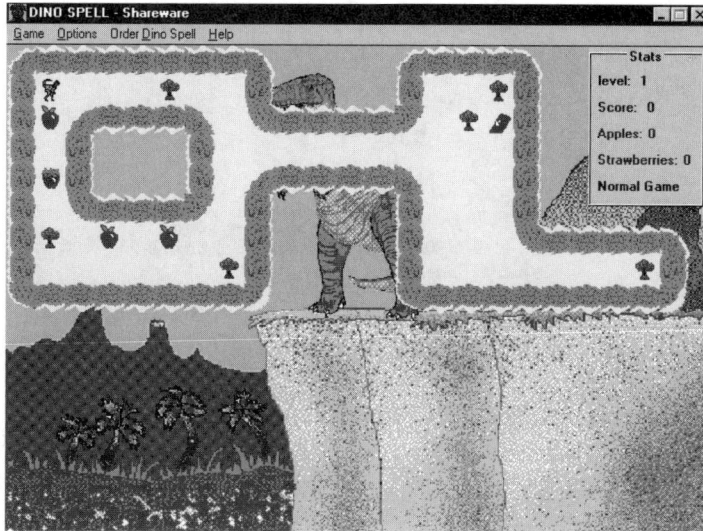

Figure 12–16   Dino Spell 4.0.

• *Ancient Ivory 3.1*

Ancient Ivory is based on a centuries-old Caribbean dice game of strategy and luck. With an intuitive interface and high-quality graphics, it allows you to play against another player, or the computer.

File Name:	ytb.zip
Type of Software:	Shareware
Registration Fee:	$9.95
Requirements:	Windows 95
	33 MHz processor, 4-Mb hard drive space, VGA, mouse, sound card
Published by:	Lattice Work Software
	P.O. Box 362
	Lafayette Hill, PA 19444
	E-mail:
	http://members.aol.com/latticewrk/lattice.htm

- *Fruitcakes*

Build fruitcakes with falling fruit—and coax the friendly frogs into helping you keep the fruit flies away. Work fast to avoid the early frost or an unexpected harvest!

File Name:	fruit11.zip (1.32 MB)
Type of Software:	Shareware
Registration Fee:	$20.00
Requirements:	Windows 95 or Windows 3.1, 4 Mb, 6-Mb free hard drive space, mouse, VGA; sound card recommended
Published by:	Neon Games c/o Dyno Tech Software 1105 Home Avenue Waynesville, MO 65583-2231 1-800-396-6832 E-mail: Dtgames@aol.com

Windows 3.1 Shareware Library

In some cases, the Windows 95 programs discussed above will also work under Windows 3.1; in most cases, we've provided another piece of software designed specifically for Windows 3.x.

Word Processing

- *Yeah Write 1.0 (Unregistered version)*

Yeah Write 1.0 (see Figure 12-17) is a free word processor by a group of developers who were once part of the WordPerfect development team. If you like it, you can upgrade to the commercial version, Release 1.1.

File Name:	yw10.exe (836K)
Type of Software:	Freeware
Registration Fee:	None
Requirements:	Windows 3.1
Published by:	WordPlace Corporation
	11 East 200 North, Suite 201
	Orem, UT 84057
	www.wordplace.com
	801-221-7777

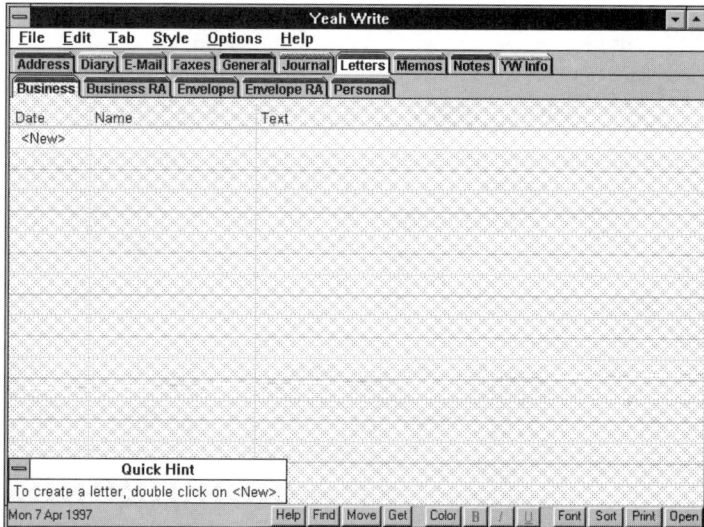

Figure 12–17   Yeah Write 1.0

Also included: WordExpress 2.0 Trial Version for Windows 3.1. (See Windows 95 description, but use the following file:

File Name:	Please run Setup.exe in the Win3X\MVD16 folder.
Type of Software:	Shareware
Registration Fee:	$49.95
Requirements:	Windows 3.1, 4-Mb RAM, 3-Mb hard disk space, VGA
Published by:	MicroVision Development, Inc.
	P.O. Box 3010
	Carlsbad, CA 92009
	1-800-998-4555
	www.mvd.com

Spreadsheet

• *FlexEasy for Windows*

FlexEasy is a spreadsheet without the familiar rows and tables. You place the information wherever you want, adding cells, labels, ranges, and graphs as you go. This may take a while to get used to, but once you do, you may really like this—and it's surprisingly powerful.

File Name:	flexw.zip (354K)
Type of Software:	Shareware
Registration Fee:	$10.00
Requirements:	Windows 3.1
Published by:	Edward Bale
	Free and Easy Software
	688 Farmbrook Crescent
	Orleans, Ontario K4A 2L2 Canada
	(613) 834-1738
	E-mail: 74660.3406@compuserve.com

Personal Information Manager

● *1st Contact 1.02*

1st Contact (see Figure 12-18) tracks pretty much everything you'll need to track on up to 65,000 contacts: name, address, phones, e-mail, company info, Web site, last-date contacted, relationship, and ten categories you define. You can speed dial any number you list, automatically time-stamp notes you make, even divide your contacts into personal "white pages" and business "yellow pages."

File Name:	con3x102.zip (769K)
Type of Software:	Shareware
Registration Fee:	$15.00
Requirements:	Windows 3.1 (A Windows 95 version is available at **http://gsanet.com/www/jsoft**)
Published by:	Jesse Roberge
	1702 W. Camelback Rd. #241
	Phoenix, AZ 85015-3347
	http://gsanet.com/www/jsoft

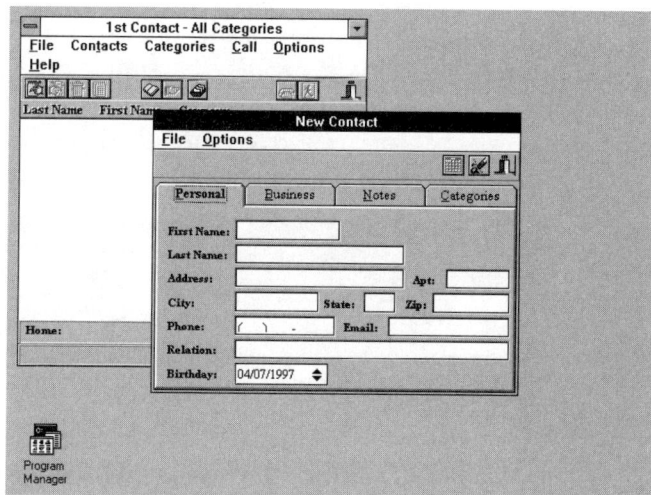

Figure 12–18   1st Contact 1.02.

449

Painting

- *PaintShop 3.11 (Shareware version)*

Similar to the PaintShop 4.12 program discussed under Windows 95, but with fewer features.

File Name:	psp311.zip (1888K)
Type of Software:	Shareware
Registration Fee:	$69.95
Requirements:	Windows 3.1
Published by:	Jasc, Inc.
	P.O. Box 44997
	Eden Prairie, MN 55344
	612-930-9171
	www.jasc.com

File Viewer

- *Drag and View Gold*

Just drag a file to the icon that appears on the bottom of your screen, and poof—the file opens. It's that simple. File formats include Excel 5, Word 6 for Windows, Works, ASCII, Lotus, Quattro, Symphony, WordPerfect, AmiPro, Q&A Write, BMP, PCX, TIF, GIF, ZIP, LZH, and many others. Wow!

File Name:	dragvu.zip (540K)
Type of Software:	Shareware
Registration Fee:	$35.00
Requirements:	Windows 3.1
Published by:	Canyon Software
	1537 4th St., Suite 131
	San Rafael, CA 94901

Compression

• *WinZip 6.2 for Windows 3.1 Shareware Evaluation Version*

See the discussion for WinZip for Windows 95.

File Name:	Please run the Setup program in the Win3X\WinZip\Win16 folder.
Type of Software:	Shareware
Registration Fee:	$29.00
Requirements:	Windows 3.1
Published by:	Nico Mak Computing
	P.O. Box 919
	Bristol, CT 06011
	www.winzip.com

Web Browser

• *Microsoft Internet Explorer*

See the description for Windows 95. However, use the file listed below instead. To see if there's a newer version than this one, visit **www.microsoft.com/ie.**

File Name:	dlmin30f.exe (2.94 MB)
Type of Software:	Freeware
Registration Fee:	None
Requirements:	Windows 3.1
Published by:	Microsoft Corp.
	www.microsoft.com

Web Authoring

- *Anansi*

See the description under Windows 95. However, use the following file instead.

File Name:	an16b3f2.zip (673K)
Type of Software:	Freeware
Registration Fee:	None
Requirements:	Windows 3.1
Published by:	Harry Bosma
	www.xs4all.nl/~hbosma/anansi/
	E-mail: hbosma@xs4all.nl

Web Utility

- *Free Agent 1.11 (16-bit)*

See the description of Free Agent (see Figure 12-19) for Windows 95. However, use the following file instead.

File Name:	fa16-111.exe (1071K)
Type of Software:	Freeware
Registration Fee:	None
Requirements:	Windows 3.1
Published by:	Forte, Inc.
	2114 Palomar Airport Road, Suite 100
	Carlsbad, CA 92009
	619-431-6400
	www.forteinc.com

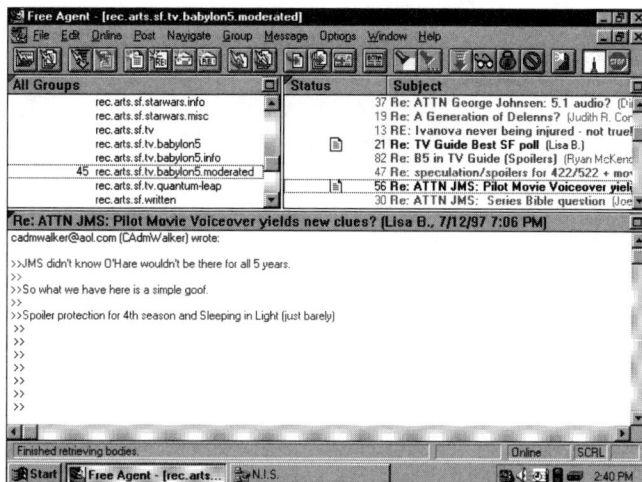

Figure 12–19   Free Agent (32-bit).

Copyright© 1995, 1996, 1997 Forte Advanced Management Software, Inc. All Rights Reserved.

Personal Finance

• *Wealth Management System 8.48*

Wealth Management System (see Figure 12.20) is a neat little financial planning program that can help you make projections for retirement, track your savings, loans and mortgages; track your net worth, and much more.

File Name:	wmstr848.zip (330K)
Type of Software:	Shareware
Registration Fee:	$28.45
Requirements:	Windows 3.1 (also runs under Windows 95)
Published by:	William W. Odlum
	105, 35 Ormskirk Avenue
	Toronto, Ontario, M6S 1A8, Canada
	1-416-767-4797

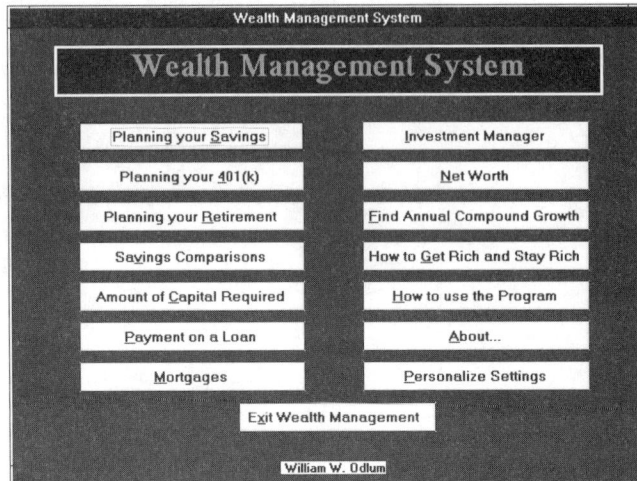

Figure 12–20   Wealth Management System 8.48.

Children's Educational

- *Roxie's Reading Fish 2.0*

See the description of Roxie's Reading Fish under Windows 95. However, use the file listed below instead.

File Name:	rreafa.zip
Type of Software:	Shareware
Registration Fee:	$9.95
Requirements:	Windows 3.1
Published by:	Lattice Work Software P.O. Box 362 Lafayette Hill, PA 19444 E-mail: 74453.2112@compuserve.com

Utilities

- *VBRUN300.DLL*

This .DLL file is needed to run some of the Windows 3.1 software on this CD-ROM.

File Name:	vbrun300.zip (226K)
Type of Software:	Freeware
Registration Fee:	None
Requirements:	Windows 3.1
Published by:	Microsoft Corporation

MS-DOS Software Library

You never hear about it any more, but there are plenty of full-featured, sophisticated, stable programs running under DOS—and a whole sub-culture of shareware developers and users keeping their DOSware going. Here are a few of the better shareware programs we've found.

Word Processing

- *Easy Word 10.2*

Easy Word (see Figure 12-21) is a convenient word processor with tables, macros, spellchecker, and more.

File Name:	ew102.zip (747K)
Type of Software:	Shareware
Registration Fee:	$35
Requirements:	DOS, 16-MHz processor
Published by:	Easy Software Ltd. 3 Brookside Ct. Prestbury Road Macclesfield SK10 3BR United Kingdom **www.ourworld.compuserve.com/ homepages/easysoftware**

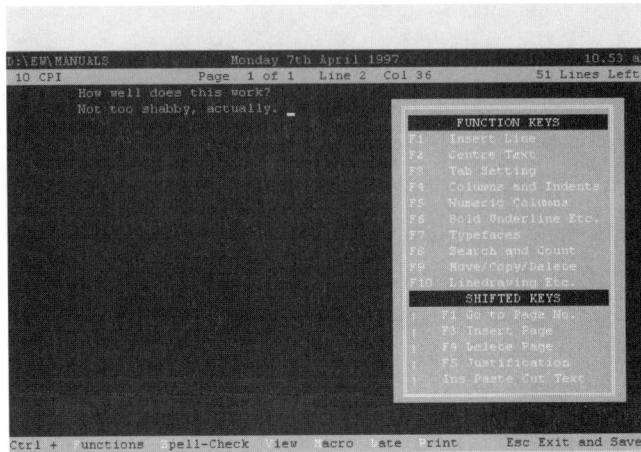

Figure 12–21   Easy Word 10.2.

Spreadsheet

● *As-Easy-As 5.70e (Shareware Version)*

As-Easy-As is a sophisticated spreadsheet program that creates Lotus-compatible files and has hundreds of math, financial, and statistical functions.

File Name:	Please run install.exe in the \DOS\AsEasyAs folder.
Type of Software:	Shareware
Registration Fee:	$75.00
Requirements:	DOS 3.1 or higher, 80286 or higher processor, 512K RAM, 1.2M hard drive space
Published by:	Trius, Inc. P.O. Box 249 N. Andover, MA 01845-0249 1-508-794-9377 www.triusinc.com

Database

● *EasyBase 11.1*

EasyBase (see Figure 12-22) is a complete, menu-based database program and application generator. Purchase it together with Easy Word for $80.

File Name:	eb111.zip (1264K)
Type of Software:	Shareware
Registration Fee:	$59.00
Requirements:	DOS
Published by:	Easy Software Ltd.
	3 Brookside Ct.
	Prestbury Road
	Macclesfield
	SK10 3BR
	United Kingdom

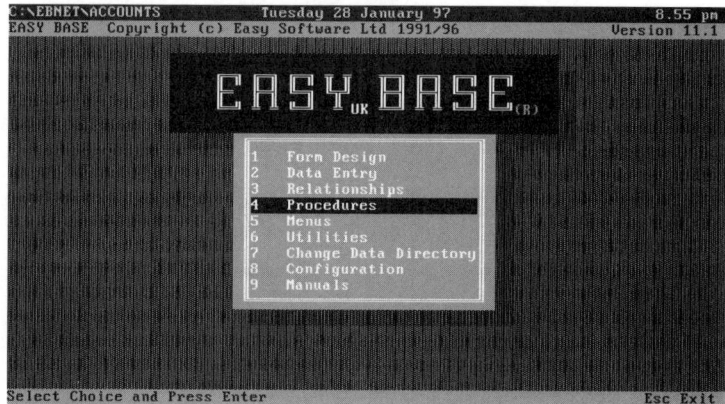

Figure 12–22   EasyBase 11.1.

Painting

• *NeoPaint 3.2b*

This powerful paint program with its own Windows-like graphical user interface provides extensive drawing tools you would expect in a high-end Windows or Mac program: brush, airbrush, eraser, fills, color conversions, Bezier lines, smudge and blend tools, charcoal pencil, stamp pad, quill pen, oil brush, and many others. It supports PCX, TIFF, BMP and GIF files. It even includes a DOS screen capture program, Neograb.

File Name:	neopt32b.zip (647K)
Type of Software:	Shareware
Registration Fee:	$45
Requirements:	DOS, mouse
Published by:	NeoSoft Corp.
	354 NE Greenwood Avenue, Suite 108
	Bend, OR 97701-4631
	541-389-5489

Personal Finance

• *Easy Money 1.4*

Easy Money (see Figure 12-23) is a simple automated ledger book which helps you track expenses in whatever categories you like. There's a macro utility that lets you automate recording of recurring expenses and income such as payroll checks, and a report utility that allows you to customize reports by category and dates.

File Name:	ezm14e.zip (254K)
Type of Software:	Shareware
Registration Fee:	$17.50
Requirements:	DOS
Published by:	WaverlyStreet
	P.O. Box 14249
	Columbus, OH 43214
	E-mail: dgjess@infinet.com

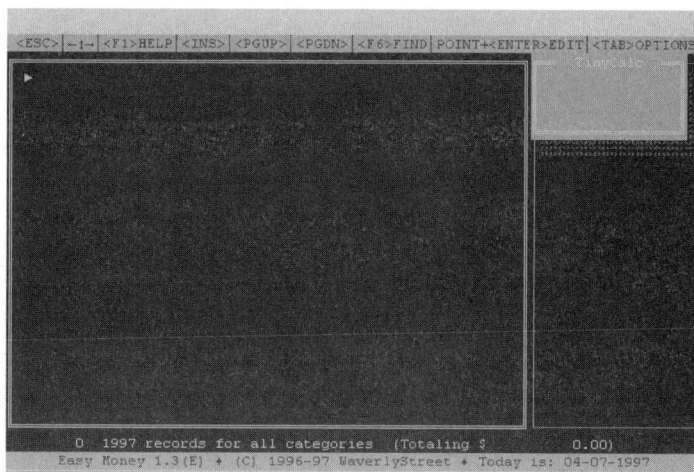

```
<ESC>|←↓→|<F1>HELP|<INS>|<PGUP>|<PGDN>|<F6>FIND|POINT+<ENTER>EDIT|<TAB>OPTIONS
                                                                TinyCalc
►




    0  1997 records for all categories  (Totaling $        0.00)
   Easy Money 1.3(E) ♦ (C) 1996-97 WaverlyStreet ♦ Today is: 04-07-1997
```

Figure 12–23   Easy Money 1.4

Children's Educational

- *Crayon Box 4.1*

Crayon Box 4.1 (see Figure 12-24) starts with a coloring and sketch book; once the kids are having fun, you can spring the built-in memory games, counting tutor, USA quiz, and, if you're lucky, maybe even the math drills on them.

File Name:	crayon41.exe (281K)
Type of Software:	Shareware
Registration Fee:	$12.00
Requirements:	DOS, EGA or VGA graphics, MS-compatible mouse, 512K memory, "one child"
Published by:	Philip Kapusta 406 Monroe Avenue Falmouth, VA 22405 **www.pc-shareware.com**

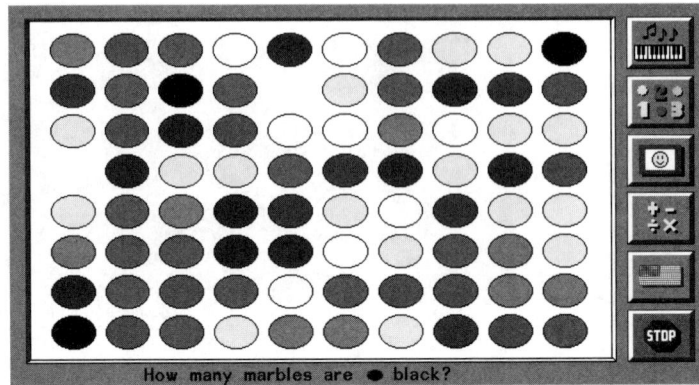

How many marbles are ● black?

Figure 12–24   Crayon Box 4.1.

Macintosh Shareware Library

Mac shareware developers have the same passion for their platform that Mac users do—and they've made available a remarkably high-quality library of shareware at equally remarkable prices. Better yet, some of the best things in life (or at least on the Mac platform) are actually *free*.

Word Processing

- *Word Edit 1.03*

Word Edit (see Figure 12-25) is what Apple's SimpleText ought to be: nuthin' fancy, but plenty to handle basic correspondence, junior high school reports, and other simple documents. It provides multiple text styles, sizes, fonts, and colors, margin and line spacing settings, tabs, and several other features, including a few surprises, like "insert current date" and a spelling dictionary. And it's free!

File Name:	word-edit-103.hqx (206K)
Type of Software:	Freeware
Registration Fee:	None
Requirements:	Macintosh; System 4.1 or later
Published by:	Quade Publishing
	P.O. Box 1576
	Fort Dodge, IA 50501-1576
	E-mail: jquade@bigfoot.com

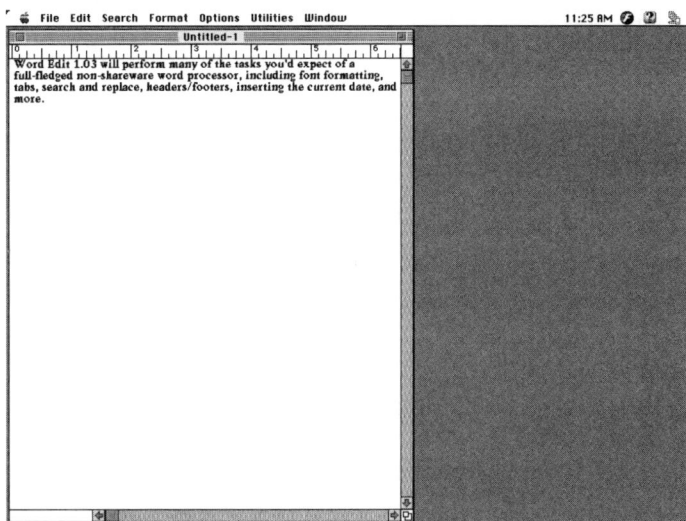

Figure 12–25   Word Edit 1.03.

Spreadsheet

• *Sum-It 1.02*

Sum-It (see Figure 12-26) is a basic spreadsheet that takes up less than a half-megabyte of disk storage with space to spare—yet it supports practically all the functions and calculations the typical spreadsheet user uses most. Remarkable.

File Name:	sum-it-102.hqx (427K)
Type of Software:	Shareware
Registration Fee:	$20.00
Requirements:	Macintosh
Published by:	Maarten L. Hekkelman
	In the U.S., send payments or credit card information to:
	Kagi Software
	1442-A Walnut Street, #392-IK
	Berkeley, CA 94709-1405
	E-mail: sales@kagi.com

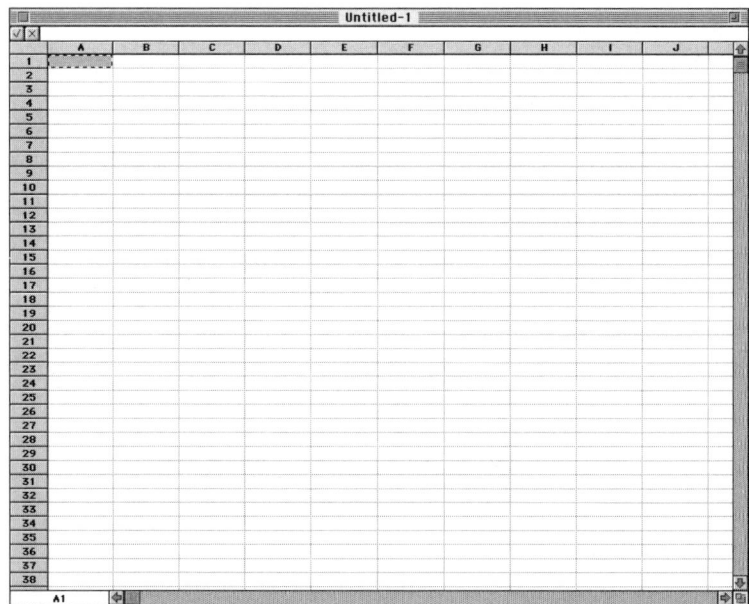

Figure 12–26   Sum-It.

Integrated Software

- *HyperWorks 3.22a*

Built on Apple's HyperCard, HyperWorks (see Figure 12-27) is minimalist integrated software: it can handle simple databases, financial management tasks, graphics, graphing, and word processing.

File Name:	hyperworks-322a.hqx (68K)
Type of Software:	Shareware
Registration Fee:	$25.00
Requirements:	Macintosh
Published by:	David & Daniel Mueller
	dsmueller@besler.org

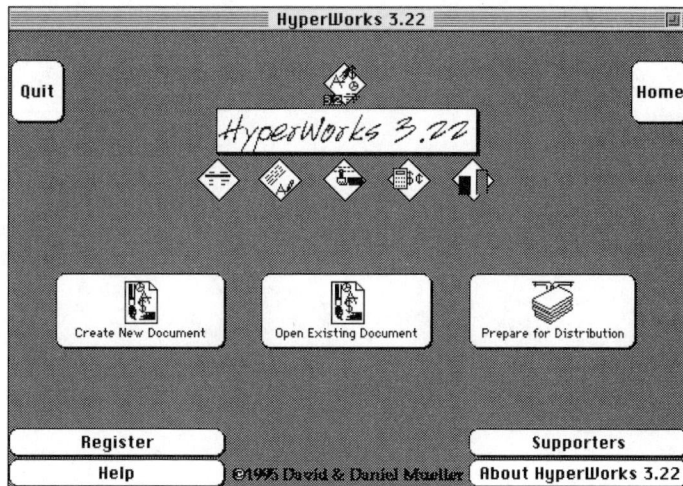

Figure 12–27   HyperWorks 3.22a.

Personal Information Manager

• *Consultant 1.42*

Consultant (see Figure 12-28) is an exceptionally slick piece of shareware for time and contact management. Use it to track your meetings and tasks; even create Gantt charts for project management tasks. This shareware is fully functional except for its export function—and one other tiny point: Files you create with it stop working one month after they're created. But this program is easily worth the $25 that's being asked for it.

File Name:	ConsultantFAT1.4.hqx
Type of Software:	Shareware
Registration Fee:	$25.00
Requirements:	"Fat" version installs on either Power Macintosh or 68x00 Macintosh
Published by:	Chronos L.C. 1092 Fir Avenue Provo, UT 84604 1-801-957-1774 **www.chronosnet.com**

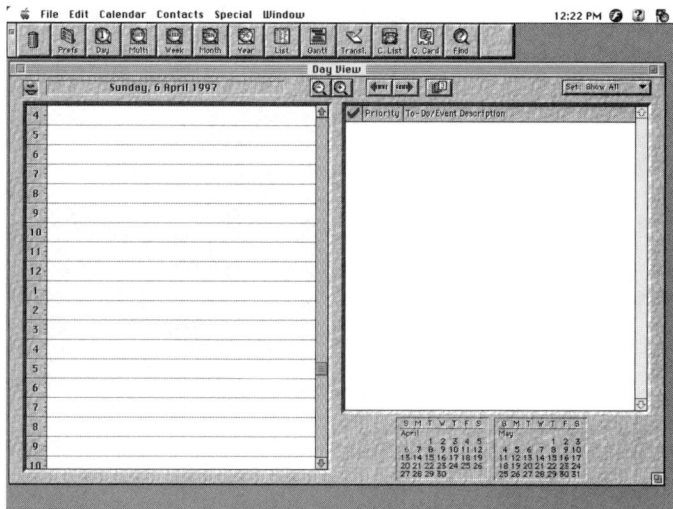

Figure 12–28   Consultant.

File Viewer

• *GraphicConverter 2.8*

When it comes to managing graphics, there's not much that GraphicConverter (see Figure 12-29) can't do. Rated "5 mice" by Mac User, this program will read, export, and manipulate files in nearly every common graphics format.

File Name:	gracon.hqx (1795K)
Type of Software:	Shareware
Registration Fee:	$35.00
Requirements:	Macintosh
Published by:	Thorsten Lemke
	Lemke Software
	thorsten_lemke@sz.maus.de

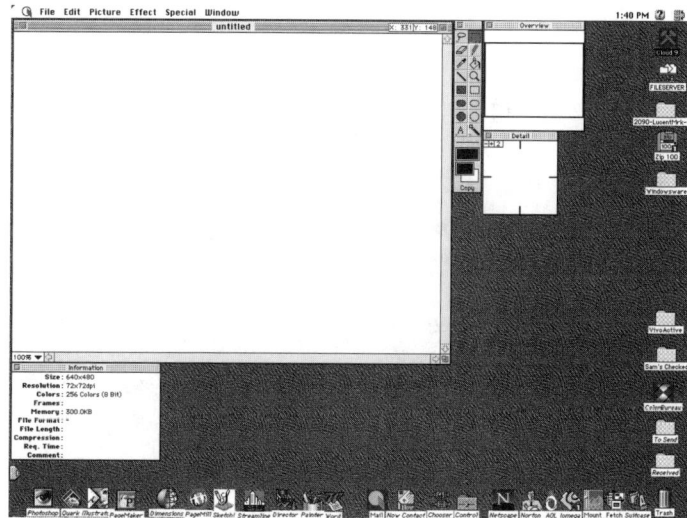

Figure 12–29   Graphics Converter 2.8.

Web Browser

● *Microsoft Internet Explorer*

Grudgingly, Mac magazines have been choosing Microsoft's Internet Explorer over Netscape's offerings: it's smaller, less buggy, easier to customize, and just as useful. To see if there's a newer version than this one, visit **www.microsoft.com/ie**.

File Name:	internet-explorer-fat-301.hqx
Type of Software:	Freeware
Registration Fee:	None
Requirements:	Macintosh
Published by:	Microsoft Corporation www.microsoft.com

Web Authoring

● *PageSpinner 1.22*

A complete, easy-to-use HTML editor, PageSpinner (see Figure 12-30) makes it convenient to insert practically every element of a Web page, including formatting, frames, image maps—even Java and JavaScript code.

File Name:	page-spinner-122.hqx (781K)
Type of Software:	Shareware
Registration Fee:	$25.00
Requirements:	Macintosh, System 7.01 or later, 3-Mb disk space, 1800K free RAM; 68020 or higher processor (68040 or PowerPC recommended)
Published by:	Optima Systems, Sweden **www.algonet.se/~optima/pagespinner.html** Send payment to: Kagi 1442-A Walnut Street, #392-PL Berkeley, CA 94709-1405 E-mail: shareware@kagi.com

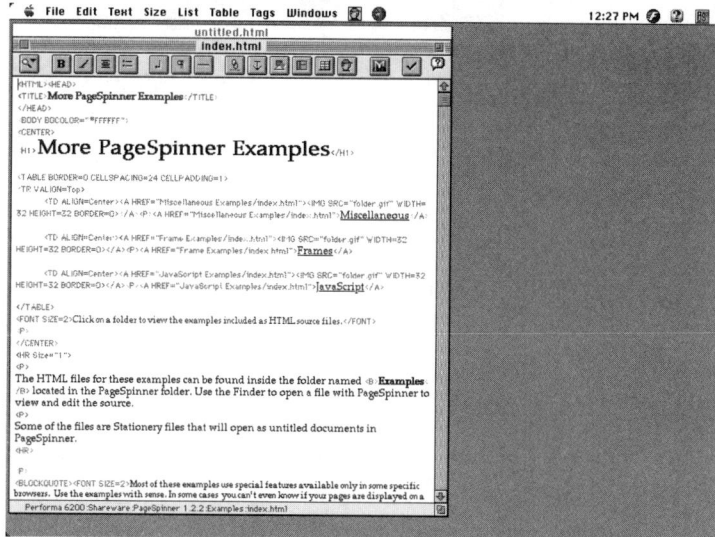

Figure 12–30   Page Spinner 1.22.

Web Utility

- *Anarchie 2.01*

Anarchie may be the world's most convenient software for handling Internet (FTP) file transfers. You can use it to search FTP sites for specific files, quickly find alternate sites that have the file you're looking for, bookmark the FTP sites you like best, and much more. Anarchie can be automated via AppleScript, and while it works with any Mac OS since System 7.01, it's even more convenient if you have System 7.5's Drag Manager installed.

Anarchie is copyright © Peter N. Lewis and licensed through Stairways Software Pty Ltd.

File Name:	anarchie-201.hqx (1089K)
Type of Software:	Shareware
Registration Fee:	$10.00
Requirements:	Macintosh

467

File Name:	anarchie-201.hqx (1089K)
Published by:	Peter Lewis
	Send payment to:
	Kagi
	1442-A Walnut Street, #392-PL
	Berkeley, CA 94709-1405
	E-mail: shareware@kagi.com

Personal Finance

● *Financial Portfolio 4.5*

The Financial Portfolio Hypercard stack (see Figure 12-31) allows you to track the purchase and sale of stocks, dividends, capital gains, and stock splits; check the value of your portfolio, and graph both your assets and liabilities. Note: Financial Portfolio must be copied to your hard drive before you can unstuff (decompress it).

File Name:	financial-portfolio-v4.5.sit (341K)
Type of Software:	Shareware
Registration Fee:	$10.00
Requirements:	Macintosh
	Hypercard Player, Hypercard 2.1, or Hypercard 2.2
Published by:	Michael Foreman
	The author requests that you send your $10 as a donation to:
	St. Jude's Children's Research Hospital P.O. Box 1818 Memphis, TN 38101-9903
	Please drop him a line telling him you've done so, at the following address:
	Michael Foreman 19 Gardenia Drive Mount Laurel, NJ 08054

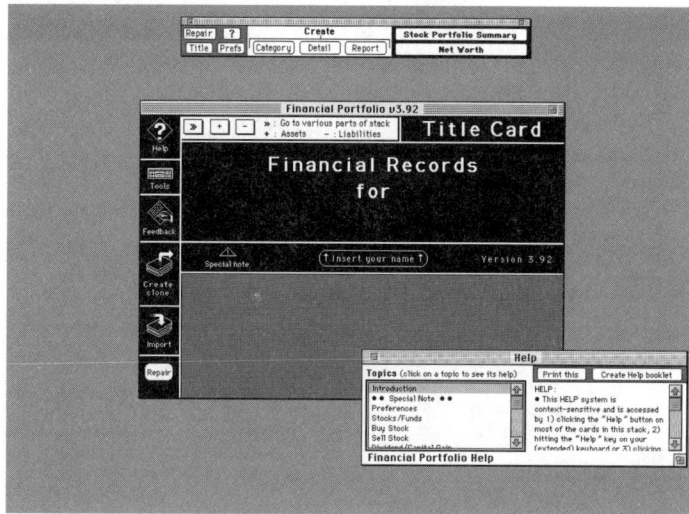

Figure 12–31   Financial Portfolio.

Project Management

- *TimeSlice Lite 3.1*

Some mainlanders may be surprised to hear that anyone in Maui needs to keep track of the time, but one of the best time-tracking programs for the Mac comes from there. TimeSlice Lite (see Figure 12-32) can help just about anyone who needs to keep track of the hours they're working on each project. You can assign tasks, track elapsed times, set different rates and categories for each project, set budgets, and export your TimeSlice documents to other software for billing and analysis purposes.

File Name:	time-slice_lite_31.hqx (462K)
Type of Software:	Shareware
Registration Fee:	$25.00
Requirements:	Macintosh

File Name:	**time-slice_lite_31.hqx (462K)**
Published by:	Maui Software
	189 Auoli Drive
	Makawao, Maui, HI 96768-9313
	1-808-573-0011
	www.mauisoftware.com

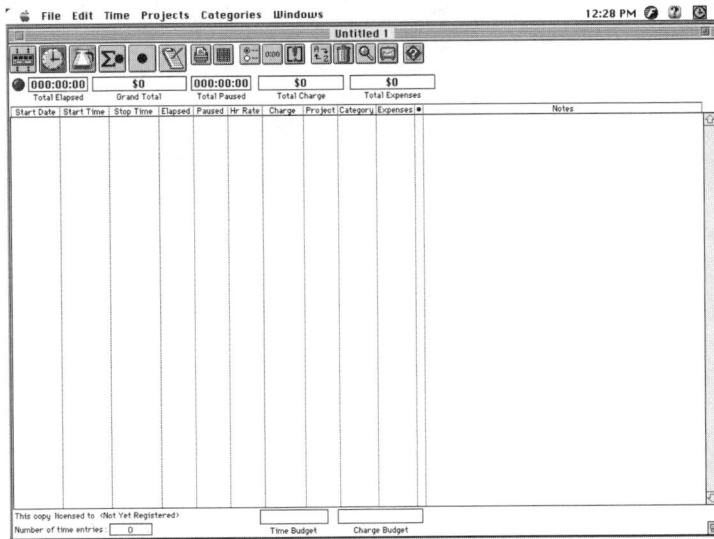

Figure 12–32　　Time Slice Lite 3.1

Children's Educational

• *TykeWriter*

Imagine a word processor for three-year-olds, and you've got the idea. With TykeWriter (see Figure 12-33), kids can either click on a letter, or type it if they know their way around the keyboard. According to the author, "for noncommercial uses, [TykeWriter] may be copied and used for free… If you send $10, we will be forever grateful." How could you say no to that?

File Name:	tyke-writer-101.hqx (207K)
Type of Software:	Shareware
Registration Fee:	$10.00
Requirements:	Macintosh
Published by:	David Lazarus
	7852 Spring Ave.
	Elkins Park, PA 19027
	http://w3.icdc.com/~lazarus/tykewriter.html

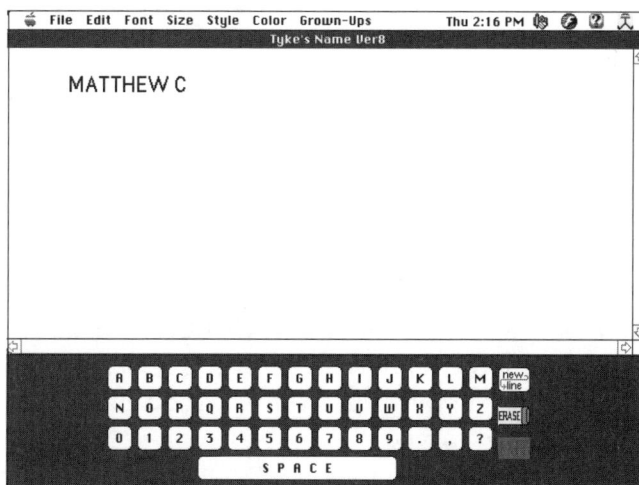

Figure 12–33   TykeWriter.

Utilities

- *SoundApp 2.23*

The essential, free Macintosh sound application, SoundApp 2.23, will play and convert nearly every common sound file found on the Mac—or the Internet. That includes System 7 sound files, MIDI type 0, 1, and 2, SoundEdit, MPEG audio, Sound Blaster VOC, WAV, AIFF, and many other formats. Just drop the file onto SoundApp and it runs. Suddenly, sound is easy.

File Name:	sound-app-223.hqx (831K)
Type of Software:	Freeware
Registration Fee:	None
Requirements:	Macintosh (68020 or higher; Power Mac recommended); Apple Sound Manager Version 3.1 or higher (downloadable, or comes with System 7.5.3). Some features require QuickTime 2.0.
Published by:	Norman Franke
	1885 Paseo Laguna Seco
	Livermore, CA 94550
	www-cs.students.stanford.edu/~franke/SoundApp/

Summary

Well, that's it: *The Cheapskate's Guide to Bargain Computing.*

I'm all cheaped out. Now it's your turn.

Let me know how you've done with the ideas (and software) in this book. And let me know what great ideas and sources *you've* come up with. (When it comes to being a Cheapskate, we're not going to read about it in the four-color magazine ads. We're going to have to help each other!)

Just e-mail me at bcamarda@nisnet. Or even better, visit my Cheapskate's Web site at **www.nis.net/camarda/cheapskate** for the up-to-date tips and sources that didn't show up in time to be included in this book! See you there.

Appendix A:
Source Quick-Reference

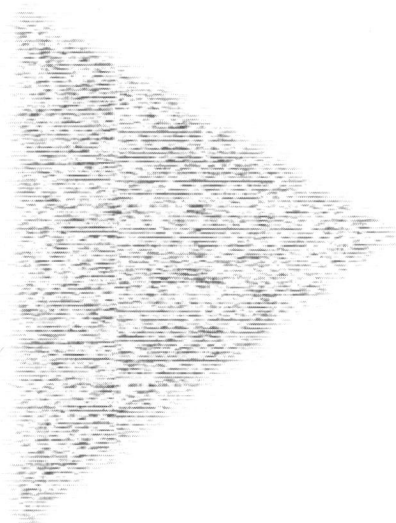

This appendix summarizes the leading Cheapskate product sources, by category—*nearly 250 sources in all*. You might also check out Chapter 11, "Where to Find Out More"—especially *the Cheapskate's top 50+ Web site list*.

Company	Phone	Web Site
PC Manufacturer's Outlets		
Acer Outlet	1-408-433-4903	www.acer.com/aac/direct/weborder.htm
AST Outlet Direct	1-800-540-7060	www.astoutlet.com
Compaq Works	1-800-318-6919	
Dell Factory Outlet	1-800-336-2891	
Gateway 2000 Factory Outlet	1-800-846-3614	
IBM Credit Corporation	1-800-IBM-5440	http://mer.shop.ibm.com/shopping/ibmcredit
IBM PC Factory Outlet	1-800-426-7015	
Micron Factory Outlet	1-208-893-7600	
NEC LikeNew	1-800-NEC-INFO	
Packard Bell Factory Outlet	1-888-474-6772	www.pbfactoryoutlet.com
Tandy Outlet Store	1-817-870-5709	
Independent Resellers of Refurbished/Used Computers		
Capital Resource Recovery	1-800-452-6670	www.remarketing.com/broker/crr/
Computer Renaissance (National franchise retailer)		www.computerrenaissance.com
Data Path Technologies, Inc	1-914-769-1999	www.data-path.com
Defense Reutilization and Marketing Service (Government stores)	1-800-468-8289	www.drms.dla.mil
Delaware Computer Center, Inc.	1-800-668-3270; 1-302-633-1500	
Dollar Computer Corporation	1-800-910-0085; 1-714-975-0542	www.earthlink.net/~dollar/
Electrified Discounters (Also Okidata printers, notebook systems)	1-800-678-8585; 1-203-787-4246	
Image Microsystems	1-800-1-800-4142; 1-310-815-1000	www.imagemicro.com
Intellysys		www.svii.com

Company	Phone	Web Site
International Marketing Associates	1-301-299-7821	www.netm.com/ima
KHI	1-800-988-1268	
Maxim Technology	1-800-755-1008; 1-316-941-0799	
Micro Exchange	1-800-284-9296; 1-201-284-1200	www.microexch.com
National Computer Clearinghouse	1-316-681-0555	www.ncc-pc.com
Tredex	1-800-899-6800	www.tredex.com
True Data Products	1-800-635-0300; 1-508-278-6555	www.truedataproducts.com
Internet-based Auctions		
Auction PC		www.auctionpc.com
Auction X		www.auctionx.com
ONSALE		www.onsale.com
Worldport Auction Board		www.worldport.com/auction/
Z Auction		www.zauction.com
Low-End Used Systems		
Alternative Computer Products Corporation	1-561-994-9899	
Breakaway Technologies, Inc.	847-265-6890	
Computer Service Point, Inc.	1-516-937-3800	
Global Computer Concepts, Inc.	1-800-411-1150	
Image Microsystems	1-800-1-800-4142; 1-310-815-1000	
Internet Clearinghouse		www.internetclearinghouse.com
Maxim Technology	1-800-755-1008; 1-316-941-0799	
NEI Computer Products	1-516-231-5845	
TII	1-203-466-1644	
Universal Sales Agency, Inc.	1-516-932-1400	
Used Computer Mall		www.usedcomputer.com

Company	Phone	Web Site
In-Person Auctions		
Internet Auction List		www.usaweb.com/auction.html
Koll-Dove	1-415-571-7400	www.koll-dove.com
Remington York	1-972-438-1737	www.remingtonyork.com
U.S. Customs Auction (Public Auction Line)	1-703-273-7373	www.ustreas.gov/treasury/bureaus/customs/
Leading PC Manufacturers Also see Table 8.2		
Compaq	1-800-345-1518; 1-281-370-0670	www.compaq.com
Dell Computer Corporation	1-800-879-8510; 1-800-289-3355	www.dell.com
Gateway 2000	1-800-846-2059; 1-605-232-2000	www.gw2k.com
Hewlett-Packard	1-800-472-5277	www.hp.com/PersonalComputing/
IBM Personal Computer Company	1-800-426-7255 (1-800-426-7235 for Aptiva and Thinkpad 365)	www.pc.ibm.com
Micron Electronics	1-800-347-3490; 1-208-893-3434	www.mei.micron.com
Superstores and Warehouse Stores		
CompUSA		www.compusa.com
Computer City		www.computercity.com
PriceCostco		www.pricecostco.com
Free Benchmark Software		
Ziff-Davis Benchmark Operation		www.zdnet.com/zdbop/winstone/winstone.html
Nonprofit Computer Recycling Organizations		
National Cristina Foundation	1-203-622-6000; 1-800-274-7876	
Non-Profit Computing Inc.	1-212-759-2368	
The East-West Education Development Foundation	1-617-261-6699	
GEOS Solutions		
Breadbox Computer	1-813-847-6996	www.breadbox.com

Company	Phone	Web Site
Academic Software Resellers		
Campus Connection	1-408-373-0323	
Focus Computer Center	1-800-223-3411; 1-718-871-7600	
PC People, Inc.	1-800-877-9761; 1-713-789-6300	www.pcpeople.com
Peripherals Plus	1-800-444-7369, 1-908-928-9600	
Premier Technology Group	1-704-391-9947	www.premiertechgroup.com/aer.html
Software Plus Academic, Inc.	1-800-377-9943; 1-201-288-7441	www.spainj.com
The Software Source	1-800-289-3275; 1-908-695-2100	www.iaswww.com/source.html
Free On-Line Clip Art Sources		
Caboodles of Clip Art		www.caboodles.com/clipart
ClarisWorks User Group	1-313-454-1969	cathy@cwug.org
Randy's Icon and Image Bazaar		www.iconbazaar.com
The Clip Art Connection		www.istnet/clipart/
Discount Software Publishers		
Essex Interactive		www.essexinteractive.com
The Learning Company		www.learningco.com
Free DOS		
Caldera OpenDOS		www.caldera.com
Previous Version Software		
Computer Reset (Also PS/2 reference disks)	1-214-276-8072	wwwipp.unicomp.net/c-reset/
Cyber Exchange		www.cyberexchange.com
Software Clearance Outlet	1-800-230-SOFT	www.softwareoutlet.com
Software Outlet	1-805-544-6616	www.greatbuy.com
Surplus Direct (Also wide variety of closeout hardware)	1-800-753-7877	www.surplusdirect.com
USoX		www.midwinter.com/usox/

Company	Phone	Web Site
Free On-Line Software Downloads		
Microsoft Free Downloads		www.microsoft.com/msdownload/
Symantec Free Downloads		www.symantec.com
LINUX Suppliers		
InfoMagic		www.infomagic.com
Red Hat Software		www.redhat.com
Walnut Creek Software (Also provides shareware)		www.cdrom.com
Yggdrasil		www.yggdrasil.com
Memory Resellers		
Intol Computers	1-800-551-1449; 1-813-796-0806	www.intol.com
Memory 4 Less	1-800-821-3354	www.memory4less.com
MicroMall Direct	1-800-346-7172; 1-714-833-3222	
The Chip Merchant	1-800-426-6375; 1-619-268-4774	www.thechipmerchant.com
The CPU & Memory Exchange Club	1-408-654-9090	
The Memory Exchange	1-800-501-2770	www.memoryexchange.com
The Memory Liquidators	1-800-718-7755; 1-310-326-5656	
The Memory Place	1-800-306-8901	www.buymemory.com
Hard Drive Resellers		
Comp-U-Plus	1-800-287-2323	www.compuplus.com
Dirt Cheap Drives	1-800-473-0960	
Insight	1-800-INSIGHT	www.insight.com
CD-ROM Drive Sources		
A2Z Computers	1-800-983-8889	
Computer Geeks Discount Outlet	1-619-603-9242	www.compgeeks.com
Windows Sources Driver Finder		http://finders.zdnet.com
Used/Refurbished Monitors		
Chipheads Unlimited	1-972-393-4216	

Company	Phone	Web Site
Computer Discounters Inc.	1-301-595-0500 1-703-556-7782 (retail location)	www.computerdiscounters.w1.com
Computer Service Point	1-516-937-3800	
Data Trend Inc.	1-800-366-7060	
Krex Computers	1-800-222-KREX, 1-847-967-0200	www.krex800.com
Second Source Engineering	1-800-848-8700	www.second-source.com
Synnex Budget Computer Depot	1-408-249-7266	www.synnex.com/mspec.html
Fixed-Frequency Video Card Manufacturers		
Mirage	1-800-228-3349; 1-310-301-4545	www.mirage-mmc.com
PCG	1-800-255-9893; 1-310-260-4747	www.photonweb.com
Software Integrators	1-800-547-2349	www.si87.com
Discount Video Cards		
XWY Direct	1-307-745-5608	
Leading National Mail-order Hardware/Software Resellers		
Computability	1-800-554-9925	www.computability.com
Computer Discount Warehouse	1-800-608-4239	www.cdw.com
Mac Connection	1-800-800-0009	www.macconnection.com
Mac Mall	1-800-328-2790	
PC Connection	1-800-800-5555	www.pcconnection.com
PC Mall	1-800-863-3282	
PC/Mac Warehouse	1-800-255-6227	www.warehouse.com
Voltage regulators for processor upgrades		
JDR Micro Devices (Also other accessories, motherboards, etc.)		www.jdr.com
PC processor upgrade kit manufacturers		
CCT	1-800-CCT-MENU	www.cct.com
Evergreen Technologies (Also PS/2 upgrades)	1-541-752-9851	www.evertech.com
Improve Technologies	1-801-224-0355	www.transera.com

Company	Phone	Web Site
Kingston Technology (Also PS/2 upgrades)	1-800-337-8410	www.kingston.com
TrinityWorks	1-800-278-4944	www.trinityworks.com
VisionTek	1-800-726-9595, 1-847-360-7500	www.visiontek.com
Premium fans and power supplies		
PC Power & Cooling	1-800-722-6555; 1-619-931-5700	www.pcpowercooling.com
Laptop/Notebook Batteries		
Batteries Etc.	1-800-697-9900	
Mice & Pointing Devices		
Logitech Factory Outlet	1-510-795-8500	www.logitech.com
Diskettes		
American Ribbon & Toner Company	1-800-327-1013	www.icanect.net/arctoner
Best Computer Supplies	1-800-544-3472	
Diskettes Unlimited	1-800-364-DISK; 1-713-643-9939	
Exxus Direct, Inc.	1-800-557-1000; 1-408-399-7655	www.disksdirect.com
MEI/Micro Center (Also other accessories; uninterruptible power supplies)	1-800-634-3478	
Midwestern Diskette	1-800-221-6332	www.mddc.com/mdi/mdi.html
Remanufactured Laser Toner Cartridges		
A-ARVIN Toner Store	1-800-555-3150; 1-303-338-1763	www.tonerstore.com
Atsumi	1-800-889-9722	
Enviro-Charge Corp.	1-800-487-0447; 1-914-232-9582	
Environmental Laser		www.toners.com
Laser Technology Systems, Inc.	1-888-389-3704	
Laserlux	1-800-366-4053; 1-210-565-9596	www.laserlux.com
Marlborough Supplies	1-800-777-2949	

Company	Phone	Web Site
Nu'life Cartridge Corporation	1-412-331-7553	
Pendl Company	1-800-869-7973; 1-414-896-8888	www.pendl.com
Quality Laser Alternatives	1-610-373-0788	www.qla.com
Toner Charge, Inc.	1-800-301-9298; 1-703-560-7800	
Tonerworks	1-301-297-4340	
Ultimate Image, Inc.	1-800-459-9876; 1-602-966-8973	www.ultimateimage.com
Inkjet Refills		
Computer Friends	1-503-626-2291	www.sourcedata.com/500/000183.htm
Micro Center/SoftCentre Inc.	1-800-366-3311	
Nu-Jet	1-800-216-7850; 1-210-599-7045	www.nujet.com
Cables		
CableNet	1-800-788-8488	
Cables America	1-800-348-8724	
Computer Gate International	1-408-730-0673	www.computergate.com
Dalco Electronics	1-800-445-5342	www.dalco.com
Discount Computer Books		
All Publishers' Outlet	1-888-255-7826	www.tucson.com/allpub/all-pub-outlet.html
Amazon.com		www.amazon.com
Paradise Books Wholesale Discount Outlet		www.paradisebooks.com/menu_computer.shtml
Readme.Doc	1-800-678-1473	readmedotdoc.com
Discount Internet service		
Baltimore Public Library	1-410-887-3297	
Bigger.Net	1-800-228-1992; 1-408-283-3703	www.bigger.net
FreeRide Media		www.freeride.com
FreeNets	See listings starting page 264	

Company	Phone	Web Site
Cheapskate's Internet Software		
DosLynx		ftp://ftp2.cc.ukans.edu/pub/DosLynx/readme.htm
Microsoft Internet Explorer		www.microsoft.co/ie/download
Netscape Navigator/ Communicator		www.netscape.com
NetTamer		http://people.delphi.com/davidcoloston/
Peak Net.Jet		www.peak-media.com
WebWhacker		www.ffg.com/whacker/
Free Web Pages for Business		
Inc. Online		www.inc.com/createsite/
Free Web Servers		
Apache		www.apache.org
Free E-Mail		
Hotmail		www.hotmail.com
Juno	1-800-654-5866	www.juno.com
NetAddress		www.netaddress.com
TravelTales		www.traveltales.com
Free News		
Individual Newspage		www.individual.com
Mercury Mail		www.merc.com
Pointcast		www.pointcast.com
More Net Freebies		
See Table 7.2, page 288		
Discount Diagnostics Software		
American Megatrends		www.megatrends.com/utilities/amidiag50.html
Windsor Technologies		www.tufftest.com
PC Batteries		
Powerline	1-800-234-2444	www.powerline-battery.com
PS/2 products and information		
Advanced Microcomputer Systems, Inc.	1-800-972-3733; 1-305-784-0900	
ComputerCraft PS/2 Resource Center	1-201-946-1178; 1-201-795-0909	www.computercraft.com

Company	Phone	Web Site
General Technics	1-800-GT-SALE-8	www.gtweb.net
Index Computer Remarketing	1-954-730-0900	
Netstream International	1-972-664-0383	www.wwtrading.com/ps2.htm
Page Computers	1-800-886-0055	
Solutronix (PS/2 repair)	1-800-875-2580	
Free PC Technical Support via E-Mail		
Jim Aspinwall		wb9gvf@raisin.com
PC Discount Network Card Manufacturers		
Addtron	1-800-998-4638; 1-510-668-5186	www.addtron.com
Allied Telesyn	1-408-730-0950	www.alliedtelesyn.com
Linksys	1-714-261-1288	www.linksys.com

MAC SOURCES

Leading Mac OS Manufacturers		
Apple	1-800-766-2333	www.apple.com
APS Technologies (Also Mac hard drives)	1-800-235-8935	www.apstech.com
Motorola StarMax	1-800-359-1107; 1-512-434-1526	www.mot.com/GSS/MCG/products/systems/ds/ starmax/SMfamily.html
Power Computing	1-800-999-7279; 1-512-388-6868	www.powercc.com
PowerTools Corp. (Also Mac upgrades)	1-800-891-4307; 1-512-891-0646	www.pwrtools.com
UMAX	1-510-651-9488	www.supermac.com/products/
Discount Resellers (Macs & clones)		
CompuAmerica	1-800-533-9005	www.compu-america.com
ComputerTown	1-800-613-0622	www.computertown.com
Other World Computing	1-800-275-4576	
Power On Computer Services (Also used monitors)	1-800-673-6227; 1-916-652-1880	www.poweron-line.com
Small Dog Electronics (StarMax specialist)	1-802-496-7171	www.smalldoggy.com
SoftClub Computer Systems	1-888-MACS-NOW	www.softclub.com

Company	Phone	Web Site
Used Macs		
CRA Systems	1-800-375-9000	www.cra-sys.com
DataTech Remarketing	1-800-281-3661	www.datatech-rmkt.com
GE Capital	1-800-431-7713	tms.crsinfo@capital.ge.com
Mac Sale International	1-800-729-7031; 1-602-858-0900	www.macsaleint.com
Mac Solutions	1-800-80-WE-BUY	www.macsolutions.com
MacResQ	1-888-44-RESCUE; 1-510-689-9488	www.macresq.com
Macstuff	1-520-747-7625	www.macstuff.com
Pre-Owned Electronics	1-800-274-5353	
Que Computers	1-612-623-0903	www.quecomp.com
Rentex Computer Rentals	1-800-545-2313	www.rentex.com
Sun Remarketing	1-800-821-3221; 1-801-755-3360	www.sunrem.com
United Computer Exchange	1-800-755-3033	www.uce.com
User Group Connection		www.ugstore.com
Mac Internal Batteries		
Resource 800	1-800-430-7030	www.iitexas.com/gpages/resource.htm
Free PowerMac Performance Enhancement Software		
Motorola		www.mot.com/SPS/PowerPC/library/fact_sheet/libmoto.html
Mac Upgrades		
MicroMac Technology	1-800-600-6227; 1-714-362-1000	www.micromac.com
Newer Technology	1-800-678-3726; 1-316-943-0222	www.newertech.com
Sonne Technologies	1-800-786-6260	www.sonnettech.com
Cache		
Components Direct	1-888-4-COMPONENTS	www.componentsdirect.com
Processor Accelerators		
PowerLogix		www.powerlogix.com

Company	Phone	Web Site
Free Mac E-Mail Technical Support		
MacAssist Web Site		www.mac4hire.com/biz/macassist/
Monitor Adapters		
Griffin Technologies	1-615-255-0990	www.nashville.net/~griffin
Used Monitors		
Silver Reef	1-714-366-6864	www.billboards.com/sreef1.html

Appendix B:
The CD-ROM

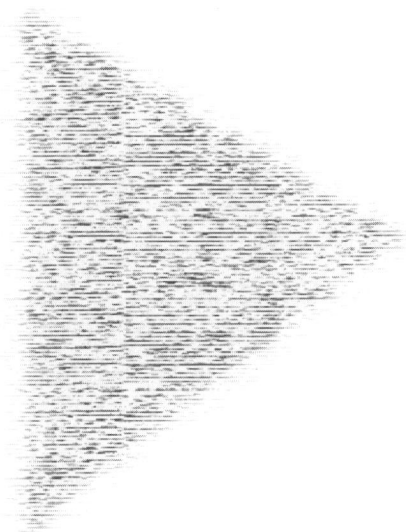

How This CD-ROM Is Organized

The Cheapskate's CD-ROM will run on both Macintosh and Windows/DOS machines. Software is organized as follows:

Type of Software	Folder (Directory) Name
Windows 95	Win95
Windows 3.x	Win31
DOS	DOS
Macintosh	MAC

You'll also find an additional folder, **www,** which contains the Cheapskate's Web site—with links to many of the world's best Cheapskate sources. To use the Cheapskate's Web site, open your Web browser and browse your computer to the file **\www.html\index.htm** on your CD-ROM drive. (In Netscape Communicator, you can display a Web page stored on your computer through File, Open Page command. In Microsoft Internet Explorer, use the File, Open menu item instead.) You don't have to be connected to the Web to access the Cheapskate's Web site, but you will need to establish a connection in order to reach the linked Web sites.

Virtually all the software on this CD-ROM is compressed, both to save space and to provide a convenient way to make sure all the files you need "travel" together.

Getting Decompression Software

In case you do not have decompression software, the shareware evaluation version of WinZip for Windows 95 and Windows 3.1 is included on the CD-ROM. If you need decompression software for Macintosh or for DOS, the CD-ROM's Web page includes links to Aladdin Systems (www.aladdinsys.com) where you can download the leading shareware decompression software for Macintosh; and to PKWARE, Inc. (www.pkware.com) where you can download the leading shareware decompression software for DOS.

Decompressing the files

Once you have installed decompression software for Windows or for the Macintosh, you can simply double-click on a .ZIP (Windows[1]) or .HQX (Macintosh BinHex) file to decompress it. You may need to specify where you wish the decompressed files to be placed, as they cannot be stored on the CD-ROM itself.

In DOS, you will need to use a PKUNZIP command from the DOS command line. For example, let's say there's a file you want to decompress, FILE.ZIP, stored on your D drive (possibly your CD-ROM). Let's say you want to place the decompressed files in a temporary folder you've created for them, C:\ZIPTEMP. The command you would use is:

pkunzip h:\file.zip c:\ziptemp

This will work only if the directory where you place PKZIP is in the path stored in your AUTOEXEC.BAT file. If not, include the entire path-name to your pkunzip utility; for example:

c:\pkzip\pkunzip h:\file.zip c:\ziptemp

In a few cases (WinZip, WordExpress, AsEasyAs, and Neopaint), the software publishers have provided their own installation routine. Rather than decompressing a ZIP file, you install these programs by double-clicking a SETUP.EXE or INSTALL.EXE. These applications and setup files are stored in their own directories within the Win31, Win95, and DOS directories.

Running the Software

For Macintosh programs, once the .HQX file is decompressed, all the files it contains are stored in a new folder on your hard drive. In most

▲ ▲

1.   If you have trouble decompressing a file by double-clicking on it in Windows, check to make sure that WinZip is "associated" with the .ZIP file extension.

cases, you can immediately run the program by double-clicking on the application file within that folder.

For most DOS and Windows programs, and for a few Macintosh programs such as Microsoft Internet Explorer, you will have to run installer software before you can run the application itself. Once Windows software is installed, you can run it by double-clicking its icon. In DOS, you will need to run it from the command line, including the entire path in your command, as in the following example:

c:\folder\sharewre.exe

More Important Information About This Software

All software on this disk is copyrighted and owned by its developers. You may not change it, and if you get permission to redistribute it, you must include all files. While freeware is, of course, free, please remember again that shareware is provided for evaluation only. If you choose to continue using it after the evaluation period is over, you must pay the shareware developer.

Shareware and freeware developers often release upgrades that provide new features or fix software defects noted by users. In most cases, you can use the Web page on this CD-ROM to link to the developer's locations and see if there have been any upgrades since this book went to press.

Index

LICENSE AGREEMENT AND LIMITED WARRANTY

READ THE FOLLOWING TERMS AND CONDITIONS CAREFULLY BEFORE OPENING THIS CD PACKAGE, *CHEAPSKATE'S GUIDE TO BARGAIN COMPUTING.* THIS LEGAL DOCUMENT IS AN AGREEMENT BETWEEN YOU AND PRENTICE-HALL, INC. (THE "COMPANY"). BY OPENING THIS SEALED CD PACKAGE, YOU ARE AGREEING TO BE BOUND BY THESE TERMS AND CONDITIONS. IF YOU DO NOT AGREE WITH THESE TERMS AND CONDITIONS, DO NOT OPEN THE CD PACKAGE. PROMPTLY RETURN THE UNOPENED CD PACKAGE AND ALL ACCOMPANYING ITEMS TO THE PLACE YOU OBTAINED THEM FOR A FULL REFUND OF ANY SUMS YOU HAVE PAID.

1.   **GRANT OF LICENSE:** In consideration of your purchase of this book, and your agreement to abide by the terms and conditions of this Agreement, the Company grants to you a nonexclusive right to use and display the copy of the enclosed software program (hereinafter the "SOFTWARE") on a single computer (i.e., with a single CPU) at a single location so long as you comply with the terms of this Agreement. The Company reserves all rights not expressly granted to you under this Agreement.

2.   **OWNERSHIP OF SOFTWARE:** You own only the magnetic or physical media (the enclosed CD) on which the SOFTWARE is recorded or fixed, but the Company and the software developers retain all the rights, title, and ownership to the SOFTWARE recorded on the original CD copy(ies) and all subsequent copies of the SOFTWARE, regardless of the form or media on which the original or other copies may exist. This license is not a sale of the original SOFTWARE or any copy to you.

3.   **COPY RESTRICTIONS:** This SOFTWARE and the accompanying printed materials and user manual (the "Documentation") are the subject of copyright. The individual programs on the CD are copyrighted by the authors of each program. Some of the programs on the CD include separate licensing agreements. If you intend to use one of these programs, you must read and follow its accompanying license agreement. You may not copy the Documentation or the SOFTWARE, except that you may make a single copy of the SOFTWARE for backup or archival purposes only. You may be held legally responsible for any copying or copyright infringement which is caused or encouraged by your failure to abide by the terms of this restriction.

4.   **USE RESTRICTIONS:** You may not network the SOFTWARE or otherwise use it on more than one computer or computer terminal at the same time. You may physically transfer the SOFTWARE from one computer to another provided that the SOFTWARE is used on only one computer at a time. You may not distribute copies of the SOFTWARE or Documentation to others. You may not reverse engineer, disassemble, decompile, modify, adapt, translate, or create derivative works based on the SOFTWARE or the Documentation without the prior written consent of the Company.

5.   **TRANSFER RESTRICTIONS:** The enclosed SOFTWARE is licensed only to you and may not be transferred to any one else without the prior written consent of the Company. Any unauthorized transfer of the SOFTWARE shall result in the immediate termination of this Agreement.

6.   **TERMINATION:** This license is effective until terminated. This license will terminate automatically without notice from the Company and become null and void if you fail to comply with any provisions or limitations of this license. Upon termination, you shall destroy the Documentation and all copies of the SOFTWARE. All provisions of this Agreement as to warranties, limitation of liability, remedies or damages, and our ownership rights shall survive termination.

7.   **MISCELLANEOUS:** This Agreement shall be construed in accordance with the laws of the United States of America and the State of New York and shall benefit the Company, its affiliates, and assignees.

8.   **LIMITED WARRANTY AND DISCLAIMER OF WARRANTY:** The Company warrants that the SOFTWARE, when properly used in accordance with the Documentation, will operate in substantial conformity with the description of the SOFTWARE set forth in the Documentation. The

Company does not warrant that the SOFTWARE will meet your requirements or that the operation of the SOFTWARE will be uninterrupted or error-free. The Company warrants that the media on which the SOFTWARE is delivered shall be free from defects in materials and workmanship under normal use for a period of thirty (30) days from the date of your purchase. Your only remedy and the Company's only obligation under these limited warranties is, at the Company's option, return of the warranted item for a refund of any amounts paid by you or replacement of the item. Any replacement of SOFTWARE or media under the warranties shall not extend the original warranty period. The limited warranty set forth above shall not apply to any SOFTWARE which the Company determines in good faith has been subject to misuse, neglect, improper installation, repair, alteration, or damage by you. EXCEPT FOR THE EXPRESSED WARRANTIES SET FORTH ABOVE, THE COMPANY DISCLAIMS ALL WARRANTIES, EXPRESS OR IMPLIED, INCLUDING WITHOUT LIMITATION, THE IMPLIED WARRANTIES OF MERCHANTABILITY AND FITNESS FOR A PARTICULAR PURPOSE. EXCEPT FOR THE EXPRESS WARRANTY SET FORTH ABOVE, THE COMPANY DOES NOT WARRANT, GUARANTEE, OR MAKE ANY REPRESENTATION REGARDING THE USE OR THE RESULTS OF THE USE OF THE SOFTWARE IN TERMS OF ITS CORRECTNESS, ACCURACY, RELIABILITY, CURRENTNESS, OR OTHERWISE.

IN NO EVENT, SHALL THE COMPANY OR ITS EMPLOYEES, AGENTS, SUPPLIERS, OR CONTRACTORS BE LIABLE FOR ANY INCIDENTAL, INDIRECT, SPECIAL, OR CONSEQUENTIAL DAMAGES ARISING OUT OF OR IN CONNECTION WITH THE LICENSE GRANTED UNDER THIS AGREEMENT, OR FOR LOSS OF USE, LOSS OF DATA, LOSS OF INCOME OR PROFIT, OR OTHER LOSSES, SUSTAINED AS A RESULT OF INJURY TO ANY PERSON, OR LOSS OF OR DAMAGE TO PROPERTY, OR CLAIMS OF THIRD PARTIES, EVEN IF THE COMPANY OR AN AUTHORIZED REPRESENTATIVE OF THE COMPANY HAS BEEN ADVISED OF THE POSSIBILITY OF SUCH DAMAGES. IN NO EVENT SHALL LIABILITY OF THE COMPANY FOR DAMAGES WITH RESPECT TO THE SOFTWARE EXCEED THE AMOUNTS ACTUALLY PAID BY YOU, IF ANY, FOR THE SOFTWARE.

SOME JURISDICTIONS DO NOT ALLOW THE LIMITATION OF IMPLIED WARRANTIES OR LIABILITY FOR INCIDENTAL, INDIRECT, SPECIAL, OR CONSEQUENTIAL DAMAGES, SO THE ABOVE LIMITATIONS MAY NOT ALWAYS APPLY. THE WARRANTIES IN THIS AGREEMENT GIVE YOU SPECIFIC LEGAL RIGHTS AND YOU MAY ALSO HAVE OTHER RIGHTS WHICH VARY IN ACCORDANCE WITH LOCAL LAW.

ACKNOWLEDGMENT

YOU ACKNOWLEDGE THAT YOU HAVE READ THIS AGREEMENT, UNDERSTAND IT, AND AGREE TO BE BOUND BY ITS TERMS AND CONDITIONS. YOU ALSO AGREE THAT THIS AGREEMENT IS THE COMPLETE AND EXCLUSIVE STATEMENT OF THE AGREEMENT BETWEEN YOU AND THE COMPANY AND SUPERSEDES ALL PROPOSALS OR PRIOR AGREEMENTS, ORAL, OR WRITTEN, AND ANY OTHER COMMUNICATIONS BETWEEN YOU AND THE COMPANY OR ANY REPRESENTATIVE OF THE COMPANY RELATING TO THE SUBJECT MATTER OF THIS AGREEMENT.

Should you have any questions concerning this Agreement or if you wish to contact the Company for any reason, please contact in writing at the address below.

Robin Short

Prentice Hall PTR

One Lake Street

Upper Saddle River, New Jersey 07458